D1534799

MARXIST POLITICAL ECONOMY AND MARXIST URBAN SOCIOLOGY

Marxist Political Economy and Marxist Urban Sociology

A Review and Elaboration of Recent Developments

Kieran McKeown

Social Research Centre
National Institute for Higher Education
Limerick, Ireland

St. Martin's Press New York

Scholarly & Reference Division,
St. Martin's Press, Inc., 175 Fifth Avenue, New York, NY 10010

First published in the United States of America in 1987

Printed in Hong Kong

ISBN 0-312-51794-7

Library of Congress Cataloging-in-Publication Data
McKeown, Kieran, 1951–
Marxist political economy and Marxist urban sociology.
Bibliography: p.
Includes index.
1. Marxian economics. 2. Business cycles.
3. Marxian school of sociology. 4. Sociology, Urban. i. Title.
HB97.5.M365 1987 335.4 86-15544
ISBN 0-312-51794-7

To Grace, Colm, Clara and Catriona

Contents

List of Tables and Figures xiii

Acknowledgements xv

General Introduction xvii

PART I MARXIAN POLITICAL ECONOMY

1 Marx's Labour Theory of Value **3**

1.0 Introduction 3
1.1 Marx's Labour Theory of Value 3
1.2 The Transformation Problem 7
1.3 Marx's Solution to the Transformation Problem 9
1.4 The Errors in Marx's Transformation Solution 12
1.5 The Correct Solution to the Transformation Problem 14
1.6 The Sraffian Approach to Prices and Profit 18
1.7 Conclusion 23

2 Marxian Crisis Theory **24**

2.0 Introduction 24
2.1 The Law of the Falling Rate of Profit 26
2.1.1 Introduction 26
2.1.2 Marx's Formulation of the Law 27
2.1.3 The Possibility of a Fall in the Maximum Rate of Profit 29
2.1.4 The Possibility of a Fall in the Actual Rate of Profit 30
2.1.5 Technical Change and the Rate of Profit 33
2.1.6 Conclusion 35

2.2 Realisation Crises 35
2.2.1 Introduction 35
2.2.2 The Possibility of a Realisation Crisis 36
2.2.3 Realisation Crisis Caused by Absence of Macroeconomic Planning 38
2.2.4 Realisation Crisis Caused by Technical Innovation. 42
2.2.5 Realisation Crisis Caused by Variable Weather Conditions 44
2.2.6 Realisation Crisis Caused by Scarcity of Labour 46
2.2.7 Conclusion 47
2.3 Crises Caused by Rising Real Wages 47
2.3.1 Introduction 47
2.3.2 The Difference between Labour Power and a Commodity 48
2.3.3 The Mechanism Regulating the Level of Wages 50
2.3.4 The Long-term Trend in Wages 50
2.3.5 The Role of Trade Unions in Wage Determination 53
2.3.6 Conclusion 54
2.4 Conclusion 55

3 Marx's Theory of Rent **56**

3.0 Introduction 56
3.1 Differential Rent I 58
3.2 Differential Rent II 61
3.3 Monopoly Rent I 64
3.4 Monopoly Rent II 67
3.5 Conclusion 68

4 Marx's Theory of Productive and Unproductive Labour **70**

4.0 Introduction 70
4.1 'Definition I' of Productive and Unproductive Labour 70
4.2 'Definition II' of Productive and Unproductive Labour 72
4.3 Conclusion 76

PART II FRENCH MARXIST URBAN SOCIOLOGY: THE CASE OF MANUEL CASTELLS AND JEAN LOJKINE

5 The Different Marxist Traditions of Castells and Lojkine: Althusserianism and State Monopoly Capitalism **81**

5.0 Introduction 81
5.1 The Althusserian Framework 81
5.2 The Theory of State Monopoly Capitalism 85
5.3 Conclusion 88

6 The Marxist Urban Sociology of Manuel Castells **89**

6.0 Introduction 89
6.1 The Critique of Urban Sociology 90
6.1.1 Introduction 90
6.1.2 Science' and 'Ideology' in Urban Sociology 90
6.1.3 Urbanism 92
6.1.4 Urbanisation 94
6.1.5 Conclusion 95
6.2. Collective Consumption 95
6.2.1 Introduction 95
6.2.2 Defining an Urban Area as an Area of Collective Consumption 96
6.2.3 The Effects of Collective Consumption 98
6.2.4 Conclusion 101
6.3 The Urban System 101
6.4 Urban Politics 104
6.5 Urban Planning 105
6.5.1 Introduction 105
6.5.2 The Typology of Urban Actors 106
6.5.3 The Causes of and Constraints upon Urban Planning 106
6.5.4 Conclusion 108
6.6 Urban Social Movements 109
6.6.1 Introduction 109
6.6.2 The Definition of an Urban Social Movement 109
6.6.3 A Framework for the Analysis of Urban Social Movements 111
6.6.4 Conclusion 113
6.7 Empirical Research 114
6.7.1 Introduction 114

6.7.2 Research on Industrial Location in the Paris region 115
6.7.3 Research on Urban Renewal in Paris 118
6.7.4 Research on Protests against Urban Renewal in Paris 121
6.7.5 Research on Urban Protests in Montreal 123
6.7.6 Research on Urban Development in Dunkirk 125
6.7.7 Research on Immigrant Workers in Western Europe 134
6.7.8 Research on Urban Protests in Paris 136
6.7.9 Conclusion 138
6.8 Conclusion 139

7 The Marxist Urban Sociology of Jean Lojkine 141
7.0 Introduction 141
7.1 The Definition of an Urban Area 142
7.2 The Collective Means of Consumption 143
7.2.1 Introduction 143
7.2.2 The 'Collective' Nature of the Collective Means of Consumption 143
7.2.3 The 'Unproductive' Nature of the Collective Means of Consumption 144
7.2.4 The Unprofitable Nature of the Collective Means of Consumption 147
7.2.5 The 'Durable', 'Immobile' and 'Indivisible' Nature of the Collective Means of Consumption 148
7.2.6 Conclusion 149
7.3 The Three Problems associated with Capitalist Urban Development 150
7.3.1 Introduction 150
7.3.2 The Problem of Financing Urban Expenditure 150
7.3.3 The Problem of the Locational Strategy of Capitalist Firms 154
7.3.4 The Problem of Urban Land Rent 154
7.3.5 Conclusion 159
7.4 Urban Planning 160
7.5 Social Movements 163
7.6 Empirical Research 167
7.6.1 Introduction 167
7.6.2 Research on Urban Policy in Paris in the Period 1945–72 167

7.6.3 Research on Urban Policy in Lyon in Period 1945–72 174
7.6.4 Conclusion 179
7.7 Conclusion 180

PART III AN ALTERNATIVE APPROACH TO MARXIST URBAN SOCIOLOGY

8 From Marxist to Post-Marxist Urban Sociology 185
8.0 Introduction 185
8.1 The Marxist Urban Sociology of Manuel Castells and Jean Lojkine 185
8.1.1 Introduction 185
8.1.2 The Definition of an Urban Area Contained in the Writings of Castells and Lojkine 185
8.1.3 The Analysis of Collective Consumption in the Writings of Castells and Lojkine 187
8.1.4 The Analysis of Urban Planning in the Writings of Castells and Lojkine 189
8.1.5 The Analysis of Urban Movements in the Writings of Castells and Lojkine 190
8.1.6 Conclusion 191
8.2. A Conflict Approach to Urban Sociology The Constrained-Actor Model 192
8.3 Urban Areas and Urban Processes: The Field of Urban Sociology 195
8.4 The Production of Urban Areas: The Process of Property Development 196
8.5 State Property Development 197
8.6 Private Property Development 200
8.6.1 Introduction 200
8.6.2 Constraints upon the Interests of Private Property Developers 200
8.6.3 Constraints upon the Interests of Landowners 204
8.6.4 Constraints upon the Interests of the State Planning Authority 205
8.6.5 Summary 207
8.7 Production in an Urban Area 208
8.7.1 Introduction 208
8.7.2 The Supply of Labour in an Urban Area 208
8.7.3 The Demand for Labour in an Urban Area 211
8.7.4 Summary 213

8.8 Consumption in an Urban Area 214
 8.8.1 Introduction 214
 8.8.2 A Typology of Consumption Goods 215
 8.8.3 The Spatial Dimension of Consumption 217
 8.8.4 The Dwelling Unit 220
 8.8.5 Tenure Groups and Changes in the Site Value of Dwelling Units 222
 8.8.6 Individual and Collective Reaction to Changes in Consumption 223
 8.8.7 Resignation 225
 8.8.8 Migration 225
 8.8.9 Collective Action 226
 8.8.10 Summary 229
8.9 Conclusion: New Directions for Marxist Urban Sociology 229

Notes 231

Bibliography 253

Name Index 274

Subject Index 277

List of Tables and Figures

TABLES

4.1 Marx's 'Definition I' of productive and unproductive labour 73
4.2 Marx's 'Definition II' of productive and unproductive labour 75
6.1 Castells's concept of the urban system 103
6.2 The sub-elements in Castells's urban system 104
6.3 Castells's typology of urban actors 106
6.4 Castells's typology of practices and their effects 110
6.5 Castells's typology of industrial establishments 117
6.6 The index of differentiation for 23 renewal areas in Paris on selected variables 119
6.7 Correlations between the areal size of renewal operations and selected variables in Paris 120
6.8 Some characteristics of Dunkirk and the Nord Region according to Castells 128
6.9 Castell's description of the fractions of the capitalist class and their interests in Dunkirk 130
6.10 Castells's description of the fractions of the working class and their interests in Dunkirk 131
6.11 Castells's typology of urban protests in Paris, 1968–1973 137
7.1 Lojkine's analysis of different types of rent in different urban situations 156
8.1 The constraints and conflicts generated in the process of private property development: sources of constraints on actors in the development process 202
8.2 A typology of consumption goods 216
8.3 A typology of the reactions of residents to a negative consumption good in their area 224

Tables in Notes

N1 Number of citations per year of the works of Manuel Castells and Jean Lojkine and the average number of citations of each cited author in the Social Science Citation Index (1969–84) 231
N2 A typology of land 238
N3 A typology of private and public goods 250

FIGURES

1.1 The relationships between physical value and price quantities 22
2.1 The relationship between wages and profit for different techniques of production 34
2.2 The shares of profits and wages in net output 51
2.3 Marx's view of the effect of an increase in net output upon the shares of profits and wages 53
3.1 The relationship between output and type of land 59
3.2 The relationship between output, type of land and rent 61
3.3 The relationship between output, technique of production and rent 63
3.4 The incidence of monopoly rent I on different types of land 65
6.1 The determinants of urban culture according to Castells and Wirth 93
8.1 The process of property development 197
8.2 The externality gradient of a negative communal consumption good 218
8.3 The externality field of a negative communal consumption good 218
8.4 The externality gradient of a consumption good with both positive and negative effects 219
8.5 The externality field of a consumption good with both positive and negative effects 219

Figures in Notes

N1 The growth of population and resources according to Malthus 237
N2 Reasons for household relocation 249

Acknowledgements

I am very grateful to Chris Pickvance of the University of Kent at Canterbury for his painstaking and constructive comments on earlier drafts of this book. He is not, of course, responsible for any errors that remain nor does he necessarily share all the views expressed in it. I would also like to thank Mary O'Malley for her careful typing at every stage in the preparation of the book.

KIERAN MCKEOWN

General Introduction

Marxist urban sociology, though a relatively recent development, is currently a major school within urban sociology (see Lebas, 1982, for a comprehensive bibliography of the literature constituting this school). The school emerged in the late 1960s largely as a result of growing academic disenchantment with the prevailing approaches to urban sociology. The new approach – sometimes referred to as 'the political economy approach' (Harloe, 1979, p. 5; Lebas, 1981, p. xi; 1982, p. 20) – is now entering its second decade and this is an appropriate time to evaluate it. This book focuses upon the writings of Manuel Castells and Jean Lojkine, who have made centrally important contributions to this new body of literature while at the same time representing different approaches within it. Thus their work represents, to some extent, both the unity and the diversity of the new school.

Manuel Castells and Jean Lojkine are sociologists whose writing has attempted to apply a Marxist perspective to the analysis of urban areas. Throughout the 1970s and early 1980s their writings have generated considerable and growing interest within the social sciences generally.[1] In the present study their writings will be analysed and discussed in detail. Their work will be located in their respective traditions of Marxism and evaluated from the point of view of Marx's political economy. Having identified inadequacies in their understanding and application of Marx's political economy, the book will attempt to provide an alternative to the approach of Castells and Lojkine. This will be done by redefining the field of urban sociology in terms of three basic processes, namely, the process by which urban (that is, built-up) areas are produced, the process by which they are used for the production of commodities and the process by which they are used for final consumption. These three processes will be analysed using a constrained-actor model of society. This results in an analysis of urban processes which, although it is not strictly Marxist, nevertheless maintains the Marxian emphasis upon the role of interests and conflicts in social interaction.

The critique of the work of Castells and Lojkine which is presented in this book is made from a particular point of view based upon the premise that the validity of a Marxist analysis of urban areas is ultimately dependent upon the validity of Marxism itself. Since, in turn, the validity of Marxism is dependent upon Marxist political economy, the critique of Castells and Lojkine will focus upon the major issues of political economy which are suggested, implicitly or explicitly, by their work.

The book is written in three parts. Part I, containing Chapters 1, 2, 3 and 4, provides an overview of Marxian political economy. Marx's theories of value, crisis, rent and productive labour are analysed in detail. It will be shown that significant difficulties exist with virtually every substantive aspect of Marx's political economy. This finding will be the basis for appraising the way in which Castells and Lojkine use this political economy.

Part II, containing Chapters 5, 6 and 7, examines the French Marxist urban sociology of Manuel Castells and Jean Lojkine. The examination begins in Chapter 5 by locating the work of Castells and Lojkine within their respective traditions of Marxism. In the case of Castells that tradition is normally referred to as 'Althusserianism' and in the case of Lojkine it is 'State Monopoly Capitalism'. The purpose of this chapter is less to evaluate these traditions than to provide the reader with the necessary background information and terminology for understanding the work of Castells and Lojkine. The main thrust and focus of the critique is contained in Chapters 6 and 7 where the entire works of Castells and Lojkine are discussed successively. In each of these chapters the strategy is to outline and evaluate the conceptual framework of each author and follow this with an assessment of his empirical research.

Part III, containing Chapter 8, presents an alternative approach to Marxist urban sociology. This alternative, which avoids the major difficulties associated with the work of Castells and Lojkine, begins from the premise that urban areas are essentially built-up areas. A constrained-actor model of society is then applied to understand how these built-up areas are produced in a capitalist society and how, in turn, they are used both for the production of commodities and for final consumption. This new formulation of the field of urban sociology contains an analysis of urban space which tries to advance our understanding of the constraints and conflicts generated by the production and use of urban areas in a capitalist society.

Part I

Marxian Political Economy

1 Marx's Labour Theory of Value

1.0 INTRODUCTION

The purpose of this chapter is to provide an over-all assessment of Marx's labour theory of value. The analysis begins by outlining the main elements of Marx's labour theory of value and by defining its central concepts (section 1.1). Marx regarded these concepts as essential to understanding prices and profit in a capitalist society and it is for this reason that the problem arises of transforming values and surplus value into prices and profit. The precise nature of this problem will be outlined in section 1.2, along with Marx's attempt to solve it (section 1.3), and the errors associated with that solution (section 1.4). The correct solution to the transformation problem will then be presented in section 1.5

The analysis will then show that, despite the formal correctness of the transformation procedure, the labour theory of value does not provide the only or even the best explanation of the formation of prices and profit within a capitalist society. The reason for this is that there is an alterative to the labour theory of value which treats the same issues in a more rigorous and less problematic way. This is the Sraffian approach whose main features will be outlined in section 1.6. It will be seen that the weight of the arguments is in favour of the adoption of the Sraffian approach and the rejection of the labour theory of value.

1.1 MARX'S LABOUR THEORY OF VALUE

The purpose of Marx's labour theory of value is to explain how the wealth of a capitalist society is produced and distributed. Since, in Marx's view, this wealth consists of commodities he draws the logical inference that 'our investigation must therefore begin with the analysis of a commodity' (Marx, 1974a, p. 43.).

Marx defines a commodity as a combination of two independent characteristics: on the one hand it is a use value, and on the other it is an exchange value. Commodities are use values in the sense that their consumption satisfies certain wants, and are exchange values in the sense that they are products of labour and exchange according to the quantity of socially[1] necessary abstract labour embodied in them. Every commodity, according to Marx, must have these two characteristics (Marx, 1974a, Chapter 1, section 1, pp. 43–8).

Marx pointed out that labour, or rather labour power (to use his preferred term – see notably Marx 1975, section 7, pp. 43–6)[2] was also a commodity within capitalist society and was therefore also a use value (in the sense that its performance led, directly or indirectly, to the satisfaction of some want) and an exchange value (in the sense that it too was the product of the socially necessary abstract labour required to produce it and therefore exchanged accordingly). Marx argued that the exchange value of labour power was equal to the bundle of commodities forming the wage since these were necessary for the subsistence, and hence the production, of labour power (see section 2.3).

The problem which Marx then confronts is to show how it is possible for the exploitation of labour to occur when every commodity (including labour power) is exchanged according to the quantity of socially necessary abstract labour required to produce it. This problem arises because Marx characterises capitalist production in the following way:

$$M\, C_{MP}^{LP} - \boxed{P} - C' - M'$$

where:

M = the amount of money which the capitalist owns at the beginning of the production process;

C_{MP}^{LP} = the commodities of labour power and means of production purchased by the capitalist at the beginning of the production process;

$\boxed{P}$ = the production process;

C' = the new commodity

M' = the money which the capitalist receives from the sale of the new commodity;

M' $= M + \Delta M >$.

The typical process of capitalist production, as Marx saw it, is that, a capitalist invests money (M) with a view to making a profit. He does this by purchasing a certain quantity of labour power and means of production based upon the technical requirements and the scale of the production process. These two sets of commodities (C_{MP}^{LP}) are then put to production ($\boxed{P}$) to produce a given output (C'). This output is then sold and the capitalist recoups his initial investment (M) plus a profit or surplus (ΔM). If there was no surplus at the end of the production process, then the entire exercise would be pointless from the capitalist's point of view. Thus the pursuit of profit is the underlying rationale of all capitalist production.

Marx's problem is to explain the origin and nature of this surplus in a way which is consistent with the proposition that all commodities exchange in proportion to their value. His explanation is that the surplus arising in production is due to the commodity labour power which he regarded as a 'special commodity' (Marx, 1974a, p. 164). The special quality of labour power derives from the fact that its use value can create a quantity of value which is greater than its exchange value (in contrast to every other commodity whose use value can only create a quantity of value which is equal to its exchange value). Marx explained this special quality of labour power in the following way: the capitalist purchases labour power at its value and then proceeds to consume its use value by putting it to work (in the same way as he/she will consume the use value of the means of production by putting them to work). If the capitalist is to make a profit from the purchase of labour power he/she must ensure that the value of the output created is greater than the exchange value of that labour power. Marx emphasised that capitalists will always ensure, through various forms of coercion, that the value created by the use value of labour power will always be greater than its exchange value. It is this difference between what Marx terms 'the value of labour power and the value which that labour power creates' (ibid., p. 188) which is the origin of profit. The size of the profit, in turn, is determined by the productivity of labour and by the length and intensity of the working day.

This is the theroretical core of Marx's theory of exploitation. This theory highlights two important points about capitalist exploitation. The first is that capitalists receive an unearned income, that is, a profit which is based solely upon their ownership of the means of production, in contrast to workers whose income has to be earned through work. The second point is that the income which the capitalist receives consists in the surplus labour which the worker is obliged to perform over and above that which is necessary to produce the wage. Thus, in his theory of exploitation, Marx was not content to point out simply that workers earned their share of society's wealth while capitalists did not, but in addition, that the capitalists' share was nothing less than the surplus labour of the workers.

This basic conceptual framework is then elaborated by introducing the concepts of constant capital (C), variable capital (V) and surplus value (S) where:

C = the value of the means of production used in the production process;[3]
V = the value of the labour power used in the production process;
S = the value of the surplus output produced in the production process.

Marx explained the connections between these three concepts by asserting that, in the production process, the value of constant capital is simply transferred to the final output while the value of variable capital, in addition to being transferred to the final output, also creates additional value, equal to surplus value, which, itself, is also transferred to the final output. Thus, the value of any output is equal to $c_i + v_i + s_i$, where i is any commodity between 1 and n (see Marx, 1974c, Chapter 8, p. 150).[4] Thus, if two commodities have the same value they can both be exchanged for one another or for the same amount of money. The amount of money, following Marx's analysis (see Marx, 1974a, pp. 74ff) will be a quantity of gold whose production required exactly the same amount of direct and indirect labour to produce as either of the two commodities with which it exchanges.[5]

Marx continues the analysis by deriving two important ratios. The first is:

$\frac{c_i}{v_i}$ = the organic composition of capital in sector i where i is any sector between 1 and n.

This ratio is a measure of the capital or labour intensity of a particular sector (Marx, 1974a, Chapter 25, pp. 574ff; 1974c, Chapter 8, pp. 145ff) and is assumed to vary between sectors so that:

$$\frac{c_i}{v_i} \neq \frac{c_j}{v_j}$$

where i and j refer to any sector between 1 and n.

The second ratio is:

$\frac{s_i}{v_i}$ = the rate of surplus value or exploitation in sector i, where i is any sector between 1 and n.

This ratio is a measure of the quantity of surplus value produced per unit of labour power. It can be raised by increasing 'absolute surplus value' (that is, by increasing the length and intensity of the working day: increasing the numerator) or by increasing 'relative surplus value' (that is, by increasing the level of productivity in the wage-goods sector: reducing the denominator) (see Marx, 1974a, p. 299). Marx assumed (though see Desai, 1979, p. 51) that the rate of surplus value was uniform throughout all sectors of the economy since, he claimed, the reproduction of labour power is the same for all workers (that is, a uniform subsistence wage) while the length and intensity of the working day also tends to uniformity. Thus:

$$\frac{s_i}{v_i} = \frac{s_j}{v_j}$$

where *i* and *j* refer to any sectors between 1 and *n*.

The important relationship between the organic composition of capital and the rate of surplus value is that those sectors with a high organic composition of capital will produce less surplus value than those sectors with a low organic composition of capital. This result, which follows consistently from the preceding analysis, is highly significant because, as will now be seen, it gives rise to the transformation problem.

1.2 THE TRANSFORMATION PROBLEM

The analysis up to this point has centred around the concepts of the value of a commodity and the surplus value generated in the course of producing that commodity. Marx regarded this analysis as a fundamental prerequisite to the explanation of profit and prices in capitalist society. This is indicated implicitly in the layout of *Capital* (broadly speaking from values and surplus value in Volume I to prices and profit in Volume III) and explicitly by the following quotation: 'If you cannot explain profit upon this supposition (that is, that on average, commodities are sold at their real values and that profits are derived from selling them at their values) then you cannot explain it at all' (Marx, 1975, p. 42; see also 1974c, pp. 43, 157).

The logic of this dualism in his economic analysis (between value and surplus value on the one hand and price and profit on the other) required Marx to show that there was, in fact, a systematic and quantifiable relationship between these two levels of reality.[6] To this end he attempted to transform value and surplus value into price and profit, thereby proving that the latter were derived from, and determined by, the former. His attempt to do this gave rise to the transformation problem.

This problem is the *pons asinorum* of Marx's economic analysis (Robinson, 1973, p. 61) and has been variously described as 'a bare contradiction' (Böhm-Bawerk, 1949, p. 30), 'a quantitative incongruity' (Bortkiewicz, 1952, p. 5), 'a great contradiction' (Blaug, 1962, p. 230) and 'an interesting theoretical problem' (Sweezy, 1942, p. 69) in Marx's work. Marx anticipated the problem as early as 1862 (see Marx and Engels, 1955; see also Marx, 1969, Chapter 10, section 4 (a), pp. 173ff) before he ever wrote Volumes I and III of *Capital* between 1863 and 1867 (see Marx, 1974a, 1974c), though he never provided a satisfactory solution to it. It is now necessary to outline precisely the nature of the problem which Marx encountered when he attempted to transform value and surplus value into price and profit.

Marx defined the price of production of a commodity as equal to 'cost price plus profit' (Marx, 1974c, pp. 36, 165). In turn he defined the rate of profit as:

$$r_i = \frac{s_i}{c_i + v_i}$$

where *i* refers to any sector or commodity between 1 and *n* (see Marx, 1947c, pp. 49ff).

It follows from this, if Marx's labour theory of value is correct, that the value of commodity $i\ (= c_i + v_i + s_i)$ must be proportionate to the price of commodity $i\ (= (c_i + v_i)(1 + r))$. However, this is not in fact the case since, with equal rates of exploitation ($s_i/v_i = s_j/v_j$) and variable rates of profit between sectors ($r_i \neq r_j$), the value of commodities will be greater than their prices in those sectors with a low organic composition of capital (c_j/v_{ji}) and will be less than their price in those sectors with a high organic composition of capital. In other words, Marx's analysis leads to the result that prices are not proportional to their values which means that there is not a consistent relationship between values and prices. This raises the problem of the connection of values to prices – in short, the transformation problem.

In algebraic terms, this can be expressed as follows:

if: $\frac{s_i}{v_i} = \frac{s_j}{v_j}$

and if: $\frac{c_i}{v_i} = \frac{c_i}{v_i}$

then: $r_i \neq r_j \neq r$

then: $c_i + v_i + s_i$ is not proportional to $(c_i + {}_i)\ (1 + r)$

Marx acknowleged this problem by pointing out that prices could only be proportional to values if the rate of profit varied between sectors according to the amount of surplus value produced in each sector. Alternatively, prices would be proportional to values if the organic composition of capital was the same in every sector.

Marx appreciated that this result was highly anomalous since 'differences in the average rate of profit in the various branches of industry do not exist in reality and could not exist without abolishing the entire system of production' (Marx, 1974c, Part II, Chapter 8, p. 153). Indeed, at this point Marx contemplated the possibility – largely for rhetorical effect given his intended and subsequent argument – that 'the theory of value is incompatible with the actual process' (ibid.)

It is now necessary to examine Marx's solution to this problem.

1.3 MARX'S SOLUTION TO THE TRANSFORMATION PROBLEM

There are essentially two components involved in the transformation of value and surplus value into price and profit. The first component involves transforming the values of constant and variable capital into their corresponding cost price; the second component involves transforming surplus value into profit. Marx largely neglected the first component: in particular, he did not indicate precisely how the value of the inputs of constant and variable capital might be transformed into their corresponding prices even though he recognised that they needed to be transformed (Marx, 1974c, pp. 159–64). In his actual numerical examples he assumed that the value and price of these inputs were the same.

Marx concentrated most of his energies on the second component since, in his formulation of the transformation problem, this is the major source of the difficulty. In his solution he focused on the problem of how to ensure that a uniform rate of profit existed throughout the economy in a way which was consistent with the basic proposition that this profit was derived from, and determined by, surplus value.

Marx's solution involved changing his definition of the rate of profit and working out the ramifications of this change. Thus, in place of the definition of the rate of profit in the previous section:

$$r = \frac{s_i}{c_i + v_i}$$

Marx put forward the following:

$$r = \frac{\sum_{i=1}^{n} s_i}{\sum_{i=1}^{n} c_i + \sum_{i=1}^{n} v_i} = \frac{S}{C+V}$$

This definition of the general rate of profit in terms of the arithmetic average rate of profit seemed to offer Marx the solution he required because it appears to clarify the relationship between surplus value and profit as well as the relationship between values and prices. According to this definition, the aggregate quantity of surplus value equals the aggregate quantity of profit, although the quantity of surplus value produced in each sector is not necessarily equal to the quantity of profit appropriated in that sector (except in the singular case where the organic composition of capital in a sector is equal to the social average). This fact can, following the above notation, be written as follows:

$$\sum_{i=1}^{n} s_i = \left[r \sum_{i=1}^{n} (c_i + v_i) \right]$$

but

$$s_i \neq r\,(c_i + v_i)$$

Marx seems to have conceptualised the relationship between surplus value and profit along the following lines: surplus value is produced in each sector and contributes to the total fund of surplus value. This, in turn, is distributed as profit, not according to the amount produced in each sector, but according to the total capital invested in each sector. Baumol captures Marx's point when the describes the production and distribution of surplus value in each sector as follows: 'It takes from each according to its workforce, and returns to each according to its total investment' (Baumol, 1974, p. 53). Marx used the analogy of the joint stock company (Marx, 1974c, p. 158) to illustrate the point that each sector or capitalist (the two can be treated as synonymous in this context) receives a share of profit in relation to its total investment, though the analogy breaks down in relation to the contribution of each to the total fund of surplus value.

The actual mechanism which ensures that surplus value is distributed as profit is competition (Marx, 1974c, p. 158, 174ff). The competitive process ensures that a uniform rate of profit operates throughout the economy which regulates the distribution of surplus value irrespective of the amount which each produces.

Marx claimed that the particular relationship between surplus value and profit was discovered by him and 'revealed for the first time' (Marx, 1974c, p. 168) in Chapter 9 of Volume III of *Capital*. Moreover, it was a discovery which, as Marx saw it, was particularly difficult since the rate of profit acts unintentionally to 'obscure and mystify the actual origin of surplus value' (Marx, 1974c, p. 167). This is because the capitalist calculates the rate of profit on the basis of his total investment $(c_i + v_i)$ whereas surplus value originates from only part of that investment (v_i). Thus the transformation of surplus value into profit (and, by implication, the transformation of values into prices) is 'a complete mystery to the individual capitalist; all the more so, since no bourgeois theorists, the political economists, have so far revealed it' (Marx, 1974c, p. 170).

Marx's redefinition of the rate of profit also implied that the price of each commodity (or output of each sector) is not proportional to its value, that is,

$$c_i + v_i + s_i \text{ is not proportional to } (c_i + v_i)\ (1 + r)$$

The reason for this is that those commodities which are produced in sectors with a low organic composition of capital (low c_i/v_i) will have prices which are less than their value (since they produce more surplus value than they receive as profit), while those commodities which are produced in sectors with a high organic composition of capital (high c_i/v_i) will have prices which are greater than their value (since they produce less surplus value than they receive as profit).

Marx argued that the inequalities between values and prices would 'balance out one another' (Marx, 1974c, p. 157) and 'compensate one another' (ibid, p. 161) in the sense that the aggregate value of all commodities would equal the aggregate price of all commodities, even though the value and price of each individual commodity would be unequal.

This proposition can be written, following the above notation, as follows:

$$\sum_{i=1}^{n} (c_i + v_i + s_i) = \sum_{i=1}^{n} \left[(c_i + v_i)\,(1 + r) \right]$$

but

$$c_i + v_i + s_i \neq (c_i + v_i)\,(1 + r)$$

Marx described this as a 'general law' (Marx 1974c, p. 161) which acts as a 'prevailing tendency' (ibid.) and in 'a very complicated and approximate manner as a never ascertainable average of ceaseless fluctuations' (ibid.).

It is now necessary to examine the validity of Marx's solution to the transformation problem.

1.4 THE ERRORS IN MARX'S TRANSFORMATION SOLUTION

Any solution to the transformation problem effectively involves transforming each of the components of the value of a commodity ($c_i + v_i + s_i$) into its corresponding price components. Marx's strategy, as has been seen, was first to transform surplus value into profit and then to transform constant capital and viable capital into cost price (though he tended to neglect this latter aspect). In assessing Marx's solution, it is necessary to evaluate both of these aspects.

Marx defined the rate of profit as $S/(C + V)$. This formula gives the value (not the price) rate of profit since each of the aggregates C, V and S are values. However, the real and actual rate of profit in capitalist society is the price rate of profit since this is the one upon which capitalists base their economic calculations and decisions (see Steedman, 1973, p. 37; Hodgson 1974b, p. 363). It follows, therefore, that Marx's formula is only correct if the values of S, C and V are proportional to their price. This is the implicit assumption in Marx's formula.

Proceeding from this formula, Marx then derives the result that values and prices are not proportional (as a result of the way in which the rate of profit distributes surplus value according to the total capital invested in each sector/commodity). This result clearly contradicts Marx's initial assumption concerning the proportionality of values and prices. His entire argument is therefore inconsistent. Steedman succinctly summarises this point as follows: 'Marx's argument is internally inconsistent. He assumes that $S/(C + V)$ is the rate of profit but then derives the result that prices diverge from values, which means precisely in general, that $S/(C + V)$ is not the rate of profit (Steedman, 1977, p. 31; see also Desai, 1979, p. 69).

Marx did not recognise this as an inconsistency *per se*. This was because, even though prices deviated from values, the sum of these deviations was equal to zero, and therefore the aggregate formula for the rate of profit appeared to be valid. This argument is invalid, however, since it involves circular reasoning. It is circular because the only reason why the deviations sum to zero is that this is necessarily built into the formula $S/(C + V)$: Marx's formula assumes the total values of constant capital ($\sum_{i=1}^{n} c_i$), variable capital ($\sum_{i=1}^{n} v_i$) and surplus value ($\sum_{i=1}^{n} s_i$) equal their respective total prices (see Bortkeiwicz, 1952, p. 10). It is therefore arithmetically inevitable that the deviations of price from value must sum to zero, simply because of the way that Marx defined the rate of profit. The former cannot therefore, under pain of circular reasoning, be used to justify the latter.

The more general point about Marx's attempt to transform surplus value into profit is that he defined, wrongly, the rate of profit in value terms, rather than in price terms. As a result of this his explanation of the distribution of surplus value as profit lacks any micro-foundation in the actual behaviour of capitalists. This is the most serious error in his entire transformation procedure.

The second aspect of the transformation solution involves transforming input values ($c_i + v_i$) into cost prices. Marx repeatedly drew attention to this aspect of the solution (Marx, 1974c, pp. 160, 164–5; 206–7) but he never actually implemented it in any of his numerical examples; nor did he indicate how it might be undertaken. As regards this aspect of Marx's solution, therefore, it is more accurately regarded as incomplete rather than erroneous (see Morishima and Catephores, 1978, pp. 160–61). There is, however, another, more general, difficulty with Marx's solution to the transformation problem. This difficulty relates to the fact that Marx attempted to transform the various components of the value of a commodity to their corresponding price components in a successive rather than in a simultaneous manner. Bortkiewicz first made this criticism of Marx's approach (echoing Marshall's criticism of Ricardo) and gave it the term 'successivism' (Bortkiewicz, 1952, p. 24). The main criticism here is that Marx did not fully appreciate (at least in the case of the transformation problem) that the various components of the value and price of a commodity determine each other mutually and simultaneously rather than 'successively in a long chain of causation' (ibid.). For this reason he attempted to first transform surplus value into profit and then to transform constant and variable capital into cost prices rather than determining both simultaneously. To do the latter it would have been necessary to use simultaneous equations which were then being used for the first time in economic analysis. However, Marx was unfamiliar with simultaneous equations and this is probably the main reason why he failed to solve the transformation problem (see

Bortkiewicz, 1952, p. 24; Hodgson, 1973, p. 363; Morishima 1974a, pp. 611–13).[7] As will be seen presently, all 'correct' solutions to the transformation problem require, following Bortkiewicz, the use of simultaneous equations. Bortkiewicz's solution will now be examined.

1.5 THE CORRECT SOLUTION TO THE TRANSFORMATION PROBLEM

The identification of the errors in Marx's solution to the transformation problem clearly indicates that a correct solution to this problem could be established if the values of constant capital, variable capital, and surplus value, were simultaneously transformed into cost price and profit respectively. In 1907 (13 years after the publication of the third volume of *Capital*) Ladislaus von Bortkiewicz produced a correct solution to the problem along these lines (see Bortkiewicz, 1949, 1952). His solution relies, as he acknowledged (1952, p. 22), on the earlier work of Dmitriev (1974), a Russian mathematical economist.

Bortkiewicz begins with a three-sector model of the capitalist economy – similar, in this respect, to Marx's model. His model is written algebraically, using three input-output equations, to describe each of the three sectors. The model, using the above notation, is as follows:

Sector I (Capital Goods): $c_1 + v_1 + s_1 = c_1 + c_2 + c_3$
Sector II (Wage Goods): $c_2 + v_2 + s_2 = v_1 + v_2 + v_3$
Sector III (Luxury Goods): $c_3 + v_3 + s_3 = s_1 + s_2 + s_3$

In order to transform this economy from various values to prices, it is necessary that every element be transformed simultaneously. In order to do this it is necessary to multiply each of these value elements by a coefficient which converts its value to its corresponding price. Each coefficient, referred to as a price coefficent, is a ratio of the price to the value of each element. When the price coefficient of an element is multiplied by the value of that element, it will yield the price of that element. Borkiewicz proposes the following price coefficients:

x = the price coefficient of constant capital
y = the price coefficient of variable capital
z = the price coefficient of surplus value

In addition, in order to write these value equations as price equations, it is also necessary to introduce the rate of profit (in price terms) which is denoted by r.

Each of these three price coefficients, together with the rate of profit, provide all of the necessary requirements for rewriting the above value equations as price equations. These price equations can be written as follows:

Sector I (Capital Goods): $c_1x + v_1y + r(c_1x + v_1y) = c_1x + c_2x + c_3x$
Sector II (Wage goods): $c_2x + v_2y + r(c_2x + v_2y) = v_1y + v_2y + y_3y$
Sector III (Luxury Goods): $c_3x + v_3y + r(c_3x + v_3y) = s_1z + s_2z + s_3z$

In these equations, the price coefficients (x, y, z) and the rate of profit (r) have been introduced in order to make it formally possible to derive the price system from the value system. However, x, y, z, and r are unknowns in the sense that they have been added to the known datum ($c_1c_2c_3v_1v_2v_3s_1s_2s_3$) and can only be specified by being expressed in terms of the known data. To do this by simultaneous equations it is necessary that the number of unknowns equal the number of equations. In this case there are only three equations, but four unknowns (x,y,z,r). Bortkiewicz solved this problem by assuming that the value of the output of Sector III was equal to its price so that its price coefficient was equal to one ($z = 1$). In this way the number of equations is equal to the number of unknowns. From these equations it is possible to derive formulas which specify the three unknowns (x,y,r) in terms of the other known quantities ($c_1c_2c_3v_1v_2v_3s_1s_2s_3$) which can then be inserted into the three-sector model (Sweezy, 1942, pp. 116–120; Bortkiewitz, 1973, pp. 202–4; Howard and King, 1975, pp. 166–7).

There are two important implications which follow from Bortkiewicz's solution to the transformation problem. The first concerns the degree of arbitrariness involved in that solution and the second concerns the determination of the rate of profit. Each of these will now be discussed respectively.

Bortkiewicz's solution demonstrates that it is possible to derive prices and profit from values and surplus value. However, as has been seen, this solution required one arbitrary assumption to ensure that the transformed prices are absolute prices. Bortkiewicz assumed that the value of the output of Sector III was equal to its price (that is, $z = 1$). Since Sector III is entirely devoted to producing the luxury good, gold, and since its output is equal to the total quantity of surplus value produced in the economy, it follows that total surplus value (200) is equal to total profit (200). The important point to note about this assumption is that it does not 'prove' that total surplus value must necessarily be equal to total profit (as Marx believed) since this equality is only arrived at by assuming it.

A number of subsequent solutions have been put forward along the same lines to that proposed by Bortkiewicz (see notably, Winternitz, 1948; Meek, 1956; Seton, 1976) and each reveals that no solution to the transformation problem is entirely free from arbitrariness. In the solutions put forward by Winternitz and Meek it is assumed (again arbitrarily) that total value is equal to total price (in the case of Winternitz) and that total surplus value is equal to total profit (in the case of Meek). Seton in his discussion of these various assumptions refers to them as 'invariance postulates' (Seton, 1976, p. 165) essentially because they postulate (or assume) that some quantity of the value system is to remain invariant when transformed into the price system. The significant point about these invariance postulates is that, as Seton points out, 'there does not seem to be an objective basis for choosing any particular invariance postulate in preference to all others, and to that extent the transformation problem may be said to fall short of complete determinancy' (ibid., p. 167).

The second implication of Bortkiewicz's solution to the transformation problem is sometimes referred to as the 'Bortkiewicz Corollary' (see for example, Sweezy, 1942, pp. 123–5; Hodgson 1974a, pp. 366–8) and concerns the determination of the rate of profit. Bortkiewicz's argument is that Marx's original formula for the rate of profit ($S/C+V$) would still be incorrect even if its constituent elements (C,V,S) were transformed into prices (Cx, Vy, Sz). In other words:

$$r \neq \frac{S}{C+V}$$

and

$$r \neq \frac{Sz}{Cx + Vy}$$

The problem with Marx's formula (and his underlying argument) can be seen from a re-examination of the precise way in which the general rate of profit is formed in capitalist society and the way in which this, in turn, is enforced through the competitive process.

In any model of a competitive capitalist economy, the rate of profit will be uniform in every sector and will be equal to the ratio of net output to total inputs (all valued in price terms). It follows, therefore, that in the above three-sector model, the rate of profit in each sector will be the same ($r_1 = r_2 = r_3$) and will be defined as:

$$r_1 = \frac{(c_1x + c_2x + c_3x) - (c_1x + v_1y)}{(c_1x + v_1y)}$$

$$r_2 = \frac{(v_1y + v_2y + v_3y) - (c_2x + v_2y)}{(c_2x + v_2y)}$$

$$r_3 = \frac{(s_1z + s_2z + s_3z) - (c_3x + v_3y)}{(c_3x + v_3y)}$$

Marx seems to have inferred from the fact that since profit is produced in each sector that, therefore, each sector must play the same role in determining the general rate of profit. That this is not so can be seen by inspecting the inputs and outputs of each sector and the way in which they affect the rate of profit.

The level of net output in any sector, assuming a given state of technology, will be determined by the level of inputs. It follows therefore that the determinants of the general rate of profit must be found among the inputs ($c_1x + v_1y; c_2x + v_2y; c_3x + v_3y$). More specifically, the rate of profit which will prevail in every sector of the economy will be determined by those inputs which enter into each and every sector since any change in the price of these inputs will affect the rate of profit in every sector in the same way. Conversely, if an input does not enter into every sector then any change in its price would not affect the rate of profit in every sector; it could not therefore be regarded as a determinant of the general rate of profit.

An inspection of the inputs in the above three-sector model reveals that all of the inputs are produced in Sectors I and II; there are no inputs which are produced in Sector III. It is thus possible to affirm categorically that Sector III has no effect upon the general rate of profit since its output does not enter as an input into any other sector (not even itself). The rate of profit is therefore established outside this sector and imposed upon it through the competitive process. This fact alone provides adequate proof that Marx's formula for the rate of profit must be wrong since it includes the inputs and outputs of this sector in its calculation when in fact they should be excluded (see Morishima and Catephores, 1978, pp. 161–2). More generally, the rate of profit in a competitive capitalist economy is determined by those inputs which enter directly and indirectly into the production of every other commodity. In the terminology of Sraffa, it is determined by 'basic' commodities (as opposed to 'non-basic' commodities) because 'basics have an essential part in the determination of prices and the rate of profits, while non-basics have none' (Sraffa, 1960, p. 54; see section 1.6). This is the important corollary of Bortkiewicz's solution.

The Bortkiewicz solution (and all similar solutions) to the transformation problem show that it is possible, under certain assumptions, to derive prices and profit from values and surplus value. However it does not prove that the price of a commodity is determined by its value or that profit is determined by surplus value. On the contrary, the transformation solution proves that there is no constant or systematic relationship between value quantities and price quantities. Since it was precisely systematic connections of this type which Marx hoped to establish by the labour theory of value, it follows that the correct solution to the transformation problem does not in fact vindicate Marx's theory. The labour theory of value is thus an inadequate theory of profit and prices.

There is, however, an alternative to the labour theory of value which shows clearly how means of production, wages, profits and prices are all interrelated in a capitalist economy. This alternative, which was first elaborated by Piero Sraffa (1960), has now become widespread in the field of Marxist political economy (see, for example, Morishima, 1973; Steedman, 1977; Morishima and Catephores, 1978; Abraham-Frois and Berrebi, 1979; Bose, 1980; Steedman, *et al.* 1981; Hodgson, 1982; Roemer, 1981, 1982; Elster, 1985). Some of its main tenets will now be examined.

1.6 THE SRAFFIAN APPROACH TO PROFIT AND PRICES

Sraffa's book is concerned with the relationships between prices, profits and wages in a competitive capitalist economy. It is thus concerned with the same issues that are central to Marx, although it is also concerned, as the subtitle of the book indicates, with 'a critique of economic theory'.

Sraffa, like Marx, characterises capitalism as a system where commodities are produced in order to make a profit. The production of commodities, according to Sraffa, can be seen as an input-output system where each commodity is the output which results from the input of other commodities, both capital and labour. In the course of the production process profits are produced and these, along with the inputs of commodities and labour, determine the price of the output. Each and every commodity is produced in this way so that the entire system of production can be described by a matrix of *n* equations, each equation corresponding to the inputs and output of one of the n commodities in the system.

In order to write these equations, the following notation (which differs slightly from that used by Sraffa) will be adopted:

A_{ij} = the quantity of commodity i which enters into the production of commodity j;
$\sum_{i=1}^{n} A_{ij} = A$ refers, therefore, to the total means of production employed in the economy;

P_i^m = the money price of a unit of commodity i;
$\sum_{i=1}^{n} P_i^m = P^m$ refers, therefore, to the sum of the price of a unit of each commodity;

a_i = the quantity of labour employed in the production of commodity i;
$\sum_{i=1}^{n} a_i = a$ refers, therefore, to the total quantity of labour employed in the production of all commodities;

m = the money wage rate (per unit of labour);
r = the rate of profit.

The equation for each commodity can now be written as follows:

$$P_i^m = P_i^m A_{11} + P_2^m A_{21} + P_3^m A_{31} + \ldots + P_n^m A_{n1} + ma_1 (1 + r)$$
$$P_2^m = P_1^m \mathrm{A}_{12} + P_a^m A_{22} + P_3^m A_{32} + \ldots + P_n^m A_{n2} + ma_2 (1 + r)$$
$$\cdots\cdots\cdots\cdots\cdots\cdots\cdots\cdots\cdots\cdots\cdots\cdots$$
$$P_n^m = P_1^m A_{1n} + P^m A_{2n} + P_3^m A_{3n} + \ldots + P_n^m A_{nn} + ma_n (1 + r)$$

This matrix can be written more summarily, as follows:

$$P^m = P^m A + ma (1 + r)$$

The content and implications of these equations will now be explored by examining some of their basic features. The first feature is that these equations describe a system of production where commodities are used to produce other commodities. In other words, some commodities enter as inputs into other commodities (possibly including themselves), which in turn enter into the production of other commodities, and so on. Sraffa refers to such commodities as 'basics' because they enter 'directly or indirectly into the production of all commodities' (Sraffa, 1960, p. 8). However, there are also some commodities which do not enter into the production of other commodities and Sraffa refers to these as 'non-basics' (ibid.). Two important implications follow from this distinction. The first is that a basic commodity affects the price of every commodity because it enters, either directly or indirectly, into the production of every commodity. A non-basic, by contrast, has no effect upon the price of any other commodity because it does not enter into the production of any other commodity. In other words, the price of a basic commodity is mutually dependent upon the price of every other commodity whereas the price of a non-basic (or luxury) commodity is independent of the price of any other commodity. The second implication is that only basic commodities have an effect upon the rate of profit since they enter as inputs into the production of every other commodity. A change in the price of a non-basic will have no effect upon the general rate of profit and will only affect the rate of profit in those sectors where it enters as an input. Sraffa neatly summarises these two implications by pointing out that 'the chief economic implication of the distinction' is that 'basics have an essential part in the determination of prices and the rate of profits, while non-basics have none' (Sraffa, 1960, p. 54).

The second feature of the above equations is that profit in a competitive capitalist economy is distributed according to the total investment of each capitalist in means of production ($P^m A$) and labour (ma). In other words there is an equal rate of return (r) on every unit of invested capital ($P^m A + ma$). However, the amount of capital invested can only be established if the price of the means of production (P^m) and the price of labour (m) is known, since neither of the latter can be aggregated without knowing their price. Thus the existence of a uniform rate of profit implies the existence of a price for each commodity (including labour). Conversely every price, as the above equations reveal, implies the existence of a uniform rate of profit. It follows that, in a capitalist economy, the rate of profit can only be known if prices are known and prices can only be known if the rate of profit is known (Sraffa, 1960, p. 6). In other words both are mutually determined and determining so that any explanation of the rate of profit implies an explanation of prices and vice versa. This feature of the Sraffa system has two important implications: one for neoclassical theory and one for Marx's labour theory of value. The implication for neoclassical theory is that the rate of profit cannot be correctly explained by the marginal productivity of capital since the latter cannot be identified independently of the rate of profit. Since this is an essential element of the neoclassical theory of distribution it follows that this theory is inherently circular and hence untenable (see Robinson, 1965; Bhaduri, 1969; Garegnani, 1972; Nell, 1972; Nuti, 1972; Dobb, 1972; 1973, Ch. 9). The implication for Marx's labour theory of value is that the explanation of profit cannot be separated from the explanation of prices even though some Marxists have attempted to treat them separately in order to 'prove' that Marx's theory of profit is still valid even if his theory of price is faulty (see, for example, Medio, 1972, 1977; Armstrong, Glyn and Harrison, 1978). However Sraffa's analysis clearly shows that these two issues are inextricably bound together so that a faulty explanation of prices must also be a faulty explanation of profit and vice versa.[8]

The third feature of the Sraffian approach is that the proximate determinants of prices, the rate of profit and the wage rate can be seen from an inspection of the above equations. Thus, the price of a commodity is determined by the physical quantity of inputs (A) and labour (a) and by the wage rate (m) and the corresponding rate of profit (r). In turn the rate of profit is determined by the physical quantity of inputs (A and a) and by the wage rate (m) while the wage rate is determined by the same physical inputs (A and a) and the rate of profit (r). These, however, are only the proximate determinants, and it is necessary also to consider their ultimate determinants. The ultimate determinants of the physical quantity of inputs of commodities and labour are the prevailing technical and social conditions of production (that is, technology, natural resources, workers' skills, work practices, intensity of the working day, and so on) while the ultimate determinants of the rate of profit and the corresponding wage rate hinge upon the respective power of workers and capitalists *vis-à-vis* the distribution of the net output.

The fourth feature of Sraffa's system of equations is that the quantity of inputs (A, a) can all be expressed in terms of labour (a) or indeed in terms of any commodity (A). This implies that the Marxian value of any commodity (that is, the quantity of labour embodied in it) can be derived and calculated from the data specifying the physical amount of commodities (A) and labour (a) needed to produce that commodity by simply expressing the latter in terms of labour (a). In turn the amount of surplus value can be calculated if, additionally, the wage rate (m) is known. Thus, Marx's three crucial value quantities (constant capital, variable capital and surplus value) can all be calculated, either for one commodity or for the economy as a whole, if the physical quantity of commodities and labour and the wage rate are known. The reverse process (that is, converting value quantities into physical quantities) is not, however, possible since the value of constant capital cannot be reduced to the physical quantities from which it is derived.

This has two implications from the point of view of Marx's labour theory of value. The first is that Sraffa's approach is more fundamental than Marx's approach in the sense that the physical inputs of commodities and labour and the wage rate determine not only the rate of profit and prices; they also determine values and surplus value. In other words, values are not, as Marx thought, the most basic elements which determine the price of a commodity; the more basic elements are the physical quantities of commodities and labour which go to produce it. The second implication is that, if one is interested in explaining the rate of profit and prices, as Marx was, then the correct approach is not to start with values and then transform them into prices, as Marx did, but to start with the physical quantity of commodities and labour and the wage rate, and then show how the rate of profit and prices can be derived from this datum (Samuelson, 1971, pp. 419–21; Hodgson, 1977b, pp. 101–5; see Steedman, 1977, chapters 3 and 4). These considerations can be summarised, following Steedman (1975a, p.78; 1977, p.48) in Figure 1.1, which shows the relationship between physical quantities, value quantities and price quantities.

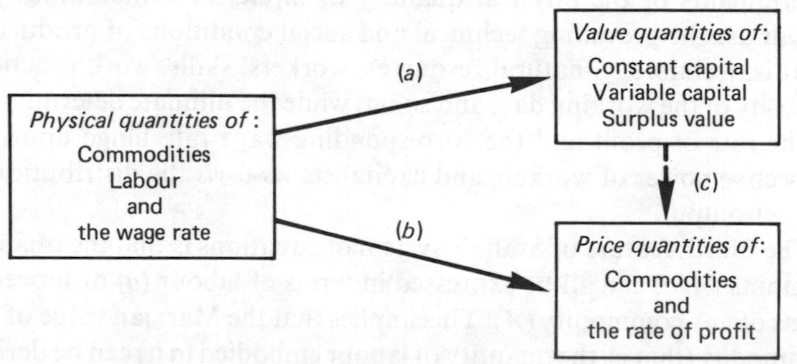

Figure 1.1 The relationships between physical, value and price quantities

Arrows (*a*) and (*b*) indicate that both value quantities and price quantities can only be derived from physical quantities. Arrow (*c*) shows that price quantities can be derived from value quantities if Bortkiewicz's transformation procedure is used (see section 1.5 above) even though, as has been seen (ibid.), there is no systematic relationship between values and prices, or between surplus value and profit. Arrow (*b*) shows the most direct way of explaining prices and profit and, for the reasons just cited, it is also the best way.

These are the main features of the Sraffian approach. As has been seen, this approach is concerned with the sames issues as Marx. The important difference between them is that the Sraffian approach is free from the difficulties associated with the labour theory of value. Thus the weight of arguments [9] is strongly in fabour of the Sraffian approach and the rejection of the labour theory of value.

1.7 CONCLUSION

Marx's labour theory of value has been examined in detail in this chapter. It was seen, in the course of examining the transformation problem and its solution, that this theory did not in fact show, as Marx had intended, that value and surplus value were related to price and profit in a constant and systematic way. The work of Sraffa was also examined in some detail and it was seen that his work deals with the same issues that are central to Marx, albeit in a more rigorous and less problematic way. There is therefore, as a consequence of this analysis, a compelling case for the rejection of the labour theory of value and the adoption of the Sraffian approach. Consequently, the Sraffian approach will be adopted, where relevant, throughout the remainder of this work.

2 Marxian Crisis Theory

2.0 INTRODUCTION

The concept of crisis is central to the entire Marxian framework even though Marx never completed and unified a systematic theory of crisis (see Sweezy, 1942, pp. 133–4; Howard and King, 1975, pp. 210–211; Alcaly, 1978, p. 17). In this chapter three types of crisis are identified and discussed. These are: the law of the falling rate of profit (section 2.1), realisation crisis (section 2.2) and rising real wages (section 2.3).

A number of features should be noted about these three types of crisis. First of all Marx only identified two possible sources of crisis; the law of the falling rate of profit and realisation crisis. There is no evidence from his writings that he ever realistically considered that rising real wages would give rise to a crisis within capitalism. However, recent evidence (Glyn and Sutcliffe, 1972;[1]Boddy and Crotty, 1975;[2] Weisskopf, 1979;[3] Heap, 1980[4]) suggests that rising real wages may be an important factor in explaining the profitability crisis within contemporary capitalism. For this reason there is a growing tendency for Marxists to distinguish three variants of Marxian crisis theory (see, for example Alcaly, 1975, 1978; Shaikh, 1978, see p. 376; Weisskopf, 1978, 1979;) in contrast to the more traditional two variants (see, for example, Sweezy, 1942; Howard and King, 1975, 1976; Sowell, 1976; Elster, 1985, pp. 154–65).

The second notable feature about these three types of crisis is that each poses a threat to the stability and growth of the capitalist system essentially because they reduce the rate of profit. However, each affects the rate of profit in different ways and this fact raises complex econometric problems. The reason for this is that it may be extremely difficult to disentangle the different chains of causation which are operative in a situation where there is a crisis of profitability, although Weisskopf (1979) appears to have successfully overcome this problem in his analysis of the US economy.

A third feature is that some of these types of crisis are secular (that is, long-run) while others are cyclical (that is, short-run).[5] In the case of the law of the falling rate of profit, it is clear that this is a secular crisis since the underlying factors which determine it are, in Marx's view, structurally irreversible. In other words, the law of the falling rate of profit is seen as endemic in the capitalist system because of the type of technical innovations which capitalists adopt. In the case of realisation crises, these are cyclical in nature since their proximate causes are inherently temporary, albeit recurring. It was in the context of a discussion of realisation crises that Marx affirmed that 'permanent crises do not exist' (Marx, 1969, p. 497). The case of rising real wages is perhaps less clear cut, although it would seem wiser to regard it as a cyclical rather than a secular crisis. This is because the growth of trade union power which is associated with rising real wages cannot strictly speaking, be regarded as a structurally inevitable and irreversible feature of the capitalist system.

The significance of Marxian crisis theory, in the present context, derives from the fact that both Manuel Castells and Jean Lojkine, whose work is examined in detail in Chapters 6 and 7 respectively, resort to different versions of Marxian crisis theory in order to explain, *inter alia*, the causes and consequences of state intervention in the area of collective consumption. The present analysis has the advantage of providing a precise clarification of Marxian crisis theory as a prelude to assessing the validity and reliability of these explanations.

The analysis of Marxian crisis theory begins with the law of the falling rate of profit. This is treated in section 2.1. The basic analytical procedure is to present Marx's own explanation of the 'law' (subsection 2.1.2.) and then to assess it in terms of its logical coherence and empirical accuracy (subsections 2.1.3 to 2.1.5). It will be seen, to anticipate, that Marx's 'law' does not have the law-like quality which he attributed to it. Moreover, while Marx's law can be shown to have an internal coherence under certain specified (though unrealistic) conditions, it is not realistically conceivable (as long as capitalists continued to be rational profit-maximisers) that the rate of profit could fall as a result of the mechanisms postulated by this variant of crisis theory. Thus the explanatory role of this variant of Marxian crisis theory is negligible.

The analysis of realisation crisis is undertaken in section 2.2. Marx's disparate references to realisation crisis are brought together and moulded to form a coherent theory. In the process, some references (notably those which could be adduced to show that Marx was a crude underconsumptionist) have had to be excised from the analysis because they are untenable *per se*, and, in addition, are inconsistent with the main thrust of Marx's theory. The discussion is divided, following Marx, into two parts; the first and shorter part is concerned with the ultimate causes which make a realisation crisis possible (subsection 2.2.2), while the second part is concerned with the proximate causes which make this possibility an actuality (subsections 2.2.3 to 2.2.7). Four proximate causes are identified and discussed; the absence of macroeconomic planning (subsection 2.2.3), technical innovation (subsection 2.2.4), variable weather conditions (subsection 2.2.5), and scarcity of labour (subsection 2.2.6). It will be observed that the first two of these proximate causes are endogenous while the final two are exogenous. This variant of Marx's crisis theory represents a possible (indeed probable) explanation of some of the crises of capitalism since it is based upon an accurate characterisation of some features of the capitalist economy. The analysis of rising real wages in section 2.3 represents a departure from Marx in that he never considered it possible for real wages to rise to a level where they would, *ceteris paribus*, threaten profits. Indeed the analysis in this section shows that Marx held a subsistence theory of wages (subsection 2.3.2 to 2.3.4) which, if this theory is to have any semblance of meaning, must imply that the share of wages in net output is likely to fall (given Marx's view of technical change) and that the share of profits (and, by corollary, the rate of profit) must rise. The crucial factor in this context is trade unions (subsection 2.3.5) whose powers have increased considerably since the time Marx was writing. This analysis, in conjunction with some recent evidence on the profitability crisis in some capitalist countries, suggests that this form of crisis may be of crucial importance.

It should be noted, finally, that the analysis below is conducted in terms of values. This is because most of the issues being considered are independent of whether one's economic categories are expressed in terms of values or prices. The retention of values has, moreover, the advantage of addressing and assessing the issues in precisely the way that Marx formulated them. However, these considerations in no way diminish from the seriousness of the critique of the labour theory of value presented in the preceding chapter.

2.1 THE LAW OF THE FALLING RATE OF PROFIT

2.1.1 Introduction

Marx regarded his 'law of the tendency of the rate of profit to fall' (Marx, 1974c, Chapter 13) as the most importance source of crisis in capitalism. This is evidenced by his assertion, in the *Grundrisse*, that 'this is in every respect the most important law of modern political economy, and the most essential for understanding the most difficult relations. It is the most important law from the historical standpoint' (Marx, 1973, p. 748).

It is not surprising that Marx should take this view given that the *raison d'être* of capitalist production is profit. By corollary, a persistent decline in the rate of profit will lead, *ceteris paribus*, to an underutilisation of existing capital equipment and to a decline in new investment which, in turn, will cause a decline in output and employment. This effectively creates a situation where there is unused (and hence excess) productive capacity in the economy or, as Marx variously put it, an 'over-accumulation of capital' (Marx, 1974c, p. 251) and an 'over-production of capital' (ibid). (Some contemporary Marxists, notably those who adhere to the state monopoly capitalism thesis, have slightly modified Marx's terminology by referring to such situations as a crisis of 'over-accumulation-devalorization' (see section 5.2).

In order to evaluate the validity of Marx's law of the falling rate of profit, it is first necessary to summarise the law as Marx formulated it in *Capital*, Vol. III, Part III (Marx 1974c, pp. 211–66). This is done in subsection 2.1.2. Two issues then arise in respect of the validity of this law. The first issue is whether there are any circumstances where it would be possible for the rate of profit to fall in the manner predicted by Marx's law. This issue is considered in subsection 2.1.3 where it will be seen that, if the actual rate of profit is equal to the maximum rate of profit, then a rise in the organic composition of capital will cause the rate of profit to fall. The second issue is whether a fall in the actual rate of profit is inevitable in the course of capitalist development. In subsection 2.1.4, it will be shown that it is not inevitable. Finally, a definitive refutation of Marx's law is presented in 2.1.5.

2.1.2 Marx's Formulation of the Law

Marx's law of the falling rate of profit begins from the assumption that in the capitalist system of production there will be a predominant tendency for capitalists to continually introduce labour-saving/capital-using technical innovations in order to increase productivity, profit, and, ultimately, capital accumulation. Marx based this assumption on two related claims. First, he claimed that technical change would result in an increase in the mass of the means of production (that is, machines, buildings and so on) relative to the mass (or size) of the labour force. Marx expressed this by saying that the technical composition of capital would rise. Second, he claimed that this would, in turn, result in a more or less corresponding increase in the value of the means of production (that is, constant capital) relative to the aggregate value of labour power (that is, variable capital). Marx expressed this by saying that the organic (or value) composition of capital would rise.

Marx then argued that as the value composition of capital tended to rise the rate of profit would tend to fall, irrespective of whether the rate of exploitation remained 'the same' (Marx 1974c, pp. 212, 213) or was 'rising' (ibid, p. 213). The logic of Marx's argument was that, since all surplus value (and hence profit) could only be derived from living labour (that is, variable capital), the latter's relative decline *vis-à-vis* dead labour (that is, constant capital) implied that surplus value (and hence profit) must also ultimately decline.

Marx realised, indeed insisted, that although the predominant tendency would be for the rate of profit to fall as capitalism developed, there were a number of 'counteracting influences' (Marx, 1974c, Chapter 14) which could diminish or even halt (albeit temporarily) the decline in the rate of profit. These tendencies and counter-tendencies can be seen more clearly in the light of an examination of Marx's formula for the rate of profit. Marx defined the rate of profit (r) as:

$$r = \frac{S}{C + V}$$

where S = total surplus value; C = total constant capital and V = total variable capital. Marx's formula can be rewritten as:

$$r = \frac{\frac{S}{V}}{1 + \frac{C}{V}}$$

From this expression, it is apparent that the rate of profit (r) will only fall if the organic composition of capital (C/V) increases at a faster rate than the rate of surplus value (S/V). In other words Marx's law of the falling rate of profit can be formally stated in the following way: there will be a tendency within capitalism for the organic composition of capital to rise at a faster rate than the rate of exploitation such that the net effect, in the long run, is to reduce the rate of profit (Howard and King, 1976, p. 37).[6] This net effect is assumed to be both necessary and inevitable even though it may encounter certain 'counteracting influences' which may cause the organic composition of capital to fall (for example, productivity increases, foreign trade) or cause the rate of exploitation to rise (for example, a reduction in real wages, an increase in the length and intensity of the working day, foreign trade, relative overpopulation) or both.

In assessing the validity of this law, it is necessary to consider two issues. The first issue is whether there are any circumstances in which a rising organic composition of capital could lead to a falling rate of profit despite the counteracting influence of a rising rate of exploitation. The second issue is whether the rate of profit will inevitably fall in the manner and for the reasons described by Marx. It will be apparent that the first issue focuses on the question of whether the outcome predicted by Marx's law is possible while the second focuses on whether it is inevitable. These issues will now be considered in turn.

2.1.3 The Possibility of a Fall in the Maximum Rate of Profit

Marx argued that technical change was an integral part of capitalist development. Technical change, he argued, would take the form of adopting capital-using/labour-saving innovations, the effect of which would be to increase the organic composition of capital. The effect of this, in turn, would be that the relative quantity of labour employed would be reduced leading, *ceteris paribus*, to a decline in the relative quantity of surplus value produced and ultimately to a decline in the rate of profit. Marx recognised that capitalists would attempt to compensate for this effect by increasing the rate of exploitation (through increases in productivity and in the length and intensity of the work day), thereby offsetting the decline in the rate of profit. However, Marx also pointed out that the possibility of increasing the rate of exploitation in order to compensate for the effects of the rise in the organic composition of capital had certain 'insurmountable limits'. As a consequence, he argued, the rate of profit must ultimately fall if the organic composition continues to rise.

Marx's analysis up to this point is internally consistent although it is incomplete in the sense that it fails to specify precisely the limits beyond which it becomes impossible to increase the rate of exploitation and hence to specify the point beyond which each increase in the organic composition of capital will result in a fall in the rate of profit.

The limit beyond which it is not possible to increase the organic composition of capital without causing a fall in the rate of profit arises when the rate of profit has reached a maximum. In capitalist society, the (theoretically) maximum rate of profit is that corresponding to zero wages. As Sraffa has pointed out 'the notion of a maximum rate of profit corresponding to a zero wage' (Sraffa, 1960, p. 94), was suggested by Marx in his discussion of the falling rate of profit when he referred to the fact that a rise in the organic composition of capital would lead to a fall in the rate of profit even if workers 'could live on air' (Marx, 1974c, p. 247).

This fact can be illustrated by inspecting the formula for the maximum rate of profit (in value terms). If the rate of profit is at a maximum, this means that wages must be zero and the entire output of direct labour must count as surplus. Thus the maximum rate of profit may be defined as:

$$r_{\max} = \frac{S+V}{C+V}$$

Any inspection of this formula reveals that if variable capital is zero ($V=0$) and if it is not possible to increase the rate of surplus value by increasing absolute surplus value (since it is already impossible to increase relative surplus value because variable capital is zero) then every increase in constant capital (C) will lead, *ceteris paribus*, to an increase in the organic composition of capital (C/V) and this will lead, in turn, to a fall in the maximum rate of profit (see Dickinson, 1957; Meek, 1976a, pp. 217–18; Steedman, 1977, Chapter 9).

This result is highly formal in the sense that the possibility of a fall in the maximum rate of profit does not necessarily imply a fall in the actual rate of profit. This analysis simply proves that there are certain circumstances where a rising organic composition of capital would inevitably lead to a falling rate of profit. However, the fact that this is theoretically possible does not imply that it is actually possible or likely. It is therefore necessary to examine if a rising organic composition of capital and a falling rate of profit are actually possible or likely.

2.1.4 The Possibility of a Fall in the Actual Rate of Profit

It will be apparent from an inspection of Marx's formula for the rate of profit, that the actual movement of the rate of profit in the course of capitalist development will be crucially dependent upon the direction of change in the organic composition of capital and the rate of exploitation; only if the former increases more rapidly than the latter will there be a tendency for the rate of profit to fall. Thus, consideration will now be given to Marx's analysis of the long-term direction of change in the organic composition of capital and the rate of exploitation, respectively.

Marx asserted that the organic composition of capital would tend to rise in the course of capitalist development. This assertion involves two related assumptions. The first is that technical change will tend to be labour-saving and capital-using, and the second is that this type of technical change will result in a rising organic composition of capital.

Both of these assumptions will now be critically examined.

Marx's assumption that capitalists, in the pursuit of increased productivity and profit, will tend to adopt labour-saving/capital using technical innovations is an assumption about the actual behaviour of capitalists. When Marx wrote *Capital* this was probably an accurate empirical generalisation of capitalist behaviour; and this may explain Marx's reason for making this assumption. However, this assumption is very difficult to justify since there would seem to be no good reason for assuming that capitalists will necessarily and inevitably adopt either labour-saving or capital-using technical innovations. It simply depends upon which is the most profitable at the time. Since capitalists are concerned, in general, with minimising costs and maximising profits, it follows that the nature of technical innovation will be highly contingent on such factors as the availability of a cheap and docile labour force, government grants, new technology, the scale of production, the type of product being produced, etc. The more general point is that Marx's assumption about the nature of technical change, whatever its historical justification, is unwarranted (see Sweezy, 1973, p. 28; Howard and King, 1975, p. 203; Wright, 1978; p. 136).

Marx's second assumption was that capital-using technical change would lead to a rising organic (or value) composition of capital. His argument was that technical change would give rise to an increase in the total quantity of constant capital (thereby causing an increase in what he termed the technical composition of capital) and to an increase in the total value of constant capital (thus causing, *ceteris paribus*, a rise in the organic composition of capital).

There are basically two difficulties with this argument. The first is that Marx's concept of the technical composition of capital is extremely vague, essentially because heterogeneous physical objects are incommensurable, and hence their physical quantity cannot be aggregated (at least not meaningfully and sensibly). There is, in other words, no way of establishing whether the 'mass' or 'quantity' of constant capital has increased or decreased between two points in time except by aggregation in terms of values or prices. It is thus conceptually unclear what Marx meant when he claimed that the technical composition of capital would tend to rise in the course of capitalist development (see Howard and King, 1976, p. 38, fn 27; Steedman, 1977, pp. 132–6).

The second difficulty is Marx's claim that the value/organic composition of capital will tend to rise as a result of capital-using technical change. The difficulty with this claim is that it is (equally) possible for the organic composition of capital to fall as a result of such technical change. This possibility follows from the fact that increases in productivity in those industries which actually produce the means of production can result in a given type of machine being produced with less and less embodied labour time (that is, less and less value). In this case technical change would lead to a fall rather than a rise in the organic composition of capital. Although Marx referred to this possibility, he assumed, without any rigorous justification, that this occurred only in 'isolated cases' (Marx, 1974c, p. 236; see also p. 212). It is thus not possible to affirm, *a priori*, what precise effect technical change will have on the organic composition of capital (see Purdy, 1973).

The more general point to emerge from this analysis is that Marx's assertion about the tendency for the organic composition of capital to rise cannot be shown to be either necessary or inevitable. This, of course, does not exclude the possibility that it may rise; it simply demonstrates that there is no inherent or inevitable tendency for it to change (that is, increase or decrease) in any given direction within capitalism.

The same general result also applies with respect to the rate of exploitation. Marx argued that a rising organic composition of capital would lead to a falling rate of profit, irrespective of whether the rate of exploitation remained 'the same' (Marx, 1974c, pp. 212, 213) or was 'rising' (ibid., p. 213). His own assumptions about the future development of capitalism (notably the prospect of technical change coupled with subsistence wages) must have obliged Marx to expect that the rate of exploitation would continue to rise (see subsection 2.3.4). Given this expectation therefore, there does not seem to be any realistic reason for expecting this rise to be constrained by some upper limit (as Marx's law requires) unless the limiting case of zero wages (see subsection 2.1.3) is regarded as realistic. Thus, even on the basis of Marx's own expectations, his assumption that the rise in the rate of exploitation will not 'compensate' for the rise in the organic composition of capital does not seem to be firmly and realistically grounded. The more general point, therefore, is that there is no reason to expect the rate of exploitation to move in the precise direction required by Marx's law.

It has now been established that Marx's expectations about the way in which the organic composition of capital and the rate of exploitation must inevitably change in the course of capitalist development, do not have any solid or realistic basis. The logical implication of this is that his expectation that the rate of profit would tend to fall in the course of capitalist development does not have any solid or realistic basis either.[7]

2.1.5 Technical Change and the Rate of Profit

The analysis so far has discussed the law of the falling rate of profit within the parameters set down by Marx. In other words, it has focused on whether the decisions and actions of capitalists in relation to technical innovation would be such as to raise the organic composition of capital and the rate of exploitation in such a way as to lead ultimately to a fall in the rate of profit. On the basis of this analysis it has been shown that technical change affects the organic composition of capital and the rate of exploitation simultaneously, and that the net effect of this technical change cannot be ascertained *a priori* (see Bortkiewicz, 1952, p. 47.) There is, however, a further piece of analysis which also shows Marx's law to be invalid. This analysis is usually referred to as 'Okishio's theorem' (Okishio, 1961, though the argument has also been attributed to Samuelson; see Howard and King 1975, p. 232, fn 31).

The basic argument is that no rational calculating capitalist would ever knowingly introduce a technical innovation which would cause a fall in the rate of profit; if, due to unforeseen and unintended consequences, a new technique reduced the rate of profit, capitalists would, *ceteris paribus*, revert to the previous technique. The reasons for this can be illustrated as follows.

For any given technique of production, there is an inverse relation between the real wage rate and the rate of profit. This is illustrated in Figure 2.1 (adapted from Steedman, 1977, pp. 127–8; see also Howard and King, 1975, pp. 208–9).

The line *AB* shows the different possible combinations of the rate of profit and the real wage rate for that technique (Technique I). If an additional technique (Technique II) is introduced, it too can be described by its own particular combination of wage and profit rates represented by the line *CD*.

The capitalist confronted with any two techniques will have to decide which is the most profitable at any given wage rate. In this example, it can be seen that if the real wage rate is below w^* then Technique I will be chosen, while if it is above w^*, Technique II will be chosen. If the real wage is equal to w^* then the capitalist will be indifferent as to which technique he adopts since both are equiprofitable at that point.

If technical innovation occurs again in this economy, then at least some part of the line describing this new technique (Technique III) must lie to the right of the wage-profit frontier (*AED*). This is because, for it to be an innovation, the attainable rate of profit must be higher, for at least

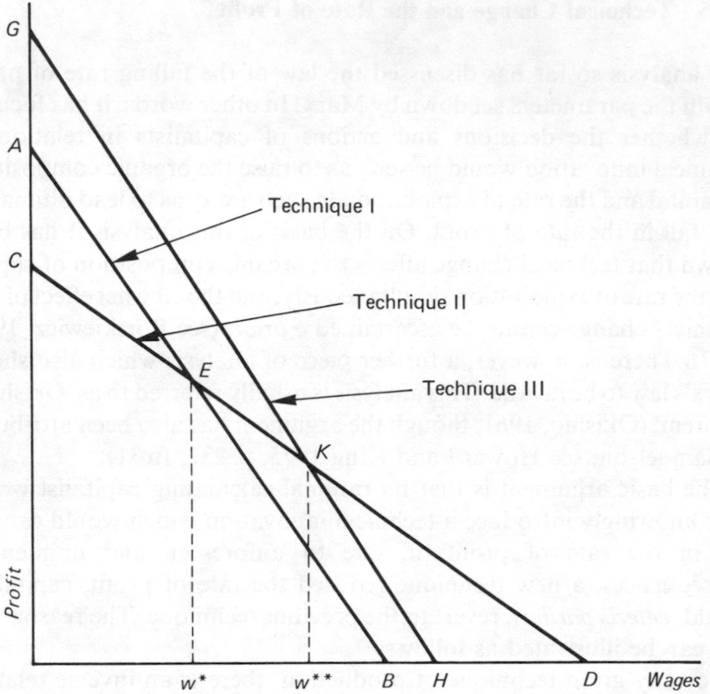

Figure 2.1 The relationship between wages and profit for different techniques of production

certain real wage rates, than the rate of profit attainable by the preceding techniques (Techniques I and II). If the line describing this new technique is *GKH* then it can be seen that, at any wage below w**, the new technique (Technique III) will be more profitable than any of the previous ones, and will therefore, *ceteris paribus*, be adopted. In other words, the new Technique III will be more profitable, at any point on the line *GK*, for any wage level below *w***. If, however, the real wage should rise above *w*** then the capitalist will find that this new technique becomes unprofitable (by comparison with the rates of profit attainable using Technique II) and he/she will revert to the older Technique II (on the line *CP*). The more general point is that no technique will ever be adopted, if and once it is known that its effect is to reduce the rate of profit. It is perhaps ironic that Marx should have made precisely this argument in *Capital*, Vol. III, Chapter 15 where he discusses the falling rate of profit. He writes: 'No capitalist ever voluntarily introduces a new method of production, no matter how much more productive it may be, and how much it may increase the rate of surplus value, so long as it reduces the rate of profit' (Marx, 1974c, p. 264). However, he subsequently rejected this argument – wrongly – on the ground that the aggregate effect of innovations was to increase the organic composition of capital, thereby causing, *ceteris paribus*, the rate of profit to fall. For all of the preceding reasons, there is no justification for assuming that technical innovation will lead to a fall in the rate of profit.

2.1.6 Conclusion

The analysis in this section has shown that there is no 'law' by which it is either necessary or inevitable for the rate of profit to fall in the course of capitalist development, as Marx claimed. This is not to deny that such a fall is a possibility; it simply denies that it is inevitable.

This result is not particularly novel, having already been established and repeated by numerous writers (see notably, Bortkiewicz, 1952, pp. 37–50; Steedman, 1972, 1975a, pp. 79–80; 1977, Chapter 9; Hodgson, 1974a, 1975; Howard and King, 1975, pp. 203–9; Roemer, 1977, 1978b, 1979, 1981, Chapter 5; Weisskopf, 1979; Van Parijs, 1980; Harris, 1983). However, it is a result which has not yet made an impact on the recent French Marxist urban sociology of Manuel Castells (see Chapter 6) or Jean Lojkine (see Chapter 7) for whom Marx's law of the falling rate of profit has considerable importance, particularly in the explanation of collective consumption (see sections 6.2, 7.2 and subsection 7.3.2).

2.2 REALISATION CRISES

2.2.1 Introduction

There are various references in Marx's work to realisation crises, though nowhere does he give a systemic and comprehensive analysis of them. The main sources are: *Theories of Surplus Value*, Part 2, Sections 6–14 (1969, pp. 492–535) and *Capital*, Vol. 2, Chapters 20 and 21 (1974b, pp. 396–527). Although this type of crisis is often referred to as a crisis of overproduction and underconsumption (see notably Sweezy, 1942, Chapter 10; Howard and King, 1976, p. 34; Alcaly, 1978, p. 18; Shaikh, 1978, p. 226; Weisskopf, 1978, p. 246) it is more accurately described as a realisation crisis for two reasons. The first is that it arises because of an inability by the capitalist to use or sell his/her commodities and hence realise the profit for which they were originally produced. The second reason is that overproduction and underconsumption are the effects of this realisation crisis (rather than the cause) in the same way that they are the effects of the (alleged) tendency of the rate of profit to fall (see subsection 2.1.1).

It should be emphasised that the term overproduction, as used by Marx, refers to the production of a quantity of commodities in excess of the quantity which can be sold at the going price of production, that is, in excess of effective demand (see Marx, 1974b, pp. 414–15). 'It is not a question' Marx emphasises, 'of absolute overproduction – overproduction as such in relation to absolute need or desire to possess commodities' (Marx, 1969, pp. 506, 527; see also 1974c, pp. 255–7). Thus it is perfectly possible (given this terminology) for a crisis of overproduction to coexist with a famine in a given capitalist country. A similar reasoning also applies to Marx's use of the term 'overpopulation' (see section 2.3.3).

Realisation crises are essentially cyclical (that is, short-run) in nature. As Marx insisted in this context: 'Permanent crises do not exist' (Marx, 1969, p. 497).

The major difficulty with any attempt to outline Marx's theory of realisation crisis is, as numerous writers and critics have pointed out, that Marx never systematically worked out his theory (Sweezy, 1942, pp. 133–4; Howard and King, 1975, pp. 210–11, 1976, p. 33; Alcaly, 1978, p. 17; Morishima and Catephores, 1978, p. 118, fn10; Elster, 1985, pp. 154, 161; for a contrary view see Sowell, 1976, pp. 56–7). The present section is, therefore, an attempt to present a systematic and coherent account of Marx's theory of realisation crisis. The analysis begins, following Marx, by indicating those factors which make a realisation crisis possible (subsection 2.2.2). This is followed by an analysis of the four proximate causes of realisation crises; the absence of macroeconomic planning (subsection 2.2.3), technical innovation (subsection 2.2.4), variable weather conditions (subsection 2.2.5), and scarcity of labour (subsection 2.2.6).[8] Each of these will now be discussed respectively.

2.2.2 The Possibility of Realisation Crisis

Every realisation crisis expresses itself in the fact that the act of sale is separated, in time and space, from the act of purchase. 'If purchase and sale coincided', Marx affirms, 'the possibility of crisis would under the assumptions made, disappear' (Marx, 1969, p. 508). This separation of purchase from sale is possible in any system of commodity production, simple or capitalist, and is the result of the fact that every commodity must be transformed into money and vice versa, and it is this 'metamorphosis of commodities' (ibid., p. 500) which creates the possibility of crisis.

Marx contrasts this situation with that of barter, where the possibility of realisation crises does not exist. 'In Barter this contradiction does not exist: no one can be a seller without being a buyer – or a buyer without being a seller' (ibid., p. 509).

The possibility of a realisation crisis can be revealed more fully by looking at the typical circuit of capital. This can be represented as follows:

$$M \rightarrow C^{LP}_{MP} \rightarrow \boxed{P} \rightarrow C^1 \rightarrow M^1$$

or

$$M \rightarrow C + V \rightarrow \boxed{P} \rightarrow C + V + S \rightarrow M^1$$

where:

M = the amount of money which the capitalist owns at the beginning of the production process;
C^{LP}_{MP} = the commodities of labour power and means of production purchased by the capitalist at the beginning of the production process;
$C + V$ = constant capital plus variable capital;
$\boxed{P}$ = the production process;
C^1 = the new commodity;
$C + V + S$ = constant capital plus variable capital plus surplus value;
M^1 = the money which the capitalist receives from the sale of the new commodity;
M^1 = $M + \Delta M = S$.

The possibility of a realisation crisis exists in this case if the capitalist is unable to sell C^1 (and hence realise profit) or if, having sold C^1 (for M^1) (s)he cannot purchase the same quantity of commodities as formerly (C^{LP}_{MP}) at the same price, and hence cannot reinvest his/her money at the same rate of profit. In this case, sale and purchase 'become separated' (ibid., p. 514), 'get bogged down' (ibid., p. 494) and are 'falling asunder' (ibid., p. 510).

Having established that the possibility of a realisation crisis is contained in the form of commodity exchange (thereby refuting Say's law (ibid., p. 493)), Marx immediately emphasises that 'the factors which turn this possibility of crisis into an actual crisis are not contained in this form itself: it only implies that the framework for a crisis exists' (ibid., p. 509). It is now necessary to look at the second part of Marx's analysis which identifies some of the factors by which this 'possibility can develop into actuality' (ibid., p. 512).

It is possible, following Marx, to identify at least four proximate causes of a realisation crisis.[8] These four causes are the absence of macroeconomic planning, technical innovation, variable weather conditions and scarcity of labour.

Each of these situations can give rise to a crisis of overproduction and underconsumption. The processes by which this occurs, in each case, will now be examined respectively.

2.2.3 Realisation Crisis Caused by the Absence of Macroeconomic Planning

One of the characteristic features of competitive capitalism is that production is owned and controlled by individual capitalists. These capitalists, in turn, are independent and autonomous of each other and, as a result, there is no ex-anté co-ordination or regulation of their separate investment decisions. In this sense, capitalism does not produce 'according to a plan' (Marx, 1969, p. 529). This fact, Marx pointed out, can lead to a realisation crisis. To understand Marx's reasons for making this claim, it is necessary to examine his two-sector model as outlined in *Capital*, Vol. II, Chapters 20 and 21 (Marx, 1974b, pp. 396–527) (for a useful discussion of this part of Marx's work, see Naqvi, 1960).

Marx's model of simple reproduction (that is, a stationary state) distinguishes between Sector I which produces means of production and Sector II which produces consumption goods.[9] Following the usual notation this two-sector model can be written as follows:

Sector I : $M_1 \rightarrow C_1 + V_1 \rightarrow \boxed{P} \rightarrow C_1 + V_1 + S_1 \rightarrow Y_1 \rightarrow M_1$
Sector II: $M_2 \rightarrow C_2 + V_2 \rightarrow \boxed{P} \rightarrow C_2 + V_2 + S_2 \rightarrow Y_2 \rightarrow M_2$

where

M_1, M_2 = the total quantity of money at the beginning of production in Sectors I and II;
C_1, C_2 = the quantities of constant capital in Sectors I and II respectively;
V_1, V_2 = the quantities of variable capital in Sectors I and II respectively;

$\boxed{P}$ = the production process;
S_1, S_2 = the quantity of surplus value produced in Sectors I and II respectively;
Y_1, Y_2 = the value of the output of Sectors I and II respectively;
M_1, M_2^1 = the quantity of money at the end of the production process in Sectors I and II respectively.

A number of features should be noted about this model. First of all it is, by assumption, a model of simple reproduction, that is, there is zero economic growth. This means that there is no technological change and the same quantity of inputs and outputs are produced and reproduced each year. The second feature is that a number of inter- and intra-sectoral exchanges have to take place to ensure that production actually continues. In effect this means that the output of both sectors (Y_1 and Y_2) will have to be distributed in such a way that each has the amount of means of production and consumption goods which they require to continue production on the same scale.

In the case of Sector I, its output (Y_1) must be such as to ensure that the input requirements of both sectors for means of production (C_1 and C_2) are satisfied. If this occurs then:

$$Y_1 = C_1 + C_2$$

In the case of Sector II, its output (Y_2) must be such as to ensure that the input requirements of both sectors for consumption goods (V_1,S_1,V_2,S_2) are satisfied. If this occurs then:

$$Y_2 = V_1 + S_1 + V_2 + S_2.$$

These two conditions, taken together, imply that simple reproduction is only possible if the quantity of consumption goods required by Sector I ($V_1 + S_1$) is equal to the quantity of means of production required by Sector II (C_2). In other words, the equilibrium condition for simple reproduction is:

$$C_2 = V_1 + S_1 \qquad \text{(see Marx, 1974b, Chapter 20)}$$

It is now possible, using this model, to specify one reason why a realisation crisis is possible within capitalism. This reason derives from the fact that the output produced by each of the two sectors in this model is the result of independent and uncoordinated decisions by a large number of capitalists. The question therefore arises (as Marx rhetorically put it): 'How is it possible to achieve the necessary balance and interdependence of the various spheres of production, their dimensions and the proportions between them, except through the constant neutralization of a constant disharmony?' (Marx, 1969, p. 529; see also Marx, 1974b, p. 499).

Marx's rhetorical question draws attention to the fact that the correct proportions which must be maintained between the different departments of production, if production is to remain in equilibrium, are likely to be upset simply because there is no ex-ante, calculated, co-ordination between the various production units. In turn, the calculations which each capitalist undertakes as to his/her anticipated level of input and output are likely to be inaccurate, essentially because he/she does not have access to the plans of other production units upon whom he/she depends for the purchase of inputs or the sale of outputs. The capitalist is thereby precluded, as a general rule, from any calculated co-ordination with other production units. As a result 'disproportionate production' (Marx, 1969, p. 521) is 'not only possible but very probable' (ibid., p. 531). This is true, *a fortiori*, in the case of expanded reproduction, as will now be seen.

Marx discusses expanded reproduction in *Capital*, Vol. II, Chapter 21 (Marx, 1974b, pp. 493–527). Expanded reproduction refers to the situation where there is positive economic growth. The difference between simple and expanded reproduction therefore centres on the use to which the surplus is put at the end of the production process: in the case of simple reproduction the surplus is entirely consumed whereas in the case of extended reproduction the surplus is only partly consumed, the remainder being used for reinvestment. Following the notation adopted above, the nature of expanded reproduction in a two-sector model can be described as follows:

Sector I:

$$M_1 \rightarrow C_1 + V_1 \rightarrow \boxed{P} \rightarrow C_1 + V_1 + (S_{01} + S_{C1} + S_{V1}) \rightarrow Y_1 \rightarrow M_1^1$$

Sector II:

$$M_2 \rightarrow C_2 + V_2 \rightarrow \boxed{P} \rightarrow C_2 + V_2 + (S_{02} + S_{C2} + S_{V2}) \rightarrow Y_2 \rightarrow M_2^1$$

where, in addition to the usual notation:

S_{01}, S_{02} = the quantity of surplus value which is consumed by capitalists in Sectors I and II respectively;

S_{C1}, S_{C2} = the quantity of surplus value which is reinvested by capitalists in constant capital in Sectors I and II respectively;

S_{V1}, S_{V2} = the quantity of surplus value reinvested by capitalists in variable capital in Sectors I and II respectively;

$(S_{01} = S_{C1} + S_{V1})$ = the total quantity of surplus value produced in Sector I;
$(S_{02} + S_{C2} + S_{V2})$ = the total quantity of surplus value produced in Sector II;

In this model, the total output of Sector I is equal to the total means of production required by the economy:

$$Y_1 = C_1 + C_2 + S_{C1} + S_{C2}$$

Similarly, the total output of Sector II is equal to the total consumption goods required by the economy:

$$Y_2 = V_1 + (S_{01} + S_{V1}) + V_2 + (S_{02} + S_V 2).$$

From these two statements, it is possible to infer that the equilibrium condition for expanded reproduction is

$$C_2 + S_{C2} = V_1 + S_{01} + S_{V1}$$

It is further possible to infer that the over-all rate of growth in the economy is equal to:

$$\frac{S_{C1} + S_{C2} + S_{V1} + S_{V2}}{C_1 + C_2 + V_1 + V_2}$$

The significance of expanded reproduction in the present context is that it increases the probability of a realisation crisis by comparison with simple reproduction. The precise reasons for this will now be explored by examining the consequences which follow when 'too much' of a particular commodity is produced in relation to effective demand. (A similar type of analysis could also be applied to the analagous case where 'too little' is produced in relation to effective demand.)

The existence of too much of a particular commodity (for example, cotton, yarn) can arise when, in a period of expanded reproduction, capitalists in one sector only (for example Sector I) invest in new and additional fixed capital, the net effect of which is that the output of the commodity in question exceeds that required by other departments as inputs. The consequence of this is that all of the output of Sector I cannot be sold, or can only be sold at a loss. In either case, each and every capitalist is unable to simultaneously cover all his/her costs (wages, depreciation, interest, rent, and so on) and make the going rate of profit and, as a result (assuming all costs are paid at the beginning of the production period) the rate of profit must fall.

This fall in the rate of profit can only be restored in the subsequent period of production if, *ceteris paribus* (that is, assuming a closed economy and no increase in domestic demand), the productive capacity in this sector is reduced. This can only be done by reducing the labour force and destroying the excess fixed capital in the sector. In this way, the overproduction of one commodity leads to the overproduction of yet other commodities, that is, wage goods and fixed capital goods. This in turn necessitates a reduction in capacity in the wage goods sector and in the sector producing fixed capital goods, and a corresponding reduction in those departments which supply these with inputs, and so on. In this way, the partial realisation crisis in one sector of production spreads as a result of the interdependence of production. Whether this partial crisis becomes a general crisis depends, in the first place, on the amount by which the original commodity is overproduced and, in the second place, on the extent to which this sector is dependent upon other sectors of production.

The implication of this analysis is that balanced economic growth within capitalism can only be achieved through rigorous planning based upon a systematic calculation of the projected level of inputs and outputs in the various departments in each period of production. The Russian economist, Michael Turgan-Baranowsky cogently demonstrated this point in 1901 (see Sweezy, 1942, pp. 158ff). He wrote:

> If social production were organized in accordance with a plan, if the directors of production had complete knowledge of demand and the power to direct labour and capital from one branch of production to another, then, however low social production might be, the supply of commodities could never outstrip the demand (ibid., p. 166).

The more general conclusion is that realisation crises are highly probable given the unplanned nature of the capitalist economy, irrespective of whether one assumes simple or expanded reproduction.

2.2.4 Realisation Crisis Caused by Technical Innovation

It is possible, from Marx's work, to identify two ways in which technical innovation can lead to a realisation crisis. Both cases reveal how technical innovation can result in the overproduction of a given commodity so that it cannot be sold at its price of production. In other words, the link between the commodity and money ($C-M$) becomes broken. Both of these cases (analysed separately here but not necessarily separate in reality) will now be dealt with.

The first case refers to a technical innovation which is adopted by all capitalists in a particular sector of production. The effect of this technical innovation is to double output, although there is no corresponding increase in the demand for this output from other sectors. In this situation there is a crisis of overproduction. Marx cites the following example of this: 'When spinning machines were invented, there was an overproduction of yarn in relation to weaving' (Marx, 1969, p. 521), adding that 'this disproportion disappeared when mechanical looms were introduced into weaving' (ibid.).

By definition this overproduction of spun cotton affects all capitalists involved in the spinning of cotton since it is the net, combined effect of their separate actions. The consequence of their overproduction is that all of the output of spun cotton cannot be sold or can only be sold at a loss. In either case, each and every capitalist is unable to simultaneously cover all his/her costs (wages, depreciation, interest, rent, and so on) and make the going rate of profit. As a result (assuming all costs are paid at the beginning of the production period) the rate of profit must fall. This fall in the rate of profit can only be restored if, *ceteris paribus* (that is, assuming a closed economy and no increase in domestic demand), the productive capacity in the cotton-spinning sector is reduced both by laying off labour and by destroying the excess fixed capital in this sector.

The actions and reactions of capitalists in this situation will lead to a reduction in the production capacity of those sectors producing spinning machines and, in turn, to a reduction in the production capacity of those sectors which provide the inputs for making spinning machines, and so on. In this way, the partial realisation crisis in one sector of production spreads, as a result of the interdependence of production, to other sectors. Whether this partial crisis becomes a general crisis depends on the size of the overproduction in the first place and, in the second place, on the extent to which other lines of production are dependent upon this sector (see Marx, 1969, pp. 523, 529).

The second case, which would seem to be implicit in one of Marx's statements (Marx, 1969, p. 495) refers to a technical innovation in a particular sector of production which is adopted only by some capitalists in the current period of production. As a result two methods of production now coexist: the old method and the new. This new technology is twice as efficient as the old and hence produces the commodity for half the price of production of the old technology.

If it is assumed that the total output in the current period of production is twice that of the preceding period of production (half of it being produced by the new technology and half by the old) and if it is further assumed that there is no change in demand, then it will be apparent that only the output produced by the new technology will be sold and, by corollary, that produced by the old technology will not (since the former is cheaper than the latter and is equal to the entire demand). There is thus an overproduction of commodities and, by implication, an overproduction of fixed capital (that is, the old technology). The consequence of this is that the production capacity of those producing with the old technology is useless.

There are two main consequences of this technical innovation: the first is that it will result in workers being laid off which will lead to a decline in the demand for wage goods, leading, in turn, to overcapacity and overproduction in this sector; second, it will result in a fall in demand for the output of those sectors which produced the old technology and in those sectors which produced inputs for this sector, and so on. These departments will have a similar effect on yet other sectors whose output they consume. The extent to which a partial crisis in one sector can develop to a general crisis throughout the economy depends, as has already been seen, upon the size of the overproduction in the first place and on the extent to which other sectors are highly interdependent with it.

2.2.5 Realisation Crisis Caused by Variable Weather Conditions

Marx explicitly acknowledged that 'weather conditions – play such an important part in modern industry' (Marx, 1969, p. 533). This is because weather can directly affect the quantity and quality of those commodities which are grown and produced on the land. This, in turn, can give rise to a realisation crisis if too little or too much is produced in relation to demand. It will now be shown how both these possibilities can arise. The first case refers to a commodity where, 'as a result of bad harvests' (ibid, p. 515) too little is produced in relation to demand. This results, *ceteris paribus*, is an increase in the price of production of the commodity since, with the same amount of labour and capital, the weather conditions adversely affect the productivity of labour. The effect of this, in turn, can be seen when the commodity enters as an input into the production of another commodity.[10]

If the commodity enters as an input into the production of another commodity then the capitalist purchasing this input will be unable, *ceteris paribus*, to obtain the same quantity of the input as in the preceding period since its price of production has increased. The consequence of this (assuming simple reproduction) is that the capitalist will have to reduce the quantity of some of his inputs by comparison with the quantity of inputs employed in the preceding production period. If it is assumed that the price of the commodity in question doubles, and if the capitalist spends the same share of money (*M*) on the various inputs as in the preceding production period, then he will only be able to purchase and process half the quantity of the raw material by comparison with that in the preceding period.

The consequence of this is that the capitalist has excess capacity in the form of fixed capital equipment and labour, since the quantity of raw material to be processed has been halved. As a result 'a part of fixed capital stands idle and a part of the workers is thrown out on the streets' (ibid., p. 516). This in turn causes the rate of profit to fall, assuming that the capitalist has certain fixed costs and wage costs which must be paid at the beginning of the production period. By corollary, the price of the finished product will increase.

The implications of this rise in price will be felt subsequently in those sectors where this commodity enters as an input. As Marx put it 'the rise in its price will result in the same disturbances in reproduction in these spheres' (ibid., p. 516). In short then, a rise in the price of a commodity, as a result of bad weather, can give rise to a realisation crisis since it creates a situation where there is relative overproduction and underconsumption of yet other commodities.

The second case refers to the situation where too much of a given commodity is produced in relation to demand as a result of favourable weather conditions. The consequences of this are crucially dependent upon whether one assumes simple reproduction or extended reproduction.

If one assumes simple reproduction, and if one further assumes that the favourable weather has the effect of doubling output (and hence halving the price of production), then the effect of the bumper harvest will be that only half the output of this commodity will be sold. This, in turn, means that the revenue of the capitalist will be halved, which has the effect (assuming that all fixed and wage costs are paid at the beginning of the production period) of reducing the rate of profit. The consequence of this is that in the next period of production, the capitalist will have to reduce the quantity of labour and capital employed. This, in turn, will lead to a reduction in the capacity in those sectors producing wage and capital goods respectively and to a corresponding reduction in those sectors which supply them with inputs, and so on. In short, the effect of the favourable weather conditions, under conditions of simple reproduction, is that it leads to an overproduction of commodities which, in turn, results in an overproduction of yet other commodities (that is, fixed capital and wage goods). The full extent of this realisation crisis will depend on the size of the overproduction of the original commodity and on the extent to which this commodity is interdependent with other sectors (as well as on the weather conditions in subsequent production periods).

If one assumes expanded reproduction, and if this expansion is able to absorb the increase in output as a result of the bumper harvest, then no realisation crisis will arise. Indeed, if the price of production is halved (as assumed above), this will have the effect, *ceteris paribus*, of raising the rate of profit in those sectors which use the commodity as an input which will further increase the expansion of reproduction.

2.2.6 Realisation Crisis Caused by Scarcity of Labour

There is evidence that Marx regarded relatively low population growth as a factor which could trigger off a realisation crisis (Marx, 1974c, pp. 250ff; see also Morishima and Catephores, 1978, pp. 117–18). Marx's argument was that if economic growth continued to grow at a faster rate than population growth then, assuming no surplus labour and a maximum rate of exploitation, a point would be reached where 'There would be . . . overproduction of capital . . . as soon as capital would . . . have grown in such a ratio to the labouring population that neither the absolute working-time supplied by this population, nor the relative surplus working-time, could be expanded any further' (Marx, 1974c, p. 251).

There would seem to be two different mechanisms, suggested by Marx, by which this disparity between population growth and economic growth could trigger off a realisation crisis with its consequent overproduction. The first mechanism is that the shortage of labour renders it impossible for a certain amount of capital equipment to be productively utilised, giving rise in effect to an excess of capital or, as Marx terms it, an 'overproduction of capital' (Marx, 1974c, p. 252). This will lead to a fall in the rate of profit in those departments where this excess occurs (since the capitalists in these departments will not be able to cover all their fixed costs and make the going rate of profit) and can only be reversed by cutting back on the excess capital. This, in turn, will have repercussions on those departments whose output enters as an input into this department, thereby leading to further cut-backs. Similar repercussions will occur in other departments which are part of this input-output chain.

The second mechanism is that the shortage of labour leads to a rise in wages. This rise in wages leads, *ceteris paribus*, to a reduction in the rate of profit in those sectors employing this labour, leading, in turn, to a cut-back in the labour and capital employed in these sectors, with consequent repercussions in those sectors which are connected, by the input-output chain, to this sector.

The net effect of the realisation crisis, in both of these cases, is to reduce the amount of capital employed to the point where there is again a relative surplus population and a return to the previous level of profitability.

2.2.7 Conclusion

The analysis in this section has attempted to organise most of Marx's references to realisation crises into a coherent, consistent and cogent framework. However, in doing this a number of references which indicate that Marx also had a crude underconsumptionist theory were edited out (these references are Marx, 1974b, Chapter 16, Section 3, p. 320, fn 32 and Marx, 1974c, Chapter 15, Section i, pp. 244–5). These references were edited out because they are based upon the fallacious Malthusian idea that realisation crises can arise from the poverty of the masses. (The fallacy in this idea is clearly demonstrated in Blaug, 1962, pp. 165–7, 283–4; Howard and King, 1975, p. 216; Shaikh, 1978; Walker, 1978, pp. 50, 51, 181). The advantage of separating Marx's various references to realisation crises in this way is that it clarifies the acknowledged confusion in Marx's work on this point and highlights those aspects which contain the core of a defensible theory of realisation crisis. In addition this section provides a basis for evaluating Castells's claims that collective consumption serves the function of solving the realisation crises of capitalism (see subsection 6.2.3).

2.3 CRISES CAUSED BY RISING REAL WAGES

2.3.1 Introduction

The possibility of crises being caused by rising real wages, as a result of their effect on profitability, has received some attention from Marxists in recent years (see notably, Glyn and Sutcliffe, 1972; Boddy and Crotty, 1975; Roemer, 1977, 1978a, 1978b, 1979; Weisskopf, 1978, 1979) though there is little evidence that Marx ever realistically considered this as a possible long-term source of crisis. Nevertheless, it does seem necessary to consider this possible source of crisis in the present context for two reasons. The first is that there is some empirical evidence which suggests that this form of crisis is particularly operative in some contemporary capitalist countries (ibid.). The second reason is to consider whether this fact can be incorporated into Marx's framework of analysis without altering some of the basic elements of that framework.

The present section critically examines Marx's theory of wages as outlined in *Capital*, Vol. I, Chapters 6, 19 and 25 (Marx, 1974a) and in *Value, Price and Profit* (Marx, 1975). The analysis begins by pointing out some of the important differences between a commodity and labour power (subsection 2.3.2). The most important difference is that the mechanism which regulates the production, and hence the value, of labour power is the industrial reserve army. The nature of this mechanism is discussed in subsection 2.3.3, followed by a discussion of its effect upon the long-term trend in real wages in subsection 2.3.4. The role of the trade unions within this framework will then be considered in subsection 2.3.5. The over-all conclusion of this section is that Marx's theory of wages cannot adequately deal with the possibility that real wages may rise as a result of trade union power and threaten profitability. It is suggested that a bargaining power theory of wages might offer a more realistic (if theoretically less determinate) explanation of wages.

2.3.2 The Difference Between Labour Power and a Commodity

Marx insisted, unlike the classicals, that labour power was a commodity like any other and that its value (that is, the wage) was determined in the same way as any other commodity (Marx, 1974a, Chapter 6, pp. 164–72; Chapter 19, pp. 501–7; 1975, Section 5, pp. 50–3). His argument was developed as follows. The value of any commodity is determined by the quantity of socially necessary abstract labour required to produce it (that is, the labour required under the prevailing technical and social conditions of production) (see section 1.1). The value of labour power – also a commodity – is similarly determined by the quantity of socially necessary labour required to produce it and is equal to a given quantity of wage goods. These wage goods are necessary to 'produce, develop, maintain and perpetuate' (Marx, 1975, p. 46) the worker's labour power. They are 'the means of subsistence necessary for the maintenance of the labourer' (Marx, 1974a, p. 167).

However, on closer inspection, the value of labour power is not determined in exactly the same way as the value of any other commodity. It differs in at least two respects. On the one hand the production process is owned and controlled by the capitalist in the case of a commodity but by the worker in the case of labour power. On the other hand exploitation occurs in the course of the production of a commodity but not in the course of the production of labour power. However, the more fundamental difference arises because the mechanisms which regulate supply and demand are quite different for commodities and labour power. This can be seen by considering the outcome which typically occurs when demand exceeds supply (and vice versa) in the case of a commodity and labour power respectively.

In the case of a commodity, an excess of demand over supply would lead, according to Marx, to an increase in the price of the commodity over and above its value, the effect of which would be that the capitalists producing this commodity would receive a higher than average rate of profit. This would lead, in turn, via the process of competition between capitalists, to increased investment in the production of that commodity up to the point where the rate of profit was restored to the competitive average. In short, an excess of demand over supply for any commodity would lead, in the long run, to an increase in the production of that commodity up to the point where supply and demand are in equilibrium.

In the case of labour power, an excess of demand over supply would lead to an increase in the price of labour power (that is, wages). However, unlike the production of a commodity, the excess demand would not have the effect of making the production of labour power more profitable (since no profit is produced in the production process); nor, by corollary, would it lead capitalists to increase the output of labour power (since capitalists do not produce labour power). What typically occurs in this case is that the demand itself is reduced (through the adoption, by capitalists, of capital-using/labour-saving technical innovations) or supply will be increased (through natural increase or immigration) or both. The more general point is that the imbalance between demand and supply in the case of labour power is not regulated by changes in the production of labour power but by changes in all of the other factors affecting demand and supply. A similar type of reasoning can also be applied to the case where supply exceeds demand.

The more general point is that labour power is not a commodity like any other, as Marx claimed, essentially because it is not produced in the same way as any other commodity. Ironically Marx recognised that the mechanism regulating the production and value of labour power is different from the mechanism regulating the production and value of commodities, yet he did not draw the logical inference that labour power is not therefore a commodity like any other (see Bortkiewicz, 1952, pp. 56–7; Lange, 1968, pp. 82–4). It is now necessary to explore more thoroughly the nature of the mechanism which regulates the production and value of labour power.

2.3.3 The Mechanism Regulating the Level of Wages

The mechanism which regulates the production and value of labour power is, as Marx variously terms it, 'a relative surplus population or industrial reserve army' (1974a, p. 589). This mechanism, he argues, is the direct outcome of capital accumulation because capital accumulation is characterised by the adoption of capital-using/labour-saving technical innovations whose net effect is to create a surplus of labour power (ibid., p. 590; 1975, pp. 76–7). In other words, the rise in the organic composition of capital, which Marx believed to be an inevitable feature of capitalist development, would bring with it a high level of unemployment. This would result in a relative surplus population in the sense that it is surplus to the requirements of capital accumulation: 'a population of greater extent than suffices for the average needs of the self-expansion of capital, and therefore a surplus population' (Marx, 1974a, p. 590).

Marx described the formation of this relative surplus population as 'a law of population peculiar to the capitalist mode of production' (Marx, 1974a, pp. 591–2). His basic point was that the supply of labour in capitalist society was not determined solely by natural increase (as Malthus claimed)[11] but also by the nature of technical change within capitalist society (see Marx, 1973, p. 604; 1974a, pp. 591–2; see also Sweezy, 1942, pp. 83–95;[12] Lange, 1968, pp. 83–4).

The significance of this relative surplus population in the present context is that it is the mechanism which, Marx believed, regulated the production and value of labour power. This is because unemployed workers will compete with each other for jobs, the effect of which will be to push wages down to their minimum level which is just equal to the value of labour power. Thus, in Marx's view, 'the general movements of wages are exclusively regulated by the expansion and contraction of the industrial reserve army' (Marx, 1974a, p. 596).

It is now necessary to examine the implications which follow from this view, particularly in relation to the long-term trend in wages.

2.3.4 The Long-term Trend in Wages

Marx defined wages as a share of net output. This definition is rendered explicit in *Wages, Price and Profit* (Marx, 1975, Section 12, pp. 60–2) where Marx defined net output (albeit without using that term) as that which remains after deductions have been made for 'the value of the raw materials and other means of production used upon it' (Marx, 1975, p. 60). Net output, he continues, is the 'fund from which both he (the worker) and the capitalist have to draw their respective shares or dividends, the only value to be divided into wages and profits' (ibid., p. 60).

There is consequently an inverse relation between wages and profit for a given level of net output which can be graphically illustrated as follows:

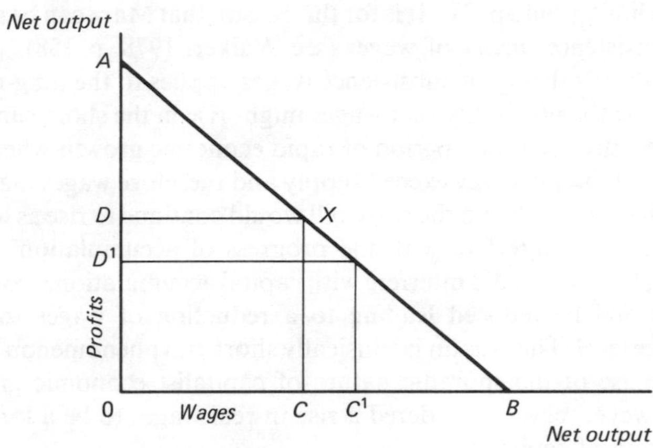

Figure 2.2 The shares of profits and wages in net output

In this diagram, net output is plotted on the two co-ordinates *OA* and *OB* and the line *AB* is the set of possible combinations of wages and profits. *OC* is the share of wages and *OD* is the corresponding share of profits. Any change in the share of wages, for example, from *OC* to OC^1, will result, *ceteris paribus*, in a fall in the share of profits from *OD* to OD^1.

Marx argued that the share of wages in net output could, in turn, be divided into two components: the first component refers to the basic 'necessaries absolutely indispensable for living and multiplying' (Marx, 1975, p. 72) (for example, food) and the second component refers to that portion of the wage which is determined by 'historical tradition and social habitude' (ibid.) (for example, alcohol and tobacco) (see also Marx, 1974b, p. 407). The first component forms the 'ultimate limit' (ibid.) below which wages could not fall without endangering the reproduction of the labour force. It is, in other words, 'the physical minimum of wages' (ibid., p. 74). It follows, as Marx correctly pointed out, that the rate of profit corresponding to this basic minimum wage is 'the maximum rate of profit' (ibid.) (not to be confused with the concept of the maximum rate of profit used in a previous subsection (2.1.3) which is the rate of profit corresponding to zero wages).

Marx points out that a fully-developed capitalist society, 'in which capital domineers over the whole process of production' (Marx, 1975, p. 75), wages will be kept to this basic minimum. In short 'the general tendency of capitalistic production is not to raise, but to sink the average standard of wages, or to push the value of labour more or less to its minimum limit' (ibid., p. 77). It is for this reason that Marx can be said to have a subsistence theory of wages (see Walker, 1978, p. 158).

While Marx's theory of subsistence wages applies to the long-run he did allow for the possibility that wages might rise in the short-run. This would typically occur in a period of rapid economic growth where 'the demand for labourers may exceed supply and therefore wages may rise' (Marx, 1974a, p. 575); and the wage bill would continue to rise as long as 'its rise does not interfere with the progress of accumulation' (ibid., p. 580). If, however, it did interfere with capital accumulation, economic growth would be reduced leading to a reduction of wages to their subsistence level. This was an intrinsically short-run phenomenon which arose because of the sporadic nature of capitalist economic growth; Marx, however, never considered a rise in real wages to be a long-run phenomenon of capitalism.

It is implicit in Marx's analysis that the total wage bill (that is, the real wage multiplied by the number of workers) will represent a diminishing share of net output as economic growth proceeds (Howard and King, 1975, pp. 132–5, make a similar point; Robinson, 1967, p. 36, and Sowell, 1960, give a contrary view). This is implicit because of Marx's views on the nature and consequences of technical change. This is because the rate of growth of net output would be increased by the adoption of new capital-using/labour-saving technology while the rate of growth of the total wage bill would be reduced by a fall in the value of the real wage as a result of productivity increases in the wage goods sector (although the latter may be increased by the employment of additional workers). While the precise outcome of this remains indeterminate it would seem, nevertheless, that the thrust of Marx's argument implies that the share of wages in net output would tend to decrease while the share of profits (though not necessarily the rate of profit)[13] would tend to increase. This is illustrated in Figure 2.3.

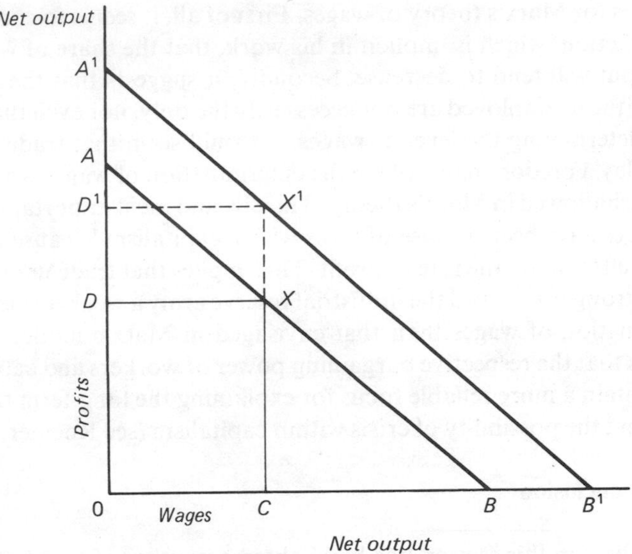

Figure 2.3 Marx's view of the effect of an increase in net output upon the shares of profits and wages

2.3.5 The Role of Trade Unions in Wage Determination

The role of trade unions, according to Marx, was to prevent wages from falling below their minimum, subsistence, level. It is in this context that Marx states that 'trade unions work well as centres of resistance against the encroachments of capital' (Marx, 1975, p. 78). On the same page Marx describes such struggles over wages as merely 'retarding the downward movement, but not changing its direction' (ibid).

Marx's view of the role of trade unions was probably an accurate reflection of their role and strength at the time when he was writing. Moreover, the crucial role which the reserve army of unemployed played in his explanation of wages precluded him from attributing any fundamental importance to trade unions. However, trade unions have now achieved considerably more power than in Marx's time and it appears that, in at least some capitalist countries (notably in the UK and in the US) the share of wages in net output has been increasing. These facts, based upon the researches of Glyn and Sutcliffe (1972)[14] in the UK, Boddy and Crotty (1975)[15] and Weisskopf (1979)[16] in the US, and Hill (1979) and Heap (1980)[17] in OECD countries, raise a number of problems for Marx's theory of wages. First of all, it seems to contradict the prediction, which is implicit in his work, that the share of wages in net output will tend to decrease. Secondly, it suggests that the reserve army of the unemployed are not necessarily the only, nor even the main, factor determining the level of wages; it would seem that trade unions today play a predominant role in the determination of wages which was not foreshadowed in Marx's theory. Thirdly, and most important, rising real wages have been a cause of crisis within capitalism because of their adverse effect upon the rate of profit. This implies that trade unions may have a stronger role, and the industrial reserve army a weaker role, in the determination of wages than that envisaged in Marx's model. It also suggests that the respective bargaining power of workers and capitalists may contain a more reliable focus for explaining the long-term trend in wages and the possibility of crisis within capitalism (see Roemer, 1978).

2.3.6 Conclusion

The analysis in this section has highlighted a number of problems with Marx's theory of wages. It has shown that his analogy between commodities and labour power breaks down essentially because both are produced in very different ways and their values are determined in very different ways. In addition it would seem that, in many sectors of the advanced capitalist economy, trade unions have replaced the industrial reserve army as a crucial determinant of wages. Finally, as regards the long-term trend in wages which, according to Marx, would represent a declining share of net output, the currently available evidence from some capitalist countries is that the share of wages in net output has increased rather than decreased. All of this suggests that Marx's theory of subsistence wages can no longer be regarded as a cogent explanation of the way in which wages are determined or the level at which they are determined.

This suggests that wages may be more adequately explained in terms of the relative bargaining strength of workers and capitalists, and that rises in real wages, as a result of the growing strength of trade unions could, *ceteris paribus*, threaten profits and thereby cause a crisis within capitalism.

2.4 CONCLUSION

This chapter has focused upon the three basic theories of crisis that are contained in Marx's writings. Although other theories of crisis have been developed by Marxists in recent years – notably theories of fiscal crisis (O'Connor, 1973) and of legitimation crisis (Habermas, 1976) – these were not considered here, essentially because they do not figure in Marx's work nor do they play an important part in the writings of Castells and Lojkine. Castells and Lojkine rely, in various ways and to varying degrees, upon the three variants of Marxian crisis theory examined above. As a consequence this chapter provides a bench-mark against which to assess how they have used these theories in their writings (see Chapters 6 and 7).

It is now necessary to examine another element of Marx's political economy – the theory of rent – in order to prepare the way further for the critique of the writings of Castells and Lojkine.

3 Marx's Theory of Rent

3.0 INTRODUCTION

Marx devoted considerable attention to the discussion of land and rent (Marx, 1969; 1974c, pp. 614–813; 1977, pp. 309–21) which suggests that he regarded it as an important element in the analysis of capitalism. However, his theory of rent is based entirely upon the analysis of agricultural production even though the rest of his theory of capitalism is based upon the analysis of industrial production. In this sense Marx's analysis of rent is not integrated tightly into the remainder of his analysis.

The purpose of this chapter is to provide a rigorous formulation of Marx's theory of rent which will be used subsequently to evaluate the Marxian concept of rent found in the writings of Jean Lojkine (see subsection 7.3.4). The formulation presented here will involve severing Marx's theory of rent from his labour theory of value (because of the difficulties associated with the latter – see Chapter 1) and recasting it within the linear equation approach outlined above (see section 1.6).

Marxists have not, until recently, devoted much attention to the analysis of land or rent. Those who have considered the topic tend to fall into two categories (see Gibson and Esfahani, 1983) – those who maintain an intimate connection between Marx's theory of rent and his labour theory of value – and those who, abandoning Marx's theory of value, follow the approach pioneered by Sraffa. The former, sometimes referred to as Fundamentalists, include, Harvey, 1973, 1982; Harvey and Chatterjee, 1974; Walker, 1974, 1975; Broadbent, 1975; Breugel, 1975; Byrne and Beirne, 1975; Clarke and Ginsburg, 1975; Edel, 1976; Ball, 1977, 1980; Markusen, 1978; Murray, 1977, 1978; Massey and Catalano, 1978; Fine, 1979, 1980; Lauria, 1984. The latter, sometimes referred to as NeoRicardians, include, Scott, 1976a, 1976b, 1979, 1980, Chapter 3; Kurz, 1978; Abraham-Frois and Berrebi, 1979, pp. 93–102; Bose, 1980, Chapter 13; Quadrio-Curzio, 1980; Bandyopadhyay, 1982; Gibson and Esfahani, 1983; Gibson and McLeod, 1983. The analysis presented here relies heavily upon the 'NeoRicardian' approach.

The most important feature about land in any system of production is that it is essential to the production of every commodity but is not itself produced.[1] In fact land cannot be produced at all (with the possible exception of land reclamation). The significance of this fact is that the price of land is not the same as the price of any other commodity and hence cannot be explained in the same way. However the fact that it is a constituent element in the price of each commodity means that it must be explained within the framework of the determinants of the price of each commodity. This means that, although rent will emerge in any system of production where land is scarce and/or variable in quality,[2] the precise way in which this occurs will depend upon how prices are determined in that system of production.

In capitalist society, land is usually owned privately and this will be assumed throughout the analysis in this chapter. More specifically, it will be assumed that land is owned by landowners and leased to capitalists who use it, in turn, to produce commodities. This was the framework within which Ricardo (1970, Chapter 2; 1966) and Marx developed their analyses of rent. The results of this analysis will not be affected if allowance is made for the fact that the state, capitalists, and even workers, own land, since the conceptual status of income derived from the ownership of land (that is, rent) is not in any way affected by the characteristics of its recipients.

The analysis below differentiates four different types of rent. These are: differential rent I, differential rent II, monopoly rent I and monopoly rent II. These four types of rent are all present in Marx's work, and the present analysis demonstrates that there is a firm conceptual basis for this fourfold typology, even though there may be some difficulties in rigorously applying them to empirical situations.

It will be shown (in section 3.1) that differential rent I arises if land is scarce and variable in quality and suitable for different uses – a fairly typical real-world situation. This will be demonstrated in the simplest possible case where one agricultural commodity is produced on two different types of land. This result can then be readily generalised to the case where *n* different commodities are produced on *n* different types of land. Differential rent II will be shown (in section 3.2) to be inherently temporary and transient in the sense that it arises when there is a change in the technology for producing a given commodity, such that the change is temporarily unknown to all landowners or unavailable to all capitalists. Monopoly rent I (for which Marx used the term 'absolute rent') will be seen (in section 3.3) to arise if landowners form a cartel in order to impose a rent (independently of differential rent I and II) on the use of all land essential for the production of basic commodities. Finally, monopoly rent II will be shown (in section 3.4) to be a special type of rent in the sense that it arises only on land which produces a special type of commodity, that is, a commodity which can only be produced on one unique plot (or set of plots) of land and whose output cannot be increased above a fixed upper limit.

3.1 DIFFERENTIAL RENT I

In a capitalist economy rent arises when land is scarce and/or variable in quality (quality depending on fertility or situation or both – see Ricardo, 1970, p. 70; Marx, 1974c, p. 650; Smith, 1976, p. 250). If it is assumed that corn is the only commodity that is produced in the economy, and if it is produced by combining the inputs[3] of corn and labour (itself produced by wages which consist of corn) and if it is produced on only one plot of land which is also the most fertile (and is designated as type (i) land)[4] then the production conditions of corn on this land can be written as follows:

$$P^m_{1\,(i)} = P^m_1 A_{11(\mathrm{i})} + P^m_2 A_{21(\mathrm{i})} + \ldots P^m_n (A_{n1(\mathrm{i})} + ma_{1(\mathrm{i})} (1 + r_{(\mathrm{i})})$$

where

$P^m_{1,2,n}$ = the money price of a unit of commodity 1, 2, n, where commodity 1 is corn;

A_{11}, A_{21}, A_{n1} = the quantity of commodity 1, 2, n which enters into the production of commodity 1 (that is, corn). It follows from the above assumptions that A_{21}, A_{n1}, are zero;

m = the money wage rate per unit of labour;

a_1 = the quantity of labour employed in the production of commodity 1 (that is, corn);

r = the rate of profit;

(i) = the plot of land on which commodity 1 is produced and whose fertility is known to be the best.

The relationship between output and type of land, which is expressed by this equation, is illustrated in Figure 3.1. In this diagram the output on type (*i*) land is broken down into its constituent parts: the inputs of corn ($P^m A_{(\mathrm{i})}$) and labour ($ma_{(\mathrm{i})}$) and the quantity of profit ($r\,(P^m A_{(\mathrm{i})} + ma_{(\mathrm{i})})$). The possibility of differential rent I now arises if type (i) land and, by implication, the corn produced on it, becomes scarce.[5] This scarcity can be overcome in one of two ways: either by introducing a technical innovation such that the increased output can be produced on the same plot or by extending production to an inferior plot. If the second option

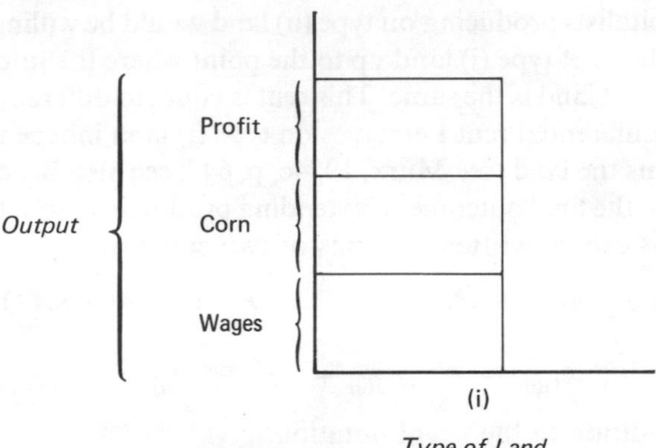

Figure 3.1 The relationship betwen output and type of land

is adopted,[6] and if it is assumed that the second plot is less fertile than the first (and is designated as type (ii) land), then the production conditions of corn on type (ii) land can be written, using the above notation, as follows:

$$P^m_{1(\text{ii})} = P^m_1 A_{11(\text{ii})} + P^m_2 A_{21(\text{ii})} + \ldots P^m_n A_{n1(\text{ii})} + ma_{1(\text{ii})} (1 + r_{(\text{ii})}).$$

It follows from the preceding assumptions that the basic difference between the production of corn on type (i) land, and the production of corn on type (ii) land is that the same input of commodities ($P^m_1 A_{n1} = P^m_1 A_{n1(\text{ii})}$) and labour ($ma_{1(\text{i})} = ma_{1(\text{ii})}$) produce a smaller output on type (ii) land, which may result in higher prices or lower profits, depending on the assumptions made about the nature of the commodity being produced (that is, basic or non-basic) and the wage and profit rates (that is, whether they are constant or flexible). If it is assumed, following Ricardo and Marx, that the commodity being produced (in this case corn) is a basic (see section 1.6) and that the wage rate is constant while the profit rate is flexible, then it is possible to infer that the effect of extending production from type (i) to type (ii) land will be to reduce the general rate of profit in the economy.[7] This reduction in the rate of profit will first occur for those capitalists producing on type (ii) land since, with constant real wages and hence constant prices for basics, the diminished returns experienced by those capitalists producing on type (ii) land (by comparison with those producing on type (i) land) will inevitably lead to a lower rate of profit (that is, $r_{(\text{ii})} < r_{(\text{i})}$). This lower rate of profit will then spread, via competition, to those capitalists producing on type (i) land, since the capitalists producing on type (ii) land would be willing to pay a rent for the lease of type (i) land up to the point where the rate of profit on both types of land is the same. This rent is equal to differential rent I. In this way differential rent I emerges on type (i) land independently of whoever owns the land (see Marx, 1974c, p. 647; see also Benetti, 1976, p. 12).[8] Thus, the final outcome of extending production from type (i) to type (ii) land can be written in terms of two equations:

$$P^m_{1(i)} = P^m_1 A_{11(i)} + P^m_2 A_{21(i)} + \ldots P^m_n A_{n1(i)} + ma_{1(i)} (1 + r) + DRI_{(i)}$$

$$P^m_{1(ii)} = P^m_1 A_{11(ii)} + P^m_2 A_{21(ii)} + \ldots P^m_n A_{n1(ii)} + ma_{1(ii)} (1 + r)$$

where, in addition to the usual notation:

$DRI_{(i)}$ = differential rent I on type (i) land.

These two equations are expressed diagrammatically in Figure 3.2. This diagram, together with the above equations and the analysis underlying them, illustrates that when land is scarce and/or variable in quality it will yield a rent, and hence a price, since the price of land is nothing more than the discounted annual rent over a number of years. The origin of this price is the surplus profit which emerges when a given commodity is produced on a more fertile plot of land. This price of land constitutes, in turn, an income for the owners of that land, and it is in this sense that it is possible to speak of an inverse relationship between the income of landowners and the income of capitalists (that is, profits) – as long as real wages are assumed to be constant.

Differential rent I would also emerge if production, instead of being extended to land of inferior quality, were extended to land of superior quality. In this case those capitalists producing on the superior land would, under the above assumptions, obtain an above-average rate of profit. However, this would only be temporary since those capitalists producing on the inferior land would be willing to pay a rent up to the point where the difference in the rates of profit was abolished. In this way differential rent I would emerge on the superior land without, however, any concomitant fall in the rate of profit: the rate of profit would remain the same. Marx made this point – a correct but minor point – in criticism of Ricardo, West and Malthus, who assumed that differential rent I only emerged when production was extended from superior to inferior land (see Marx 1974c, p. 658).[9]

Marx's analysis of differential rent I is substantially identical to that developed here which, in turn, is identical with that developed by Ricardo (though Ricardo does not make an explicit distinction between

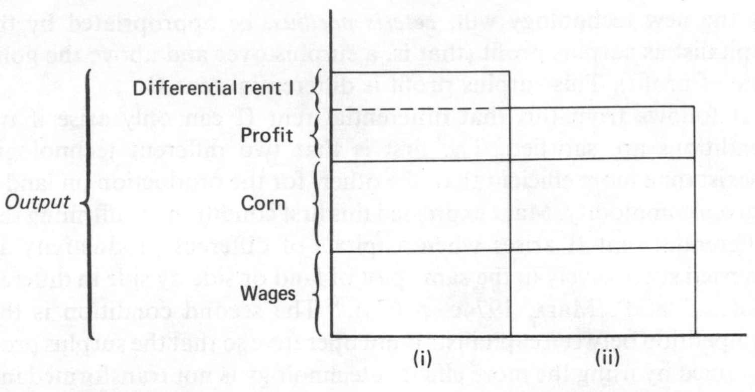

Figure 3.2 The relationship between output, type of land and rent

differential rent I and II despite its implicit presence in his work (see notably Ricardo, 1970, Chapter 2).

3.2 DIFFERENTIAL RENT II

The essential features of differential rent II can be brought out most easily in the simple case of a capitalist economy where corn is the only commodity being produced (that is, the same model which was used to explicate the nature of differential rent I). In this economy it can be shown that differential rent II will arise (over and above differential rent I) if there is a change in technology such that, *ceteris paribus*, the rate of profit is increased on at least one plot, and perfect competition is hindered, temporarily.

If a new technique is invented for the production of a given commodity (in this case, corn), this effectively means that there are two different technologies for the production of that commodity: the old technology (technique I) and the new technology (technique II). If it is assumed that the new technology is more efficient than the old then it follows, given the assumptions made in the preceding section (that is, that the commodity being produced is a basic, and that the real wage is constant), that the new technology will give rise to a higher rate of profit than the old. If, in turn, it is assumed that competition between capitalists is hindered and that (for example) only one capitalist has access to the new technology, then the increased rate of profit obtained by the new technology will, *ceteris paribus*, be appropriated by this capitalist as surplus profit (that is, a surplus over and above the going rate of profit). This surplus profit is differential rent II.

It follows from this that differential rent II can only arise if two conditions are satisfied. The first is that two different technologies coexist (one more efficient than the other) for the production on land of a given commodity. Marx expressed this first condition by affirming that differential rent II arises when 'capitals of different productivity are invested successively in the same plot of land or side by side in different plots of land' (Marx, 1974c, p. 674).[10] The second condition is that competition between capitalists is not operative so that the surplus profit obtained by using the more efficient technology is not transformed into differential rent I and appropriated by the landowner; it is appropriated by the capitalist as differential rent II.

There are two possible reasons why competition between capitalists may be hindered, even if only temporarily. The first is that there may not be a perfect flow of information throughout the system so that a new and more efficient technology for producing a particular commodity may not be universally known or universally available to all capitalists.

The second reason, and this is the one cited by Marx, is the leasing system. This could hinder competition between capitalists in the situation where one capitalist secures a long lease, in the course of which a new and more efficient technology is invented and applied by the leasing capitalist, giving rise to a surplus profit, that is, differential rent II. Marx referred to this possibility in the following terms:

> Rent is fixed when land is leased, and after that the surplus profit arising from successive investments of capital flows into the pockets of the tenant as long as the lease lasts. This is why the tenants have fought for long leases, and, on the other hand, due to the greater power of the landlords an increase in the number of tenancies at will has taken place, that is, leases which can be cancelled annually (Marx, 1974c, p. 675).

This analysis can be readily expressed in terms of the above notation. The two equations describing the conditions of production of the commodity in question (that is, corn) using two different techniques of production (technique I and technique II) can be written as follows:

$$P^m_{1(\mathrm{I})} = P^m_1 A_{11(\mathrm{I})} + P^m_2 A_{21(\mathrm{I})} + \ . \ . \ . \ P^m_n A_{n1(\mathrm{I})} + ma_{1(\mathrm{I})}(1+r)$$
$$P^m_{1(\mathrm{II})} = P^m_1 A_{11(\mathrm{II})} + P^m_2 A_{21(\mathrm{II})} + \ . \ . \ . \ P^m_n A_{n1(\mathrm{II})} + ma_{1(\mathrm{II})}(1+r)$$

where, in addition to the usual notation, the subscripts:

I = technique I (that is, the old technique of production)
II = technique II (that is, the new technique of production)

On the basis of the assumption that technique II is more efficient than technique I (that is, that the commodity being produced is a basic and that the real wage is constant) it follows that, *ceteris paribus*, the rate of profit obtained by producing with technique II will be higher than that obtained by producing with technique I. This difference constitutes differential rent II for the capitalist producing with technique II. This fact can be brought out more clearly by rewriting the two equations as follows:

$$P^m_{1(\mathrm{I})} = P^m_1 A_{11(\mathrm{I})} + P^m_2 A_{21(\mathrm{I})} + \ldots P^m_n A_{n1(\mathrm{I})} + ma_{1(\mathrm{I})}(1+r)$$
$$P^m_{1(\mathrm{II})} = P^m_1 A_{11(\mathrm{II})} + P^m_1 A_{21(\mathrm{II})} + \ldots P^m_n A_{n1(\mathrm{II})} + ma_{1(\mathrm{II})}(1+r) + DR\,\mathrm{II}.$$

where, in addition to the usual notation,

$DR\,\mathrm{II}$ = differential rent II.

These equations, and the analysis underlying them, are expressed diagramatically in Figure 3.3.

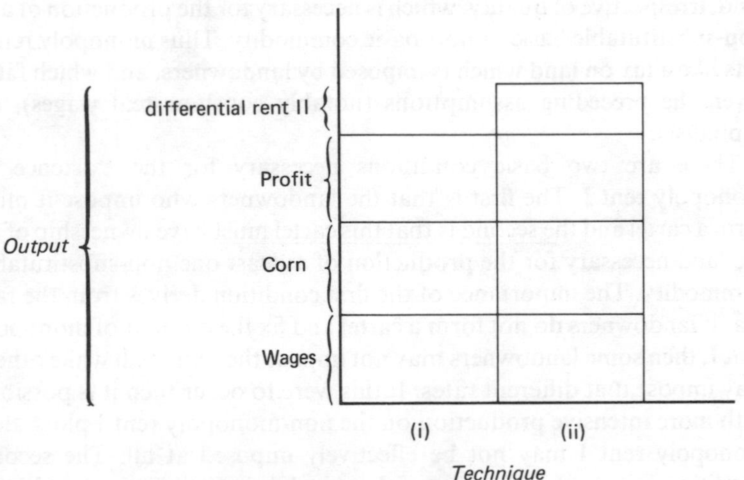

Figure 3.3 The relationship between output, technique of production and rent

From this analysis it is possible to affirm that differential rent II is a temporary form of rent, that is, it is an income which goes to the capitalist (not the landowner) only so long as the conditions of perfect competition do not operate. Once, however, the obstacle to competition is removed, then differential rent II will disappear as such and become part of differential rent I, and appropriated by landowners.

This analysis of differential rent II is substantially identical to that developed by Marx: the only difference is that Marx's analysis is much more detailed. In fact Marx devotes five chapters (1974c, Chapters 40–44) to the analysis of differential rent II in order to show the effect of using different methods of production when prices of production are constant (the 'first case' examined in Chapter 41), falling (the 'second case' examined in Chapter 42) or rising (the 'third case' examined in Chapter 43). In turn, each of these three cases have three variants depending on whether the new methods of production have constant, falling or rising productivity. All of these details are entirely consistent with the analysis presented here.

3.3 MONOPOLY RENT I

Monopoly rent I (for which Marx used the term 'absolute rent')[11] arises when the owners of land form a cartel and impose a rent on the use of all land, irrespective of quality, which is necessary for the production of any non-substitutable basic or non-basic commodity. Thus monopoly rent I acts like a tax on land which is imposed by landowners, and which falls, given the preceding assumptions (notably constant real wages), on capitalists.

There are two basic conditions necessary for the existence of monopoly rent I. The first is that the landowners who impose it must form a cartel and the second is that this cartel must have ownership of all the land necessary for the production of at least one non-substitutable commodity. The importance of the first condition derives from the fact that if landowners do not form a cartel and fix the amount of monopoly rent I, then some landowners may not impose the rent at all while others may impose it at different rates. If this were to occur then it is possible, with more intensive production on the non-monopoly rent I plots, that monopoly rent I may not be effectively imposed at all. The second condition is important because if the cartel does not have ownership of all the land essential to the production of at least one non-substitutable commodity, then capitalists will cultivate that land which is owned outside the cartel, thereby avoiding monopoly rent I. Thus both of these

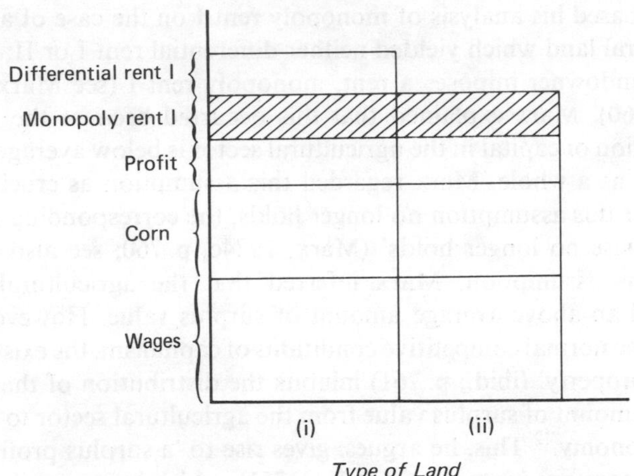

Figure 3.4 The incidence of monopoly rent I on different types of land

conditions must be satisfied for monopoly rent I to exist.

The effect of monopoly rent I on wages, profits and prices will depend upon whether the commodity being produced is a basic or a non-basic and on the assumptions made about the variability of wages and profits. These effects will now be analysed, first in the case of basics and second in the case of non-basics.

If monopoly rent I is imposed upon land producing at least one non-substitutable basic commodity and if it is assumed that the real wage is constant (as Marx assumed), then its effect will be to reduce profits by the amount of the monopoly rent I. This effect is illustrated in Figure 3.4 (which is an adaptation from Figure 3.2).

The real wage may, however, be variable and, in this case, the effect of monopoly rent I on wages and profits will depend upon the relative bargaining power of workers *vis-à-vis* capitalists and the ability of one to force the other to bear the cost of monopoly rent I. If, on the other hand, the commodity is a non-basic, then the effect will be to raise prices by the amount of the rent, producing no effect on either wages or profits. In this way monopoly rent I acts entirely like a tax and, a tax on luxuries (that is, non-basics) raises the price of luxuries by the amount of tax.

Marx's analysis of monopoly rent I is significantly different to the analysis developed here and is seriously flawed. The reasons for this emerge from a close examination of his analysis.

Marx based his analysis of monopoly rent I on the case of a plot of agricultural land which yielded neither differential rent I or II. On this plot, a landowner imposes a rent, monopoly rent I (see Marx 1974c, pp. 748–60). Marx explained that this occurred because the organic composition of capital in the agricultural sector is below average for the economy as a whole. Marx regarded this assumption as crucial since 'whenever this assumption no longer holds, the corresponding form of rent likewise no longer holds' (Marx, 1974c, p. 760; see also p. 765). From this assumption, Marx inferred that the agricultural sector produced an above-average amount of surplus value. However, contrary to the normal competitive conditions of capitalism, the existence of 'landed property' (ibid., p. 761) inhibits the distribution of the above-average amount of surplus value from the agricultural sector to the rest of the economy.[12] This, he argues, gives rise to 'a surplus-profit which could be converted into rent' (ibid., p. 761), which is monopoly rent I.

This is the essence of Marx's analysis. There are a number of difficulties with it, three of which may be noted. The first is that Marx did not know that the organic composition of capital in the agricultural sector was higher than in the rest of the economy (a fact he curiously acknowledges – Marx, 1974c, p. 760). Thus the basic premise of Marx's argument is based upon an assumption, not a fact, and no evidence is adduced to either confirm or refute this assumption. The second difficulty is that landowners are equally ignorant about the organic composition of capital in the agricultural sector, and hence are also ignorant of the above-average quantity of surplus value which is allegedly produced in that sector. Consequently they cannot act upon this information (even if it were correct) although Marx's argument requires them to do so. The third and more general difficulty relates to the labour theory of value which underlies this analysis. The difficulty is that an above-average amount of surplus value is not necessarily associated with an above-average amount of profit; it may even be associated with a negative amount of profit (see Chapter 1). Consequently, the existence of an above-average amount of surplus value in the agricultural sector (even if correct) cannot be taken as proof of the existence of above-average profits, which are supposed to be the basis of monopoly rent I. These three reasons provide a compelling case for rejecting Marx's analysis of monopoly rent I. However, it has also been shown in this section that the concept of monopoly rent I is amenable to a clear and rigorous formulation and this formulation should therefore be adopted.

3.4 MONOPOLY RENT II

It is possible, following Marx, to distinguish a second type of monopoly rent which, for convenience, I shall term monopoly rent II. Marx referred to this possibility when he cited the case of 'a vineyard producing wine of very extraordinary quality which can be produced only in relatively small quantities' (Marx, 1974c, p. 775; Adam Smith also examined this case – see Smith, 1976, Chapter 9, pp. 259–60). As will be seen, Marx's analysis of monopoly rent II (though he did not use this term) is substantively identical to that presented here.

In order to understand the nature of monopoly rent II it is necessary to make a distinction between two different types of commodity:

(a) reproducible commodities (and their substitutes) whose output can be increased in response to an increase in demand. Most commodities produced in capitalist economies (in fact in every economy) are reproducibles and it is this set of commodities which is the central focus of Marxian political economy. The important characteristic of reproducibles in the present context is that their market price tends to equal their price of production;

(b) non-reproducible commodities (which have no substitutes) whose output cannot be increased in response to an increase in demand. Such commodities include antiques, oil paintings by 'grand masters' and rare wines. The important characteristic of non-reproducibles, in the present context, is that their market price tends to exceed their price of production.

The significance of this distinction in the present context is that monopoly rent II arises only on land which produces non-reproducible commodities. Marx's example of 'a vineyard producing wine of very extraordinary quality' represents a typical example of a non-reproducible commodity. This is because an increase in demand for this commodity simply results in an increase in its market price with no increase in output. As a result, its market price will tend to exceed its price of production. Marx refers to this market price as 'a monopoly price' (Marx, 1974c, p. 775) because it is determined by 'the purchasers' eagerness to buy and ability to pay, independent of the price determined by the general price of production' (ibid.).

Monopoly rent II is determined entirely by this difference between market price and price of production. This is because the commodity (for example, wine) can only be produced on this land (that is, the vineyard) and it (or a suitable substitute) cannot be produced on any other land. Since this land is limited it follows, *ceteris paribus* (that is, assuming the land cannot be cultivated more intensively) that an increase in the demand will lead to an increase in monopoly rent II. The reason for this is that the increase in the market price for this commodity creates the possibility of a higher rate of profit for the production of this commodity by comparison with that obtainable in other spheres of production. However, competition between capitalists will ensure that a rent (that is, monopoly rent II) is paid to the owner of this land up to the point where the difference in the rates of profit disappears. In this way, the difference between market price and price of production is converted, via competition between capitalists, to monopoly rent II for landowners.

If it is assumed that the land in question (that is, the vineyard) is not just uniquely suited, but only suited, to the production of wine, then it can be affirmed that the rent on this land (that is, monopoly rent II) will be determined independently of the differential rent (I or II) on any other land. The landowner may also levy a monopoly rent I on this land, irrespective of whether or not this is levied on other land.

The effect of monopoly rent II on wages, profits and prices depends upon whether the land in question produces a basic (for example, oil) or a non-basic (for example, wine) and on the assumptions made about the variability of wages and profits. Its effects are identical to those produced by monopoly rent I, as outlined in the preceding section.

3.5 CONCLUSION

The analysis in the preceding sections has illustrated how the price of land is determined under four different sets of conditions, thereby giving rise to four different types of rent. The basic insight conveyed by this analysis is that the price of land – which is 'nothing but the capitalized and therefore anticipated rent' (Marx, 1974c, p. 808; see also Keiper, *et al.*, 1961) – is an income which landowners receive from capitalists for the use of land (assuming that wages are constant and that neither workers nor capitalists own land).

The price of any plot of land is thus conceptually decomposable into its various rental components (that is, differential rent I and II, monopoly rent I and II) some of which may be zero. Thus differential rent I exists when the output per unit of input on a plot of land is greater than the output per unit of input on those plots which yield no rent. In practice this means that, in a competitive capitalist economy, the price of a plot of land is the capitalised value of differential rent I. Differential rent II, by contrast, exists when the difference in output between two otherwise identical plots of land is due entirely to the different types of technology employed on them. In this situation, the land which employs the more efficient technology, that is, yields a higher net output, will yield differential rent II. In the urban context, this new technology may be a new and taller building (for example, a larger office block) or an old but renewed one (for example, as a result of gentrification). Monopoly rent I arises when landowners form a cartel to raise the price of certain plots above that prevailing for identical plots elsewhere. In the urban context, this type of rent can arise through land-use zoning, particularly when the zoning is exclusionary (see Williams and Norman, 1971) and its effect is to raise the price of land above that which would prevail in a competitive market. Finally, monopoly rent II exists when (a) the land is uniquely (and perhaps only) useful for producing a particular commodity and (b) the quantity of the commodity being produced cannot be increased above a fixed upper limit and (c) there is no suitable substitute for this commodity within the system of production. In the urban, as in the agricultural context, there are few examples of this type of rent. However, a residential area in a city which was highly 'exclusive' and for which there was no other substitute in terms of 'exclusivity' could have an element of monopoly rent II in its land prices.

The analysis in this chapter, in short, has attempted to place Marx's rent categories on a firm conceptual footing so that they can be usefully applied to both rural and urban contexts. The chapter also provides a basis for evaluating how the categories of rent are used in the work of Jean Lojkine (see section 7.3.4).

The next chapter will now examine one final element in Marx's political economy, namely, the distinction between productive and unproductive labour.

4 Marx's Theory of Productive and Unproductive Labour

4.0 INTRODUCTION

Marx considered the distinction between productive and unproductive labour to be of the 'greatest importance' (Marx, 1969, p. 396) even though his writing on the topic is rather confused. Nevertheless, the distinction continues to be used in Marxist writing and is given some prominence in Lojkine's recent attempt to develop a Marxist urban sociology (see section 7.2). For this reason it is essential to establish the precise meaning of the distinction.

This chapter provides a thorough exegesis of Marx's use of the distinction and reveals that there are two different and inconsistent usages implicit in his work. The first usage is outlined and examined in section 4.1. This usage, referred to for convenience as 'Definition I',[1] is then shown to give rise to certain anomalies which provide the basis for a more general definition. In section 4.2 Marx's second definition of productive and unproductive labour – 'Definition II'[2] – is examined and explained. Two fundamental problems associated with this definition are then identified which render it untenable. It is concluded, therefore, in section 4.3, that the most consistent, tenable and heuristically useful formulation of the distinction is Marx's slightly modified first definition.

4.1 'DEFINITION I' OF PRODUCTIVE AND UNPRODUCTIVE LABOUR

The basic criterion for distinguishing between productive and unproductive labour, according to this definition is whether it contributes to capital accumulation. Labour which contributes to capital accumulation is productive; labour which does not is unproductive. This criterion is explicit in the following definition:

> Productive labour, in its meaning for capitalist production, is wage-labour which, exchanged against the variable part of capital (the part of the capital that is spent on wages), reproduces not only this part of

capital (or the value of its own labour power) but in addition produces surplus value for the capitalist . . . only that wage-labour is productive which produces capital' (Marx, 1969, p. 152).

Unproductive labour, by corollary, is defined as 'labour which is not exchanged with capital, but directly with revenue, that is, with wages or profit' (ibid., p. 157). In other words, if labour results directly in capital accumulation it is productive,[3] otherwise it is unproductive.

The distinction between productive and unproductive labour implies a further distinction between a capitalist sector (where labour is exploited and accumulated as capital) and a non-capitalist sector (where labour, irrespective of whether it is exploited, is not accumulated as capital).[4] The examples which Marx used of, *inter alia*, actors, tailors, cooks, musicians, dancers, poets and prostitutes, illustrate that the 'same labour' (Marx, 1969, p. 401) is productive if performed in the capitalist sector and unproductive if performed in the non-capitalist sector. In other words, only labour performed in the capitalist sector is productive since it results directly in capital accumulation; labour performed in the non-capitalist sector is unproductive because it does not directly result in capital accumulation.

The distinction between productive and unproductive labour is further reinforced by the distinction between capital and revenue. Capital refers to the quantity of profits[5] which is exchanged against dead and living labour for the purpose of capital accumulation. Revenue by contrast refers to that quantity of profits and wages which is exchanged entirely for consumption goods. Thus, labour which is exchanged against capital is productive labour, whereas labour which is exchanged against revenue is unproductive (ibid., p. 157).

Marx insisted, contrary to Smith's view,[6] that the distinction between productive and unproductive labour (as used in 'Definition I') had 'absolutely nothing to do with the determinate content of the labour' (ibid., p.401). The distinction depends rather upon the 'social relations of production, within which the labour is realized' (ibid., p 157). Since the social relations of capitalism are characterised by the exploitation of labour and its accumulation as capital, it follows that this is the basic criterion for differentiating between productive and unproductive labour.

Combining these different dimensions of the distinction, Marx's first definition of productive labour may be formulated as follows: productive labour is labour which is exchanged against capital, is performed in the capitalist sector and results directly in capital accumulation; unproductive labour, by corollary, is defined as labour which is exchanged against revenue, is performed in the non-capitalist sector and does not give rise to capital accumulation.

This definition of productive and unproductive labour gives rise to one important anomaly which must now be considered: the case of labour which is exchanged against revenue, is performed in the non-capitalist sector, but nevertheless results, not directly, but indirectly, in capital accumulation. This anomaly, which Marx did not consider, is typified by the case of state expenditure on real wages (that is, on education, health, housing, social welfare, and so on). This case is anomalous whenever the net effect of state expenditure on real wages is either to reduce the total cost of the wage bill for capitalists or to increase the productivity of labour employed in the capitalist sector. In either of these cases the effect of state expenditure upon real wages is to increase the rate of profit and hence the rate of capital accumulation in the capitalist sector.

The significance of this is that labour which is employed by the state, is exchanged against revenue (that is, taxes) and is performed in the non-capitalist sector (that is, the state sector), may nevertheless have the effect of increasing the rate of profit in the capitalist sector. It could therefore, under these conditions, be classified as productive labour, according to Marx's first definition.[7] Thus, it is necessary to modify Marx's definition by stating that labour is productive if it directly or indirectly increases the rate of profit and capital accumulation; conversely, it is unproductive if it directly or indirectly decreases the rate of profit and capital accumulation. In Sraffian terms, labour is productive if it produces 'basics' (that is, commodities which enter directly or indirectly into the production of other commodities) and is unproductive if it produces 'non-basics' (that is, commodities which do not enter directly or indirectly into the production of other commodities) (see Sraffa, 1960, p. 54 and section 1.6; see also Hunt, 1979, pp. 311, 320 ff). This criterion provides a clear dividing line between the two types of labour which is at once consistent with Marx's first definition while nevertheless free from its anomalies. The main features of this reformulated version of 'Definition I' are summarised in Table 4.1.

4.2 'DEFINITION II' OF PRODUCTIVE AND UNPRODUCTIVE LABOUR

The distinctive feature of Marx's second definition is his characterisation of circulation costs as unproductive. In order to understand this

Table 4.1 Marx's 'Definition I' of productive and unproductive labour

	Productive	*Unproductive*
Criterion	Labour which, directly or indirectly, maintains or increases the level of capital accumulation (i.e., basics)	Labour which, directly or indirectly, decreases the level of capital accumulation (i.e., non-basics).
Mechanism	(i) Capital exchanged against labour in the capitalist sector (ii) Revenue exchanged against labour in the non-capitalist sector whose net effect is to increase capital accumulation.	Revenue exchanged against labour in the non-capitalist sector whose net effect is to reduce capital accumulation.
Examples	Respectively, (i) All labour performed in capitalist enterprises. (ii) Labour performed in the state provision of certain types of collective consumption.	Labour involved in performing the legislative, judicial and executive functions of the state.

definition it is necessary to recall Marx's characterisation of the typical process, or cycle, of capitalist production (see section 2.2.2). Marx characterised the process as follows:

$$\underbrace{M - C^{L}_{MP}}_{(1)} - \underbrace{P - C'}_{(2)} - \underbrace{M'}_{(3)}$$

where M represents the amount of money at the beginning of the production cycle; C^{LP}_{MP} is the labour power and means of production necessary for production; P represents the production process proper; C^1 represents the new commodity at the end of the productive process; M^1 is the monetised form of the new commodity and is greater than M thus indicating the amount of the surplus created in the production process.

This process of production, according to Marx, takes place in three stages (see Marx, 1974b, p. 25). The 'first stage' (1) is the stage of circulation where money is transformed into commodities. The 'second stage' (2) is, according to Marx, the stage of 'productive consumption' (ibid., p. 25) where a new commodity is produced from the combination of labour and means of production. The 'third stage' (3) is the final stage of circulation, and the inverse of the first stage, where the new commodity is converted back into money.

Marx attempted to show that the two stages of circulation were unproductive, and that only the production stage was productive. He put forward the 'general law' that 'all costs of circulation which arise only from changes in the forms of commodities do not add to their value' (ibid., p. 152). Circulation costs (such as accounting costs, advertising costs, packaging costs, storage costs, wholesaling costs, retailing costs, and so on) are 'an unavoidable evil' (ibid., p. 153) and 'intrinsically' (ibid., p. 134) unproductive, because they are expenses which must be met if surplus value is to be realised. In the aggregate they are 'a deduction from surplus value' (ibid., p. 152) and 'unproductive expenses as far as society is concerned' (ibid., p. 140).[8]

Marx further explained why he regarded circulation costs as unproductive:

> a certain amount of labour-power and labour-time must be expended in the process of circulation . . . A part of the variable capital must be laid out in the purchase of this labour-power functioning only in circulation. This advance of capital creates neither product nor value. It reduces *pro tanto* the dimensions in which the advanced capital functions productively. It is as though one part of the product were transformed into a machine which buys and sells the rest of the product. This machine brings about a reduction of the product (ibid., p. 138).

According to most commentators (Baran, 1957; Gillman, 1957; Gough, 1972; Harrison, 1973; Hunt, 1979) the precise reason why Marx classified circulation costs as unproductive is that they are 'costs which are occasioned solely by the fact that the goods are being produced and distributed under the capitalist mode of production' (Harrison, 1973, p. 73). In other words, 'the critical distinction is between those activities necessary to production in general, and those activities peculiar to commodity production' (Gough, 1972, p. 57; see also Marx, 1974b, pp. 146–52).

The implication of this is that those costs which are technically necessary for the production of a commodity in any mode of production are productive, while those which are peculiar to the capitalist mode of production are unproductive. Since circulation costs are assumed to be

Table 4.2 Marx's 'Definition II' of productive and unproductive labour

	Productive	*Unproductive*
Criterion	All labour whose performance is technically necessary in any mode of production	All labour whose performance is necessary only in the capitalist mode of production.
Example	Wage costs as well as the cost of produced and unproduced means of production.	Circulation costs and certain supervisory costs.

peculiar to the capitalist mode of production they are defined, therefore, as unproductive.

This definition of productive and unproductive labour is schematically outlined in Table 4.2.

Marx's second definition of productive and unproductive labour faces two fundamental problems. The first is that it is inconsistent with the previous definition ('Definition I') and by implication with other, more important, aspects of Marx's work. The second problem is that it is impossible to apply empirically. Both of these problems will now be considered.

Marx's second definition is inconsistent with his first since circulation costs are unproductive according to one (the second) but productive according to the other (the first). This is because, according to the first definition, the labour involved in the circulation process produces commodities (that is, use values and exchange values) which are financed by capital and produced in the capitalist sector and hence are vehicles of capitalist exploitation and accumulation.

Marx seems to have been aware of this inconsistency and attempted to resolve it with two different arguments. He argues, 'in the first place' that the labour performed in the process of circulation' is used up in a mere function of circulation. It cannot be used for anything else, not for productive labour' (Marx, 1974b, p. 135). However, this argument is tautological since it fails to show why the 'function' of circulation is 'unproductive' (in the first sense). Marx argues 'in the second place' that 'society does not appropriate any extra product or value' (ibid.) as a result of circulation. In fact, however, the opposite would appear to be the case (unless it is assumed, erroneously, that 'immaterial' commodities cannot result in capital accumulation). The services produced in the process of circulation are commodities like any other, are produced and financed in the capitalist sector, and result in capital accumulation and are thus productive (according to the first definition). There is thus an inconsistency between Marx's two definitions of productive and unproductive labour.[9]

The second problem with Marx's definition is that it is impossible to apply empirically. This is because the criterion implied by Marx's second definition involves a comparison between that labour (that is, productive labour) which is technically indispensable for the production of a given output, using the same technique, in any mode of production and that labour (that is, unproductive labour) which is specific to, and necessitated solely by, the particular features of the capitalist mode of production. The problem with this criterion is that it assumes that it is possible to establish the amount of labour which is technically indispensible for a given output, independently of the mode of production in which the production takes place. This assumption is untenable because in a situation where there is choice of technique, no one technique (or method of production) can be regarded as technically indispensable except in the context of a particular set of criteria which are likely to be specific to each particular mode of production. For example, in the capitalist mode of production, the criteria of cost minimisation and profit maximisation would probably make one technique of production 'technically' indispensable, though only in terms of those criteria. It is conceivable that in a different mode of production, certain criteria (such as the optimising of labour inputs, or machinery inputs, or raw material inputs, or the optimising of spatial and social equity) would make altogether different techniques of production 'technically' indispensable. This means that techniques of production will tend to be specific to each mode of production – thereby ruling out the possibility of empirically applying the criteria implicit in Marx's second definition (see Harrison, 1973, pp. 74–5).[10] It would seem therefore, on the basis of these arguments, that Marx's 'Definition II' should be rejected.

4.3 CONCLUSION

The analysis in this chapter has argued that Marx's second definition of productive and unproductive labour ought to be rejected and that his first definition ought to be retained. It has also argued that the first definition ought to be modified to allow for the possibility that certain forms of state expenditure (for example, expenditure on infrastructure, education, health, social welfare, and so on) may have a positive effect on capital accumulation. The value of this analysis in the present context is that it provides a basis for evaluating how this distinction is used in the writings of Jean Lojkine and thereby assessing his claim that certain forms of state expenditure (which he refers to as the 'collective means of consumption') are unproductive (see section 7.2.3).

Part II

French Marxist Urban Sociology: The Case of Manuel Castells and Jean Lojkine

5 The Different Marxist Traditions of Manuel Castells and Jean Lojkine: Althusserianism and State Monopoly Capitalism

5.0 INTRODUCTION

The works of Manuel Castells and Jean Lojkine are written within different Marxist traditions and it is necessary to understand these traditions in order to assess their work. Castells's work – at least that written prior to 1983 (see Castells, 1983a, pp. 289–336) – is located within the Althusserian framework, while that of Lojkine is located within the framework of state monopoly capitalism (although in one place Castells attempts to combine elements of both frameworks – see Castells and Godard, 1974). Each of these frameworks will be briefly outlined as they impinge upon the work of Castells and Lojkine respectively.

5.1 THE ALTHUSSERIAN FRAMEWORK

The Althusserian school of Marxism is the name usually given to the works of Althusser (1969; 1971; Althusser and Balibar, 1970), Balibar (Althusser and Balibar, 1970) and Poulantzas (1972, 1973, 1975, 1976). Castells, in numerous places, openly acknowledges his debt to the writings of this school (Castells, 1969a, p. 420; 1976a, p. 43; 1976c, p. 149; 1977a, pp. ix, 125). This 'debt' is evident throughout all of Castells's work but particularly in his concept of the urban system and in his theories of urban politics, urban planning and urban social movements (See sections 6.3, 6.4, 6.5 and 6.6 respectively). In those parts of his work the Althusserian penchant for taxonomies of structures, elements and sub-elements is particularly evident.

The Althusserian framework can be seen as an attempt to provide an alternative to the crude determinism which is implicit in the Marxian distinction between the base and the superstructure and the Marxian claim (as expressed in Marx, 1976) that the history of any society can be understood solely by reference to changes occurring in the economic base.[1] Althusser rejects this 'spatial metaphor of the edifice' (Althusser, 1971, p. 130) by asserting that the superstructure has 'relative autonomy' (ibid.). As a result, he claims that every mode of production should be characterised, not in terms of its base and its superstructure, but in terms of three relatively autonomous elements: the economic, the political and the ideological. These elements (or instances, levels or systems as the terms are interchangeably used) are said to be combined in a specific way according to each mode of production. It is the 'specific combination' (Poulantzas, 1973, p. 13) of instances which permits the various modes of production to be differentiated.

Every mode of production is said to have one instance which is 'dominant' (Poulantzas, 1973, p. 14) and it is this instance which characterises the mode of production in question and determines its laws. In the capitalist mode of production, the economic system is said to be dominant. Also, in every mode of production there is a 'determinant' instance (Poulantzas, 1973, p. 14) and this, it is claimed, is invariably the economic system. Thus in the capitalist mode of production, the economic system is both dominant and determinant.

Each of the elements (or instances) of any mode of production (that is, the economic, the political and the ideological) is said to form a structure which, in turn, is made up of a number of elements and a number of relations. According to Balibar, every economic system is a structure which is made up of three elements and two relations and it is the specific combination of these elements and relations which differentiate one economic structure from another (see Althusser and Balibar, 1970, pp. 212ff).

The three elements which make up any economic structure are labour, means of production, and non-labour, and the relations which combine these elements are the relations of property (or ownership) and real appropriation (or control) (see Althusser and Balibar, 1970, pp. 212–14; Poulantzas, 1973, pp. 28–30). In the capitalist economic system, the relations of property and real appropriation are said to be such that the capitalist (that is, non-labour) owns labour power and means of production (relation of property) and also controls the production process by which these two elements are combined (relation of real appropriation). Thus, in the capitalist economic system the relations of property and real appropriation are said to 'overlap and coincide' (Althusser and Balibar, 1970, p. 215) and are described by Castells as 'homologous' (Castells, 1976a, p. 180).[2]

At any particular point in history, a society will have a combination of different modes of production, one of which will be dominant. This 'complex unity' (Poulantzas, 1973, p. 15), in which a number of different modes of production coexist, one of them being dominant, is called a 'social formation' or a 'conjuncture'.

The analysis of any mode of production thus involves, according to the Althusserian School, an analysis of the three 'regional' (Poulantzas, 1973, p. 12) structures which comprise it (that is, the economic structure, the political structure and the ideological structure). In the case of the capitalist mode of production, only the economic structure has yet been systematically analysed – by Marx himself. Thus Althusserians see the analysis of the political and ideological structures of capitalism as a major priority. They argue that such an analysis must, following the example of Marx's pioneering economic analysis, be in terms of structures, that is, in terms of elements and relations.[3] Poulantzas attempts to develop this type of structural analysis[4] in relation to the political structure of the capitalism. Thus the Althusserian school simultaneously outlines the various 'regional theories' that need to be developed as part of the analysis of the capitalism, as well as stipulating the methodological procedures, gleaned from Marx's economic analysis, by which these theoretical advances may be achieved (see Glucksman 1974, p. 293).

One additional feature of the Althusserian framework may be noted. This feature concerns the distinction between 'structures' and 'practices', and is fundamental to the whole Althusserian problematic. Althusser explains the two concepts in the following way: 'All the levels of social existence are the sites of distinct practices: economic practice, political practice, ideological practice, technical practice and scientific (or theoretical) practice. We think the content of these different practices by thinking their peculiar structure' (Althusser and Balibar, 1970, p. 58).[5]

The basic idea here is that there are two levels in reality: the superficial level (of practices) and the fundamental level (of structures). The relationship between these two levels is that the underlying reality of structures determines the more superficial reality of practices (but not entirely, since practices can vary within given structural limits). This is what Poulantzas means when he describes a structure as defining 'the limits of variation' (Poulantzas, 1973, p. 95) of practices. The same idea is implicit in the following quotation: 'The determination of the practices by the structure, consists in the production by the structure of the limits of variation of the class struggle: it is these limits which are the effect of the structure' (Poulantzas, 1973, p. 95).[6]

These are some of the basic concepts and terms which make up the Althusserian framework. Before completing this account, however, it is necessary to outline briefly Poulantzas's theory of the capitalist state, since this too is relevant to understanding Castells's work. According to Poulantzas, the function of the state is to act as 'the factor of cohesion between the levels of a social formation' (Poulantzas, 1973, p. 44). It does this in two ways: through repression and through ideology. On this basis, Poulantzas, following Althusser, classifies the institutions of the state (which are renamed state apparatuses) according to whether they contribute to cohesion through repression or through ideology. These two types of state apparatus are referred to as the repressive state apparatus and the ideological state apparatus respectively (Poulantzas, 1972, p. 25; see also Althusser, 1971, pp. 131–40).

The term repressive state apparatus is used to designate those institutions of the state which, within capitalism, serve the function of repressing any serious threat to the system of capitalist exploitation and accumulation. For Poulantzas and Althusser, the repressive state apparatus contains the following elements: the head of state, the Government, the administration, the army, the police, the courts and the prisons (Althusser, 1971, p. 131; Poulantzas, 1972, p. 151). Each of these institutions is classified as 'repressive' because they can have recourse, if need be, to the use of violence, in the course of their functioning. For Marx and Lenin, the state was identified exclusively with the repressive state apparatus, but Althusser and Poulantzas propose to extend the definition of the state to include other institutions which also play a role in the maintenance and cohesion of the capitalist system. These institutions are referred to as the ideological state apparatus.

The term ideological state apparatus covers a wide gamut of institutions which include, according to Poulantzas, the church, the schools, the mass media, the arts, the political parties, the unions ('with the exception of course, of the revolutionary part of trade union organizations' (Poulantzas, 1972, p. 251)) and the family ('from a certain point of view' (ibid.)). Despite the plurality, diversity and 'relative autonomy' of these various institutions, both Althusser and Poulantzas feel justified in classifying them together as part of the state apparatus since anything which constitutes a 'factor of cohesion' between the levels of a social formation must, they argue, be part of the state (Althusser, 1971, p. 139; Poulantzas, 1972, pp. 251–2).[7]

The significant point about the apparatuses of the state within capitalist society is that their 'structure' is such that they serve the interests of the dominant capitalist class while at the same time being 'relatively autonomous' from this class. Poulantzas argues that the state serves the interests of the dominant class through a 'power bloc' (Poulantzas, 1973, p. 230) which unites the various fractions of the dominant class and ensures that the state is subordinated to their interests. However, within the power bloc there is one class fraction which is dominant and this is called the 'hegemonic class or fraction' (Poulantzas, 1973, p. 237). Within advanced capitalist societies, this hegemonic class fraction is monopoly capital and it unites the various fractions of the capitalist class and ensures that the state operates in the interests of the entire capitalist class.

These are the main features of Poulantzas's theory of the state. This account and the account of the Althusserian framework which preceded it are designed to provide the conceptual and terminological background necessary for an understanding of Castells's work. This account has not tried to assess the Althusserian framework since this will be undertaken, in so far as it is directly relevant, within the specific context of Castells's work. It is now necessary to examine an alternative Marxist tradition – the theory of state monopoly capitalism – since this is the conceptual background to the work of Jean Lojkine.

5.2 THE THEORY OF STATE MONOPOLY CAPITALISM

Lojkine's work is situated within the Marxist tradition known as state monopoly capitalism (henceforth, SMC).[8] This tradition has been the official doctrine of the European Communist parties for many years, including the French Communist Party of which Lojkine is a member (see Pickvance, 1977a, p. 220; see also Lebas, 1983, pp. 14ff). Thus the theory of SMC considerably predates the more recent Althusserian approach. Indeed these two approaches to Marxism are in conflict on a number of important issues as this section reveals.

Four elements of the theory of SMC are highlighted in Lojkine's work, and together these constitute the main core of the theory. Each of these four elements will now be briefly outlined.

The first element of the theory is that there are three stages in the history of capitalist development. The three stages are: classical competitive capitalism, simple monopoly capitalism and state monopoly capitalism (Lojkine, 1977a, p. 122; see also 1977c, p. 21). In Lojkine's view the capitalist countries of Western Europe and America have passed through the first two stages and are now in the third and final phase of capitalist development. In the case of France the transition from competitive to monopoly capitalism occurred at the end of the nineteenth and the beginning of the twentieth century (Lojkine, 1977d, p. 259). The methodological implication of this is that a correct understanding of any capitalist society must begin from a correct 'periodization' (ibid., p. 120) of the history of that society. Indeed the failure to respect this methodological point is one of the criticisms which Lojkine directs at Poulantzas's analysis of the capitalist state which (implicitly) assumes that 'political domination is identical in capitalist states . . . whether these states are at the stage of competitive capitalism . . . or at the monopoly stage' (1977a, p. 277).

The second element of the theory is the claim that monopolistic firms[9] entirely dominate the economy and the state in the period of SMC. The dominance of monopolies in this period, according to Lojkine, is reflected in the fact that they receive a higher rate of profit than non-monopolistic firms (Lojkine, 1977a, p. 112). In addition, their interests are given special protection by the state since 'the whole of the organization of the economy and of the society is under the thumb of the large monopolies' (ibid., p. 118). The implication of this, Lojkine argues, is that the primary class conflict in SMC is between monopoly groups and non-monopoly groups (the latter consisting of medium and small capitalists and landowners and workers). The central Marxian conflict between capitalists and workers still remains, but it is secondary rather than primary (see Lojkine, 1972b, p. 143; 1977a, p. 113 and Chapter 5, pp. 275–311; 1977b, pp. 143–4; 1977c, p. 22; 1977d, pp. 257, 260, 261; 1978, pp. 46, 50). The party political implications of this, as Jessop points out, is that SMC is 'often associated with the political programme of an anti-monopoly front' which 'would embrace small and medium capital as well as the petit bourgeoisie and wage-earning class, and would attempt to capture the state apparatus for its own use' (Jessop, 1977, pp. 360–1). This element of the theory presents yet another source of disagreement between Lojkine and Poulantzas. Poulantzas, as has just been seen (section 5.1), argues that the capitalist class are united in a 'power bloc' while Lojkine argues that they are divided into two opposed groups: monopolies and non-monopolies (see Lojkine, 1977a, pp. 275–311).

The third element of the theory is that the rate of profit will tend to fall in the course of capitalist development and this becomes most acute in the period of SMC. This arises because of the tendency for constant capital to increase relative to variable capital thereby giving rise to what Lojkine terms an 'overaccumulation' of constant capital and its subsequent 'devalorization' (Lojkine, 1977a, pp. 96–101, 122). This characteristic of the theory of SMC is based directly upon Marx's law of the falling rate of profit (see section 2.1). It is the basis of the claim that the chronic crisis of capitalism is deepest in the period of SMC, where non-monopoly groups are particularly adversely affected (Lojkine, 1977e, pp. 116–18).

The fourth element of the theory is that state intervention in the economy is 'a growing necessity' (Lojkine, 1976a, p. 140). The ultimate purpose or function of this intervention is 'to maintain the cohesion of the social formation as a whole' (ibid., p. 139) and it does this by attempting, as Lojkine variously puts it, 'to regulate' (1977a, p. 178), 'to attenuate' (ibid.), 'to suppress' (ibid., p. 179) and 'to resolve' (ibid.) the profitability crisis of the capitalist economy. The effect of this intervention, it is claimed, is to regulate the problem in the short term while exacerbating it in the longer term (Lojkine, 1977a, pp. 180, 353; 1977e, pp. 116–17). It exacerbates the problem in the long term because it increases the organic composition of capital (as a result of state investment in physical and social infrastructure – see section 7.3.2) which leads, *ceteris paribus*, to further falls in the rate of profit, and to yet further interventions by the state. Thus state intervention becomes a permanent feature of the monopolistic stage of capitalist development; hence the term state monopoly capitalism.

It is the question of the state and state intervention which represents the source of greatest disagreement between Lojkine and the Althusserian school, particularly Poulantzas (see Pickvance, 1977a, pp. 219–27).[10] Lojkine rejects the Althusserian theory of instances and hence rejects the notion that the state has 'relative autonomy' from the economic base (Lojkine, 1975, p. 28 fn23; 1977a, pp. 78–9, 275–311; 1977b, pp. 141, 142, 147; 1977e, p. 113). In turn he rejects the notion that the state acts in the interests of the entire capitalist class. In his view the state is 'determined' by the economic base (1977a, p. 257) and is an 'active reflection' of it (1977b, pp. 141ff) and hence is an active reflection of the class struggle. Since the monopolies dominate the other class fractions in the class struggle, it follows, on Lojkine's premises, that they also dominate the state to which they are united by a 'unique mechanism' (1972b; 1977a, p. 116; 1977e, p. 119; Lojkine and Preteceille, 1970, p. 80). Thus the state tends to reflect and protect the interests of the monopolies in the current stage of capitalism.

These are the four characteristics which constitute the core of the theory of SMC as seen by Lojkine. This theory plays an important role in his analysis of collective consumption and urban development (which are discussed in sections 7.2 and 7.3) and it is in that context that an assessment of the theory of SMC will be made.

5.3 CONCLUSION

This chapter has briefly outlined two different traditions of Marxism namely Althusserianism and State Monopoly Capitalism. These two traditions are the contexts within which the respective works of Castells and Lojkine are located. No attempt was made to assess these two traditions, however. This will be done, where relevant, in the course of assessing the work of Castells and Lojkine. The aim of this chapter was simply to provide the essential conceptual and terminological background necessary for a proper understanding of their work. It is now necessary to undertake a systematic examination of that work.

6 The Marxist Urban Sociology of Manuel Castells

6.0 INTRODUCTION

The purpose of this chapter is to assess, systematically, the writings of Manuel Castells. These writings date from 1967 and, as the bibliography reveals, they are extremely copious. They represent one of the first attempts within urban sociology to develop a Marxist analysis of urban areas. Castells's writings can be classified into three different categories: those concerned with a critique of conventional urban sociology; those concerned with formulating an alternative Marxian approach for urban analysis; and those concerned with empirical research. While this classification is not watertight it is broadly accurate and will be adopted in this chapter. Thus, Castells's critique of conventional urban sociology will be discussed in section 6.1; his formulation of a Marxist approach to urban analysis in sections 6.2 to 6.6; and his empirical research will be examined in section 6.7.

This threefold classification of Castells's work corresponds broadly to the chronological sequence in which it was published. The first stage represents his early writings in the late 1960s in which he advanced his critique of conventional approaches to urban sociology. The second stage involved the formulation of a Marxist approach to the analysis of urban areas, which was quite a new approach within urban sociology when it first appeared in the late 1960s and early 1970s. The third stage represents the application of this new perspective to empirical research which led to the publication of a large number of research reports authored and coauthored by Castells throughout the 1970s (see section 6.7.1).

It is necessary to assess the value of Castells's intellectual endeavours, not only because of their comparative novelty, but also because they have become influential within the social sciences generally (as the number of citations to his work reveals – see General Introduction, note 1). The assessment presented in this chapter will focus primarily, though not exclusively, upon issues in Marxian political economy essentially because this is the ultimate foundation upon which Marxist analysis rests. Thus the analysis presented in Part 1 (Chapters 1 to 4) is central to the arguments presented in this and the next chapter. The crucial question, therefore, which will be addressed to Castells's work, is whether it is based upon a valid Marxian political economy and whether the latter, in turn, is conceptually capable of handling the spatial dimension necessitated by an urban analysis.

6.1 THE CRITIQUE OF URBAN SOCIOLOGY

6.1.1 Introduction

Castells's critique of urban sociology was first published in French in 1968 (Castells, 1968 – republished in English in Castells, 1976a). It has subsequently been repeated, extended and translated in a number of different publications. It was repeated and extended in French in 1969 (Castells, 1969c – republished in French in Castells, 1971b – republished in English in Castells, 1976b) again in French in 1972 (Castells, 1972c – republished in English in Castells, 1977a), and in English in 1975 (Castells, 1975c – republished in English in Castells, 1976d). This critique attempts to assess the 'scientific relevance' (Castells, 1976a, p. 33) of urban sociology with a view to identifying those areas of it which, in Castells's view, have 'produced knowledge' (Castells, 1976b, p. 84). Castells's critique, which acknowledges that many of his criticisms were made by previous writers, was enthusiastically received by many commentators and has been variously described as 'brilliant' (Pickvance, 1978, p. 174), 'rigorous and comprehensive' (Harloe, 1977, p. 2), 'convincing' (Reynaud, 1974, p. 617), 'systematic' (Garnier, 1974, p. 124) and 'radical' (Pickvance, 1974a, p. 205).

Castells concentrates his critique on the twin topics of urbanism and urbanisation and these are outlined and discussed below in subsections 6.1.3 and 6.1.4. Prior to that, however, it is necessary to clarify the terms 'science' and 'ideology' which Castells uses in his critique before considering the more substantial issues involved. This will now be done.

6.1.2 'Science' and 'Ideology' in Urban Sociology

Castells's critique (with the exception of Castells, 1977a, Parts I and II) begins from the proposition that any science must possess one of two criteria if it is to be truly scientific. It must have either a 'specific theoretical [or scientific] object' or a 'specific real object' (Castells, 1976b, p. 60). If it does not possess one of these two criteria then it 'does not exist as a science' and hence is 'ideological' (ibid.).

On the basis of this syllogistic formulation of the relations between science and ideology Castells argues that urban sociology is unscientific – first, because it lacks a 'specific real object' due to 'the absence of any clear delimitations' of the term 'urban' (ibid., p. 73), and secondly, because it lacks a 'specific theoretical [or scientific] object', since the 'themes around which urban sociology has historically attempted to constitute itself as a science' (that is, urbanism, urbanisation and the ecological system) 'do not possess the characteristics of theoretical distinctiveness' (ibid.). Castells concludes, therefore, that 'urban sociology is an ideology' (ibid., p. 60).

He argues further that urban sociology is unscientific because, while possessing a 'theoretical [or scientific] object', it is both 'non-specific' and 'non-explicit' (Castells, 1976a, p. 38) and hence, according to his definition, is unscientific. Castells claims that a close examination of the main works of the Chicago school, which foreshadowed 'all the subsequent developments of the discipline' (Castells, 1976b, p. 61), reveals their concern with 'the processes of social disorganization and individual maladjustment, the persistence of autonomous sub-cultures, deviant or otherwise, and their resistance to integration' (Castells, 1976a, p. 37). For Castells, these studies in the 'sociology of integration' (ibid., p. 39) are 'perfectly legitimate' (ibid.) though limited from the point of view of 'understanding urban social life' (ibid.). He concludes by rejecting urban sociology as unscientific and ideological.

Castells's definition of science in terms of a specific theoretical object and a specific real object originates in the writings of Louis Althusser (Althusser and Balibar, 1970; see also Castells, 1970c; Castells and de Ipola, 1976 – republished in 1979). Two distinctive features should be noted about this definition. The first is that the distinction between a theoretical (or scientific) object and a real object is used by Althusser and Castells to emphasise the crucial role played by theory in the production of scientific knowledge: it is the theoretical object which provides the conceptual map for understanding the real object. This view, according to Althusser and Castells, contrasts with the empiricist view which characterises scientific knowledge as a process of abstraction from the real object.

The second feature of this definition of science is the claim that Marxism is scientific because Marx's writings constitute a radical epistemological break with Hegel and the classicals, whose theoretical object is essentially ideological. For both Althusser and Castells, as indeed for Marx, the distinction between science and ideology corresponds to the division between Marxist and non-Marxist thought respectively. It is this particular (and somewhat controversial)[1] usage which Castells employs in his critique of conventional urban sociology; hence his claim that the latter is ideological should be understood in this peculiarly Marxist sense (see Pickvance, 1974b, pp. 203–5). It is now necessary to consider the more substantive issues involved in Castells's critique, namely urbanism and urbanisation.

6.1.3 Urbanism

Castells devotes considerable attention to criticising the theory of urbanism of Louis Wirth (1951), since this theory provides, he believes, 'the essential theoretical basis of urban sociology' (Castells, 1976b, p. 65; see also Castells, 1976a, pp. 36–40; 1977a, Chapter 5, pp. 75–85). Wirth's theory is that the spatial characteristics of urban areas (as defined by size, density and heterogeneity) determine, to a large degree, the cultural characteristics of urban dwellers (as defined by secondary relations, role segmentation, anonymity, isolation, instrumental relations, the absence of direct social control, the diversity and transcience of social commitments, the loosening of family ties and individualistic competition). Unlike the traditional criticisms of Wirth (whch have focused upon the fact that his description of urban culture was ethnocentric and temperocentric) Castells's criticism is that the real determinant of urban culture is not the spatial form of urban areas but the mode of production in which it is situated. In the case of urbanism, it is capitalism rather than spatial form which is its ultimate cause.

Castells accuses Wirth of making a 'spurious correlation' (Castells, 1976b, p. 69) between the spatial characteristics of urban areas and the culture of urban residents since both, in fact, are simultaneously determined by capitalism. He suggests further that Wirth's treatment of urban areas, as entities which exist independently of the mode of production, represents 'too impoverished a vision of sociological theory to be seriously defended' (Castells, 1976b, p. 68).

Castells's own position, however, contains an ambiguity. On the one hand he claims that the mode of production is the determinant of the spatial and cultural characteristics of urban areas (see Castells, 1976a, pp. 38, 54, 55; 1977a, pp. 81–2). On the other hand he claims that industrialisation is also the determinant of these spatial and cultural characteristics. This ambiguity was first pointed out by Pickvance (1974b, pp. 212–16) and is illustrated in Figure 6.1 (which is a slight

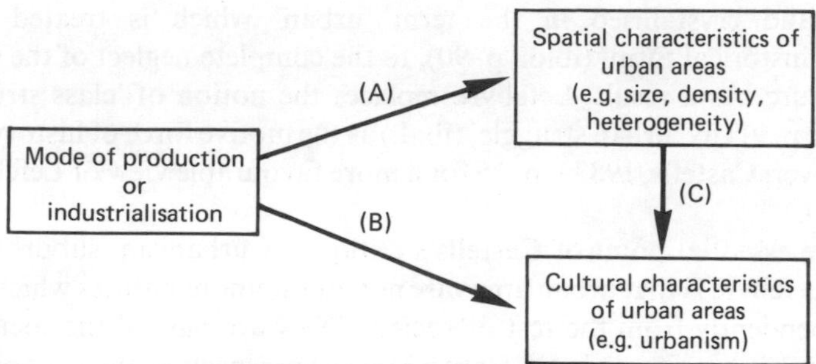

Figure 6.1 The determinants of urban culture according to Castells and Wirth

modification of Figure 1 in Pickvance, 1974b, p. 213). In terms of Figure 6.1, where the arrows indicate the direction of causality, Wirth's position corresponds to arrow (C) while Castells's position vacillates between arrows (A) and (B). (Pickvance, 1974b, pp. 213–14, in a more generous, if exegetically more questionable interpretation, characterises Castells's position in terms of arrows (A) and (C).)

Apart from the ambiguity in Castells's position, his critique of Wirth is cogent and useful. This is particularly so from the Marxist point of view since it opens up the possibility of developing a Marxist approach to the analysis of urban areas.

Castells extends his critique of urbanism to include the sociological literature on 'suburbanism' as well as the urban analysis of Henri Lefebvre (1968, 1972, 1973). He rejects all of these as 'urban ideology' because they treat the city as causally autonomous and as the 'most important' (Castells, 1977a, p. 87) reality. He criticises the thesis that a certain suburban culture is associated with a certain (suburban) 'ecological unit' (ibid., p. 101) since this involves the same assumptions and errors as Wirth's thesis. These assumptions, he states, imply an 'implicit link between an ecological context and a cultural context' (ibid., p. 104).

The work of Henri Lefebvre is of a different tradition to urbanism and suburbanism but is nevertheless 'very close to Wirth's thesis concerning the way social relations are produced' (ibid., p. 90). Although Lefebvre is of the Marxist tradition, Castells finds his urban analysis objectionable because it is conducted in terms of the category 'urban' rather than in terms of modes of production. Thus Lefebvre is criticised for referring to 'urban contradictions' (ibid., p. 86) rather than to contradictions stemming from the dominant mode of production. The 'whole problem' (ibid., p. 89) with Lefebvre's analysis, according to Castells, is summarised and crystallised in the term 'urban' which is treated as a 'transhistorical form' (ibid., p. 90), to the complete neglect of the social structure. As a result, Lefebvre replaces the notion of 'class struggle' (ibid., p. 91) by 'urban struggle' (ibid.) as the motive force of history (see, however, Castells, 1983a, p. 15 for a more favourable view of Lefebvre's work).

The essential point of Castells's critique of urbanism, suburbanism and Lefebvre is that urban areas are not autonomous entities which exist independently from the rest of society. They are part of the society in which they are situated and, from a Marxist perspective, they can only be properly understood in terms of the dominant mode of production prevailing in that society. In this sense Castells's critique prepares the way for the explicit application of a Marxist perspective to the analysis of urban areas.

6.1.4 Urbanisation

Urbanisation refers, *inter alia*, to the process by which urban areas grow and to the resulting spatial structure of those areas. Castells is particularly critical of two themes that have been part of the conventional approach to the study of urbanisation: the concentric zone model of Burgess and the concept of 'overurbanization' (see Castells, 1970a; 1970b; 1976a, pp. 40–41; 1977a, Chapter 3, pp. 39–63). His criticism of both these themes is that they treat urbanisation as if it were a uniform, unilinear and universal process.

The assumption that urbanisation follows an inevitable and universal pattern is typified, according to Castells, by the work of Burgess who depicts all urban growth by a series of concentric zones and explains them as the outcome of ecological processes: competition, concentration, centralization, segregation, invasion and succession. Castells's criticism of Burgess and this 'school' is that it treats 'as a universal feature a social process which is found only under particular conditions' (Castells, 1976a, p. 40). Castells is also critical of the concept of 'overurbanization' which has been developed for the purpose of understanding the process of urbanisation in 'dependent' societies (see Castells, 1970a, pp. 1168–90; 1971a; 1977a, pp. 43–63). His criticism, which is not original (see Sovani, 1964), is that if urbanisation and industrialisation have occurred simultaneously in advanced capitalist society, this does not imply that the pattern must be either universal or inevitable. Indeed an historical investigation of dependent societies would reveal why the process of urbanisation is likely to be systematically different from that which occurred in advanced capitalist societies.

As in his critique of urbanism, Castells's critique of urbanisation emphasises the necessity of relating urbanisation to the mode of production in which it is occurring. It is a valid critique and a useful antidote to those studies which tend to treat urban areas as autonomous entities unrelated to the society in which they are located (Castells, 1970a, p. 1156).

6.1.5 Conclusion

Castells's critique of urban sociology is significant, not because of its originality, but because it is tied to the promise of a new Marxian approach to the analysis of urban areas. Since Marxism has never before been applied to the analysis of urban questions (apart, possibly, from Engels's (1958) precedential study of Manchester), this represents a new departure for both Marxism and urban sociology. It is for this reason that the value of Castells's work must be judged, not by the perspicacity of his critique, but by the Marxist alternative which he proposes. It is this alternative which is examined in the subsequent sections.

6.2 COLLECTIVE CONSUMPTION

6.2.1 Introduction

In 1972 Castells's book, *La Question Urbaine*, was published in French (Castells, 1972c) and in 1977 it was translated and published in English (Castells, 1977a). This is probably Castells's best-known work and has been described by one reviewer as 'one of the most significant works in urban sociology ever written' (Pickvance, 1978, p. 173).[2] In this book Castells restates his critique of conventional urban sociology (Castells, 1977a, Chapters 1 and 2, pp. 7–112) and replaces it by what he terms 'an adaptation of Marxist concepts to the urban sphere, using a particular reading of Marx given by the French philosopher Louis Althusser' (Castells, 1977a, p. ix; see also p. 125). It is this 'adaptation' which will be examined in this and subsequent sections.

Castells's first step in this 'adaptation' is to select the theme of 'collective consumption' – which he rescues from 'the murk of urban sociology' (Castells, 1976b, p. 75) – and treat it as the major defining characteristic of urban areas within capitalism. There are two important aspects to this part of Castells's analysis which will be discussed in this section. The first concerns the way in which he arrives at this definition of an urban area (discussed in subsection 6.2.2) while the second concerns his analysis of the role and function of collective consumption in capitalist society (discussed in subsection 6.2.3). Before proceeding to an examination of these topics, however, it may be useful to first clarify the meaning of the term collective consumption as it is used by Castells.

The term 'collective consumption' – which is frequently used interchangeably with 'collective means of consumption' (Castells, 1978a, p. 42) and 'means of collective consumption' (Castells, 1977c, p. 64) – is defined by Castells as follows: 'We class as "collective means of consumption" expenditure on education and culture, social welfare, transport, housing and urbanization' (Castells, 1978a, p. 42). On the basis of this definition and from the way in which he uses the term in various other places (Castells and Godard, 1974, pp. 228–9; 1976b, p. 295; 1977a, pp. 451, 460; 1977b, p. 64; 1978a, pp. 41–2; 1981b, pp. 8, 9; 1983b, p. 9) it is reasonable to infer that, for Castells, the term collective consumption refers to the state provision of the 'indirect salary' (Castells, 1975a, p. 175). In other words, collective consumption refers to that part of the real wage which is paid, indirectly (by the state) to the worker in contrast to that part which is paid directly (by the employer). Thus the workers' wage contains at least two elements: the element paid by the employer and the element paid by the state. There may also be a third element if workers receive goods and services from voluntary welfare organisations (though Castells does not consider this possibility). This definition of collective consumption is quite straightforward and can be easily handled within the conventional Marxian framework (as will be seen in subsection 6.2.3).

On the basis of these clarifications, it is now possible to proceed to an examination of the way in which the concept of collective consumption is used in Castells's urban sociology.

6.2.2 Defining an Urban Area as an Area of Collective Consumption

Castells claims that an urban area – 'the urban', 'urban space' and 'urban unit' (Castells, 1977a, pp. 234–5) being synonyms of same – should be defined as an area of collective consumption since this definition would allow the entire urban question to be investigated in a 'theoretical way' (ibid., p. 236). The procedure by which he arrives at this definition can be summarised in terms of four separate propositions, as follows:

(i) An urban area should be defined in terms of one of the instances of the social structure (Castells, 1977a, p. 235). Given that Castells follows the Althusserian definition of social structure (see section 5.1) this translates to the proposition that an urban area should be defined as either an economic, a political or an ideological entity.
(ii) An urban area, at least within capitalist societies, should be defined in terms of the economic instance since this is the dominant instance in the capitalist mode of production (ibid., p. 235).
(iii) The economic instance consists of two elements, namely, means of production and labour power, and an urban area should be defined in terms of the latter, not the former. The reason for this is that 'the urban seems to me to connote directly the process relating to labour power' (ibid., p. 236) and is an area 'delimited by a job market and by the relative unity of its daily life' (ibid.) as measured by 'the map of commuter flows' (ibid.). Means of production, by contrast, are said to correspond to the domain of regional problems (ibid.).
(iv) The reproduction of labour power consists of two elements namely, individual consumption, and collective consumption, and the city should be defined in terms of the latter (ibid., p. 445). The reason for this is that collective consumption contains 'most of the realities connoted by the term urban' (ibid.; see also Castells, 1976h, pp. 180ff; Castells and Godard, 1974, pp. 174, 192).

Castells's arguments are extremely cursory and unconvincing (as indeed various commentators have already noted – Harloe, 1979, p. 22; Pahl, 1977, p. 314; 1978; Pickvance, 1978, p. 175). The main difficulty is that he places too much importance on collective consumption as the distinctive and defining characteristic of urban areas to the neglect of other 'urban' processes (for example, production, property development, and so on). Moreover, the boundary of an urban area cannot consistently be defined, as he suggests, in terms of the job market since the areal size (and hence the boundary) of the job market varies considerably for workers of different skills (see section 8.7). It would seem that a more cogent and comprehensive definition of an urban area would treat it as a built-up area, that is, a spatial concentration of physical structures consisting of buildings (for example, houses, factories, offices, shops, and so on) and infrastructure (for example, roads, water sewerage, electricity, parks, and so on) (see Chapter 8). In turn, three basic processes are associated with every urban area. The first is the process by which the physical structures of the urban area (that is, the buildings and infrastructure) are produced and reproduced. This process includes, *inter alia*, the production of collective consumption. The second is the process by which these physical structures are used for the production of other commodities. The third is the process by which these physical structures are used for final consumption. It is these three processes taken together which constitute an urban area. Collective consumption is only one item in these processes. Thus the 'urban question' is much broader in scope than the issue of collective consumption as Castells's claims.

6.2.3 The Effects of Collective Consumption

It is possible, on the basis of various *obiter dicta* in Castells's writings, to identify three different theories by which he attempts to explain the 'strategic role' and 'decisive place' (Castells, 1977a, pp. 457, 458) of collective consumption within the capitalist economy. His first theory is that collective consumption plays an important role in the 'constant battle against the tendency toward a lower rate of profit (Castells, 1975a, p. 176; 1977a, p. 461) by 'counteracting' (Castells, 1978a, p. 19) this tendency. Castells's second theory is that collective consumption serves the function of alleviating the problem of deficiency of aggregate demand because 'the economy of advanced capitalist societies rests more and more on the process of consumption, i.e. the key problems are located at the level of the realisation of surplus value' (Castells, 1976d, p. 294; 1976h, p. 182; 1977a, p. 63; 1981b, p. 8). The third theory is that collective consumption is a response to the 'development of the class struggle and the growing power of the workers' movement that extends its bargaining power to all areas of societal life' (Castells, 1975a, p. 176; 1976h, p. 184).

These three explanations of the role and function of collective consumption correspond to the three types of Marxian crisis which were analysed above (see section 2.2). In other words, Castells links collective consumption and, by implication, the state, to the major crisis points of capitalist society. Unfortunately, however, he does not elaborate in sufficient detail any of these three explanations. It may therefore be useful to consider some of the major issues which arise in each case.

The first explanation, as has been seen, claims that collective consumption performs the role and function of 'counteracting' the tendency for the rate of profit to fall (Castells, 1978a, p. 18; see also 1980a, pp. 51–2, 69–70). The tendency for the rate of profit to fall refers to Marx's famous 'law' which he outlined in the third volume of *Capital*

(Marx, 1974c, Part III, Chapter 13–15, pp. 211–60), and which he regarded as the major source of crisis in capitalist societies. This 'law' or tendency was thoroughly examined above (see section 2.1) and it was seen that it could only occur if the organic composition of capital increased more rapidly than the rate of surplus value. (It was also seen, that there is nothing in the nature of capitalism to ensure that this tendency will necessarily and inevitably occur, thereby refuting the idea that this is a 'law' as distinct from a possibility.)

It follows from this that if collective consumption is to counteract the tendency for the rate of profit to fall, it must do so either by reducing the organic composition of capital or by increasing the rate of surplus value or by a combination of both. Castells argues that it has the effect of reducing the organic composition of capital. His argument (which can only be reconstructed from *obiter dicta*, since it is nowhere clearly developed) is that collective consumption counteracts the falling rate of profit by removing 'unprofitable' (Castells, 1978a, pp. 41–2; 1976h, pp. 184–5) sectors from capitalist production. Since these are unprofitable because they have a higher than average organic composition of capital,[3] it follows that their removal from the capitalist sector has the net effect of reducing the organic composition of capital in that sector and hence, *ceteris paribus*, counteracting the falling rate of profit. Castells explains the effect of state expenditure and investment as follows: 'By investing at a loss the general rate of profit of the private sector holds steady or increases' (Castells, 1978a, p. 19) and concludes: 'social expenditures of the state not only thus favour big capital, but they are also indispensable to the survival of the system' (ibid.) and are 'one of the principal cogs of monopoly capitalism' (Castells, 1977a, p. 161).

Castells presents no empirical evidence to support any of these claims, however. Moreover, the relevant evidence could only be produced after extensive and complex econometric analyses. His claims are thus based upon conjecture rather than on fact.[4]

Castells's second explanation seems to involve the claim that collective consumption performs the function of solving the realisation crises which periodically occur within capitalism. This is possibly the most conventional view held about the nature of collective consumption in the sense that it refers (implicitly, in this case) to the basic Keynesian notion that expenditure by the state can have the effect of increasing the level of aggregate demand, thereby allowing firms to increase output and produce to full capacity. It is now part of the conventional wisdom that Keynesian policies can only be effective in a capitalist economy if that economy is undergoing what Marx termed 'a realisation crisis' (see section 2.2). Such a crisis will express itself in the existence of unsold stocks of finished commodities (beyond what is normal to ensure a steady flow of same) as well as the underutilisation of the economy's capacity (that is, every firm will not be using its productive potential to the full). In such a situation state expenditure can have the effect of increasing the level of aggregate demand, thereby allowing firms to realise the profits which are crystallised in their existing stocks of unsold commodities and to increase their output up to the level of full capacity. If, however, a particular capitalist economy is already at full capacity (that is, every firm is producing the maximum possible output), then an increase in state expenditure on (for example) collective consumption would simply lead, at least in the short term, to inflation.

This seems to be the unstated argument behind Castells's claim about the relationship between collective consumption and realisation crises. In the light of these remarks, therefore, it is possible to outline more formally the precise empirical conditions which would have to be satisfied if Castells's claim were to be tested and proven correct. There are three such conditions:

(a) that there is a realisation crisis in at least one capitalist country which expresses itself in the existence of unsold stocks of commodities and the underutilisation of productive capacity;
(b) that this realisation crisis preceded in time, the introduction of, or a major increase in, collective consumption;
(c) that the realisation crisis in the country in question was solved by the introduction of or the increase in, collective consumption.

It is possible that the rapid growth in collective consumption in the 1930s and 1940s operated in this way, though whether this continues to be the case is an interesting empirical question which Castells does not discuss.

The third explanation claims that the growth of collective consumption is a response to 'the growing power of the workers' movement' (Castells, 1975a, p. 176). At the theoretical level, this claim emphasises the respective bargaining power of workers *vis-à-vis* capitalists and the state in the determination of wages. In this sense it effectively and correctly involves a rejection of Marx's theory of subsistence wages (see section 2.3). At the empirical level, Castells presents no evidence to support his claim. The relevant evidence in this case would have to show that the genesis of collective consumption was the outcome of the growing bargaining power of workers. It would also have to show that variations over time and place in the quality and quantity of collective consumption were a reflection of variations in that bargaining power. In addition it would also involve establishing if in fact collective consumption increases or decreases real wages, and for which group of workers (and this would be done by subtracting the amount which each worker pays in taxes from the amount of collective consumption which each receives).

These then are the three nascent theories about collective consumption which are alluded to in Castells's work. The brief analysis undertaken here reveals that there are complex theoretical and empirical issues beneath each of these theories. It also reveals how unwise it is to make intemperate claims, such as Castells does, about the role and function of collective consumption without first considering these issues.

6.2.4 Conclusion

The theme of collective consumption is central to Castells's work. However, he attributes an inordinate importance to it by claiming that urban areas derive their specificity from the organisation of the reproduction of labour power and are accordingly structured round the process of collective consumption. Castells also claims that collective consumption plays a key role in solving the major crises of capitalism although this claim is a matter of belief rather than a matter of fact. This aspect of Castells's analysis is lacking in a solid grounding in Marxist political economy and its empirical implications. In general, therefore, this section of Castells's analysis is not particularly useful from the point of view of developing a Marxist urban sociology. It is now necessary to examine his concept of the urban system.

6.3 THE URBAN SYSTEM

The term 'urban system' refers to the set of concepts produced by Castells for understanding urban areas (see Castells, 1969d, p. 92; 1976b, p. 78; 1976c, p. 153; 1977a, pp. 237ff; 1981a, pp. 385ff; Castells and Godard, 1974, pp. 192ff). These concepts are the result of his efforts to 'extend in the field of the analysis of space the fundamental concepts of historical materialism' (1977a, p. 125).

Castells extends the conceptual framework of Marxism, not by extending the basic concepts of Marxian political economy (as outlined in Part I) but by elaborating the Althusserian notion of a mode of production. According to the Althusserian view (see section 5.1), a mode of production consists of three interrelated elements or systems: the economic, the political and the ideological. Castells argues that these three systems need a more detailed 'specification' (1976c, p. 153) if they are to be of any use in understanding urban areas. He begins this 'specification' with the economic system by arguing that this can be decomposed into three elements: production (*P*); consumption (*C*) and exchange (*E*). The specification of the political system involves redefining it as Administration (*A*) because it refers to the regulation and control of the relations between *P*, *C* and *E* (for example, local government, urban planning agencies, and so on). Finally, the ideological system becomes the Symbolic element (*S*).

In summary then, Castells's urban system contains five elements: Production (*P*), Consumption (*C*), Exchange (*E*), Administration (*A*) and Symbolic (*S*).[5]

Castells then argues that these five elements of the urban system must be further broken down into sub-elements, since the former are 'much too general to be translated into explanatory propositions' (Castells, 1976c, p. 157). The procedure by which this is done is rather obscure: each sub-element is 'defined by the refraction on it of other elements (including itself) and/or other instances of the social structure (Castells, 1977a, p. 238). The outcome is that the five elements of the urban system are broken down into sub-elements as illustrated in Table 6.1.

The taxonomy in Table 6.1 is further elaborated 'by specifying, within each sub-element, levels and roles' (ibid., p. 240). Castells shows, in Table 6.2, how this might be done in the case of two sub-elements (C_1 and P_3).

This is Castells's concept of the urban system. It is, he insists, 'only a concept and, as such, has no other use than that of elucidating social practices and concrete historical situations in order both to understand them and to discover their laws' (ibid., p. 241). In terms of this criterion Castells's concept does not seem to achieve the purpose for which it was intended since it is an elaborate taxonomy apparently without any heuristic use. The reason for this is that the processes by which the elements, sub-elements, levels and roles are 'internally' related is as unclear as is their 'external' relation to the decisions and actions of the main actors in a capitalist society (that is, capitalists, workers, landowners, and the state). As a consequence Castells's classification of such phenomena as raw materials, green spaces and historic buildings as, respectively, P_2, C_2 and E_6 appears rather pointless and uninformative.

The concept of the urban system is also unsatisfactory because it does

Table 6.1 Castells's concept of the urban system

Elements	*Sub-elements*		*Example*
Production (P)	*Instruments of work*	P_1	Factories
	Objects of work	P_2	Raw materials
	Objects of work	P_3	Industrial environment
	Objects of work	P_4	Administration, Information
Consumption (C)	*Simple reproduction of labour power*	C_1	Housing and minimal material amenities (drains, lighting, roads, etc.)
	Extended reproduction of labour power	C_2	Green spaces, pollution, noise, etc. (environment)
	Extended reproduction of labour power	C_3	School amenities
	Extended reproduction of labour power	C_4	Socio-cultural amenities
Exchange (E)	*Production*→Consumption	E_1	Commerce and distribution
	Consumption→Production	E_2	Commuting (urban transport)
	Production→Production	E_3	Goods transport
	Consumption→Consumption	E_4	Circulation (residential mobility)
	Consumption→Ideological	E_5	Emission of information, shows, etc.
	Production→Ideological	E_6	Historic buildings
	Consumption→Political	E_7	Decision-making centres
	Production→Political	E_8	Business centres
Administration (A)	*Global/local* *Specific/general*		
Symbolic (S)	*Failure to recognise/ recognition/ communication* *Effect of legitimation*		

Source: Castells, 1977a, pp. 238–40.

not achieve the other purpose for which Castells intended it, namely an extension of the Marxian framework to incorporate the analysis of urban areas. The basis of the Marxian framework resides ultimately in Marx's political economy, particularly as elaborated in the three volumes of *Capital* (Marx, 1974a, 1974b, 1974c) and any elaboration of the Marxian framework should probably start from, or be directly

Table 6.2 The sub-elements in Castells's urban system

Sub-element	*Levels*	*Roles*
C_1 (Housing)	Luxury housing Social housing, (+, −) Slums, etc.	Lodger Tenant Co-owner Owner
P_3 (Industrial zone)	Well-equipped Badly-equipped	Articulation of industry with the: natural environment (water, space) Communications (network of transportation) Social milieu technology (industrial interdependencies)

Source: Castells, 1977a, pp. 240–41.

related to, this basis. The Althusserian concept of a mode of production bears only a tenuous relation to Marxian political economy and Castells's elaboration of it clearly illustrates the ultimate aridity to which it can lead. In this sense the failure of the concept of the urban system is due to the fact that it is not anchored in Marx's political economy.

6.4 URBAN POLITICS

Castells, following the Althusserian school (see section 5.1), makes a distinction between structures and practices. The relevance of this distinction in the present context is that the concept of the urban system, which has just been outlined, is a concept for understanding the structure, but not the practices, of urban areas. In order to understand the practices which occur in urban areas it is necessary to analyse the class struggle and the relationship of this struggle to the state. It requires, in Castells's terminology, an analysis of 'urban politics' (Castells, 1977a, pp. 243–5, 261–75) and this, he argues is 'the heart of the sociological analysis of the urban question' (ibid., p. 244).

Urban politics consists of two different fields: urban planning and urban social movements. These two topics are the main focus of Castells's analysis of urban areas, particularly his empirical analysis (see section 6.7). His interest in these two topics reflects his preoccupation with the mechanisms by which urban areas in a capitalist society are maintained (through urban planning) or transformed (through urban social movements). In this way Castells establishes the link, however tenuous, between the preceding analysis of the urban system and the subsequent analysis of urban planning and urban social movements. It is now necessary to examine Castells's conceptual treatment of these two topics.

6.5 URBAN PLANNING

6.5.1 Introduction

Castells has written relatively little, at a conceptual level, on the nature of urban planning, even though it is an important theme throughout his work and is particularly important in his empirical research (see Castells *et al.*, 1970, Godard, Castells *et al.*, 1973 and Castells and Godard, 1974 which are discussed in subsections 6.7.3 and 6.7.4 respectively). The basic concepts of his original article in 1969 (Castells, 1969a – republished in English in Castells, 1981a) have been repeated on a number of occasions without any major alteration (see notably Castells, 1976c and 1977a, Chapters 10 and 12 respectively).

Urban planning, according to Castells, refers to state intervention in an urban area which has been necessitated by the contradictions of the capitalist mode of production. It is a political response to what he variously terms 'a contradiction' (1977a, p. 260), a 'dislocation' (ibid.), a 'displacement' (1969a, p. 426) and an 'irregularity' (1977a, p. 427) in the social structure. Its effects are described in equally varied terms: to 'regulate' (1977a, p. 269), to 'counterbalance' (ibid., p. 425) and to 'go beyond' (ibid., p. 427) the contradictions of the capitalist system.

Castells's definition of urban planning clearly refers to any form of state intervention in an urban area. Thus it does not differentiate between, for example, state land use planning and state property development, even though both are different types of intervention in terms of their purposes and effects (see sections 8.4 to 8.6). The adoption of such a broad definition, while not excluding the possibility of finer distinctions being made between different types of state intervention, has the disadvantage of not focusing upon the particular features of any.

Castells's conceptual analysis of urban planning can be divided into two parts: the first concerns the definition of urban actors and the second concerns the causes of and constraints upon urban planning. Both of these will now be examined.

Table 6.3 Castells's typology of urban actors

Theoretical structural combination	*Example of a 'concrete' actor*
$O-G-P$	Large international firms
$O-G-C$	Trade unions
$O-L-P$	Chambers of Commerce and Industry
$O-L-C$	Neighbourhood associations
$A-G-P$	Organs of planning
$A-G-C$	
$A-L-P$	Committees of concerted action or regional expansion
$A-L-C$	Municipal institutions

Source: Castells, 1969a, p. 424.
O = organisation; G = global; P = centred on production; C = centred on consumption; L = local; A = authority.

6.5.2 The Typology of Urban Actors

Urban actors, according to Castells, are defined in relation to 'the different elements and sub-elements of the urban system' (Castells, 1969a, p. 423). In addition to the elements of the urban system outlined in section 6.3 – that is, *P*, *C*, *E*, *A*, and *S* – Castells adds four other 'sub-elements' namely, Authority (*A*), Organisation (*O*), Local (*L*) and Global (*G*). Without any explanation Castells proceeds to construct a typology of urban actors. His typology is contained in Table 6.3. Castells does not explore further the uses to which this taxonomy of urban actors might be put, stating that they are only 'illustrations' (Castells, 1969a, p. 442, fn. 39) though precisely what they illustrate is left unclear. In its existing form Castells's taxonomy seems rather useless and pointless.[6] A simpler approach, and one more directly related to the methodology of Marx's political economy would define urban actors in terms of their economic and political interests and would reveal that the most important urban actors include private property developers, state property developers, landowners, state land-use planning authorities, and so on. This approach is adopted in Chapter 8, and seems to be more effective in revealing some of the processes which take place in urban areas.

6.5.3 The Causes of and Constraints upon Urban Planning

Urban planning arises, as Castells frequently insists, because there is one central contradiction within the capitalist system, namely, the contradiction between 'the private control of labour power and means of production on the one hand, and the collective character of the reproduction of these two elements on the other' (Castells, 1976c, p. 166; 1977a, p. 269; 1981a, p. 388). At the urban and regional level, this contradiction is expressed as a contradiction between 'the increased profit a firm can obtain by selecting a location in an established industrial zone within a previously built-up area and the dysfunctional consequences of generalized behaviour of this kind' (Castells 1976c, p. 166). Elsewhere Castells restates the latter point: 'each individual firm profits by pushing towards greater concentration whereas organized decentralization would bring the greatest overall technical advantages' (Castells, 1976c, p. 152). In this situation the state must intervene in order to solve the problems which ensue.

This, in essence, is Castells's explanation of the cause of urban planning. It is an extremely summary and mechanistic explanation. The implicit assumption seems to be that the existence of this contradiction is itself sufficient to trigger off interventions by the state. In reality the process is much more complex and a fuller conceptualisation of the process would require an analysis of how this contradiction affects the interests of different groups of capitalists and workers and how this, in turn, is transmitted to the state in such a way that it is impelled to intervene on behalf of one group or another or both. Viewed in this light there is nothing as automatic about state intervention as Castells's presentation seems to imply.

However, Castells's analysis is deficient, not just because it fails to establish the connection between urban planning and (as he sees it) the central contradiction of capitalism, but also because his analysis of the latter is erroneous in a number of ways. Three errors may be noted in his formulation of this contradiction. The first is that it is not necessarily the case, contrary to Castells's claim, that every firm will obtain increased profit by locating in an established industrial zone in a previously built-up area. Indeed Castells's research on industrial location in Paris showed that there was a tendency for large manufacturing firms to decentralise from established industrial zones (Castells, 1967; Touraine *et al.*, 1967, 1968; Castells, 1969b; 1975d, Chapter 2; 1977a, pp. 137–45; see subsection 6.7.1 for a critical assessment of this research).

Secondly, although there may be dysfunctional consequences from the location of a firm in a particular area (for example, congestion, pollution, and so on), there may equally be highly positive consequences (for example, backward and forward linkages with other firms, and so on). Since both consequences are equally possible, it is clearly an error to cite only one of them, as Castells's does, and treat it as the only possible consequence.

Thirdly, organised decentralisation would not necessarily bring the greatest over-all technical advantages relative to highly-centralised locations, as Castells claims. It all depends upon such factors as the level and efficiency of infrastructural facilities, the type of industrial activity, the distribution of the population in the various urban areas, and so on. It is not possible, without considering these factors, to make broad generalisations about the 'technical' merits of centralisation versus decentralisation.

These three errors reveal the deficiency of Castells's economic analysis which is a feature of his entire work. In other words his work is not firmly grounded in any political economy, Marxist or otherwise.

Castells also examines the constraints under which the state operates in a capitalist society. In this context he introduces the important concept of 'limits' (Castells, 1976c, p. 166; 1977a, p. 269; 1981a, p. 389) to convey the notion that the state (like every other interest in society) operates within a set of constraints. He cites two limits which constrain the state. The first is that the state cannot alter the ownership relation, and the second is that there can be no direct intervention by the state in production, although interventions in such matters as zoning, financial incentives and collective consumption are possible (Castells, 1981a). Castells seems to be rather confused about the nature of these limits since zoning, for example, involves reduction in the private property rights of landowners (see section 8.8), which effectively proves that the ownership relation is not inviolable within capitalism. Moreover, the ownership relation and production itself are constantly being altered by the state through regulations relating to the quality, the safety, the sale, the price, the advertising and the labelling of commodities. These regulations affect the production process itself, and are effective reductions in the private property rights of the producers of those commodities (that is, capitalists). It would thus seem that the limits to state intervention in a capitalist society are not those identified by Castells. Nevertheless, there are limits to the actions of the state and, as will be shown (see section 8.5) they can be listed specifically.

6.5.4 Conclusion

This section has shown that Castells's concept of urban planning does not provide a useful framework for the analysis of this type of state intervention. There are three reasons for this. The first is that Castells treats urban planning as synonymous with all forms of state intervention so that its particular features (such as zoning development control, state property development, and so on) are lost from view. Secondly, the concept of urban actors (as defined by Castells) seems to be useless from the point of view of understanding urban planning. Thirdly, the analysis of the causes of, and constraints upon, urban planning was seen to contain a number of errors at the level of political economy. Despite these defects, however, Castells's subsequent analysis of urban planning in Dunkirk (Castells and Godard, 1974) contains a number of very useful insights on the political and ideological effects of urban planning, largely because it does not rely upon the type of analysis developed in this section (see subsection 6.7.6).

6.6 URBAN SOCIAL MOVEMENTS

6.6.1 Introduction

Castells's first and fullest conceptual treatment of urban social movements was presented in 1970 to the Seventh World Congress of Sociology at Varna in Bulgaria (Castells, 1976c)[7] and the main elements of his approach have been repeated, and added to, in a number of subsequent publications (Castells, 1972b, republished in Castells, 1972d, pp. 6–17; 1977a, Chapter 12; Castells, *et al.*, 1974, republished in 1978). His concern in these writings is with producing a Marxist conceptual framework for understanding urban social movements. The analysis in this section will be primarily concerned with outlining and evaluating that framework (subsection 6.6.3). However, it is necessary first to clarify precisely the meaning of the term urban social movement as it is used by Castells (subsection 6.6.2).

6.6.2 The Definition of an Urban Social Movement

An urban social movement, as Castells uses the term, has two characteristics. The first is that it must produce a major change in the capitalist system, and the second is that it must be related to other movements in the society (Castells, 1976c, p. 155; 1977a, p. 263).

As regards the first characteristic, Castells distinguishes an urban social movement from other types of practices. To this end he constructs a typology of practices and their corresponding effects. These are summarised in Table 6.4.

In terms of this typology, urban social movements are the cause of major change in a capitalist society. Indeed Castells insists that they are

Table 6.4 Castells's typology of practices and their effects

Practices	*Effect*
Regulation	Reproduction of the urban system
Reform	Change in one element of the system
Maintenance of order	Reproduction of another structural instance through the urban system
Urban social movement	Transformation of the structural law of the urban system
Social movement, with an urban base	Challenge to the political system
Demogogic movement	No effect, apart from the practice itself

Source: Castells, 1976c, p. 163; 1977a, p. 268.

the 'true source of change and innovation in the city' (1972d, p. 14) because they produce 'a qualitatively new effect on the social structure' (1976c, p. 151). This qualitatively new effect must involve radical changes in either the capitalist relations of property and real appropriation, or in the system of authority (ibid.).

As regards the second characteristic of an urban social movement Castells emphasises that 'one of my central hypotheses . . . is that there is no qualitative transformation of the urban structure that is not produced by an articulation of the urban movements with other movements, in particular (in our societies) with the working class movement and with the political class struggle' (1977a, p. 453). Thus, for Castells, the linking and fusion of different movements is the crucial catalyst for producing radical change in a capitalist society.

Two issues arise in relation to this definition. The first is that it may be difficult to apply empirically since the criteria for identifying 'true' and 'radical' change are not made clear. Castells states that radical change must involve, *inter alia*, a change in the property relation in a capitalist society. However, the rights of private property (that is, the property relation) in a capitalist society can be, and are, changed in a wide variety of ways through state regulations relating to the use of land, the pollution of the air, the construction of buildings, and so on, as well as regulations relating to the price, quality, safety, marketing, and so on, of commodities. The point is that all of these regulations involve changes in the property relation within capitalism (because they reduce the rights of private property) though they may not necessarily be regarded by Castells or others as 'radical'. In other words, 'true', 'radical' change is not a clear-cut phenomenon, not even within the Marxist perspective.

The second issue is that Castells is primarily interested in urban social movements because of his optimistic belief in the possibility of radical change through the fusion of urban protests with other struggles. However, it would seem that many of the protest movements which typically take place in urban areas are unlikely to achieve the status of an urban social movement in Castells's sense because many of them tend to be concerned exclusively with purely local issues (for example, the provision of schools, transport, public lighting, police protection, and so on). Castells's own research actually confirms this (see subsections 6.7.4, 6.7.5 and 6.7.8) which suggests that his emphasis on urban social movements, as distinct from protests generally, is somewhat misplaced. These considerations suggest that Castells's preoccupation with urban social movements is excessively narrow and is therefore not very useful. Indeed, as will be seen below (subsections 6.7.4, 6.7.5 and 6.7.8), his actual researches into the empirical reality of urban protest clearly reveal that the typical urban protest does not develop into an urban social movement.

6.6.3 A Framework for the Analysis of Urban Social Movements

Castells's framework for the analysis of urban social movements consists of the concepts of the urban system and urban actors as well as a set of methodological rules to guide empirical research on this topic. Since the former have been thoroughly examined already (see section 6.3 and subsection 6.5.2), the analysis in this section will be concerned above all with Castells's methodological rules.

It is possible to construct, from Castells's writings (1972d, pp. 42–5; 1976c, pp. 163–5; 1977a, pp. 268–9), six different methodological rules which should guide empirical research on urban social movements. Although these rules are not listed as such in Castells's work, each of them is nevertheless present in his writing, albeit in a less systematic form that that presented here.

The first methodological rule is to identify what Castells variously terms the 'problems', 'stakes' or 'issues' involved (1972d, p. 42; 1976c, p. 173). The issues, he argues, must be identified and coded in structural terms. This would seem to mean, given Castells's concept of structure, that if a particular issue concerns, for example, a claim for better housing, then this will be classified 'structurally' as C_1 (see section 6.3). This methodological rule is cryptically crystallised in Castells's advice to: 'Give it a name' (1976c, p. 163).

The second methodological rule is to identify the characteristics of the population affected by the issue, that is, 'the social base' (Castells, 1972d, p. 42). The latter must, in turn, be distinguished from that fraction of the population which mobilises round the issue, that is, 'the social force' (ibid.).

The third methodological rule is to identify 'the adversary' (ibid.), which the social force must confront.

The fourth methodological rule is to identify the politico-ideological orientation of the organisation through which the social base is mobilised into a social force (ibid.). Castells places considerable emphasis on the difference between those organisations which are solely concerned with specific but limited issues (for example, tenants' organisations) and those which attempt to link specific issues to broader political issues (for example, a radical political organisation). In Castells's view, it is only organisations of the latter type which can, strictly speaking, give rise to an urban social movement.

At a more general level Castells insists that organisations are methodologically secondary in the analysis of urban social movements. He states – with the implicit purpose of differentiating his approach from what Pickvance terms 'the Anglo-Saxon tradition of "participation" studies' (Pickvance, 1976, p. 198; Castells, 1977a, p. 324) – that the usual starting point for the study of urban social movements, to wit, 'organizations' is the 'wrong one' (Castells, 1976c, p. 171). This is because 'the genesis of an organization does not form part of the analysis of social movements, for only its effects are important' (Castells, 1976c, pp. 169–70). The correct approach, he argues, 'must start by identifying the contradictions ('problems') or drawing attention to the mobilizations specific to those problems' (ibid., p. 171).

The fifth methodological rule is to identify the strategy or 'type of action' (Castells, 1972d, p. 43) by which the organisation pursues its claim. These strategies can be classified into legal actions (for example, petitions, demonstrations, delegations, and so on) and illegal actions. Any analysis should examine the relative success of each of these means in attaining their end.

The sixth and final methodological rule is that the 'effects' of the movement must be analysed (ibid.). Castells distinguishes three different situations: those where there are no effects; those where there are 'urban effects' (that is, the effect is limited to one specific issue); and those where there are 'political effects' (that is, the effect alters the relationship of the successful group *vis-à-vis* other groups and the state). For Castells, a truly urban social movement will produce both urban effects as well as political effects.

This is the essence of Castells's approach to the study of urban social movements. Apart from the taxonomic character of the concepts of the urban system and urban actors which are unlikely to be of any use in the understanding of urban social movements, Castells's methodological rules for empirical research are, by contrast, likely to prove useful. The above outline of Castells's framework, in the form of methodological rules, has the advantage of showing how that framework might be applied in empirical research.

There is, however, one important element missing from Castells's conceptual analysis, namely, the spatial dimension. Many protest movements in urban areas are locality-based and arise because the residents in an area are all equally affected by a particular issue (for example, inadequate public transport, crime, redevelopment, and so on). In other words the spatial sphere of influence of many issues is likely to be limited to specific geographical areas so that only the inhabitants of that area are directly and immediately affected by it. This fact (which is conceptualised more formally in section 8.8) is a crucial element in explaining the size of the social base affected by a particular issue and, depending upon the level of mobilisation, the resulting social force. In addition it may explain why many protest movements in urban areas are issue-specific and are unconcerned with broader political issues. It would thus seem that a more rigorous analysis of the spatial dimension would considerably strengthen and deepen Castells's analysis. In addition, it would offer the possibility of developing a more explicitly spatial dimension to Marxian political economy, a step which has not yet been undertaken.

6.6.4 Conclusion

The analysis in this section has shown that while Castells's definition of an urban social movement is seriously deficient, his methodological rules for the study of the latter have some merit. Castells's analysis could, however, be improved by introducing a spatial dimension and by incorporating this within the framework of Marxian political economy. As is demonstrated in Chapter 8, this offers a real possibility for developing a Marxist analysis of urban protest. It is now necessary to examine how Castells applies this framework in empirical research.

6.7 EMPIRICAL RESEARCH

6.7.1 Introduction

Castells has undertaken at least 18 different pieces of research, usually in collaboration with other researchers and research assistants. These are listed below in approximate chronological order, according to their date of original publication:

1. Industrial location in the Paris region (Castells, 1967; Touraine, *et al.*, 1967, 1968; Castells, 1969b; 1975d, Chapter 2; 1977a, pp. 137–45).
2. New towns in Britain (Castells, 1969a, pp. 429–32; 1977a, pp. 277–83).
3. Urban renewal and other urban problems in the United States (Castells, 1969a, pp. 433–6; 1970b; 1976e; 1976f; 1977a, pp. 379–420).
4. Urban renewal in Paris (Castells, *et al.*, 1970; Castells, 1972a; Godard, *et al.*, 1973; Castells, 1977a, pp. 304–22; 1978a, pp. 93–125).
5. Retirement and old age in France (Castells and Guillemard, 1971).
6. Protests against urban renewal in Paris (Castells, 1972c, pp. 406–30; 1972d, pp. 19–45; 1977a, pp. 326–48);
7. Protests in Montreal (Castells, 1972c, pp. 431–44; 1972d, pp. 49–67; 1977a, pp. 348–60);
8. Shanty town dwellers in Santiago, Chile (Castells, 1972c, pp. 444–71; 1972d, pp. 91–116; 1977a, p. 360–75).
9. Urban development in Dunkirk (Castells and Godard, 1974; Castells, 1975d, Chapter 3, pp. 141–97; 1975e; 1977c, pp. 66–78; 1978a, Chapter 4, pp. 62–91).
10. Urban protests in Paris (Castells, *et al.*, 1974, 1978; Castells, 1983a, Part 2, pp. 73–96).
11. Immigrant workers in Western Europe (Castells, 1975b).
12. Urban protests in Paris (Castells, 1977b, 1978a, Chapter 6, pp. 126–51).

13. The service sector in the US (Castells, 1976g).
14. Shanty town dwellers in Monterrey, Mexico (Castells, 1977d).
15. Neighbourhood groups in Madrid, Spain (Castells, 1978b, 1983a, Part 5, Chs 21–7, pp. 213–88).
16. The economic crisis in the US (Castells, 1980a).
17. Latin and gay communities in San Francisco (Castells, 1983a, Section III).
18. Squatter movements in Peru, Mexico and Chile (Castells, 1983a, Section IV).

These research publications vary, not only in terms of their theme and its location, but also in terms of their size and quality. Some are major pieces of research based upon a systematic collection and analysis of data (for example, those listed as 6, 7, 8, 12, 14 and 15). Some are reviews of concepts and data which already exist in the literature (for example, those listed as 2, 3, and 13), while others are on topics quite unrelated to urban questions (for example, 5). Faced with this diversity it has been necessary, for the purpose of this book, to select and assess those research reports which simultaneously represent Castells's major research endeavours, as well as the range of urban themes that are covered in his work. On this basis seven different pieces of research have been selected (those listed as 1, 4, 6, 7, 9, 11 and 12) and will be assessed below. Each will be discussed in their approximate order of original publication. The strategy will be to assess the concepts, data, methods and results of each piece of research in order to discern if it contributes to a Marxist analysis of urban issues.

6.7.2 Research on Industrial Location in the Paris region

This research was carried out by four researchers (including Castells) and the results were published in preliminary form in 1967 (Touraine, *et al.*, 1967). They were also submitted for Castells's doctoral thesis (Doctorat de 3 ème Cycle en Sociologie: 1967). They were published in final form in 1968 (Touraine, *et al.*, 1968) and have been published subsequently, at varying lengths, on three occasions (Castells, 1969b; 1975d, Chapter 2, pp. 49–139; 1977a, pp. 137–45).

The research involved an examination of 940 industrial establishments which were located in the Paris region between January 1962 and

July 1963 (Touraine, *et al.*, 1967, p. 375; Castells, 1977a, p. 137). The basic purpose of this research was simple: to show that different types of industrial establishment were located in different parts of the Paris region. The methodological procedure adopted for this purpose involved classifying industrial establishments into nine different types, and classifying the communes of Paris into three different types of area and examining the frequency distribution of each type of industrial establishment in each type of area. (Touraine, *et al.* (1967, p. 376) refer to these industrial establishments as the independent variable, and the areas of location as the dependent variable, although this is evidently a misuse of terms since there is no causal connection between these two variables.)

The criterion according to which industrial establishments are classified into different types is autonomy: 'technical' autonomy and 'economic' autonomy (Touraine, *et al.*, 1967, pp. 373ff). According to Castells there are three types of 'technical' autonomy:

Type A refers to industrial establishments which have low technical autonomy since they are small family firms producing a specialised product and are 'entirely subordinated, from the technological point of view, to other industrial sectors; for example general engineering companies' (Castells, 1977a, p. 138).

Type B refers to industrial establishments which are highly mechanised and which mass-produce a highly standardised product (for example, motor cars).

Type C refers to industrial establishments which are highly autonomous and are concerned with the creation of new products (for example, electronics).

Similarly there are three types of 'economic' autonomy:

Type 1 refers to industrial establishments which have low economic autonomy because they are dependent upon a specific market.

Type 2 refers to industrial establishments whose means of production have a fixed location.

Type 3 refers to industrial establishments which have high economic autonomy since they are 'without spatial constraint from the point of view of their functioning' (Castells, 1977a, p. 138).

Castells proceeds from this to construct a typology of nine different types of industrial establishments according to their autonomy. These are illustrated in Table 6.5 where each of the symbols in the table have already been defined.

Table 6.5 Castells's typology of industrial establishments

A1	A2	A3
B1	B2	B3
C1	C2	C3

Source: Castells, 1977a, p. 138.

This typology of industrial establishments is rather unsatisfactory since the concept of 'autonomy' is ill-defined, as is the distinction between 'technical' and 'economic' autonomy. As a result the precise meaning of each type remains unclear.

The next stage of the research was to classify all the communes in the Paris region into different types (Touraine, *et al.*, 1967, p. 386). These types are:

Type α which refers to areas of high density, close to the centre of the Paris agglomeration.

Type β which refers to areas where there is a strong concentration of transportation networks.

Type γ which refers to areas of high social status.

(Touraine, *et al.*, 1967, pp. 384–5; Castells, 1977a; pp. 139–40).

The basic hypothesis of the study was that industrial establishments A1, B3 and C3 would tend to locate in areas α, β and γ respectively. A number of other subsidiary hypotheses were also put forward for each of the other types of industrial establishments (see Touraine, *et al.*, 1967, pp. 384–5; Castells, 1977a, pp. 140-41). The basic rationale for these hypotheses was that firms which were highly dependent upon a centralised market (A1) would tend to locate in the centre (α), while firms which were concerned with access to locationally fixed inputs (B2) would tend to locate in areas with a strong concentration of transportation networks (β) and, finally, firms concerned with research and development (C3) would tend to locate in prestigious areas (γ) (for example, the southern and western suburbs). The date showing the frequency distributions of each type of industrial establishments in each type of area is broadly consistent with these hypotheses (see Touraine *et al.*, 1967, pp. 394–402; Castells, 1977a, p. 43). The same result is also revealed more simply and straightforwardly by the maps showing the location of the different types of industrial establishments (Touraine *et al.*, 1967, pp. 367–83, 388–93).

This was Castells's first piece of published research and predates his subsequent Marxist writings. In the light of the research that has since been carried out on industrial location in the 1970s and early 1980s (see section 8.7), Castells's failure to distinguish between industrial establishments which are branch plants of multiplant firms and those which are uniplant firms now appears as a striking and serious limitation. The research is now of little theoretical or practical interest essentially because the relationship between different types of firms and their corresponding location behaviour is poorly formulated (possibly because the form of the research was more influenced by data availability than by theoretical considerations).

6.7.3 Research on Urban Renewal in Paris

A preliminary report of this research was published in 1970 (Castells, *et al.*, 1970) and the final report was published in 1973 (Godard, *et al.*, 1973). In addition, a summary of the results has been published in three different places (Castells, 1972a; 1977a, pp. 304–322; 1978a, p. 93 –125). The results have thus been exhaustively reported.

The research was carried out in 1970 by a team of six researchers who were, according to Castells, 'under our direction' (1972a, p. 95). The research, which took six months (Castells, 1974, p. 241), attempted to assess the effects of urban renewal in Paris from 1954 to 1970. The basic research procedure was to establish why certain areas in Paris had been selected for renewal projects and what were the social consequences of those projects. Thus the research involved an examination of the pre-renewal and the post-renewal characteristics of the areas in which renewal projects were located.

Castells attempted to measure the pre-renewal characteristics of the renewal areas in three ways: first, he computed the 'index of differentiation' for the areas in which the renewal projects were located; secondly, he correlated a number of variables with the size of the renewal projects in each area; and thirdly, he compared the areas within which renewal occurred with Paris as a whole on a number of selected variables. Each of these measures will now be examined.

Castells devised an 'index of differentiation for urban renewal (IDUR)' in order to establish the degree of association between the renewal areas and a number of variables. The formula for the index is:

$$\text{IDUR} = \frac{\text{Value of the variable (\%) in the renewal areas}}{\text{Value of the variable (\%) in the whole of the city of Paris}} - 1$$

(see Castells, *et al.*, Castells, 1972a, p. 111; Godard, *et al.*, 1973, p. 25; Castells, 1977a, p. 308).

This index was calculated for 23 of the 30 renewal operations and the results are presented in Table 6.6.

Table 6.6 The index of differentiation for 23 renewal areas in Paris on selected variables

Variable	*Index*
Proportion of Algerians in the population	+ 1.20
Proportion of upper management and liberal professions	− 0.57
Dwellings without water	+ 0.36
Proportion of semi-skilled and unskilled workers	+ 0.50
Overcrowding in the dwellings	+ 0.47
Dwellings without WC	+ 0.31
Proportion of foreigners	− 0.30
Proportion of persons over 65	− 0.19
Rate of women's activity	− 0.13
Proportion of craftsmen and tradesmen	+ 0.04
Proportion of persons under 19	+ 0.02
Rate of activity of the population	+ 0.06

Sources: Godard, *et al.*, 1973, p. 26, Table 6; Castells, 1977a, p. 308, Table 54. (It is noteworthy that there is considerable discrepancy in the indexes contained in each of these tables even though both are based upon the same research. It is assumed that the first table (Godard, *et al.*, 1973, p. 26, Table 6) is the correct one.)

Castells interprets this table as follows: 'They [that is, the renewal areas] are sectors in which housing has deteriorated, of course, but they are also sectors strongly marked by the presence of immigrant and unskilled, and by the absence of the upper strata of the population' (Castells, 1977a, p. 308). The difficulty with this interpretation is that it is impossible to assess if it is an accurate account of the various renewal areas. The reason for this lies in the index of differentiation itself which could have the same value in two entirely different situations for example, 80%/40% – 1 = 1; 8%/4% – 1 = 1). This fact raises serious doubts about the usefulness of this index as a way of isolating the distinctive characteristics of the renewal areas. In these circumstances a more accurate characterisation of the various renewal areas could probably be gleaned by simply inspecting the actual percentage values of the various variables in each area and in Paris as a whole. However, this information, although used by Castells to calculate the index of differentiation, does not appear in any published account of this research.

Castells then correlates each of the above variables with the areal size of each renewal operation in order to establish more precisely the distinguishing characteristics of the renewal areas. The results of this Spearman rank correlation test are tabulated in Table 6.7.

Table 6.7 Correlations between the areal size of renewal operations and selected variables in Paris

Selected variable	*Correlation*
Proportion of persons over 65	+ 0.28
Proportion of semi-skilled and unskilled workers	+ 0.18
Proportion of foreigners plus active women	+ 0.14
Proportion of Algerians in the population	+ 0.20
Proportion of craftsmen and tradesmen	+ 0.09
Proportion of upper management and liberal professions	+ 0.04
Overcrowding in the dwellings	– 0.09
Rate of activity of the population	– 0.05
Dwellings without water	– 0.27
Dwellings without WC	– 0.06
Proportion of persons under 19	– 0.17

Source: Godard, *et al.*, 1973, p. 27, Table 7; Castells, 1977a, p. 309, Table 54. (Once again there are considerable discrepancies between these two tables. It is assumed that the first table is the correct one.)

These results, according to Castells, indicate that the renewal operation was 'all the more important in that it concerned old people, semi-skilled and unskilled workers, foreigners, working women and Algerians. And, on the other hand, there was a low but inverse relation with the variables concerning the deterioration of the housing' (Castells, 1977a, p. 309). This interpretation is broadly consistent with the figures, although two points should be noted: first, all of the correlations are extremely low, thus indicating a weak association; secondly, the correlations for some of the variables (notably proportion of persons over 65, overcrowding in dwellings and dwellings without WC) are the opposite of that suggested by the index of differentiation. Both of these points reveal that the evidence is inconclusive.

Castells also examined other characteristics of the renewal areas and found that the latter tended to be areas of industrial decline and areas where the majority of the residents tend to be politically left-wing (Godard, *et al.*, 1973, pp. 28–34).

The research also examined the post-renewal characteristics of the renewal areas. Because many operations were still in progress while the research was being carried out, this aspect of the research is incomplete. However, two findings are of considerable importance. The first relates to housing, where it was found that renewal frequently resulted in 'eviction of most of the former residents and the occupation of the new space by social categories of higher status' (Castells, 1977a, p. 313). The second finding was that 62 per cent of all land under renewal was being converted to office use (Godard, Castells, *et al.*, 1973, p. 52) thereby accentuating the industrial decline in those areas. These results have in fact been confirmed by more recent investigations of urban renewal in Paris (see notably Zetter, 1975; Bentham and Moseley, 1980).

The main feature of this research is that it is concerned with the characteristics of certain areas in Paris, and with the way in which the characteristics of those areas have changed as a result of urban renewal. This methodological procedure was adopted in order to reveal what Castells terms 'the social logic at work in the operation' (1977a, p. 306). While this methodological procedure is useful it is limited. It is limited because it does not investigate the actions of each of the actors involved in the renewal process (developers, planners, landowners, residents, and so on, since it is ultimately their actions, each pursuing their respective interests, which determine the outcome of the renewal process. Castells's analysis would need to proceed to this level to ensure that the 'social logic' of the renewal process is in fact revealed.

6.7.4 Research on Protests against Urban Renewal in Paris

This research was carried out in 1970 in Paris with the assistance of two other researchers (F. Lentin and J. Olives) (Castells, 1972d, p. 24, fn 2). The results were published twice in 1972 (Castells, 1972c, pp. 406–30 –

translated to English and republished in 1977a, pp. 326–48, and 1972d, pp. 19–45).

This study is closely linked to Castells's study of urban planning in Paris (see subsection 6.7.3 above), since the urban protests under investigation here were a direct response to the urban renewal as analysed in that study.

One of the areas studied was given the fictional name of 'Cité du Peuple' and its population was predominantly working class with a high proportion of immigrants. The area was scheduled for redevelopment and, as a result of this, a protest action was organised in 1965 by the national tenants association to protect residents from the threat of eviction (Castells, 1972d, p. 26). The demand was made, supported by petitions, meetings, speeches and demonstrations, that a larger proportion of HLMs (the French equivalent of local authority housing) be built in the redeveloped area. This demand was acceded to in 1966, although the new HLMs were subsequently allocated to residents from outside the area and this led to the disintegration of the movement (Castells, 1972d, p. 29; 1977a, pp. 326–30).

Subsequently, a group of architecture students ('strangers to the district', Castells, 1977a) attempted to mobilise the residents into opposing evictions by denouncing the redevelopment plan and calling for revolutionary struggle. This, however, had no effect upon the residents and the students left (1972d, pp. 29–30).

In another part of the 'Cité du Peuple' – 'a slum largely inhabited by unskilled workers, immigrants or North African Jews' (Castells, 1972d, p. 32) – an organisation was formed by young workers and working-class students from the area, with the aim of linking the demand for 'rehousing in the same district with moderate rents' (ibid., p. 33), with a general political struggle (that is, the denunciation of the bourgeoisie (ibid., p. 34). Gradually, however, the movement dwindled as fewer people attended meetings and residents left the area.

In another part of Paris – the 'Midi' district – there was no mobilisation against the evictions even though this district had a strong left-wing tradition (Castells, 1972d, p. 36). A revolutionary group of young workers and students set up a local committee, distributed a news bulletin and held a rent strike. However, the movement finally collapsed because the revolutionary group had to leave to carry out revolutionary work elsewhere (ibid., p. 37).

Finally, in the 'Cité d'Aliarte' district a movement, supported by revolutionary students and a left-wing party, managed to halt, albeit temporarily, the evictions necessitated by redevelopment. A number of immigrant workers who were threatened with eviction occupied seven houses, but they were ultimately dislodged by the police (ibid., p. 39).

This is a brief summary of Castells's research on the resistance to redevelopment in Paris (as reported in Castells, 1972d, pp. 19–45). The research is interesting, though highly impressionistic and lacking in detail on crucial questions such as the chronology of events as they occurred in the district, the size of the social base affected in each area, and the size of the social force which emerged from this base. In addition to these deficiencies, the duration of the research and the research procedure itself remains obscure. In the introduction Castells states that his results are based upon 'precise research, personal experience and sometimes by sharing in the struggle' (ibid., p. 16) although the connection between the former and the latter are not clearly brought out. In this sense Castells's research would seem to conform neither to the standard procedures of sociological research, nor indeed to his own methodological procedures as outlined in subsection 6.6.3. In short, it is an interesting, but very inadequately executed, piece of research.

6.7.5 Research on Urban Protests in Montreal

This research, carried out between 1969 and 1971, examined what Castells regards as 'one of the most important urban struggles of recent years' (1972d, p. 49). The results of the research were published twice in 1972 (1972d, pp. 49–67 and 1972c, pp. 431–44 – translated to English and republished in 1977a, pp. 348–60). The information upon which the research is based comes, Castells states, 'from several sources' (1977a, p. 348, fn 17). These sources are listed as follows:

> personal experience, especially in the *Mouvement d'Action Politique Municipale* during my stay in Montreal in 1969; the work of Quebec students in my urban politics seminars at Montreal University in 1969 and at the University of Paris in 1970 and 1971; long discussions with Evelyne Dumas, author of a series of articles on this theme in the Montreal Star; continual exchange of information and ideas with Ginette Treusdell, a Quebec sociologist who has written a study on this theme; bulletins, tracts, publications and internal reports of FRAP and Montreal citizens' committees. (Ibid.; see also Castells, 1972d, pp. 66–7).

The movements which Castells examined originated in 1963 in 'citizens' committees' which were set up in various parts of Montreal for the purpose of solving the problems of unemployment and the lack of adequate housing and communal facilities. In 1970 these committees were united under an umbrella organisation, FRAP (*Front d'Action Politique*), and were renamed CAPs (*Comité d'Action Politique*). Castells examined the viscissitudes of four of these CAPs in four different districts of Montreal.

The first district was Sainte-Anne, a working-class slum area with 20 per cent unemployment. Castells found that the attempt to establish an urban protest here was a complete failure because 'a discrepancy soon became apparent between the "locals" solely concerned with problems of facilities, and the militant "outsiders" . . . 'who wanted to bring politics into every action' (Castells, 1977a, p. 355). Castells explains this failure as follows:

> on the one hand the social base, lower proletarian, was a favourite area for charitable organizations and had a very long way to go before political awareness could emerge from daily oppression; on the other hand it was partly a consequence of the characteristics of that district; the issues were seen in the context of social work and the balance of power was never questioned (Castells, 1977a, p. 356).

The second district examined by Castells was Saint-Jacques, which had similar social characteristics to Sainte-Anne. In this district the CAP was initially concerned with social problems and formed a co-operative and clinic for which they gained 'the respect of a large section of the population' (Castells, 1977a, p. 356). However, the CAP was also, and increasingly, committed to 'a rigorous Marxist line' (ibid.) which they attempted to propagate, through militants, by taking 'advantage of the local base obtained through urban claim actions' (ibid.). As in the district of Sainte-Anne, there seems to have been no fusion of urban and political issues in this district, and hence no urban protest developed.

The third district of Montreal which Castells examined was Cotes-des-Neiges. This district was inhabited largely by students and professors and was 'an extremely petty-bourgeois district' (ibid., p. 357). The aim of CAP was to develop an urban protest (through the fusion of urban and political struggles) by remaining 'close to the local level' (ibid.) while maintaining a long-term revolutionary view. This approach resulted in failure because 'the CAP found itself out of line with its local base, an upwardly mobile petty-bourgeoisie' (ibid., p. 358).

The fourth and final district investigated by Castells was Hochenlaga-Maisonneuve. In this district, according to Castells 'there was a combination of all the elements necessary for the desired unification of struggle' (ibid. – these elements being the presence of a majority of unionised workers and a citizens' committee. In 1971 an urban protest was initiated in order to oppose the realisation of a proposed motorway plan which threatened to demolish 'thousands of homes' (ibid.). An organisation was formed which combined 'unions and working-class organizations' (ibid.). Castells described the campaign which ensued in the following way: 'Information sheets were circulated, meetings held, a petition taken from door to door and signed by thousands of people; mass demonstrations were organized, including one where the demonstrators drove along the proposed motorway route' (ibid.). The result of the campaign was nevertheless a 'total failure' (ibid., p. 359) because, according to Castells, the interests in favour of the motorway plan were 'so powerful' (ibid.) and support for the campaign 'dwindled and the local population lost interest' (ibid., pp. 358–9).

Castells states that this research is 'necessarily summary and schematic' (ibid., p. 348), presumably because much of it is based upon second-hand accounts, rather than upon systematic observation, of the events which he is analysing. In this sense, the value of the research is necessarily limited by the limitations of the data. Nevertheless, its results may prove useful, if only in showing that urban social movements, in Castells's strict sense (see subsection 6.6.2) are rare occurrences indeed.

6.7.6 Research on Urban Development in Dunkirk

Castells's research into the urban development of Dunkirk was undertaken in collaboration with Francis Godard and Vivian Balanowski. The results of the research were published in full in 1974 in *Monopolville* (Castells and Godard, 1974) and have been subsequently published, in more abbreviated form on four occasions (Castells, 1975d, Chapter 3, pp. 141–97; 1975e; 1977c, pp. 66–78; 1978a, Chapter 4, pp. 62–91).

The data used in the research was gleaned from a wide range of sources:

documents (census, research reports, planning documents etc);
the daily press and periodicals;
letters from firms, associations and the administration;
120 interviews;
contacts with key informants;
participant observation;
a forty-minute film;
photographs.
(see Castells and Godard, 1974, p. 418).

The authors present no discussion whatever of the methodological issues which arose in the gathering and coding of this varied collection of data on Dunkirk. This is a serious omission in a book which regards itself as a contribution to 'scientific research' (Castells and Godard, 1974, p. 441) (Lojkine's comment on this book is thus strange when he writes: 'in this study methodology is the object of a very precise consideration' (Lojkine, 1981b, p. 92). In the introductory section entitled 'Theoretical Problematic and Methodology of the Research' (Castells and Godard, 1974, pp. 7–20) Castells and Godard emphasised that the ideas and concepts of *La Question Urbaine* must be 'put to the test of observation' (ibid., p. 14) and that, in turn, these 'observations must be coded and reinterpreted with the aid of concepts' (ibid., p. 13). Yet, as will be seen, Castells is often quite careless and cavalier in his handling of the data.

Monopolville is divided into five large chapters. The first two chapters present the theoretical orientation of the book as well as a considerable amount of information on Dunkirk and the Nord region. The third chapter presents an outline of the class structure of the town while the fourth discusses some of the pressing urban problems which it is currently experiencing. The fifth and final chapter discusses, *inter alia*, the nature of urban planning and urban protest in Dunkirk. Each of these chapters will now be briefly reviewed and assessed.

The first two chapters (pp. 21–104) present a considerable amount of information on Dunkirk, as well as a synopsis of the theoretical orientation of the book. The entire book is stamped by Castells's theoretical approach which has been systematically analysed here in the preceding sections (6.2 to 6.6). However, in the first chapter Castells and Godard add a new dimension to that approach by referring to the state monopoly capitalism thesis (see section 5.2 for an outline of the main tenets of this thesis). This is the first time in Castells's work where the state monopoly capitalism thesis is explicitly mentioned. However, the Althusserian approach continues to predominate and, for Castells, the state monopoly capitalism thesis seems to involve no more than acknowledging the necessity of 'periodization' within capitalism (Castells and Godard, 1974, pp. 22–3) and the fact that the current period of capitalism is dominated by a combination of monopolistic firms and state intervention. (Castells, like Lojkine, seems to use the term monopoly as a vague indicator of size rather than as an indicator of market share. For convenience Castells's and Lojkine's usage will be retained.)

The essence of Castells's theoretical approach is based upon what he regards as one of the 'basic contradictions of capitalism' (Castells and

Godard, 1974, p. 23) which is the law of the falling rate of profit. The consequences of this law are twofold: on the one hand it leads to a growing concentration of capital in huge monopolistic firms in order to counteract this fall; on the other it leads to increased intervention and expenditure by the state in order to make necessary but unprofitable investments (for example, infrastructure). These two consequences of the falling rate of profit are said to be clearly visible in Dunkirk which has recently undergone a rapid transformation, as a result of the joint actions of the monopolies and the state; hence the sub-title of *Monopolville: L'éntreprise, L'état, l'urbain*) (The Firm, the State, the Urban).

Although *Monopolville* is a serious attempt to show how the town of Dunkirk is being moulded and transformed by the combined actions of capitalist firms and the state, it is not, as its theoretical orientation might suggest, an attempt to show how the actions of capitalist firms and the state respond to the law of the falling rate of profit. Indeed the actual rate of profit enjoyed by the various firms in Dunkirk, although possibly very difficult to obtain in the case of the branch plants of multi-plant firms, is one piece of information that is conspicuously missing from Castells's and Godard's book, as is the effect of state expenditure on these different rates of profit. This fact confirms again (see subsection 6.2.3) that for Castells, the law of the falling rate of profit is a dogma rather than an explanation and, moreover a dogma which is erroneous (see section 2.1). The same remark, as will be seen, applies with equal force to the work of Lojkine (see notably subsection 7.3).

Dunkirk was chosen as one of the 'new poles of industrial development' (Castells and Godard, 1974, p. 8) under the aegis of the Fifth (1966–70) and Sixth (1971–5) French economic plans. These plans, like the economic plans of other EEC countries in this period, placed great emphasis on the necessity of restructuring and revitalising key manufacturing industries in order to make them nationally and internationally competitive. Dunkirk was selected as a coastal growth pole with this aim in mind for the propulsive iron, steel and petrochemical industry.

The iron and steel industry is the main activity in Dunkirk and is owned and controlled by Usinor (a French firm first founded in 1948) who located there in 1960 (Castells and Godard, 1974, p. 10). The other French steel giant, Wendel-Sidelor, has moved most of its operations to the coastal site of Fos-sur-Mer and this site has become a growth pole analogous in many ways to Dunkirk (see Castells and Godard, 1974, p. 66).) The petrochemical industry in Dunkirk is not as developed as the iron and steel industry, but the signs are that the French petroleum

Table 6.8 Some characteristics of Dunkirk and the Nord Region according to Castells

Characteristic	*Score*
Occupational structure	Above average percentage of manual workers
Education and training	50% of young people (14–17) receive no skilled training
Salaries	Below average
Quality of housing	Below average
Female participation in labour force	Below average

Source: Castells and Godard, 1974, pp. 62–3.

company, Total, is on the verge of a major expansion there (see Castells and Godard, 1974, p. 81). As a result, the economic growth of Dunkirk is coming to depend increasingly on monopolistic enterprises.

The selection of Dunkirk as a growth pole, according to Castells and Godard, is due not only to its advantages as a coastal site suitable for industries of primary transformation (such as iron and steel and petrochemicals) where imported raw materials can be readily processed and re-exported (see Castells and Godard, 1974, pp. 43–55, 61). It is also due to the decline of many traditional industries (notably coal and textiles) in the populous hinterland of Dunkirk and the Nord region (see Castells and Godard, 1974, pp. 55–69) and to the fact that Dunkirk and the Nord region are relatively disadvantaged in terms of a number of characteristics (see Table 6.8).

One consequence of this pattern of disadvantage is that today Dunkirk suffers from a shortage of skilled labour which is being met by a combination of immigration and long-distance commuting (Castells and Godard, pp. 101–2) with the result that skilled workers are more than ordinarily privileged in comparison with unskilled workers.

During the past few decades the population of Dunkirk has grown rapidly, though not as rapidly as was earlier predicted (see Coing, 1977, p. 184). Its growth rate, throughout the 1960s and 1970s, has been exceptional by comparison with the growth rates for the total French population and the total urban population in France (see House, 1978, pp. 125–40).

In Chapter 3 (and in the latter part of Chapter 2), Castells and Godard identify the various class fractions and their interests in Dunkirk. This is one of the most interesting and commendable parts of the entire book, essentially because it is central to any Marxist analysis. Tables 6.9 and 6.10 give a schematic summary of the main fractions of the capitalist and working classes and their corresponding interests.

According to Castells, it is the non-monopoly class fractions (notably those numbered (4a), (5) and (6)) which are most in crisis and he cites as evidence (albeit without citing the source) the 'fact' that 1000 small and medium-sized firms disappeared between 1964 and 1968 (see Castells and Godard, 1974, p. 90).

This analysis is one of the most promising parts of Castells's and Godard's book, though it is not developed as systematically, nor as exhaustively, as the topic requires. One of the interesting findings to emerge from this analysis, in view of Castells's references to state monopoly capitalism, and in view of Lojkine's adherence to this thesis (see notably section 5.2), is that the central class conflict in Dunkirk does not seem to be between the monopolies on the one hand and all other non-monopoly groups (that is, medium and small capital and all workers) on the other (see Tables 6.9, 6.10).

Three pieces of evidence in particular seems to indicate this:

(a) Certain groups of non-monopoly capitalists (notably subcontractors, numbered (4a) in Table 6.9) benefit considerably from the presence of monopolies.
(b) Certain groups of workers (notably skilled workers, numbered (1) in Table 6.10) also benefit from the presence of monopolies.
(c) All workers benefit from the expansion of monopolistic supermarkets through lower prices (see Castells and Godard, 1974, p. 124).

These three cases seem to reveal that an anti-monopoly alliance between all non-monopoly groups is not an inevitable – nor even a highly probable – feature of state monopoly capitalism, at least as found in Dunkirk. (This point, however, is not made by Castells and Godard.)

In addition to identifying the different class fractions, their interests, and the conflicts between them, Castells and Godard also investigate the ideology of these different class fractions (Chapter 3, pp. 150–72). This analysis is based upon 'various observations' (Castells and Godard, 1974, p. 161) of the daily life of these class fractions and on the 'general information' (ibid.) which Castells and his collaborators possess of the Dunkirk agglomeration. On the basis of this evidence Castells identifies four different ideologies:

(1) The ideology of consumption and the nuclear family.
(2) The ideology of class solidarity and conflict.

Table 6.9 Castells's description of the fractions of the capitalist class and their interests in Dunkirk

Fractions of the capitalist class	*Interests*
(1) The integrated monopoly sector for iron and steel. The production of steel, for example, is integrated with the production of ships, boilers, pipes, etc. (see Castells and Godard, 1974, pp. 74, 76–9, 85–6, 114–15).	(1) Smooth and efficient system of production; (b) Reserving space for expansion and storage, preferably as close as possible to the quays; (c) a rail network within the industrial-port complex; (d) no competition for its skilled labour force
(2) The non-integrated monopoly sector. The refining of petrol, for example, is currently not integrated with any other activity (see Castells and Godard, 1974, pp. 74, 79–82, 87, 115).	(a) a deep-water port capable of taking oil-tankers of 400 000 + tons; (b) storage space close to the quays; (c) Efficient road and rail network for transporting the petrol throughout France and Europe
(3) Large (monopoly) companies specialising in port activities – e.g. port authority, ship owners, freight owners (see Castells and Godard, 1974, pp. 75, 82–4, 87)	(a) Increase in port traffic; (b) Increase in the capacity of the port; (c) Efficient road and rail network for linking Dunkirk with the rest of France and Europe
(4) Small and medium enterprises specialising in port activities (a) subcontractors with strong financial backing (e.g. building companies) (b) autonomous family enterprises (Castells and Godard, 1974, pp. 75, 82–4, 87–8, 115)	(a) continued development of the port and the monopolies (b) their existence is threatened by the monopolies
(5) Agriculture: (a) small farmer (b) large farmer (c) market gardener	Urban expansion is absorbing agricultural land and removing a number of farmers and market gardeners off the land. The small farmer suffers most from the sale of his land while the larger farmer is likely to set up an alternative business either in the building or transport industry.
(6) Shopkeepers and artisans	Their interest is to stay in business but (particularly in the case of small shopkeepers) their existence is threatened by the growth of large supermarkets.

Source: Castells and Godard (1974).

Table 6.10 Castells's description of the fractions of the working class and their interests in Dunkirk

Fractions of the working class	*Interests*
(1) Skilled workers in the monopoly sector (see Castells and Godard, 1974, p. 117)	In view of the scarcity of skilled labour these workers are relatively privileged and their interests lie in maintaining these privileges
(2) Workers in small and medium-sized enterprises (see Castells and Godard, 1974, p. 118)	These workers are in a weak market position and their interest is in preserving their jobs even at the expense of lower wages
(3) Building workers	These tend to be foreign workers whose interests tend to be quite different to those of French workers in Dunkirk
(4) Unskilled workers (see Castells and Godard, 1974, p. 117)	They are in a weak market position
(5) Dockers	Their jobs are being threatened by technological advances, notably containerisation.

Source: Castells and Godard, 1974.

(3) The ideology of individual artisan autonomy.
(4) The ideology of traditional rural community and extended family (Castells and Godard, 1974, pp. 162–8).

Each class fraction is said to possess its own particular combination of these different ideologies and it is this combination which constitutes its ideology. (Dockworkers, for example, combine ideology (2) with ideology (4).)

The major difficulty with this aspect of the research is that the reader has no way of assessing the empirical status and accuracy of this classification of ideologies and their distribution among the different class fractions in Dunkirk. This is a difficulty because the empirical basis of the analysis – that is, the data – is not (contrary to normal scientific practice) made accessible to the reader. There is, in other words, no indication of the set of empirical observations that were made which are so neatly summarised by these four ideologies and which, in turn, are neatly distributed among the different class fractions. Without such data there is no way of assessing the validity of this analysis; it must therefore be regarded with some scepticism.

In Chapter 4 (pp. 173–292) Castells and Godard discuss some of the problems in the 'urban system' which arise in relation to the reproduction of labour. In this chapter the housing problem is given particular attention. At the time of writing Castells found a serious housing shortage in Dunkirk (1974a, pp. 198–212) although the more recent evidence (see notably Coing, 1977, p. 184) seems to suggest that this has been reversed and that there is now an 'overproduction' (ibid.) of houses, to the extent that the 1975 census recorded 6100 houses vacant in Dunkirk.

Castells and Godard also discuss (pp. 235–59) the transport problem in Dunkirk and the transport requirements of the various class fractions and the way in which they are inadequately dealt with in Dunkirk. This discussion focuses on the demands for improved road and rail networks and on the inadequacy of the existing, privately-run, bus service.

The problems of housing and transport are referred to as problems associated with, respectively, the consumption element and the exchange element in the urban system. This type of terminology, derived from Castells's concept of the urban system, pervades and vitiates Chapter 4 of *Monopolville* and is of no real heuristic value. Castells's and Godard's treatment of the data in this chapter is also rather careless since the sources of the 'facts' related to housing and transport are rarely cited.

The third and fourth parts of Chapter 4 (pp. 364–412 and pp. 412–39 respectively) contain an analysis of urban planning and urban protests. The analysis of urban planning begins by defining the latter as all forms of state intervention (Castells and Godard, 1974, p. 365) though the subsequent discussion is largely confined to the institutional structures in France and Dunkirk for urban and regional land use planning. Castells goes through the history of the production of various planning documents and it is on the basis of this analysis that he reaches his conclusion that urban planning serves the function of reconciling, integrating and regulating the diverse interests in the city within 'the limits drawn by the structural laws of the dominant mode of production' (Castells and Godard, 1974, p. 411). Castells and Godard are particularly emphatic that urban planning never challenges the dominant interests of the capitalist class (for example, it never challenges, but always facilitates such monopolies as Usinor).

The analysis of urban planning also highlights, particularly in his later accounts of this research (1978a, pp. 82–8), the political and ideological effects of planning. The planning authority, according to Castells, is at the centre of various conflicting class interests and its role is to produce plans which demonstrate that the various types of development envisaged by the plan reflect the 'common interest' rather than the particular interest of one particular class or class fraction. The visibility of the contradictions and conflicts between classes is reduced by presenting plans as statements of 'harmony and agreement of contradictory demands, rubbing out these contradictions by colouring them differently on a map, or more seriously by separating them spatially (zoning), or temporally (phased development), thus enabling divergent or even contradictory social demands to be represented in the same scheme' (ibid., p. 84).

Viewed in this light, the planner is both a negotiator and a technician. Castells continues: 'he [sic] uses the prestige of neutrality and technical competence to present himself as a professional and "scientist" above conflict, and as such is in a comfortable position to arbitrate between various social partners' (ibid., p. 85).

On the basis of this analysis, Castells concludes that the major effects of urban planning are to be found, not in the particular types of property development which it envisages and approves but in its ideological and political effects. The ideological effect consists in the 'rationalization-legitimation' of conflicting interests, while the political effect consists in 'negotiation and mediation' between these conflicting interests (ibid., p. 86).

This is probably the most convincing part of Castells's analysis of urban planning in Dunkirk and provides a number of insights which are likely to prove relevant to understanding urban planning in other capitalist countries. Indeed, some of the empirical research on urban planning in Britain is largely confirmatory of Castells's analysis (see notably Lambert, *et al.*, 1978; Flynn, 1981).

The fifth and final chapter is concerned with 'urban politics' (in the broad sense) in Dunkirk. This chapter contains five parts. The first two parts contain a summary of the various political parties in France and Dunkirk and the various class fractions which these parties tend to represent, as well as a brief résumé of the results of the 1971 municipal elections where the Socialist Party gained control of the Dunkirk urban community (Castells and Godard, 1974, pp. 293–363).

Castells and Godard finally discuss urban protests even though these were particularly scarce in Dunkirk (ibid., p. 414). His analysis is in fact concerned with explaining the absence of urban protests. Two reasons are given for this absence. The first is that the urban problems in Dunkirk (such as the housing problem) inhibit the emergence of urban protests. For example, those living in HLMs which are of poor quality, or have excessively high rents, are discouraged from engaging in protest action since many families are obliged to live in even worse conditions such as caravans or disused barracks (ibid., p. 429). The second reason is that the trade unions and the political parties have not offered their support and organisational capacities to the development of urban protests over housing, transport, and so on (ibid., pp. 429–30). In fact, Castells and Godard found that, in Dunkirk, conflicts in the work place were never related to conflicts over urban problems (ibid., p. 423).

The preceding synopsis has highlighted the main features of the study of Dunkirk as well as its salient merits and defects. It is now necessary to briefly summarise.

The principal merit of Castells's book is that it attempts to analyse the urban growth and development of Dunkirk by focusing on the different class fractions participating in that development and the different (and often competing) interests which each has in relation to that development. It is this approach which is at the heart of any Marxist analysis of the city. Unfortunately, however, Castells and Godard do not develop this line of analysis to its fullest extent thereby neglecting some of the more interesting and complex empirical issues (such as, for example, the way in which the income of the various class fractions is affected, directly and indirectly, by the central and local state).

The main defect of this book is its carelessness with respect to the methodological details of doing research. This was seen to be the case both with respect to the use of 'official' statistics in the book, the exact source of which was rarely cited, but more particularly with respect to the data generated by the authors in the course of the research, most of which, on the basis of the information contained in this book must be regarded with some scepticism.

6.7.7 Research on Immigrant Workers in Western Europe

This research is an examination of some official statistics on immigration in Western Europe and was published in 1975 (Castells, 1975b). Most of the statistics were produced and published by the OECD, the EEC and the Governments of France, Germany and Britain, and were collected for Castells with the aid of a research assistant (ibid., p. 33). No date is given as to when the research was undertaken.

Castells's starting point is that immigration is high in certain West European countries, as measured by the percentage of foreigners in the population in 1971: Germany (5.55 per cent), France (6.87 per cent), Belgium (7.39 per cent), Luxembourg (10.81 per cent), Switzerland (15.71 per cent), Sweden (5.0 per cent), United Kingdom (3.4 per cent) (ibid., p. 37). 'We . . . want to argue', writes Castells, 'that immigration is not a conjunctural phenomenon linked to the manpower needs of expanding economies but a structural tendency characteristic of the current phase of monopoly capitalism' (ibid., p. 44).

The main structural tendency to which Castells refers is the law of the tendency of the rate of profit to fall (ibid., pp. 44ff), and immigration is seen as an important device in counteracting this tendency. The argument is that the fall in the rate of profit which results from a rising organic composition of capital is counteracted by increasing the exploitation of immigrant workers. This is done by increasing the rate of both absolute surplus value (that is, by reducing wages) and relative surplus value (that is, by increasing the length and intensity of the working day). This, in turn, has the effect, via competition, of reducing the wages of indigenous workers. From this Castells concludes that immigration causes 'a relative lowering of wages, thus contributing to the structural counter-tendency which helps delay the fall in the rate of profit' (1975b, p. 49). It should be noted that the only relevant empirical evidence which Castells presents in favour of this analysis is one table which shows that, in 1968, in France, the wages of foreign workers were less than the wages of French workers (ibid., p. 47).

The importance of immigrant workers in counteracting the tendency for the rate of profit to fall arises, Castells claims, because of the fact that thay are not unionised and united with the indigenous trade union movement (ibid., p. 53). This, in turn, is due to their 'legal-political status' (ibid.) as well as 'racism and xenophobia' (ibid.). The absence of unionisation mkes it possible for capitalists to exploit immigrant workers at a high rate of exploitation while also making it possible, via competition, to increase the rate of exploitation of indigenous workers. The only solution to this, according to Castells is 'the common discovery by immigrant and indigenous workers of their basic identity of interests' (ibid., p. 60).

This is the essence of Castells's analysis. It is essentially an attempt to explain the effects of immigration on wages and profits using Marx's law of the falling rate of profit (see section 2.1 for a critique of this law; see also subsection 6.2). However, none of the evidence presented by Castells is relevant to the proof or disproof of that explanation.

Castells's carelessness with respect to empirical evidence is also evident in this interpretation of the tables of data which are presented in the article. His interpretation of nearly half these tables (Tables 1, 2, 11, 12, 13, 14 and 15) is, strictly speaking, incorrect. Two examples may be used to illustrate this. Citing Tables 13, 14, 15 and 16, Castells states that '32% of immigrants in Germany live in temporary dwellings . . . while 98% of shanty town dwellers in France are immigrants. (See Tables 13,

14, 15, 16)' (ibid., p. 49). In fact, Tables 13, 14 and 15 refer to the socioeconomic status of employees in Germany, Switzerland and France, respectively, while Table 16 is non-existent. (In addition, four diagrams are cited as evidence but are not published in the article.) An equally striking disparity occurs in the interpretation of Tables 11 and 12, which claims to show that 'the majority [of immigrants] are unmarried or 'forced bachelors (See Tables 11 and 12)' (Castells, 1975c, p. 47). In fact, only Table 11 contains any evidence on the marital status of immigrants, and this shows that the majority of immigrants in Germany in 1970 were married, while the majority in France in 1968 were single.

In addition to these two defects there is also an internal inconsistency in Castells's position. One of the fundamental assumptions made by Marx (see section 2.3), and seemingly adopted by Castells, is that there is perfect competition in the labour market. On the basis of this assumption Castells is able to argue that the wages of immigrant workers have an effect upon the wages of indigenous workers (1975b, p. 49). However, if there is not perfect competition in the labour market because immigrant and indigenous workers operate in 'segmented labour markets' (see Cain, 1976), then the wages of the former would have no effect upon the wages of the latter. This could occur if immigrant workers had different types of jobs from indigenous workers (as Castells believes: 1975b, p. 43); if immigrant workers had lower wages than indigenous workers (as Castells believes: ibid., pp. 49, 50, 54); and if immigrant workers were non-unionised while indigenous workers were (as Castells believes: ibid., pp. 53, 59, 60). Under these circumstances, there would not be a competitive labour market, and the wages of immigrant workers could be expected to have no effect upon the wages of indigenous workers. While this does not establish empirically that the labour markets of Western Europe are competitive or segmented, it does indicate that Castells's position is inconsistent and confused.

This research therefore is of extremely limited value because Castells does not provide empirical evidence to support his empirical claims and even when empirical evidence is provided it is frequently interpreted in an incorrect way.

6.7.8 Research on Urban Protests in Paris

This research is based upon a pilot study of nearly 180 different urban protests in Paris between 1968 and 1973. The results were first published in 1977 (Castells, 1977b – translated and published in Castells, 1978a Chapter 6, pp. 126–51). The period between 1968 and 1973 was chosen

Table 6.11 Castells's typology of urban protests in Paris, 1968–1973

Type of protest	*Example of stake*	*Social base*	*Mobilisation*
Economic	Housing and urban policy	Working class	High
Political	Transport	Multiclass	Medium
Ideological	Environment	Student	Low

Sources: 1977b, p. 50; 1978b, pp. 131–2.

for study because 1968 was 'a significant historical watershed' (Castells, 1978b, p. 129) while 1973 was 'the date of the start of the research' (ibid.).

Castells explains that the data used in the study was 'obtained by a systematic analysis of newspapers and weeklies, as well as the pamphlets, documents and dossiers of unions and political organizations. In many cases field work supplemented our information' (ibid.).

The analysis begins with a typology of urban struggle. Castells distinguishes between economic struggles, political struggles and ideological struggles in terms of their stake (or issue) and their level of mobilisation. This typology can be summarised as shown in Table 6.11.

This typology is a rather loose device for differentiating between different types of protest action, since they are largely interchangeable. It is possible that a typology which focused upon the spatial dimension of different struggles (that is, the size of the area and population affected by the issue) might be a more effective device in this case. All struggles are limited, depending on the issue, to specific geographical areas (for example, a neighbourhood, an urban area or an entire society) (see section 8.8). It is quite possible that the types of issues cited by Castells may vary along this dimension.

There would seem to be three principal results which emerge from Castells's research.

The first is that a protest is likely to produce a successful economic (or 'urban') effect if it is not related to any political organisation and if it is not supported by single persons, immigrants or students (Castells, 1978b, p. 137). Castells emphasises the political aspect of this result: 'the politicization of a struggle does not increase its efficiency at the urban level' (ibid.). He cites the example of the squatting movement whose excessive politicisation led to its isolation and ultimate defeat (ibid., p. 146).

The second result is that a protest is likely to have a successful effect if it aims to be overtly political and if its social base and social force is predominantly French and does not include students or immigrants (ibid., pp. 135–9).

The third result is that a protest is likely to have a successful ideological effect (that is, challenge the dominant ideology) if it is concentrated on the housing issue and is supported by a student (rather than by a family or immigrant) social base (ibid., pp. 139–42). On the role of students Castells states: 'despite their rather negative effect on the successful outcome of protest action, [they] reveal themselves to be ideological agents par excellence' (ibid., p. 140).

Castells emphasises the political implications of these results, particularly the first one. He states that: 'a protest struggle must be kept independent of a political struggle in order to obtain positive urban effects on the one hand and positive political effects on the other' (ibid., p. 144). However, while the two types of protest must be kept separate, they should, he argues, be developed simultaneously. These are the main themes and results of Castells's research. It is virtually impossible, however, to evaluate the validity of this research since Castells provides no information on how the various variables are measured (for example, the size and characteristics of the social base, the level of mobilisation of this social base, the effects produced by the resulting social force, and so on) or on how these variables are intercorrelated. There is no quantitative evidence presented to support any of the claims made by Castells in this research report. Moreover, since nearly 180 different protest actions were studied, many of which had ceased before the research had started, it is possible (indeed likely) that accurate and comprehensive information was not available in every case. Castells provides no discussion of these issues. For these reasons his research is of extremely limited value.

6.7.9 Conclusion

Castells's research is an earnest attempt to apply his 'Marxist' urban theory to actual empirical situations. This research is moderately successful in some cases (notably in the study of Dunkirk: subsection 6.7) but in virtually every case it is blemished by serious methodological defects in the treatment of data. Castells's treatment of data is extremely careless: in some cases because his interpretation of the data is wrong (as in his study of urban renewal in Paris: subsection 6.7.3), and in his study of immigrant workers in Western Europe: subsection 6.7.7; in others because the production of the data itself, particularly in those cases where the data is based upon 'personal experience' and 'newspaper reports' is never discussed or explained (as in the study of protests in Paris: subsections 6.7.4 and 6.7.8; and in Montreal: subsection 6.7.5; in yet other cases because factual claims are made without the data source being cited (as in the study of Dunkirk: subsection 6.7.6), and finally because the full empirical implications and data requirements of his claims are not fully appreciated (as in the study of Dunkirk: subsection 6.7.6 and the study of immigrant workers in Western Europe: subsection 6.7.7).

These considerations seriously limit the validity of Castells's empirical research. In conjunction with the defects identified in his theoretical analysis, they seriously limit the value of his entire work.

6.8 CONCLUSION

Castells's writing, as has been seen, can be divided into three parts: his critique of conventional urban sociology; his formulation of a 'Marxist' urban sociology; and his empirical research. It is now necessary to summarise the main conclusions to emerge from the assessment of his work.

Castells's critique of conventional urban sociology was seen to be incisive, cogent and largely correct. His empirical research, by contrast, was seen to be blemished by a frequently haphazard use of empirical evidence. As regards his conceptual framework for the analysis of urban areas, two major sets of problems were identified. The first is the inadequacy of his definition of urban areas. This definition, which isolated collective consumption as the distinguishing and 'structuring' characteristic of urban areas, was seen to be inadequate since it placed undue emphasis on collective consumption at the expense of other urban processes. As is argued more fully in Chapter 8, an urban area is, fundamentally, a spatial concentration of physical structures, that is, buildings (for example, houses, factories, offices, shops, and so on) and infrastructure (for example, roads, water, and sewerage services, schools, hospitals, parks, and so on). Evidently collective consumption is only one part of this spatial concentration. Moreover, Castells's attempt to 'explain' collective consumption in terms of Marxian crisis theory was seen to be wholly inadequate both conceptually and empirically.

The second set of problems relates to Castells's analysis of urban planning and urban social movements. The difficulty with this analysis lies in its reliance upon seemingly useless taxonomies such as the urban system and urban actor. Moreover, it would seem that the processes of urban planning and urban protests are in fact part of more general processes constituting urban areas. As is argued in Chapter 8, urban areas consist of three basic processes: the process by which the urban area is produced; the process by which the urban area is used for further production; and the process by which the urban area is used for final consumption. From this point of view, urban planning is simply part of the process by which urban areas are produced while urban protests (or most of them) are part of the more general process by which urban areas are used for final consumption (and the conflicts inherent in that process).

The more general conclusion of this chapter is that Castells's analysis is not a significant contribution to the Marxian analysis of urban areas because it fails in its self-appointed goal 'to extend in the field of the analysis of space the fundamental concepts of historical materialism' (Castells, 1977a, p. 125). The ultimate reason for this failure seems to lie in Castells's adherence to, and elaboration of, the Althusserian framework. The consequence of this, in turn, is that Castells's analysis is highly functionalist, in the literal sense that many of his explanations take the form of identifying the (alleged) functions which particular actions or activities fulfil (for example, collective consumption or urban planning), rather than identifying the actual effects of those actions. It is only by knowing the effects of particular actions that it is possible to infer their 'functions'. The consequence of Castells's functionalism, in turn, is that he explicitly (see notably Castells, 1976b, pp. 77–8; 1974b, p. 239; 1981a, pp. 379, 380, 386) avoids any analysis which would treat urban processes (such as urban planning or urban social movements) as the outcome of the conscious and calculated decisions and actions of the actors in a capitalist society (that is, capitalists, landowners, workers, the state, and so on). Paradoxically, it is precisely Marx's focus on individual decisions, each made within a particular set of constraints and structures, and the collective outcome of those decisions, which is one of the important methodological features of his political economy.

The need for an analysis of urban areas along Marxist lines thus remains. An attempt will be made in Chapter 8 to meet that need by developing an urban sociology which avoids the major errors of Castells's approach, but which nevertheless retains the Marxian emphasis upon the role of interest and conflict in social interaction. However, before proceeding to that task, an assessment will now be made of Lojkine's attempt to develop a Marxist analysis of urban areas.

7 The Marxist Urban Sociology of Jean Lojkine

7.0 INTRODUCTION

The purpose of this chapter is to evaluate the writings of Jean Lojkine. Lojkine's writing, like that of Castells, attempts to apply a Marxist perspective to the analysis of urban areas. The corpus of his work, which is much smaller than that of Castells (see Bibliography) can be classified into two categories: his theoretical, Marxist, analysis of urban areas, and his empirical research. Unlike Castells, whose analysis develops out of a critique of conventional urban sociology, Lojkine's starting point is Marxism itself (or that variant of Marxism known as state monopoly capitalism – see Chapter 5). More specifically, Lojkine's urban analysis emerges from his analysis of the state and the urban policies of the state. It is in this sense that he regards the Marxist analysis of the state, particularly the contemporary French state, as 'the guiding thread' in all his writing (Lojkine, 1977d; also 1977a, p. 123).

There is no clear chronological sequence between the two parts of Lojkine's writing (that is, the theoretical analysis and the empirical research). In fact, his first major piece of theoretical analysis appeared in 1972 (Lojkine, 1972c – translated and published in English in 1976a), the same year in which his first major piece of empirical research was also published (Lojkine, 1972a). Nevertheless, there is a logical separation between these two parts of his work and this will be maintained in the presentation below. Thus, his conceptual analysis will be examined in sections 7.1 to 7.5, followed by an examination of his empirical research in section 7.6.

The central focus guiding this examination of Lojkine's writing is Marxian political economy as outlined in Part I. This perspective, while appropriate to any piece of Marxist writing, is particularly so in the case of Lojkine whose analysis is very explicitly based upon the assumptions and propositions of Marx's political economy. As a result most of Lojkine's work can only be adequately assessed from this perspective. Thus the crucial issue to be investigated is whether his use of Marxist political economy is rigorous and cogent, and whether it is adapted to cope with the spatial dimension which is an essential part of any urban analysis.

The analysis begins with Lojkine's definition of an urban area.

7.1 THE DEFINITION OF AN URBAN AREA

Lojkine defines an urban area as the spatial concentration of the general conditions of production (Lojkine, 1976a, pp. 120ff; 1977a, pp. 125ff). He defines the general conditions of production, in turn, as consisting of the following elements:

the means of production and reproduction;
the collective means of consumption (that is, the totality of medical, sports, educational, cultural and transport facilities);
the means of social circulation (that is, the commercial and banking institutions);
the means of material circulation (that is, the means of communication and transport).
(Lojkine, 1976a, pp. 120–21; 1977a, pp. 125–6).

Thus, within every urban area, 'the totality of general conditions of production, including collective means of consumption, have become concentrated within a limited area' (Lojkine, 1976a, p. 123).[1] Urbanisation occurs within capitalism, according to Lojkine, because of 'the tendency for capital to increase the productivity of labour by socializing the general conditions of production' (ibid., p. 124). 'The city thus appeared', he continues, 'as the direct effect of the need to reduce indirect costs of production, and the costs of circulation and consumption in order to speed up the rotation of capital and thus increase the period during which capital was used productively' (ibid., p. 127).

These quotations reveal the centrality of the concept of production in Lojkine's definition of urban areas and in his explanation of urbanisation. While this orientation is consistent with the basic premises of Marxian theory, the process by which urban areas are used in the production of commodities is only one of the processes constitutive of urban/built-up areas. As will be argued more fully in Chapter 8, there are, in addition, two other processes which are also an integral part of every urban area. These are the process by which the urban area is itself produced through property development, as well as the process by which it enters into final consumption. These two processes are neglected in Lojkine's work.

In addition to his definition of urban areas, Lojkine also argues that urban areas within capitalism have two distinctive features. He writes: 'in our opinion what does characterize the capitalist city is on the one hand the growing concentration of the collective means of consumption . . . ; and on the other hand the particular mode of concentration of the totality of means of reproduction (of capital and of labour power)' (ibid., pp. 120–21). Of these two characteristics, it is the collective means of consumption which receives the most attention in Lojkine's work since the latter, he believes, 'bring out the novelty of the urban mode of life' (ibid., p. 123) and 'gradually create a style of life, new social needs, hence the phrase urban civilization' (ibid., p. 120). It is thus necessary to examine the concept of the collective means of consumption as it is used in Lojkine's work. This will be done in the next section.

7.2 THE COLLECTIVE MEANS OF CONSUMPTION

7.2.1 Introduction

Lojkine analyses what he regards as the four most important characteristics of the collective means of consumption. For him the collective means of consumption are, first, collective; second, unproductive; third, unprofitable; and fourth, durable, immobile and indivisible. This section will analyse the cogency and rigour with which Lojkine analyses these four characteristics (subsections 7.2 to 7.2.5).

7.2.2 The 'Collective' Nature of the Collective Means of Consumption

Lojkine defines the collective means of consumption as 'the totality of material supports of the activities devoted to the extended reproduction of social labour power' (Lojkine, 1976a, p. 121). These are exemplified by reference to 'the totality of medical, sports, educational, cultural and public transport facilities' (ibid.). Lojkine refers to these facilities as 'collective' though his use of the latter term is neither clear nor consistent. In fact it is possible to identify four different usages of the term in his work.

In his first usage, Lojkine states that the collective means of consumption are 'collective' because they are provided by the state. This usage is implicit in his assertion that the 'great importance' (ibid., p. 121) of the collective means of consumption is evidenced by the proportion of 'expenditure in the budgets of the major capitalist countries' (ibid.) devoted to the provision of these facilities. This usage is identical to that of Castells (subsection 6.2.1) and is quite straightforward from a Marxist perspective.

In his second usage, Lojkine claims that the collective means of consumption are collective because 'the mode of consumption is collective and is thus by its nature opposed by individual, private appropriation' (ibid., p. 122). This is exemplified by stating that 'parks and lessons cannot be consumed individually – at least not in their current increasingly socialised form' (ibid.). In this case Lojkine uses the term collective to refer to those use-values which can be consumed simultaneously by a number of individuals. The problem with this usage, however, is that many use-values designated by the term 'collective means of consumption' are not in fact 'collective' in this sense (for example, medical services, such as operations and kidney machines, cannot be consumed simultaneously as can parks and lessons) while many use-values designated as individual consumption would in fact be 'collective' (for example, all spectator sports and entertainments). Thus the second usage of the term 'collective' in contrast to the first, fails to specify what is the quintessential characteristic of the collective means of consumption. It should therefore be rejected (see Pahl, 1978; Saunders, 1980a, p. 122; Theret, 1982, pp. 349–50).

In his third usage, Lojkine claims that the collective means of consumption are 'collective' because they satisfy needs which 'can only be satisfied collectively' (Lojkine, 1977a, p. 136). These needs refer, *inter alia*, to the need for health, education and transport. However, this claim would seem to be false since these needs can be, have been, and in some cases still are, satisfied individually. There would thus seem to be little justification for defining the collective means of consumption according to the particular need which it satisfies.

In this fourth usage Lojkine claims that the collective means of consumption are 'collective' because this represents the 'best' (ibid., p. 136) way of satisfying these social needs. While this may be the case (though it is debatable) this definition would seem to provide a justification for 'collective' consumption rather than a criterion for distinguishing between individual and collective consumption. As a result it does not grasp the specific features of the collective means of consumption.

The result of this analysis suggests that Lojkine's first definition of the collective means of consumption is the most straightforward and clear cut because it identifies the term 'collective' with state provision. Lojkine's other usages seem to be imprecise (in the case of the second), factually incorrect (in the case of the third), or irrelevant (in the case of the fourth).

7.2.3 The 'Unproductive' Nature of the Collective Means of Consumption

One of Lojkine's most important claims about the collective means of consumption is that they are 'unproductive' (Lojkine, 1977a, p. 134). He claims that the collective means of consumption are essential to the reproduction of labour and are a part of variable capital. However, they have the 'peculiarity' (ibid., p. 132) that they are 'not consumed directly by individual labour power' and hence are not directly transformed 'from variable capital to wages' (ibid.).

Lojkine distinguishes between two types or fractions of variable capital: individual consumption (which he identifies with wages), and collective consumption. He claims that individual consumption is directly consumed while the collective means of consumption have the indispensable function of transforming 'the remainder of variable capital into wages' (ibid.).

Lojkine elaborates by making a distinction between 'objects of consumption' and 'means of consumption' (ibid., p. 134). The difference is that the former are use-values which enter final consumption whereas the latter are a set of activities which make final consumption possible (ibid.). Thus, in Lojkine's usage, individual consumption comprises material objects which are consumed individually, while the collective means of consumption are activities or services which are not consumed but instead 'make consumption possible' (ibid.).

On this basis Lojkine claims that there is a 'parallelism' (ibid., p. 133) between the collective means of consumption and the means of social circulation, that is, 'commercial and banking institutions' (Lojkine, 1976a, p. 120). He claims that the collective means of consumption play an 'identical social function' (ibid.) in the capitalist system of production to the means of social circulation. This is because the means of social circulation perform the function of transforming 'value from the money form to the commodity form' (ibid.) while the collective means of consumption perform the function of transforming 'variable capital into wages and then into means for the reproduction of labour power' (ibid.).

Lojkine infers that since the means of social circulation are unproductive, as Marx claimed (Marx, 1974b, Part I), the collective means of consumption must also be unproductive. Both of these processes, according to Lojkine, are 'necessary from the social point of view but totally unproductive' (Lojkine, 1977a, p. 134). The collective means of consumption are an 'expenditure of lost funds, in so far as they create no value but, on the contrary, effect a reduction on the value already created' (ibid., p. 135). Even though they 'increase the productivity of labour' (ibid., p. 137) they nevertheless remain unproductive and 'superfluous' (ibid., p. 135) from the point of view of the reproduction of capital.

Lojkine's argument is seriously flawed in a number of ways. Five problems in particular may be identified.

The first problem is his claim that the collective means of consumption are not consumed. This proposition seems to contradict the obvious fact that the services designated by the term collective means of consumption (such as health, education, transport, and so on) are actually consumed. It is thus difficult to see the justification for this claim.

The second problem lies in the claim that the collective means of consumption perform the function of 'transforming' a fraction of variable capital into wages. This appears to be misconceived since variable capital is simply wages by another name. Correspondingly, the alleged parallelism between the collective means of consumption and the means of social circulation does not exist since variable capital does not have to be transformed into wages unlike commodities which have to be transformed, through the means of social circulation, into money and vice versa.

The third problem with Lojkine's argument concerns his central proposition that the collective means of consumption are 'unproductive'. This proposition is difficult to assess straightforwardly since, as has been seen in Chapter 4, Marx used the terms productive and unproductive labour in two different and inconsistent senses (which, for convenience, were labelled 'Definition I' and 'Definition II'). In addition, Marx's Definition II was found to be untenable (see notably section 4.2). Lojkine does not avert to this ambiguity in Marx's usage though he does appear to use the term in the sense of 'Definition II' so that it is open to the difficulties identified above. Nevertheless, it is possible that the collective means of consumption may be unproductive according to Marx's Definition I. This, however, is an empirical question which cannot be established *a priori* but can only be established by measuring the net effect of the collective means of consumption upon the rate of profit and hence upon the rate of capital accumulation. Thus it remains an open question as to whether the collective means of consumption are in fact 'unproductive'.

The fourth problem concerns the proposition that the collective means for consumption 'increase the productivity of labour' (Lojkine, 1977a, p. 137). Two issues arise in this context. The first is whether it is empirically true that the collective means of consumption increase the productivity of labour. Lojkine provides no evidence to prove that it does. The second issue is that if the collective means of consumption increase the productivity of labour then its effect (depending upon the costs, and hence the taxes, needed to produce it) may be to increase the output of the capitalist sector and hence, *ceteris paribus*, the rate of profit. If this possibility were shown to exist empirically then the collective means of consumption would in fact be 'unproductive' (according to Marx's Definition I). These considerations reveal the complex issues which are left unexplored in this part of Lojkine's analysis.

The fifth problem relates to Lojkine's assertion that the collective means of consumption are 'superfluous from the point of view of the reproduction of capital' (Lojkine, 1977a, p. 135). The difficulty with this claim is that the profitability of capitalism is dependent upon, *inter alia*, a labour force which has an adequate level of nutrition, health, education, skill, mobility, and so on. Since one of the effects of the collective means of consumption is to produce such a labour force, they would seem to be essential rather than superfluous to the reproduction of capital. The fact that capitalists attempt to minimise the costs of the individual and collective reproduction of labour power, as Lojkine points out (ibid., p. 140), only proves that these are necessary costs; it does not prove that they are superfluous.

These are the main problems with Lojkine's claim that the collective means of consumption are unproductive. As has just been seen, it is a claim which he fails to justify because his understanding of Marx's political economy seems to be seriously deficient.

7.2.4 The Unprofitable Nature of the Collective Means of Consumption

Lojkine states that the production of the collective means of consumption is unprofitable from the point of view of the individual capitalist (Lojkine, 1977a, p. 138). He explains this by referring to 'the slowness of the rotation of nonproductive capital in the consumption sector' (ibid.). This is exemplified by stating that houses, schools and hospitals 'last for many years' (ibid.). Lojkine's argument, in short, is that the collective means of consumption are inherently unprofitable because their production requires a capital investment lasting many years.

The main difficulty with this argument is that the production of many commodities (and not just the collective means of consumption) require that capital be invested for long periods. Examples of this are the investments in plant and machinery for the generation of electricity, the assembly of cars, the refining of oil, the mining of coal, the production of chemicals, and so on. The production of these commodities is not, however, normally unprofitable. Thus the period of rotation of capital in the production of the collective means of consumption does not seem to be the correct explanation for their lack of profitability.

It would seem that the reason why many of the goods designated by the term 'collective means of consumption' are unprofitable is that the level of effective demand for them (that is, those able and willing to pay for them) is too low. This is why education (and to a lesser extent medical care) can only be produced profitably if they are confined to a relatively small number of affluent consumers (and, even then, direct and indirect state subventions are frequently required to make them profitable). Thus it is only when these goods and services are produced for consumers who do not, and cannot, constitute an 'effective demand', that their production becomes unprofitable. This is typically the reason why the state in most capitalist countries, is unable to produce the collective means of consumption for a profit: the latter are normally distributed, not according to ability to pay but according to the state's definition of need. Thus the collective means of consumption are unprofitable, not because of some inherent features involved in their production but because there is a deficiency in the aggregate demand for them.

7.2.5 The 'Durable', 'Immobile' and 'Indivisible' Nature of the Collective Means of Consumption

Lojkine describes the collective means of consumption as use-values which are simultaneously durable, immobile and indivisible (Lojkine, 1977a, p, 138). Each of these three characteristics is said to be derived from the fact that these use-values are immaterial services which cannot (unlike material products) be separated from or exist independently of their act of production (ibid.). The purpose of the present analysis will be to clarify the meaning of the terms 'durable', 'immobile' and 'indivisible' and establish whether they are in fact genuine characteristics of the collective means of consumption.

The term 'durable', as used by Lojkine, indicates that the consumption of the collective means of consumption has a 'useful effect' (Lojkine, 1976a, p. 122) which is 'durable' (ibid.). This is elaborated by affirming that 'their consumption does not involve destruction as in the case of the consumption of food' (ibid.). Lojkine does not explain the matter further. The difficulty with his argument in its existing form is that there is no way of comparing the useful effects of consuming education with the useful effects of consuming food. The reason for this, in turn, is that in order to establish a comparison between two things (or in this case, two effects) it is necessary for both to be reduced to the same common denominator. But since the effects of education and food cannot be reduced to a common denominator, any more than can a quantity of education and a quantity of food, it follows that it is impossible to establish whether the effects of one are more durable than the effects of the other. For this reason Lojkine's claim that the collective means of consumption are more 'durable' than the individual means of consumption would seem to be impossible to prove.

The term 'immobile' is not explained by Lojkine, though it seems plausible to infer from the text (Lojkine, 1977a, pp. 138–9) that it refers to the fact that the services of the collective means of consumption can only be consumed at the time and place of their actual production. This is a feature of all services (which contrasts with the 'mobility' of material products with respect to the time and place of their production) and hence is not the exclusive peculiarity of the collective means of consumption.

The term 'indivisible' is not explained by Lojkine either, though it seems reasonable to assume that it is being used in the normal economic sense to designate the fact that some commodities have a minimum economic size (see Bannock, Baxter and Rees, 1972, p. 135). The usual example of this is certain types of plant and machinery which, for either engineering or cost reasons, have a minimum economic size. In designating the use-values of the collective means of consumption as highly indivisible, Lojkine is thus presumably claiming that such services as education, health and transport cannot be produced in different sizes or amounts according to individual requirements. This claim is basically correct since the equipment needed to produce the collective means of consumption (that is, buildings, roads, technical equipment, trained staff, and so on) cannot be produced in discrete units, and hence are indivisible.

The results of this analysis reveal that the collective means of consumption are immobile and indivisible, as Lojkine claims. It is however impossible to prove that they are more durable than other consumption goods, as he also claims.

7.2.6 Conclusion

The analysis in this section has examined what Lojkine regards as the four main characteristics of the collective means of consumption. Four results have emerged. The first is that the term 'collective' (as used in the expression 'collective means of consumption') is most accurately and unambiguously identified with 'state provision'. Lojkine's other usages of the term 'collective' were found to be either imprecise, factually incorrect, or irrelevant. The second result is that the collective means of consumption are not 'unproductive' in the sense claimed by Lojkine. The third result is that the collective means of consumption are unprofitable because there is a deficiency in the aggregate demand for these commodities and not, as Lojkine claims, because of the slow rotation of capital involved in their production. The fourth result is that the collective means of consumption are immobile and indivisible as Lojkine claims, but it is impossible to prove that they are more durable than other consumption goods.

7.3 THE THREE PROBLEMS ASSOCIATED WITH CAPITALIST URBAN DEVELOPMENT

7.3 Introduction

There are, according to Lojkine, three major 'crisis points' (Lojkine, 1976a, p. 143) or 'contradictions' (1977d, p. 264) associated with urban development in capitalist societies. These are: the financing of urban expenditure; the locational strategy of firms; and urban land rent. Lojkine's analysis of these problems essentially involves applying to them some traditional concepts in Marx's political economy. The details of his analysis will now be examined.

7.3.2 The Problem of Financing Urban Expenditure

The first problem associated with urban development in capitalist societies is, according to Lojkine, the limit to the financing of 'urban expenditure', that is, the means of communication and the collective means of consumption (Lojkine, 1976a, p. 128; 1977a, p. 160; 1977d, p. 264). The limit to urban expenditure arises, Lojkine argues, because the latter increases the organic composition of capital which causes the rate of profit to fall. This limits the further expansion of urban expenditure presumably because (though Lojkine does not make this explicit) the decline in the rate of profit causes a decline in investment and employment which causes a decline in the amount of revenue received by the state and this, in turn, leads to a decline in the amount of the state's urban expenditure.

Lojkine's statement of this argument may be reformulated in terms of three basic stages. In the first stage he classifies the collective means of consumption as a type of capital ('expenses capital', Lojkine, 1976a, p. 130) analogous to constant capital. The second stage of the argument affirms that both types of capital (that is, constant capital and expenses capital) have the same effect of increasing the organic composition of capital. The third stage is then to deduce that, since urban expenditure has the effect of increasing the organic composition of capital, it also has the effect of reducing the rate of profit upon which its growth depends. As a result, the financing of urban expenditure faces an inexorable limit as a result of the tendency of the rate of profit to fall. Each of these stages of Lojkine's argument will now be critically examined.

The first step of Lojkine's argument attempts to establish that one element of urban expenditure (that is, the collective means of consumption) is like 'expenses capital' (that is, the means of social circulation) in that they produce 'zero extra value' (Lojkine, 1976a, p. 131), while the other element of urban expenditure (that is, the means of material circulation) are assumed to be 'highly devalorized' (that is, produce little extra value). He claims that the collective means of consumption are like the means of social circulation in being 'a deduction from surplus value already produced' (ibid., p. 130). His argument is that both perform an 'identical social function' (Lojkine, 1977a, p. 133) within capitalism, in that the means of social circulation perform the function of transforming 'value from the money form to the commodity form' (ibid.), while the collective means of consumption, as part of variable capital, perform the functions of transforming 'variable capital into wages and then into means for the reproduction of labour power' (ibid.). In other words, the collective means of consumption and the means of social circulation are designated as 'expenses capital' since they are 'necessary to the productive utilization of capital . . . but do not transmit or add any value' (Lojkine, 1976a, p. 130).

The first step of Lojkine's argument is misconceived for at least two reasons: first because it is based upon a false analogy and second, because it is inconsistent with the value analysis which Lojkine adopts. Lojkine's analogy is misconceived because, as has already been seen (sub section 7.2.3), the collective means of consumption do not transform variable capital into wages, unlike the means of social circulation which transform commodities into money and vice versa. Variable capital and wages are simply different expressions for the same thing.

The second difficulty with Lojkine's argument is that the treatment of the collective means of consumption as expenses capital is inconsistent with Marx's value analysis which Lojkine adopts. This is because the collective means of consumption are a fraction of variable capital which means precisely that they are not a 'deduction from surplus value already produced' but an outlay of capital for the purpose of producing surplus value. In other words, if the collective means of consumption are a fraction of variable capital, they cannot, analytically speaking, be seen as a deduction from surplus value already produced since no surplus value can ever be produced without the prior outlay of variable capital.

A third difficulty is that Lojkine provides no empirical evidence whatever to show that the collective means of consumption are 'totally devalorized capital' (Lojkine, 1976a, p. 13) (that is, produce no extra value) and that the means of material circulation are 'very highly devalorized capital' (that is, produce little extra value). To establish the former would require empirical evidence to show that for each expenditure on the collective means of consumption there is an equal and corresponding reduction in the mass of profit/surplus value (as well as in the rate of profit), while to establish the latter would require evidence to show that for each expenditure on the means of material circulation there is a correspondingly smaller increase in the mass of profit/surplus value (through a decline in the rate of profit). None of this requisite evidence is provided by Lojkine.

The second step of Lojkine's argument affirms that urban expenditure acts upon the organic composition of capital in the same way as does constant capital: an increase or decrease in either expenses capital or constant capital leads, respectively, to an increase or decrease in the organic composition of capital. Lojkine's explanation is that urban expenditure 'acts on the organic composition of capital in the same way as constant capital: it raises the organic composition by increasing the mass of accumulated social capital without itself being productively utilized' (Lojkine, 1977a, p. 163).

There are two flaws in this stage of Lojkine's argument. The first which is identical to that found in Marx (see sub section 2.1 above), is that an increase in the 'mass' of aggregate (that is, social) capital does not necessarily imply a corresponding increase in the 'value' of aggregate capital. This does not follow because the concepts of constant capital and the organic composition of capital refer to value quantitities and not physical quantities (that is, masses), so that any increase or decrease in the mass of the latter (however that might measured) does not imply any corresponding increase or decrease in their value.

The second flaw is that no evidence is provided to show that the means of material circulation are 'highly devalorized'. To show this it would be necessary to demonstrate that the total value of the means of material circulation causes the organic composition of capital to increase more rapidly than the rate of exploitation. Without this evidence Lojkine's argument is seriously weakened.

The third stage of Lojkine's argument affirms that urban expenditure 'strengthens the tendency for the rate of profit to fall' (Lojkine, 1976a, pp. 131–2), because of its effect upon the organic composition of capital. The argument, following Marx, is that since all profit arises from the exploitation of labour power (that is, variable capital plus surplus value) the decline of variable capital relative to constant capital implies, assuming a constant rate of exploitation, a fall in the rate of profit. The fall in the rate of profit is said to cause, *inter alia*, an 'over-accumulation' of constant capital because it is capital which cannot be used 'to exploit labour at a given degree of exploitation' (Marx, 1974c, p. 255). In other words an increasingly larger amount of constant capital will be used to produce the same quantity of profit (see section 2.1). Lojkine refers to this as the 'devalorization' of constant capital (Lojkine, 1976a, p. 131; 1977a, p. 163ff); hence his 'over-accumulation – devalorization hypothesis' (Lojkine, 1976a, p. 131).

Lojkine's argument is that of the two components comprising urban expenditure (that is, the collective means of consumption and the means of material circulation) the former are 'totally devalorized capital producing no extra capital (expenses capital)' (ibid., p. 131) while the latter are 'very highly devalorized capital' (ibid.). Hence his conclusion that: 'the financing of the collective means of consumption, like the financing of means of material and social circulation, increase the mass of capital which is devalorized in relation to that which is productively utilised at or above the average rate of profit' (ibid.).

The main problem with this argument is the lack of any empirical evidence of where and by how much the rate of profit is falling and, if so, whether this fall is due to the effect of urban expenditure on the organic composition of capital. Lojkine assumes, independently of any empirical evidence, that urban expenditure strengthens the tendency for the rate of profit to fall. He further assumes, following Marx, that there is a tendency for the rate of profit to fall. As has been shown above (section 2.1), that assumption is unwarranted.

In this section Lojkine's claim was examined: that there is an inherent limit within capitalism to the financing of urban expenditure because the latter causes the organic composition of capital to rise and the rate of profit to fall. It was seen that this claim is without justification since Lojkine provides no evidence to show either that urban expenditure raises the organic composition of capital and even if it did, that this would cause the rate of profit to fall. In the absence of such evidence Lojkine's claim is purely an assertion.

7.3.3 The Problem of the Locational Strategy of Capitalist Firms

The second problem associated with urban development in capitalist societies stems, according to Lojkine, from the locational strategy of firms (Lojkine, 1976a, pp. 133–5; 1977a, pp. 170–71; 1977d, pp. 264–5). The problem, he argues, derives from the fact that firms tend to locate in those areas which offer the best 'situational advantage' (Lojkine, 1976a, p. 134). The consequence of this, in turn, is 'the increasing underdevelopment of the regions least well-equipped in urban infrastructure' (ibid.) on the one hand, and 'the growing congestion of the gigantic 'megalopolises' (ibid.) on the other. Lojkine concludes from this that the locational criteria and strategy of large capitalist firms is in 'contradiction with the technological and social necessities of any real territorial planning, i.e. of developed cooperation at the level of the nation as a whole' (ibid.).

Lojkine does not elaborate his analysis further. His basic and recurrent point is that the locational strategy of capitalist firms is such that they will tend to locate in developed rather than underdeveloped regions. The problem with this generalisation is that it does not accord with the facts since there is growing evidence that manufacturing firms in advanced capitalist countries are now tending to locate in smaller urban and even rural areas and in areas that were formerly regarded as underdeveloped (see, for example, Goddard, 1978, p. 311; Massey and Meegan, 1978, p. 287; Massey, 1979, p. 237; Perrons, 1981; Keeble, Owens and Thompson, 1983).

Lojkine does not consider that the locational strategy of a firm is likely to depend upon its characteristics such as size (for example, uniplant or multiplant) and product (for example, extraction, manufacturing, services) as well as upon the availability and cost of inputs in various regions. His analysis is therefore of rather limited value.

7.3.4 The Problem of Urban Land Rent

The third limit to any rational planning of urban development, according to Lojkine, derives from the existence of urban land rent. However, as will be seen presently, much of Lojkine's analysis is concerned, not with substantiating this claim, but with elaborating the concept of urban land rent (Lojkine, 1971; 1976a, pp. 135–8; 1977a, pp. 172–7).

Lojkine's analysis of urban land rent or, to use his term 'urban property rent' (Lojkine, 1971, p. 89) is essentially an attempt to show that the conceptual categories developed by Marx for understanding agricultural land rent and land prices are equally applicable in the context of urban land rent and land prices. On the basis of this analysis, he makes a number of claims about the effect of urban land rent on the rate of profit, capital accumulation and urban planning which will be examined below.

Lojkine begins his analysis by affirming that: 'In a given economic sector, two conditions determine the possibility of property rent being formed' (ibid., p. 89). These two conditions are:

1. the organic composition of capital in this sector must be below the social average organic composition of capital;
2. there must be an obstacle, within this sector, to the free circulation of capital so that the surplus profit generated in this sector (as a consequence of the low organic composition of capital) will not be redistributed to other sectors but appropriated by the landowners within this sector (ibid.).

According to Lojkine: 'Marx proved in *Capital* that these two conditions are to be found in the sector of agricultural production' (ibid., p. 89).

On the basis of his definition of rent, Lojkine then considers a number of urban situations where these two conditions might exist, with a view to establishing the existence of urban property rent. A number of different situations are referred to, though seldom is a systematic analysis developed. Before critically examining one of these situations, which Lojkine does attempt to analyse, it may be useful to provide a brief diagrammatic summary of the different situations to which he alludes. This is done in Table 7.1.

Lojkine analyses one of the situations identified in Table 7.1, namely, the case of a property developer who leases offices to capitalists for commercial, financial or administrative use. His basic strategy is to establish whether his two conditions for the existence of rent are present. In this light, he attempts to prove that his first condition is present by arguing that the capital invested in this sector, although unproductive, nevertheless allows its owner to 'appropriate a more or less large amount of surplus value (and hence profit)' (Lojkine, 1971, p. 91). Lojkine explains that this is because:

> the organic composition of capital is still relatively low in this sector given the massive employment of underpaid female labour (commercial and office employees) and the still limited introduction of mechanization (the productivity of the banking and commercial sector is far lower, despite recent progress, than that existing in the mining or industrial sector) (ibid., p. 91).

Table 7.1 Lojkine's analysis of different types of rent in different urban situations

Situations giving rise to rent	*Condition (1) for the emergence of rent: a lower than average organic composition of capital (C/U)*	*Condition (2) for the emergence of rent: an obstacle to the free mobility of capital*	*Types of rent arising: Differential rent I Differential rent II Absolute rent*
Owner of land leasing to a capitalist farmer	A lower than average organic composition of capital	The landowner acts as a barrier to investment in agriculture	Differential rent I Differential rent II Absolute rent
Owner of residential property leasing to tenants	Not specified	Not specified	Differential rent I Absolute rent No differential Rent I
Owners of a factory leasing to a capitalist	A higher than average organic composition of capital	Not specified	Not specified
Owners of commercial, financial or administrative offices leasing to capitalists	A lower than average organic composition of capital	The property developer acts as an obstacle to the free mobility of capital	Differential rent I Differential rent II Absolute rent
Owners of collective facilities (roads and railways) leasing to capitalists	A higher than average organic composition of capital	Not specified	Differential rent Absolute rent No differential Rent II

Source: Lojkine, 1971.

Lojkine argues that the second condition for the existence of urban property rent is also present because of the existence of an agent who hinders the free mobility of capital and the equalisation of the rate of profit. This agent is the 'property builder-developer' (ibid., p. 91) who, according to Lojkine, 'purchases, develops and equips the urban land and leases the commercial (or office) premises to capitalist agents' (ibid.).

According to Lojkine, this analysis is 'amply validated by contemporary facts: the leasing of commercial or office premises by private property developers' (ibid.). As further evidence he refers to property development at Parly II, La Defense and Maine Montparnasse.

Lojkine then elaborates his analysis by claiming that 'the three types of rent distinguished by Marx' (ibid.) namely, differential rent I, differential rent II, and absolute rent, coexist in the case of commercial, financial or administrative offices. In explanation, he claims that:

(1) differential rent I arises because of the situational advantages of a particular plot of urban land. According to Lojkine, 'the means of communication play a key role here in differentiating land' (ibid.) and cites the example of the proximity of the A13 motorway to Parly II;
(b) differential rent II arises because of differences in productivity arising from differences in capital investment in commercial centres and office buildings;
(c) absolute rent arises because of the ownership of land and the obstacle which this raises to the free circulation of capitals and the formation of an average rate of profit (ibid.).

There are three serious difficulties with this analysis. The first is that Lojkine's definition of rent corresponds to only one of the types identified by Marx, namely, monopoly rent I (or, as Marx termed it, absolute rent) (section 3.3). Lojkine implies that the conditions for the existence of this type of rent apply to all types which is not the case (see Chapter 3 above). Moreover, the first of these conditions (that is, a low organic composition of capital) is not even necessary for monopoly rent I.

The second difficulty is that Lojkine fails, in any case, to show that his two criteria for the existence of rent actually exist empirically. As regards the first criteria he simply affirms its existence by referring to the large numbers employed in the commercial and financial sector. But this evidence, however suggestive to some, does not establish anything about the organic composition of capital. Lojkine also fails to establish the second criterion because he fails to show in what way the developer and owner of an office block acts as an obstacle to the free mobility of capital and the equalisation of capital. This proposition is affirmed and never proven.

The third difficulty arises with respect to Lojkine's discussion of the three types of rent. Two specific difficulties may be noted here. In the first place, there are four types of rent present in Marx's work and not three as Lojkine claims (Chapter 3). Secondly, there is an inconsistency between Lojkine's initial definition of rent (in terms of two conditions) and his definition of differential rent I and II. This is because he acknowledges that the two conditions which are necessary for rent to exist are not in fact necessary for the existence of differential rent I or II.

These are the most serious problems associated with Lojkine's analysis of office property and they reveal a fundamental conceptual confusion in this part of his work.

Lojkine then makes four claims about the nature and consequences of rent in general. These four claims are:

(1) urban rent acts as 'an obstacle' to 'the development of social productive forces' (Lojkine, 1976a, p. 135), to 'monopolistic accumulation' (ibid., p. 136), and to 'economic growth' (ibid., p. 135);
(b) urban rent strengthens the tendency for the rate of profit to fall (Lojkine, 1976a, p. 137; 1977a, p. 174);
(c) urban rent is a 'structural obstacle to all real urban planning' (Lojkine, 1976a, p. 137; 1977a, p. 175);
(d) urban rent gives rise to 'economic and social segregation' (Lojkine, 1977a, p. 175).

Lojkine makes no serious attempt to substantiate or elaborate any of these four claims. As regards the first two, it is clear that they are closely related since the rate of profit determines the rate of capital accumulation and the rate of economic growth. In other words, both these claims are identical. The question therefore, is whether and, if so, under what conditions does the existence of rent lead to a fall in the rate of profit and, in turn, to a reduction in the rate of economic growth.[2] As was seen in Chapter 3, the answer to this question depends upon the type of commodity being produced (that is, a basic or a non-basic) and on the type of rent (that is, differential rent I and II, monopoly rent I and II). Moreover, the issue of whether rent is an 'obstacle' to capital accumulation, as Lojkine claims, depends essentially upon whether it arises because of the existence of the private ownership of land or independently of it. It would seem that only those types of rent which exist because of the private ownership of land (that is, monopoly rent I) can properly be regarded as 'obstacles' to capital accumulation. Rent which exists independently of the private ownership of land (that is, differential rent I and II, and monopoly rent II) is no more an 'obstacle' to capital accumulation than other costs which must be borne in the course of capital accumulation.

Lojkine's third claim is that rent is a 'structural obstacle' to all 'real' and 'rational' urban planning. It is, however, impossible to evaluate the validity of this claim without first clarifying the meaning of the terms 'real' and 'rational' planning. Unfortunately, Lojkine does not clarify these terms so that no evaluation of this claim is possible.

Lojkine's fourth claim is that urban land rent gives rise, via land prices, to 'economic and social segregation' (Lojkine, 1977a, p. 175). He distinguishes between, three different types of 'urban segregation' (ibid., p. 176):

1. an opposition between the centre where land prices are high (because of 'agglomeration effects' and the periphery where land prices are low;
2. a separation between desirable and undesirable residential areas;
3. a separation between office, industrial and residential zones.

Lojkine's main argument (ibid., pp. 176–7) is that land prices in the city centre are now so high that the centre is 'increasingly reserved for the headquarters of international firms' (ibid., p. 176). Identifying international firms with monopolistic firms, Lojkine concludes that both wage-earners (of all sizes) and non-monopoly capitalists are excluded from the city centre by monopoly capital.

Lojkine's claim is basically an empirical claim and, although no evidence is presented to substantiate it at this point, his empirical research in Paris (Lojkine, 1972a) and Lyon (Lojkine, 1974a) does provide some confirmatory evidence on this point (see subsections 7.6.1 and 7.6.2).

The analysis in this section has revealed a number of weaknesses in Lojkine's treatment of the Marxian concept of rent. This was seen, not only in his exegesis of Marx's concept, but also in his application of it to the urban context. In addition it was seen that some of Lojkine's claims about the effects of rent were quite unfounded.

7.3.5 Conclusion

Lojkine's analysis of the three problems associated with urban development in capitalist societies is seriously flawed essentially because it is based upon an inadequate understanding of the nature and limitations of Marxian political economy. It is not, therefore, a significant contribution to the Marxist analysis of urban areas.

It is now necessary to examine Lojkine's analysis of urban planning.

7.4 URBAN PLANNING

Lojkine's analysis of urban planning is an extension of his analysis of the three problems which, in his view, are inextricably associated with capitalist urban development. These problems, which have been analysed in the preceding section, are the financing of the collective means of consumption, the locational strategy of firms and urban land rent. In Lojkine's view, the 'capitalist relations of production' (Lojkine, 1976a, p. 128) which generate these problems simultaneously act as an 'obstacle' (ibid., p. 137; 1977a, p. 172), a 'limit' (Lojkine, 1976a, p. 128; 1977a, p. 160) and a 'hindrance' (Lojkine, 1977a, p. 172) to any 'real' (Lojkine, 1976a, p. 137) 'rational' (ibid., p. 128; 1977a, p. 159), 'socialized' (1977a, p. 159) urban policy.

Lojkine's analysis of urban planning is also an extension of his views on the nature and consequence of state intervention within the period of SMC (see section 5.2.). This view is essentially that all state intervention is an attempt to regulate the economic and social contradictions generated in this stage of capitalist development. However, since this intervention is subordinated to 'the logic of private capital accumulation' (Lojkine, 1977d, p. 258) it tends to exacerbate rather than regulate the problems which it attempts to solve. Thus, for Lojkine, 'all state policy acts less as an instrument of regulation than as an indicator of a society torn by the conflict of antagonistic classes' (ibid., p. 258). In short, it is an 'active reflection' (ibid., pp. 141ff) of the class struggle.

Lojkine differentiates his view of urban planning from two other views which he regards and rejects as functionalist (ibid., pp. 141, 147). These views treat urban planning as either 'a mechanism of state regulation designed to resolve the technical problems of urban development' (ibid., p. 141) or 'a form of . . . regulating social contradictions' (ibid.). The error in these views, according to Lojkine, is the assumption that the state can regulate the problems generated by capitalism within the framework of capitalism. This, in Lojkine's view, is impossible.

Lojkine develops the concept of urban planning by isolating what he regards as its three different dimensions (Lojkine, 1977a, p. 191). These dimensions are:

1. a planning dimension, which refers to the written plans, that is, the documents which reveal the planning goals being adopted by the planning authority;
2. an operational dimension, which refers to the financial and judicial interventions of the state in relation to those plans;

3. an urban dimension, which refers to the effects of the two preceding dimensions

(ibid., see also 1977d, p. 259 where urban planning is defined only in terms of the first two dimensions).

Lojkine emphasises two points in particular about this concept of urban planning. The first is that there is a 'complete opposition' (Lojkine, 1977a, p. 192) between the goals of planning as elaborated in the planning texts and documents (that is, the first dimension) and the actual implementation of those goals (that is, the second dimension). This opposition takes the form of delays or cancellations in the implementation of those aspects of the plan which are unprofitable or financially expensive (for example housing, green spaces, schools, other collective facilities; ibid., pp. 192, 195). There is thus 'a constant distortion between plans and practices' (ibid., p. 186) which tends to increase as the financial requirements of plans increase (ibid., pp. 197–8). For this reason Lojkine quotes approvingly from Castells to the effect that urban plans are, above all, 'ideological texts which in no way deprives them of their social efficacity but characterizes the intervention of the political as bearing not on the urban system but on the general ideological instance' (Lojkine, 1977a, p. 186; Castells and Godard, 1974, p. 276). (At the same time Lojkine criticises Castells for his tendency to actually identify urban planning with urban plans (ibid.).

The second point which Lojkine emphasises about his concept of urban planning is that the true 'logic' (Lojkine, 1977a, p. 203) and 'sociological content' (ibid., p. 254) of urban planning can only be identified from its effects, that is, the third dimension. On this basis he reviews the evidence on the effects of the state's urban policy in a number of French cities; Paris (Lojkine, 1972a; 1974c; Castells, 1973a; Freyssenet, Regazzola and Retel, 1971), Dunkirk (Castells and Godard, 1974, Lyon (Lojkine, 1974a) and Rennes (Huet *et al.*, 1973). All of this evidence, according to Lojkine, confirms that the state's urban policy in contemporary France is in favour of the monopolies and against the interests of all non-monopoly groups (Lojkine, 1977a, p. 273; 1977b, pp. 149ff; 1977c, pp. 21–2; 1977d, p. 259; Lojkine and Preteceille, 1970, p. 80). In other words, its effect is to 'exacerbate the principal contradiction, at the current stage of capitalism, between the monopolies and the non-monopoly social strata' (Lojkine, 1977a, p. 273). Lojkine bases this conclusion on the claim that the bulk of the state's urban expenditures are concentrated in the centre of urban areas (for example, Paris and Lyon) or in large industrial complexes (for example,

Dunkirk) which are increasingly occupied by the monopolies, to the neglect of expenditures on the reproduction of labour. In short, the effect of the state's urban policy is the 'segregative distribution of the general conditions of production' (Lojkine, 1977d, p. 258).

These are the main features of Lojkine's analysis of urban planning. Although this analysis contains the useful distinction between the three dimensions of urban planning it nevertheless remains underdeveloped and excludes some important aspects of urban planning. Three aspects in particular should be noted.

The first is that urban plans have a double purpose: they not only provide the framework for state expenditure in particular areas (as Lojkine correctly points out), but they also provide a set of guidelines through which the planning authority regulates private property development. These guidelines are then enforced by the planning authority through the process of development control. Lojkine's analysis contains no reference to development control and hence excludes an important area of interaction between the state and the private sector and hence, in turn, excludes the possibility of revealing the constraints which private property developers as well as landowners impose upon the state and vice versa.

The second aspect of urban planning which is absent in Lojkine's analysis is the process by which plans are actually produced. Plans are produced by officers and politicians of the state (whose interests may frequently be in conflict) and it is through these individuals that the constraints and conflicts engendered in a capitalist society must be interpreted and reflected in the plan. Lojkine's analysis contains no reference to the way in which plans are made and hence to the process by which class conflicts are reflected in the state.

The third aspect of Lojkine's analysis which remains weak is his treatment of the effects of the state's urban policy. Throughout this part of his analysis Lojkine nowhere takes into account the elementary fact that all state expenditure is ultimately financed from taxes on wages, profits and rents, so that a completely accurate account of the effects of the state's urban policy in a particular locality must be based upon a comparison of the distribution of taxes between the different classes, with the distribution of the subventions which they receive back from the state through urban planning. Moreover, if such a comparison were made it may well reveal that not all non-monopoly groups (that is, medium and small firms as well as professional, artisanal and manual workers) are equally affected by the state's urban policy as Lojkine in fact maintains.

These are some of the main deficiencies of Lojkine's analysis of urban planning. An attempt will be made below (in Chapter 8) to bring these considerations together into a more coherent and plausible framework for the analysis of the state's urban policy.

It is now necessary to consider Lojkine's analysis of urban social movements.

7.5 SOCIAL MOVEMENTS

Lojkine's analysis of social movements (see notably Lojkine, 1977a, pp. 312–41) is essentially concerned with clarifying the main elements which make up a social movement, and with exploring the possibility for the emergence of a 'new type of social movement' (Lojkine, 1977b, p. 153; 1977a, pp. 334ff). He defines a social movement as a mobilisation of the dominated class for the purpose of making a number of demands on the dominant class, thereby challenging their power and, possibly, overthrowing it. This definition is implicit in a number of statements made by Lojkine:

'the social movement only has significance by its capacity to oppose the dominant class and all of its hegemonic system' (Lojkine, 1977a, p. 313).

'the real historical influence of a social movement can only be defined by the analysis of its relationship to political power' (ibid., p. 320).

'the social movement is defined, in the last resort, by the capacity to change the socio-economic system in which it is born' (ibid.).

These quotations indicate that, for Lojkine, a social movement is more than just a protest or a reform movement. It is a movement with radical intent which may 'open the road to socialism' (ibid., p. 316) and may ultimately bring about a socialist revolution. As an example of a successful social movement Lojkine cites the case of the Russian Revolution of April and October 1917 (ibid., pp. 316ff). As examples of unsuccessful social movements he cites the case of 'the French social movements of 1848, 1871 and 1968' (ibid., p. 321).

Lojkine then proceeds to analyse in greater detail the basic elements of a social movement. He argues that a social movement is 'the combination of two social processes' (ibid., p. 318). These two processes or 'dimensions' (ibid., p. 319) are:

1. class mobilisation, and
2. the political stake (ibid., pp. 318–19).

Lojkine's discussion of each of these processes will now be examined. As regards the first dimension, he states that class mobilisation consists of two elements:

(a) the social base, and
(b) the organisation.

Together these form the 'social force' (ibid., p. 318). It follows from this that the extent to which a social force can be mobilised is crucially dependent on the nature of both the social base and the organisation. Lojkine points out that a social base can vary according to its size and according to its heterogeneity. It can be either large or small in size and homogeneous or heterogeneous in class composition. The social movement which led to the Russian Revolution of 1917 was, according to Lojkine, clearly a case where the social base was large in size and heterogeneous in class composition (though this is not the only possible combination for mobilising a social force). In addition, a social base can be spread over areas of different size (national, regional, urban or local) and this too can affect the mobilisation of a social force.

Lojkine makes two important points about organisations. The first is that a social movement does not occur 'spontaneously' (ibid., p. 321). It requires an organisation. The second point is that organisations can vary both with respect to their 'degree of openness' (ibid., p. 318) and according to whether they exist at a national, regional, urban or local level.

Lojkine attributes particular significance to the spatial aspect (that is, national, regional, urban, local) in the mobilisation of a social force. He argues that a national, as distinct from a regional, urban or local social movement, implies 'a different relationship to the power of the state insofar as the latter relies, in the last instance, on the capacity of the dominant class to maintain the 'national' cohesion of the whole of the social formation' (ibid., p. 319). Lojkine goes further and argues that only a national social movement is capable of attacking the political power of the dominant class (ibid.).

As regards the second dimension (that is, the political stake) Lojkine states that a social movement is crucially dependent on its 'political stake' (ibid., p. 319). The precise nature of the political stake involved in any social movement can only be ascertained through an analysis of the ideological and political content of both its claims and its actions. It is, according to Lojkine, only after the precise nature of the political stake has been established, that it is possible to assess the capacity of a social movement to actually challenge the political power of the dominant class (ibid., p. 320).

As with the first dimension, the spatial aspect is also important here. According to Lojkine, only a political stake which is national in its import has the possibility of being truly revolutionary, that is, of posing a challenge to the central, national, political power of the dominant class. Moreover, even if, in the case of a given social movement, the mobilisation of the social force is limited to a regional, urban or local level, but it has a national political stake, it could still be a revolutionary movement.

Both Lojkine and Castells share the belief that a social movement must be radical in intent and pose a challenge to the dominant class in the society. For Castells an urban protest can only be successful if it is fused with other movements (see section 6.6.2) whereas, for Lojkine, a social movement can only have a chance of success if it is not limited solely to an 'urban' issue. Thus Lojkine's position is virtually identical to that of Castells (despite Lojkine's protests to the contrary; ibid., pp. 322–5). Neither regard a local struggle over an item of collective consumption as having any potential for radical or revolutionary change, and both regard them, therefore, as politically and analytically insignificant.

Lojkine, finally and briefly, refers to 'a new type of social movement' (Lojkine, 1977b, p. 153; 1977a, pp. 334 ff) which is likely to emerge in France in the near future. He writes: 'French urban social movements have until recently been characterized by a total separation between the economic demands fought for by the working class within the work place (higher wages and the slowing down of speeds) and the 'social' demands linked to the reproduction of labour power (housing, transport, health, cultural facilities, and so on). The new feature of the 1970s is, on the contrary, a strongly expressed desire by the labour movement to make a close link between demands within the workplace and those related to the 'environment' (Lojkine, 1977b, pp. 153–5; 1977e, p. 23).

The distinctive feature of this new type of social movement, according to Lojkine, is that a number of different demands are brought together and made part of the same movement. As an example of this he cites the case of a strike which occurred in Turin in July 1969 (Lojkine, 1977a, pp. 335–6). This strike was organised by the trade unions and by political parties of the left to protest against the increase in rents and in the cost of living. In other words, a number of different demands were linked together in this movement. Social movements of this type have not yet occurred in France, according to Lojkine, with the possible exception of a strike which took place at the Rateau factory in La Courneuve, Paris, between February and April 1974.

These are the main features of Lojkine's analysis of social movements. It is similar, in many respects, to Castells's analysis (see section 6.6) so that many of the comments made in that context apply equally here. In particular, both are primarily interested in those protest actions which are radical and revolutionary in both intent and effect. However, as has been argued above in the case of Castells, this would seem to be unwise since many of the protest actions which occur in urban areas are undertaken by purely local groups (such as residents associations, tenants associations, environmental lobbies, and so on) and are concerned with purely local issues (such as schools, public transport, crime, noise, and so on). Many of these protest actions are not radical either in intent or effect yet, as is argued in Chapter 8, they are an important feature of the consumption process in urban areas. Thus Lojkine's exclusion of such protest actions, whatever its political justification, would seem to be an error.

The most important and insightful part of Lojkine's analysis is the spatial dimension. He recognises that a social base, an organisation, and an issue, have a spatial dimension in the sense that they can vary spatially from a national to a local level and this fact is of central importance in understanding not only the level of mobilisation of a social force but also the potential impact of the movement. In this respect, Lojkine's analysis is superior to that of Castells.

Lojkine's analysis concludes in the sanguine belief that a new type of social movement is emerging in the 1970s in France and elsewhere, and is likely to become even more important in the future. While this is clearly a possibility, it may not be as inevitable as Lojkine believes, essentially because neighbourhood and locality-based interests (that is, those concerned with the issues of collective consumption) do not always nor necessarily coincide with work-based interests (that is, those concerned with issues of pay, conditions of work, and so on). Thus Lojkine's new type of social movement is only likely to emerge when, *ceteris paribus*, there is a coincidence between these two sets of interests.

It is now necessary to examine how Lojkine applies the conceptual framework outlined in the preceding sections to his empirical research.

7.6 EMPIRICAL RESEARCH

7.6.1 Introduction

Lojkine has undertaken two major pieces of research: one on urban development in Paris (Lojkine, 1972a and 1974c; 1976b) and one on urban development in Lyon (Lojkine 1974a). More recently he has been undertaking research on the political aspects of urban development in Lille, the preliminary results of which are now becoming available (Lojkine, 1980, 1981b). The present section will be confined to an examination of his research in Paris and Lyon since these constitute the main corpus of his research work.

7.6.2 Research on Urban Policy in Paris in the Period 1945–72

Lojkine's study of Paris was first published in 1972 and is an attempt to reveal 'the real sociological content' (Lojkine, 1972a, p. 12) of the changes which have been occurring in the Paris region over the past few decades. These changes effectively involve the 'deindustrialization' (ibid., p. 15) of the city and its transformation into a major 'tertiary centre' (ibid., p. 12); they also involve, in addition, a growing separation and 'segregation' (ibid., p. 41) of places of work from places of residence, with consequent problems for commuters, given the inadequate transport system. Lojkine's book is essentially an attempt to describe, in broad outline, the processes which underlie these changes.

The book is divided into three chapters. The first chapter (pp. 15–81) provides a general account of the major economic changes which have been occurring in Paris since 1945. These changes are described, first, in terms of the way in which they affect the 'dominant class' and second, in terms of the way in which they affect the 'dominated class'. The second chapter (pp. 83–186) attempts to discover the role which the planning authorities have played in relation to these economic changes, with particular reference to the spatial dimension. Finally, in the third chapter (pp. 187–261), Lojkine examines a number of specific examples of urban planning which, he argues, are particularly revealing of the nature of state activity. Each of these chapters will now be briefly summarised and assessed.

The first chapter of Lojkine's book begins by looking at the relationship of the dominant class to the deindustrialisation of Paris. Lojkine notes that deindustrialisation began in the 1930s and increased rapidly after the end of the Second World War (though the actual evidence for this is only sourced and not presented (Lojkine, 1972a, p. 15, fn 1). This process effectively involved the removal of many industrial installations from Paris to either the suburbs or the provinces and their replacement by offices which tended to locate to the west of the traditional centre of Paris (for example, La Defense). These offices are usually the headquarters of large firms or centres for research and development and these, in turn, have attracted luxury shops, hotels and houses.

The main thrust of Lojkine's argument is that the deindustrialisation of Paris cannot be explained as the outcome of either technological change (ibid., p. 16) or urban planning (ibid., pp. 18–19). The explanation lies rather in the way in which different firms have responded to the changing conditions of profitability of the centre of Paris *vis-à-vis* its suburbs and the provinces. According to Lojkine, large industrial firms (such as Renault and Simca) have transferred their various plants from the centre of Paris and concentrated them in the suburbs or the provinces because this strategy offers them a number of advantages:

cheaper suburban sites with proximity to the Paris labour and consumer markets;
avoidance of the high costs of land and congestion in Paris;
a cheaper and more docile labour force;
a reduction in the costs associated with dispersal by concentrating different production units on one suburban or provincial site (ibid., p. 17).

In contrast to these large industrial enterprises, for whom relocation and spatial concentration outside Paris are rational and beneficial courses of action, medium and small firms have largely been unable to follow and relocate outside Paris because:

unlike larger industrial firms (which frequently do not require a highly skilled labour force), medium and small firms frequently depend on a highly skilled labour force which is not obtainable outside the centre of Paris;
the costs of moving are often prohibitive;
the grants system for relocating favours the larger rather than the smaller firms (since the grant is proportional to the number of jobs created);
they frequently do not have access to new finance (ibid., p. 20).

These factors, together with the fact that many of these medium and small firms are unable to afford the currently expensive sites in the centre of Paris, has had the consequence that many such firms are disappearing through voluntary liquidaton or bankruptcy (ibid., p. 20).

Thus the relocation and expansion of large firms coupled with the disappearance of many medium and small firms suggests the more general conclusion that there is, as Lojkine puts it, 'a close correlation between the movement of economic concentration and industrial decentralization' (ibid., p. 20).

Turning to the 'dominated classes' (who include all wage-earners, shop-keepers, artisans, and so on), the main consequence of the twin processes of deindustrialisation and tertiarisation is that there is now, within the Paris region, 'a growing spatial disequilibrium between place of work and place of residence' (ibid., p. 41). This disequilibrium, which Lojkine usually refers to as 'urban segregation' (ibid.), expresses itself in the fact that the centre and neighbouring suburbs of Paris are increasingly becoming places of employment while residential areas are being pushed further towards the urban periphery. The major consequence of this is that many workers are required to undergo long, twice-daily commuting journeys to work. Lojkine cites evidence (ibid., pp. 46–7) which confirms that the daily movement of commuters between Paris and its suburbs is continuing to grow apace as is inter-suburban commuting. The consequence of this, in combination with the inadequate financing of public transport generally, is that the time and the discomfort of travelling to work have increased considerably in recent years (ibid., pp. 48–9).

In the second chapter of his book, Lojkine examines various urban planning policies (particularly those relating to housing and public transport) which have been pursued between 1945 and 1971, of which, he claims, the main effect has been urban social segregation. Lojkine provides a particularly long discussion of public transport policies (ibid., pp. 100–135; see also 1974b) the essence of which is that the public transport system 'reinforces' (Lojkine, 1972a, p. 121) and 'accentuates' (ibid., p. 92) segregation: it reinforces segregation because the rail network is 'radiocentric' (ibid., p. 103) in design and, as such, facilitates long commuting journeys between the centre and the periphery of the Paris region at the expense of inter-suburban journeys; it accentuates segregation because the transport system is underfinanced (as a result of attempting to run it according to the principles of the free market) so that commuting journeys take longer and are more uncomfortable than they might otherwise be.

In Chapter 2 Lojkine also discusses three aspects of urban policies over which there has been some controversy within the state itself (ibid., pp. 135–86). The first controversial issue was whether the growth of Paris should be curtailed or whether it should be allowed to expand. Lojkine traces the various 'oscillations' (ibid., p. 141) between these two planning objectives, from the Third Republic (1870–1940) through various planning documents notably PADOG (1960),[3] SDAU (1965) (1969)[4] and the preparatory documents for the Sixth National Plan (1971–5). However Lojkine concludes that this controversy is 'above all ideological' (Lojkine 1972a, p. 146), essentially because the actual course of events in such matters as housing, employment, the location of new offices, the relocation of manufacturing industries, indicates that the growth of the Paris region (defined according to ZEAT),[5] far from being curtailed, has in fact grown more rapidly than France as a whole over the past 20 years.

The second controversial issue was whether the redevelopment and expansion of the business and commercial centre of Paris should proceed westwards, or whether it should be concentrated in the centre and east of Paris. The former approach was crystallised in PADOG (1960) in its proposal to continue the development of La Defense (to the north-west of Paris) as the locus of new office expansion (Lojkine, 1972c, p. 149); the latter approach was advocated by the Commissariat au Plan[6] and by SDAU (1965) who advocated the redevelopment of the centre and east of Paris and a cessation of the development at La Defense (ibid., pp. 149–50). The actual course of events, as measured by building and planning approvals for offices (ibid., pp. 153–8), reveals that the development at La Defense, and in the western sector generally, continued apace, which effectively proves, according to Lojkine, that the state endorses the dominant tendencies of the Paris property and office market and thereby acts 'as a means for systematizing segregation rather than as a means of suppressing it' (ibid., p. 166).

The third and final area of debate has been the mode of financing urban public transport. The main debate has been between those (notably the Ministry of Finance) who argue that it should be financed by levying the appropriate and commercially-determined fares on the users/workers (ibid., p. 183), against those (virtually all of the planning agencies) who argue that it should be financed, in part at least, by a tax on employers and property developers. In the event, it is the former option, which Lojkine describes as 'Malthusian and liberal' (ibid., p. 181), which has largely prevailed 'since 1945 even 1930' (ibid., p. 183).

The third chapter of Lojkine's book is an attempt to show how the actions of the state, particularly as expressed through various planning agencies and policies, can be understood in one of three ways: as the organisation of the hegemony of the dominant class; as the active reflection of the class struggle; as the maintenance of the cohesion of a social formation. An example of each of these three aspects of state activity will now be examined to reveal the tenor and content of this chapter.

Lojkine cites the example of the planning and development of the office complex at La Defense (of 1.6 million^2 of office space) as an example of how the state organises the hegemony of the dominant class. The idea for the development of an office complex at La Defense was effectively initiated by the state with the setting up, in 1958, of The Public Institution for the Development of La Defense (l'Etablissement Public Chargé de l'Amenagement de la Defense). At the time, this appeared 'perfectly strange' (ibid., p. 214) to the majority of large firms who have since located there, essentially because it was not until the late 1960s that the demand for office space actually began to grow rapidly (ibid., p. 219). In the light of subsequent events which have seen the transformation of La Defense into a vibrant centre for the headquarters of many large multinational firms, the actions of the state in this regard can be seen as a perfect example of 'anticipation' (ibid., p. 218) of the future needs of the dominant class and, in this sense, Lojkine regards the state as the organiser of the interests and hegemony of the dominant class.

Lojkine then cites a number of different examples to show how urban planning is also a reflection (an 'active reflection'; ibid., p. 247) of the class struggle. These examples (such as the extension of certain metro lines, the postponement of certain fare increases on public transport, the decentralisation of some office employment) are designed to show that the actions of the state can also be a response to pressure from the dominated class. Indeed Lojkine affirms that all of these measures 'directly reflect the pressure of those social classes who are victims of urban segregation' (ibid., p. 239). Lojkine does not, in fact, substantiate this claim with any evidence: there is no evidence of any protest or social movement in relation to any of these issues, nor indeed is there any indication that the state's actions were an anticipated response to such protest movements. There is, nevertheless, a more general and valid point which is implicit in Lojkine's analysis, which is that the state can (and does) respond to demands and pressures from the working/wage-earning class, without significantly altering the capitalist system of production, as long as these concessions do not seriously undermine productivity and economic growth. Finally, Lojkine gives an example of how the state, through its planning agencies, can take measures which seem to be governed above all by a concern with maintaining the cohesion of capitalist society. Lojkine's example is the project for the development of a 'Cité Financière' (ibid., pp. 199–211) in the centre of Paris (Opéra-Saint-Lazare-Chateaudun) which would rival Wall Street in New York and 'The City' in London. This project was strongly advocated by the banking and insurance industry but was strongly opposed by many of the relevant planning agencies, notably DATAR,[7] who regarded it as a measure which would further concentrate population and employment in Paris at the expense of the provinces. Writing in 1972, Lojkine argued that, in this case, the logic of the planning agencies was directly opposed, and in contradiction, to the logic of the banking and insurance industry; and on this basis he concluded that it was 'impossible to explain' (ibid., p. 209) the state's activity in relation to this project without reference to the cohesive role and function of the state. In a subsequent article, Lojkine (1974c) has examined the project more thoroughly in the knowledge that the project has gone ahead albeit with a decentralisation of a wide-range of banking and insurance activities. His interpretation in this article is that the contradiction between the banking and insurance industry and the planning agencies is in fact only apparent. This is because the revolution in information technology (notably through computers) has made it possible to have a high degree of decentralisation of 'technico-administrative functions' (ibid., p. 128) in the provinces headed by one large centre in the 'Cité Financière' in Paris for the purpose of making and implementing investment decisions in the various equity, gilt, and property markets. Lojkine's later analysis (1974c) is a considerable improvement on his earlier analysis (1972a), both in terms of its approach (that is, comparing the optimal strategy open to the banking and insurance industry, in the light of recent technical innovations, with the planning strategies of the various state agencies) and in terms of the richness of the data. As such, his 1974 interpretation of the events surrounding the 'Cité Financière' project would seem to be more accurate than that suggested in 1972.

Lojkine's book, as the preceding synopsis reveals, contains a very considerable amount of information and analysis on urban planning and development in the Paris region. It is one of the first research monographs which has attempted to examine urban planning and development from a Marxist perspective. According to one French reviewer, it is also the 'first study' (Lautman, 1974, p. 274) of the development of Paris as a whole in the post-war era. The research is based largely on an analysis of planning documents, official reports, and on a number of interviews, though Lojkine gives no information about the number or nature of those interviews (see Lojkine, 1972a, pp. 37, 207, 208). The research is unavoidably incomplete in the sense that a number of important projects (notably the one million square metres of office space at Bercy in the east of Paris) were unfinished at the time of writing.

Because of the wide-ranging nature of Lojkine's project, it is inevitable that some issues are dealt with in insufficient detail or precision. This is particularly the case with Lojkine's concept of class, which divides the entire class system into two groups: the dominant and the dominated, reflecting Lojkine's abiding belief that the central cleavage in the contemporary phase of capitalist development is between monopoly and non-monopoly groups (see section 5.2). While Lojkine does not make some attempt in Chapter 1 to differentiate between the different fractions of the dominant class (largely in terms of size: large, medium, small), he makes no attempt to differentiate between the different fractions of the dominated class which includes all wage-earners, artisans, shopkeepers, and so on. While the evidence from Lojkine's research does reveal that all of the members of this class have suffered the segregative effects of urban planning and development in Paris, it is unlikely that they have all been affected uniformly. The fact that there does not appear to have been any concerted action by them in the form of an urban social movement might be taken as indicative of this.

In terms of the over-all corpus of Lojkine's work, this book reveals that a basic division exists between much of Lojkine's theoretical work and his actual research. Lojkine's book, while providing a broad Marxist account of 25 years of planning and development in Paris, does not deal with those issues which are actually central to his theoretical writings and which are so much in need of empirical research. This is particularly the case with his analysis of collective consumption and his analysis of rent. As has been seen (subsection 7.3.3), Lojkine claims that state expenditure on collective consumption has the effect of reinforcing the fall in the rate of profit. This claim is elaborated at some length, and was first published in the same year as the present study (1972), yet no attempt is made to subject it to the test of empirical evidence. Similarly, with the concept of rent (subsection 7.3.5), which was first published in 1971, but which receives no attention in this study despite its centrality to the change in land use which has been occurring in Paris over the past 25 years. This division between theoretical and empirical research (which is also to be found in Castells – see notably section 6.7) may be the cause of many of the errors which were identified in Lojkine's theoretical analysis (sections 7.1 to 7.5) and is one of the basic weaknesses, not only of this research,[8] but of his entire work.

7.6.3 Research on Urban Policy in Lyon in the Period 1945–72

Lojkine's study of Lyon was carried out between 1970 and 1972 with the collaboration of two other researchers (Françoise Orlic and Catherine Skoda) and was published in 1974 (Lojkine, 1974a). Lyon, with a population of just over 1 million in 1976 (see House, 1978, p. 142), is the second largest city in France (though still nine times smaller than the largest, Paris), and Lojkine attempts to 'preserve the parallelism' (Lojkine, 1974a, p. 31) between this study and his previous study of Paris (see subsection 7.6.2) by confining both studies to the same historical period (1945–72), and also by attempting to analyse urban planning and development in both cities in terms of its consequences for different classes and class fractions.

Like his previous study of Paris, Lojkine's study of Lyon is based upon documentary research. This research draws upon a variety of materials: planning documents, research reports, reports of parliamentary debates and a variety of books, newspapers and magazines. Lojkine, however, does not discuss any of the methodological issues which arose from the use of these data sources.

Lojkine's book is divided into three chapters. The first chapter (27 pages) is a brief analysis of the expenditure by the various agencies of the state on the city of Lyon. The second chapter (75 pages) examines commercial capital, banking capital and industrial capital respectively, and the way in which each of these class fractions have been changing in recent years. The third chapter (48 pages) is concerned with the working class and with the way in which it has been affected by recent urban plans and policies. Each of these chapters will now be briefly summarised and assessed.

In the first chapter (ibid., pp. 29–56) Lojkine identifies four different state bodies, each of which makes a contribution to the total expenditure of the state in Lyon. These state bodies (listed according to their sphere of power and influence) are:

The City of Lyon (Ville de Lyon);
The General Council of the Rhône (Conseil General du Rhône);
The Urban Community of Lyon (La Communauté Urbaine de Lyon);
The National Government.

Lojkine discusses the expenditure of each of these four state bodies with particular reference to their expenditure on public transport and housing.

Beginning with the City of Lyon, Lojkine highlights three sets of facts about the pattern of expenditure of this body. The first is that expenditure (and the borrowing necessary to finance it) rose particularly rapidly after 1960 (ibid., p. 32). The second fact is that expenditure on public transport is inadequate. This is evidenced, according to Lojkine, by the fact that there has been a deficit on the running of the public transport service since 1963 (ibid., p. 35) and also by the fact that, in 1967, the public transport network only covered an area of 150km^2 while the size of the Lyon agglomeration is 2000km^2 (ibid., p. 37). Unfortunately, Lojkine does not indicate the actual amount or the proportion of the total budget which was devoted to public transport except to state that, since 1961, it was 'even less' (ibid., p. 34) than that spent on HLM housing – which, on the basis of data subsequently presented on page 43, means that it was below 6 per cent of the total expenditure.

The third set of facts relate to expenditure by the City of Lyon on housing. The basic data are that, in the period 1953–61, annual expenditure on housing averaged 10 per cent, but was considerably below this in the preceding and succeeding periods and in 1970 it was only 1 per cent of total expenditure (though there does appear to be a discrepancy between the two different figures which Lojkine gives for the total expenditure in 1970; see Lojkine, 1974a, pp. 32, 43). Lojkine makes no comment on the underlying causes of this fluctuating pattern of expenditure.

Turning to the expenditure of the General Council of the Rhône, Lojkine notes that 65 per cent of this expenditure was devoted to 'social aid' (ibid., p. 45), (that is, education, training, health, social action, sporting, cultural and administrative facilities), while most of the remainder was devoted to roads and airports. As a result, very little of its expenditure was devoted to public transport or housing.

Lojkine then discusses the expenditure pattern of the Urban Community of Lyon and states that this gives priority to roads and education but not to public transport or housing (ibid., p. 50). Unfortunately, Lojkine provides no data giving an itemised breakdown of this expenditure.

Finally, in Chapter 1, Lojkine briefly examines national state expenditure in Lyon and concludes that this expenditure is primarily directed at infrastructural development. In other words it is primarily directed at the means of communication (roads, motorways, airports) rather than the means of collective consumption (ibid., p. 56).

Lojkine's analysis in Chapter 1 leaves little doubt that public transport and housing receive a small share of total state expenditure. While the data is not always complete, nor always presented in the most systematic manner, this central point still forcefully emerges. However, it should be emphasised that this is the only solid fact to emerge from the first chapter. This chapter is certainly not a comprehensive analysis of state expenditure in Lyon (as its title suggests), nor indeed a comprehensive analysis of state expenditure on public transport and housing in Lyon.

In Chapter 2 (ibid., pp. 61–137) Lojkine discusses the position of the different fractions of capital in Lyon (commercial capital, banking capital, industrial capital) and the way in which they have been changing in recent years.

The first class fraction to be discussed is commercial capital. In this section (ibid., pp. 61–82) Lojkine puts forward the view that, in the Lyon region, the commercial class is undergoing 'the classical process of centralization and concentration of capital' (ibid., p. 71). This, in effect, means that small shopkeepers are being replaced by larger more monopolistic commercial enterprises. The evidence presented in this study (Lojkine, 1974a, pp. 67–71) and elsewhere (Lojkine, 1972b, pp. 159–61) strongly supports this interpretation.

Lojkine then examines banking capital and the relationship between 'urban policy and banking capital in the Lyon region' (ibid., p. 83). This section (ibid., pp. 83–97) describes the efforts of the central, regional and urban state authorities to create, in the Part-Dieu area of Lyon, a commercial and financial centre of major national and international importance. Lojkine's main argument is that at least one aspect of this policy is doomed to failure in the sense that Lyon can never become a major national or international centre for finance. This is so for three reasons. The first is that, in Lyon, most of the insurance companies (notably the Union des Assurances de Paris) and the banking groups (notably Credit Lyonnais and Banque Nationale de Paris) are subsidiaries of companies which are controlled from Paris. The second reason is that most of these groups and companies are currently reorganising to take advantage of the revolution in information technology associated with the computer and the microchip. This reorganisation has taken the form of separating purely routine administrative activities (such as compiling and issuing bank statements, processing claims, and so on) from purely commercial activities (which involve dealing directly with clients) and, in turn, the separation of these two functions from those of control and decision-making. This reorganisation has resulted in a highly-decentralised commercial and administrative operation while at the same time it is highly centralised and controlled from Paris. The third reason is that Paris is likely to remain the major control and decision-making centre in the French financial world because 'the major means of communication and exchange are to be found in Paris and in Paris only' (ibid., p. 97). For these reasons, according to Lojkine, Lyon is unlikely to supplant the traditional supremacy of Paris in the financial world.

The final section of Chapter 2 is concerned with industrial capital. The major fact which Lojkine highlights here, is that large monopolistic firms are either supplanting small and medium-sized firms (particularly in the civil engineering field – see Lojkine, 1974a, pp. 126–7) or absorbing them through mergers (as with the merger between Berliet and Michelin-Citroen – see ibid., pp. 134–6) or through employing them as sub-contractors (ibid., pp. 102, 132). This growing dominance of large monopolistic firms is, in turn, reflected in the urban and regional plans of the state which is currently (that is, since 1970 – see ibid., p. 118) making huge investments in order to provide and service large industrial estates (over 1000 hectares in size) to attract multinational monopolistic firms. Lojkine describes this 'subordination of regional political power to large industrial capital' (ibid., p. 122) as 'a new phenomenon in France' (ibid.) and is to be found not only in Lyon (where those in political power are described as 'overtly of the right or camouflaged under centrist labels' (ibid., p. 113) but throughout the entire area of the 'Grand Delta' which has become 'a pole of interest for monopolistic groups' (ibid., p. 119).

Despite the radical differences in the economic interests of small and medium industrial capital on the one hand, and monopoly capital on the other, the Lyon Chamber of Industry and Commerce manages to maintain a 'political alliance' (ibid., p. 133) between them. This is exemplified, according to Lojkine, by Satolas airport which was supported by the Chamber even though it appears to be in the interests of small and medium, rather than of monopoly, capital (ibid., pp. 130–33).

In Chapter 3 (ibid., pp. 137–84) Lojkine looks at the relationship of urban planning and policy to the working class. His discussion centres around housing, education and public transport.

As regards housing, Lojkine points out that the strongest spatial concentration of the working class is in the East and North of Lyon since this is where there is the highest concentration of HLMs and *grands ensembles*. These *grands ensembles* are located at the urban periphery and many of them were built since 1960 to rehouse those (that is, the traditional working class, but also artisans, shopkeepers and small industrialists) who were 'deported' (ibid., p. 161) from the centre of Lyon as a result of urban 'renewal' (ibid.) there.

One of the main reasons why working-class housing tends to be located at the periphery rather than the centre is that the City of Lyon leases its city centre land (which would be suitable for HLMs) to developers who build offices and commercial premises on it. Lojkine adds that the 70-year leasing arrangements granted by the City of Lyon allow the capitalist tenant to appropriate differential rent I and II and the City of Lyon to appropriate absolute rent (ibid, p. 142). Lojkine states that this is only a 'hypothesis' (ibid.) which could nevertheless be 'demonstrated' (ibid.) by comparing the value of the absolute rent with the value of differential rent I and II.

Turning to education, Lojkine points out that there is a very unequal spatial distribution of educational facilities in Lyon since they are much more heavily concentrated in the centre than in the suburbs (ibid., p. 164). However, he does not show that this unequal spatial distribution of educational facilities has an independent effect on access to, and success in, education so that this aspect of his analysis remains incomplete.

As regards public transport, Lojkine argues that the basis of the problem in Lyon is that public transport is governed and operated by what he variously terms 'the same old logic of capitalist profit' (ibid., p. 169), 'the narrowly commercial optic' (ibid., p. 167), and 'the good old marginalist logic' (ibid., p. 169). This policy, according to Lojkine, is erroneous, because public transport is inherently unprofitable (though the precise reasons for its unprofitability are not given). The adverse consequences of the public transport policies in Lyon are that buses are overcrowded; travel to the centre of Lyon from certain suburban areas can require two buses; in certain suburban areas, bus stops can only be reached after a walk of 15 minutes; there is, in certain cases, a lack of synchronisation between some buses and trains (ibid., pp. 166–7).

Lojkine also discusses and disputes the 1966 Waldman report on the metro system in Lyon (ibid., pp. 171ff). However, it is impossible to assess this section of Lojkine's analysis since the various pieces of data which are crucial to the debate do not appear to be strictly comparable and, moreover, there is no detailed map showing the location of the various places cited in the discussion.

These are the main themes of Lojkine's study of Lyon. It is a descriptive and informative study of some of the more recent developments in that city, particularly those which have occurred since the 1960s. Although the title of the book states that it covers the period 1945–72, this is somewhat misleading since most of the data postdates 1960. However, even in this reduced time-span Lojkine's book covers a wide gamut of topics – from state expenditure on housing and education to developments in the world of banking and insurance. It is this breadth of scope which is probably the main weakness of the book since it contains a relatively small amount of data upon each of the various topics. In fact, it is less rich in empirical detail than the companion volume on Paris (see subsection 7.6.2). For this reason Lojkine's study of Lyon is more a preliminary investigation than a definitive study.

Another feature of this study is that most of the major issues which are raised in Lojkine's conceptual analysis (see sections 7.0 to 7.5) do not appear here. The one exception to this is the concept of rent which is briefly alluded to, although Lojkine treats it in a very confused manner. He claims that the tenants of land in the centre of Lyon (that is, the banks and insurance companies) are able to appropriate differential rent I and II while the landowner (that is, the municipal authority of Lyon) is able to appropriate absolute rent. This claim is confused for three reasons. First, tenants cannot appropriate differential rent I; they can only appropriate differential rent II (see section 3.2). Secondly, the possibility of the City of Lyon appropriating absolute rent would require that it is the sole owner of all city centre land or that it acts in collusion with other landowners to raise land prices (see section 3.3). Thirdly, the amount and type of rent appropriated by the landowner and tenant in this case could only be established according to the method outlined above (see section 3.5), and not by comparing the size of the different rental components, as Lojkine suggests.

In summary, Lojkine's book is a useful and informative investigation of various developments in the City of Lyon since the 1960s. However, it is very preliminary in nature, not only because of the paucity of data on each topic, but also because many of the issues in Lojkine's conceptual analysis are not treated here or are treated in a rather confused manner. In short, too little data is spread over too wide a geographical, historical and conceptual area.

7.6.4 Conclusion

The central theme running through Lojkine's two major pieces of research is that the effect of urban development and redevelopment in Paris and Lyon is to advance the interests of the monopolies against all non-monopoly groups. The state presides over and facilitates this process, thus 'confirming' the thesis of state monopoly capitalism that the state protects and advances the dominance of the monopolies in the current phase of capitalism. As has been seen, Lojkine presents some evidence to support this thesis, though it is considerably less univocal than his conclusions suggest. This suggests a more general difficulty with Lojkine's research: that it is too broad in scope to allow detailed empirical analysis of one particular issue.

In his more recent researches on urban development in Lille, Lojkine has shifted his focus decisively to local politics, and is retrospectively critical of his failure, particularly in the study of Lyon, to identify the links between the economic effects of urban development on different class fractions and the political consequences of those effects (see Lojkine, 1980; 1981b, pp. 93–4). This new self-criticism may mean that Lojkine's subsequent research will be free from some of the blemishes that have been identified in this section.

7.7 CONCLUSION

It is now necessary to draw together the various findings which have emerged from the analysis in this chapter. These findings relate to both the conceptual and the empirical parts of Lojkine's work. The empirical part of Lojkine's work has just been analysed (in section 7.6) and it was found that his studies of Paris and Lyon are useful preliminary studies which, however, suffer from a lack of detail on many of the important topics. Moreover, there seemed to be a divorce between the themes covered in this research and the major issues in his conceptual analysis. For example, the effect of the collective means of consumption on the rate of profit, which is a central element in his conceptual analysis, is not even considered in his empirical research.

Lojkine's conceptual analysis not only defines the field of urban sociology but also outlines and analyses the main themes which, in his view, fall within that field: collective consumption and its financing; the locational behaviour of firms; urban land rent; urban planning and urban social movements. It is now necessary to summarise briefly the usefulness of Lojkine's analysis of these topics.

Lojkine defines an urban area as a spatial concentration of the general conditions of production (section 7.1). He then selects one of these conditions – the collective means of consumption – and claims that it is one of the most distinctive characteristics of urban areas within capitalism. In this way the collective means of consumption become one of the central themes of Lojkine's urban sociology (section 7.2).

Lojkine's definition of the field of urban sociology is somewhat narrow because it does not include all of the processes which take place within urban areas. As was argued earlier (section 7.1), urban areas are the locus of three major social processes: the process by which the urban area is produced through property development; the process by which it is used in the production of other commodities and the process by which it is used for final consumption. This definition of the field of urban sociology, which will be elaborated at length in the next part of this book (Part III, Chapter 8) shows that the field of urban sociology can be broader in scope, and richer in content, than that envisaged by Lojkine's definition.

The collective means of consumption are a central theme in Lojkine's writing although his analysis of them (section 7.2) was seen to contain a number of errors. Apart from the ambiguities surrounding his use of the word 'collective' (which was used in four different senses) his explanation of the 'unproductive' and 'unprofitable' nature of the collective means of consumption was shown to be faulty. In turn his analysis of the problems relating to the financing of urban expenditure is also untenable. The reason for this is that it relies upon Marx's law of the tendency for the rate of profit to fall which has been shown to be invalid (see section 2.1).

Lojkine's analysis of the locational behaviour of firms (subsection 7.3.3), is extremely brief and cursory and seemed to be uninformed by the literature in their field. Similarly, his analysis of rent (subsection 7.3) was based upon an inadequate and confused understanding of Marx's concept of rent and of the limitations of that concept.

In his analysis of urban planning (section 7.4) Lojkine is particularly anxious to show that the major effect of state intervention in this field is to advance the interest of the monopolies against the interest of all other non-monopoly groups. While considerable evidence is adduced to support this claim, Lojkine's apparent preoccupation with it led him to totally neglect a number of other important issues about urban planning such as the actual process by which plans are produced and the effect of the implementation of that plan, through development control, on private property development.

Lojkine has not yet carried out any empirical research on social movements although his conceptual analysis of this topic is both cogent and informative (section 7.5). In particular, his focus upon the spatial dimension of social movements highlights an important feature of these movements which is neglected in other work, such as Castells's.

These are the main findings to emerge from an examination of Lojkine's work. Most of the errors in that work can be traced directly to Lojkine's lack of a clear and rigorous understanding of Marxian political economy, and the latter's limitations, and to his lack of detailed knowledge of the processes underlying urban planning and development. For this reason his writing does not appear to be a significant contribution to Marxist urban sociology. As a result, the value of Lojkine's work, like that of Castells, lies essentially in its role as a catalyst for other work in this field leading, possibly, to the development of a more cogent analysis of urban areas. It is in this spirit that an attempt is made to develop a new approach to urban sociology in the next part of the book (Part III, Chapter 8).

Part III

An Alternative Approach to Marxist Urban Sociology

8 From Marxist to Post-Marxist Urban Sociology

8.0 INTRODUCTION

The purpose of this chapter is to make some innovations in the field of Marxist urban sociology. These innovations will attempt to avoid some of the difficulties which have been identified in the work of Manuel Castells and Jean Lojkine, while at the same time addressing many of the issues which are central to it.

The analysis begins with a synthesis of the results of the preceding chapters in order to provide a summary assessment of the work of Castells and Lojkine (section 8.1). In response to some of the problems identified in their work an alternative model will be outlined (section 8.2) and subsequently applied to the analysis of urban processes and conflicts (section 8.4 to 8.8).

8.1 THE MARXIST URBAN SOCIOLOGY OF MANUEL CASTELLS AND JEAN LOJKINE

8.1.1 Introduction

The writings of Castells and Lojkine represent a pioneering attempt to develop a Marxist urban sociology. It is now necessary to bring together the various strands of their work which have been examined in the two preceding chapters in order to provide a more summary and definitive assessment of it. This is essential before proceeding to examine the future developments in this field. To this end the central themes in the writings of Castells and Lojkine will be briefly summarised and assessed. These themes are: the definition of an urban area (subsection 8.1.2); collective consumption (subsection 8.1.3); urban planning (subsection 8.1.4) and urban movements (subsection 8.1.5).

8.1.2 The Definition of an Urban Area Contained in the Writings of Castells and Lojkine

Castells and Lojkine have two quite different definitions of an urban area. For Castells an urban area is an area of collective consumption (see subsection 6.2.2), whereas for Lojkine it is an area where there is a spatial concentration of the general conditions of production (see section 7.1).

Castells's definition is based upon his assumption that the urban area is distinguished as a unit by its 'everydayness', that is, the reproduction of labour power. Since reproduction, and hence consumption is, he argues, increasingly organised collectively, he infers that an urban area is a place of collective consumption – 'collective' being used as a synonym for 'state provision' (see Castells and Godard, 1974, pp. 228–9; Castells, 1976b, p. 295; 1977a, pp. 451, 460; 1977b, p. 64, 1978a, pp. 41–2); 1981b, pp. 8–9: 1983b, p. 9). In addition he claims that the boundary of an urban area is coterminous with the boundary of the job market and is fixed by commuting patterns (see Castells, 1977a, pp. 234–6; 1976h, pp. 180ff; Castells and Godard, 1974, pp. 174–92).

The main difficulty with Castells's definition is that it limits unnecessarily the range of issues which are considered to be 'urban' (see Harloe, 1977, p. 22; Pahl, 1977, p. 314; 1978; Pickvance, 1978, p. 175). Indeed the issue of consumption itself is considerably richer, both conceptually and empirically, than Castells's analysis suggests, as will be seen more fully in section 8.8. Moreover, the way in which the urban area is itself produced through property development, and the way in which it is used in the production of other commodities, are processes which are also neglected in Castells's framework (see section 8.4 to 8.7) although they would seem to be essential concerns to Marxist urban sociology.

Castells's definition is open to the further objection that the boundary of an urban area is not normally coterminous with the boundary of the job or labour market: labour market areas can be equal to, greater than, or less than, the boundary of an urban area, depending upon such factors as the skill level of the labour in each market (see subsection 8.7.2 below). Thus Castells's definition of an urban area is difficult to sustain.

Lojkine's definition of an urban area is much more comprehensive and convincing than that offered by Castells since it includes the main physical elements which are to be found in any urban area (that is, those things which are necessary for production and final consumption (see Lojkine, 1976a, pp. 120ff; 1977a, pp. 125ff). However, like Castells, Lojkine only considers those elements of an urban area which are either owned privately (for example, factories, offices, and so on) or by the state (for example, schools, hospitals, parks, and so on); neither of them consider the category of communal goods such as air, the visual environment, smoke, noise, congestion, and so on, which are also important elements in an urban area and which may be important sources of conflict within those areas (see subsection 8.8.6). In addition

Lojkine's analysis focuses upon the processes by which urban areas are used in capitalist production and in final consumption but neglects to consider the process by which the urban area is itself produced through property development (see section 7.1). Thus neither Castells nor Lojkine offers entirely satisfactory definitions of an urban area or of the field of urban sociology generally.

8.1.3 The Analysis of Collective Consumption in the Writings of Castells and Lojkine

Castells and Lojkine attempt to explain the role and function of collective consumption by using traditional Marxian concepts, most notably Marx's theory of crisis (see Chapter 2) and productive and unproductive labour (see Chapter 4). Although there are different emphases in both writers, the law of the falling rate of profit is central to the explanations of both. Both writers assume that the role and function of collective consumption must be related to the law of the falling rate of profit and, on this basis, Castells reaches the firm conclusion that the function of collective consumption is to 'counteract' the tendency for the rate of profit to fall (Castells, 1978a, p. 18; 1980a, pp. 51–2), 69–70; see also subsection 6.2.3) whereas Lojkine reaches an equally firm but opposite conclusion that the function of collective consumption is to 'strengthen the tendency for the rate of profit to fall' (Lojkine, 1976a, pp. 131–2; see also subsection 7.3.2). Since there is no firm evidence for either conclusion, because of the difficulty of measuring and testing Marx's law, neither claim is particularly useful. In both cases, however, there appears to be an implicit assumption that the effects of collective consumption in any capitalist country can be inferred from Marx's law of the falling rate of profit. This particular example illustrates in striking fashion how Castells and Lojkine tend to use Marxian concepts in a dogmatic and functionalist manner. Their usage tends to be dogmatic because they do not actually examine Marxian concepts to ensure that they are internally consistent or empirically accurate. (The analysis in section 2.1 reveals that this is particularly necessary in the case of Marx's law of the falling rate of profit.) Their usage also tends to be functionalist because they infer the effects of collective consumption by deduction from the functions which it is supposed to play within a capitalist society, given certain Marxian premises. The error in this procedure is that the 'function' of collective consumption can only be inferred from its effects and the latter in turn can only be established by empirical inquiry which, in this case, would be extremely difficult to undertake.

Castells also offers two additional explanations of the role and 'function' of collective consumption. He claims, on the one hand, that collective consumption alleviates the problem of deficiency of aggregate demand because 'the economy of advanced capitalist societies rests more and more on the process of consumption, i.e., the key problems are located at the level of the realization of surplus value' (Castells, 1976d, p. 294; 1976h, p. 182; 1977c, p. 63; 1981b, p. 8.). He also claims, on the other hand, that collective consumption is a response to the 'development of the class struggle and the growing power of the workers' movement that extends its bargaining power to all areas of societal life' (Castells, 1975a, p. 176; 1976h, p. 184). These are major and important, though unsubstantiated, claims about the nature of collective consumption, and the corroboration of either would involve a major research undertaking. In this, as in other contexts, Castells seems to be more concerned with defining the perspective, and setting the agenda for future research, rather than actually undertaking the research itself.

Lojkine too applies some additional Marxian concepts to clarify the nature of collective consumption. He points out that collective consumption is unprofitable (see subsection 7.2.4) as well as unproductive (see subsection 7.2.3). He explains that collective consumption is unprofitable to produce because investment in such things as houses, schools, universities, and hospitals 'lasts for many years' (Lojkine, 1977a, p. 138). As was seen above, the difficulty with this argument is that many profitable investments in the private sector, such as equipment for the extraction and refining of oil, the assembly of cars, the production of chemicals, and so on, also 'last for many years'. In addition, some forms of collective consumption are in fact produced profitably in the private sector in many capitalist countries (for example, private medicine and private education). These considerations would seem to indicate that, whatever the real reason for the unprofitability of collective consumption, it probably does not lie, like Lojkine claims, in the difficulties associated with the supply of these goods in a capitalist system.

Lojkine also claims that collective consumption is 'unproductive'. However, he does not seem to recognise that there are two quite different, and inconsistent, usages of the terms productive and unproductive in Marx's work (see Chapter 4). As a result, his claim is inherently ambiguous. In this, as in other cases (most notably in his discussion of rent – see subsection 7.3.4), Lojkine's analysis, like that of Castells, tends to be highly conjectural and speculative. Although both draw heavily upon concepts from Marx's political economy, neither gives serious consideration to the methodological problems involved in testing those concepts. As a result, the value of their analysis of collective consumption lies more in suggesting possible applications of Marxian political economy that in its rigorous application.

8.1.4 The Analysis of Urban Planning in the Writings of Castells and Lojkine

Castells and Lojkine, despite their similarities, represent quite different traditions within the Marxist paradigm (see Chapter 5) and this difference becomes particularly apparent in their discussions of urban planning. Castells's writing is part of the tradition known as Althusserianism (see section 5.1) while Lojkine's is in the tradition known as state monopoly capitalism (see section 5.2).

For Castells, urban planning is a form of state intervention whose effect is to regulate the contradictions generated by capitalist urban development (see subsection 6.5.1). In Althusserian terminology, it is an intervention of the political system on the economic system. Lojkine, by contrast, argues that urban planning reflects rather than regulates the contradictions of capitalist urban development and that, in the current stage of capitalism (that is, state monopoly capitalism), its effects are to promote the interests of monopolistic groups against those of non-monopoly groups (see section 7.4).

Castells and Lojkine differ, not only in terms of their definition of urban planning, but also in terms of the problems which they identify as necessitating it. For Castells, urban planning is necessitated by the contradiction between the private nature of production and the collective nature of reproduction (see subsection 6.5.3), whereas for Lojkine it is necessitated by three contradictions associated with urban development in capitalist societies, namely, the financing of urban expenditure, the locational strategy of firms, and urban land rent (see sections 7.3 and 7.4). The analysis of these various problems leads Castells and Lojkine to address some of the central and most important issues in Marxian political economy, yet, as was seen above (subsection 6.5.3 and sections 7.3 and 7.4) this is one of the weakest aspects of their work, essentially because they do not consider either the internal validity of these concepts or the problem of operationalising them empirically.

Despite the different emphases in their work, both Castells and Lojkine treat urban planning as part of the more general process of state intervention. While this approach has the advantage of focusing upon those features which urban planning shares with other forms of state intervention, it has the disadvantage of concealing important internal differences within the category of urban planning. As a result, their analysis tends to exclude any explicit consideration of such issues as zoning, development control, compensation, the internal and external constraints upon planners in making and implementing plans, the effect of land-use planning upon private property rights and property development, and so on. None of these issues are investigated in their writings, yet together they constitute one type of state intervention, namely, land-use planning, which has an important effect upon the urban environment and, moreover, an effect which is probably different from other types of state intervention. In this sense it would appear that there are some disadvantages with Castells's and Lojkine's definition of urban planning.

8.1.5 The Analysis of Urban Movements in the Writings of Castells and Lojkine

Castells and Lojkine are totally opposed to the capitalist system in all its forms and share a common commitment to some form of socialism. It is this fact, possibly more than any other, which accounts for the style and content of their writing. It accounts, in particular, for the approach which they adopt towards urban movements.

Castells and Lojkine both define an urban social movement as being concerned with 'true' and 'radical' change which will 'open the road to socialism' (see subsection 6.6.2 and section 7.5). They regard neighbourhood and community protests (such as those concerned with the provision of public transport, schools or housing) as unimportant, both analytically and politically, as long as they remain within the horizon of that particular neighbourhood or community. Thus both Castells and Lojkine are, in principle, interested mainly in movements that have, actually or potentially, a national and not just a purely local dimension.

This definition was criticised (see subsection 6.6.2 and section 7.5) for being too narrow, because it excluded from consideration many of the protest actions which typically occur in urban areas (for example, protest actions over such issues as rents, repairs to local authority houses, planning proposals, crime, and so on). Although many of these movements could scarcely be described as 'radical', they are nevertheless a vital part of the political interaction that takes place between the local or central state and the residents in that jurisdiction. Any definition which wishes to exclude these neighbourhood and community-based movements from the general category of urban movement is likely to miss an important part of the politics that take place within urban areas.

In his research Castells was unable to find any 'real' urban social movements (as he would define them) and was obliged, by default, to focus upon protests over such issues as housing and redevelopment whose horizons tended to be local rather than national (see notably subsections 6.7.4, 6.7.5 and 6.7.8).

Given their definition of an urban movement, Castells and Lojkine place considerable emphasis upon the fusion of struggles over collective consumption with struggles in the workplace. Indeed, Lojkine has expressed the belief that movements involving this fusion are likely to be of growing importance in the coming decades (Lojkine, 1977a, pp. 334ff; 1977b, p. 153). While this may turn out to be the case, it is likely to occur in spite of, rather than because of, a growth in protests over collective consumption. This is because the latter tend to be limited to the spatial confines of a particular externality field (see subsections 8.8.3, 8.8.6 and 8.8.9). In Britain the evidence would seem to disprove Lojkine's expectation since community movements, according to Saunders, 'are typically fragmented, localized, limited to a narrow range of concerns, and politically isolated from broader radical movements' (Saunders, 1980b, p. 551).

Although the concept of urban social movement contained in the work of Castells and Lojkine is excessively narrow, they nevertheless put forward a useful framework of concepts for the description and analysis of social movements. They argue that a social movement can best be understood by identifying: the issue or stake of the movement (that is, the problem affecting, or goal adopted by, a particular group), the social base (that is, the population affected by the particular problem or issue), the organisation (that is, the vehicle through which the social base achieves its goal), the social force (that is, that part of the social base which is mobilised into action through the organisation and the effect (that is, the outcome of the action pursued by the social force). These concepts and the methodological procedure underlying them are likely to prove useful in characterising and comparing different protest movements.

8.1.6 Conclusion

This review of the work of Castells and Lojkine suggests that their attempt to develop a Marxist analysis of urban areas must be regarded, despite its occasional insights, as having rather limited value. The evidence supporting this claim was presented systematically and exhaustively in Chapters 6 and 7 and in the preceding subsections of this chapter (8.1.1 to 8.1.5). This evidence suggests that, despite the centrality of Marxian political economy in their work, they rarely use its concepts in any methodologically rigorous or creative way. Both tend to use Marxian concepts in a rather dogmatic and functionalist way. In consequence, they fail to make some of the modifications and innovations to the Marxian framework which, as will be seen presently (in section 8.2), seem to be necessary in order to adapt it to the spatial and often highly localised nature of class and class conflict at the urban level. Nevertheless, their work is significant because of its role in generating interest and in helping to define the research agenda for the growing field of Marxist urban sociology. It is in this context that the subsequent sections of this chapter (8.2 to 8.9) will attempt to develop a more empirically-grounded, if less strictly Marxist, analysis of some of the central issues in this new field of urban sociology.

8.2 A CONFLICT APPROACH TO URBAN SOCIOLOGY: THE CONSTRAINED-ACTOR MODEL

Marxist political economy, apart from certain *obiter dicta* about the separation of town and country (Marx, 1947c, p. 333) is virtually non-spatial and this immediately creates a problem when applying it to the urban context. In addition, there is the problem that Marx's analysis of class and class conflict tends to be at a high level of abstraction, particularly in *Capital*, whereas class conflict in urban areas tends to be more locality-based. Thus, notwithstanding the lack of methodological rigour with which Castells and Lojkine use Marxist political economy, the latter itself seems to require some innovations in order to make it more amenable to the analysis of urban issues (for example, issues such as the conflicts associated with negative externalities in residential areas or the conflicts between developers and planners over property development).

The analysis developed here derives its basic thrust from the Marxian emphasis upon the role of interests, both material and ideal, in human action, and upon the conflicts of interest which usually ensue from the pursuit of those interests. However, unlike the standard Marxian approach, where classes are treated as the main actors or agents in society, the concept of actor will be broadened here to include individuals, groups and organisations which have a separate and identifiable interest and which act purposively to pursue that interest.[1] This broader concept of interest reflects the hierarchical levels of abstraction at which the concept of interest can be treated so that the approach developed here represents a change of levels rather than a change in the basic perspective. Nevertheless, the focus upon actors, whether they are individuals, groups or organisations, is not strictly Marxist, and is probably closer to Weber. For this reason the term 'constrained-actor' will be used as a label of convenience for the model developed and applied here.

The constrained-actor model focuses upon instrumentally rational, self-interested action to the exclusion of other types of human action, notably, altruistic, affective and traditional action. The reason for this is that it is assumed that instrumentally rational self-interested action is the most salient type of action in the various urban contexts discussed below (while acknowledging that other types of motivations are likely to operate in other urban contexts). This view of society which is complementary to, though less deterministic than, the Marxian view, can be stated more systematically in terms of four basic propositions.

The first proposition is that an actor is defined by the particular interest which it pursues. Those interests may be material (for example profits, wages, subventions from the state, neighbourhood facilities, and so on) or ideal (for example, political and ideological influence and legitimacy). In turn an actor may be a single individual (for example, a capitalist, worker, landowner, resident, and so on) or an organisation (for example, a union of employers or workers, the central or local state, a resident's association, and so on). It follows from this that a sociological analysis of any social process must begin by identifying the actors involved, and the interests which they are pursuing. This typically was Marx's procedure, for whom the three main actors were capitalists, workers and landowners, each defined by their respective interest, namely, profits, wages and rents.

The second proposition is that the material interests of actors are determined by their legally defined rights over resources (for example, capital, labour, land, subventions from the state, houses, and so on) and the pursuit of their self-interest typically involves maximising the gains from those resources within the limits set by the law and upheld by the state (see Saunders, 1980a, pp. 45–8). This, it will be recalled, is the fundamental basis of Marx's theory of class: capitalists have property rights over capital, workers have property rights over labour and landowners have property rights over land. However, the constrained-actor model, unlike the strict Marxian model, allows for the fact that the interests of an individual organisation are also determined by their legally defined property rights over items of final consumption (for example, dwellings).

The interests of the state (that is, its policies and goals) are more difficult to define than those of other actors, and can vary within and between capitalist countries, depending upon such factors as its organisational structure, the values and attitudes of its incumbents and the relative power of the various classes and interest groups in that society. These factors, in turn, are reflected in the law which defines the scope of state power as well as the manner in which the power can be exercised.

The third proposition is that actors in advanced capitalist societies tend to act in an instrumentally rational way and hence to calculate the efficiency of the means used to attain their self-interest. This, as Weber observed, is part of the process of 'rationalisation' of western societies (Weber, 1974, pp. 13–31), an assumption that is also implicit in Marx's *Capital* (Marx, 1974a, 1974b, 1974c).

The fourth and final proposition is that the pursuit of self-interest takes place through interaction with other actors, equally in pursuit of their self-interest, so that the interests of one actor are typically constrained and limited by the interests of another. In this way conflicts of interest arise which are a characteristic feature of capitalist societies. The relationship between workers and capitalists, so exhaustively analysed by Marx, is a perfect example of the operation of these constraints: workers' interest in higher wages (for example) are continually constrained by capitalists' interest in higher profits and vice versa. There are, however, many other types of conflict, notably conflicts in the sphere of final consumption, which were not investigated by Marx. As will be seen below, these can be adequately analysed within the framework of the constrained-actor model outlined here.

The analysis below focuses primarily upon the micro-level conflicts which take place in the urban context (for example, conflicts associated with property development, or over negative externalities in residential areas) although it is not intended to exclude consideration of the more macro-level issues which are central to Marxist analysis generally. In other words, the analysis here leaves open the question of the connection between classes and various interest groups such as residents' association, environmental lobbies, local planning authorities, landowners, developers, and so on. Thus, although the approach developed here does not solve all of the problems identified in the writings of Castells and Lojkine, it does have the advantage of using concepts that can be operationalised more easily while aware of the need to subsequently relate those concepts to more abstract levels of analysis (see Pickvance, 1984, especially pp. 43–7; see also Castells, 1983a and 1983b where the latter seems to be moving in this direction).

Before applying the constrained-actor model to urban analysis proper, however, it is necessary to define as precisely as possible the nature of urban areas, and the urban processes which typically take place within them. This will be done in the next section.

8.3 URBAN AREAS AND URBAN PROCESSES: THE FIELD OF URBAN SOCIOLOGY

An urban area is a built-up area consisting of physical structures, that is, buildings (for example, houses, offices, factories, schools, hospitals, churches, theatres, and so on) and infrastructures (for example, roads, railways, water and sewerage systems, electricity, telecommunications, parks, streets, and so on). It is, in other words, a spatial concentration of land-using, humanly-created property.[2] (A similar stress upon the built environment is also to be found in some of the writings of Harvey – 1976, republished in 1978a; 1978b, republished in 1981.)

Urban areas are essentially dynamic in the sense that the size and composition of their stock of property typically changes over time. Some of the existing stock of property becomes obsolete and is replaced while additional new buildings and infrastructures are produced at the edges of the built-up area. In addition, the use to which property is put can itself change over time (for example, from residential to office) as can the social class of the users (for example, from lower to middle income group through gentrification).

Urban areas are typically produced by private developers using private and state capital. In turn, they are used for both producing other commodities and for final consumption. Urban sociology, as defined here, is essentially concerned with understanding how the property concentrated in an urban area is produced and used. To be more precise, it is concerned with understanding three processes which together constitute an urban area. The first is the process by which an urban area is produced through private and state property development. The second is the process by which an urban area is used to produce goods and services as a result of the location decisions of firms and agencies and the migration and commuting decisions of workers. The third is the process by which an urban area is used for final consumption through the use of houses, schools, parks, theatres, museums, and so on.

This formulation of the field of urban sociology is broader and more comprehensive than that found in the writings of either Castells or Lojkine. As will be seen in sections 8.4 to 8.8, this formulation not only incorporates the main issues which are to be found in their work (that is, collective consumption, industrial location, urban planning, urban social movements) but also includes a number of other issues (notably property development and the spatial nature of final consumption) which are not found in their writings but which are nevertheless an integral part of the processes taking place within urban areas.

The three processes constitutive of an urban area will now be analysed using the constrained-actor model. The methodological procedure in each case will be to identify the various actors involved in each process, the interests which they are pursuing, and the constraints which they encounter in trying to achieve them. The analysis begins with an investigation of the process of property development (sections 8.4 to 8.6) followed by the process by which urban areas are used in production (section 8.7) and in final consumption (section 8.8).

8.4 THE PRODUCTION OF URBAN AREAS: THE PROCESS OF PROPERTY DEVELOPMENT

The majority of buildings and infrastructure which constitute the physical fabric of an urban area in advanced capitalist societies is produced by capitalists and the state through the process of property development. Property development can arise in a number of ways: sometimes it is a direct response to the demand for buildings and infrastructures; at other times it is an indirect response, in anticipation of future demand; at yet other times, it is a response to a demand which is itself created by property developers. Thus property development is a major force affecting the quantity, type and location of buildings and infrastructures in an urban area.

A number of different actors or agents are involved in the process of property development. These include the private property developer whose role typically involves organising the finance, assembling the sites and contracting the construction company; the various state agencies which hire development companies to carry out property development; the financial institutions which provide the finance capital; landowners, who provide the sites; the state land-use planning authority whose permission is necessary for most development to occur; various professional agents such as architects, engineers, surveyors, planners, and so on; and finally the construction companies who actually built the physical structures. These various actors, each of which operates within a particular set of constraints or 'structures', represent operationally distinct parts of the development process.

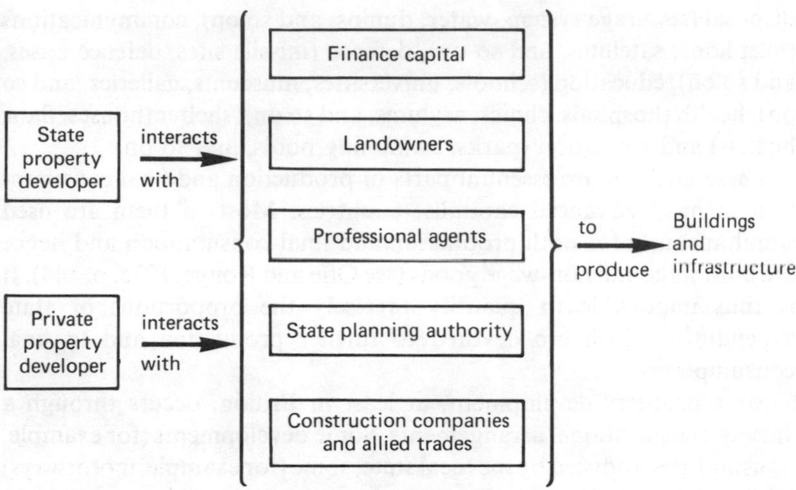

Figure 8.1 The process of property development

The relationship of these different actors to the over-all process of property development is outlined, in highly simplified form, in Figure 8.1 (see Lorimer, 1972, p. 19 and Ambrose, 1977, p. 42, for a slightly different diagram of the same process).

It is now necessary to analyse separately the process of state property development (section 8.5) and the process of private property development (section 8.6). This analysis is very similar to that of Ambrose and Colenutt whose book, *The Property Machine*, provides a detailed empirical analysis of the activities of the various actors involved in property development in Britain and its resulting costs and benefits (1975; see also Ambrose, 1977). Lorimer (1972) has done a similar analysis for Canada. The analysis of Lamarche (1976), by contrast, is primarily concerned with the nature of the income derived from property development rather than with the process itself and is thus less relevant in this context.

8.5 STATE PROPERTY DEVELOPMENT

The state is probably the largest property developer in most advanced capitalist countries. Its property developments include the production of facilities (that is, buildings and infrastructure) for transport (roads, railways, airports, and so on), energy (electricity, gas, and so on), waste disposal (sewerage system, water, dumps, and so on), communications (telephone, satellites, and so on), defence (missile sites, defence bases, and so on), education (schools, universities, museums, galleries, and so on), health (hospitals, clinics, asylums, and so on), shelter (houses, flats, hostels) and recreation (parks, swimming pools, and so on).

These facilities are essential parts of production and final consumption in most advanced capitalist countries. Most of them are used simultaneously for both production and final consumption and hence are both wage and non-wage goods (see Offe and Ronge, 1975, p. 144). It is thus impossible to quantify precisely the proportions of state expenditure which are devoted to further production and to final consumption.

State property development, at least in Britain, occurs through a variety of institutional arrangements. Some developments (for example, housing) are produced by the local state; some (for example, motorways) by the central state; some (for example, water and sewerage treatment) by regional state bodies; and some (for example, railways) by nationalised industries. Thus the over-all process is characterised by considerable organisational complexity.

In order to understand the nature of state property development, it is necessary, following the methodological principles of the constrained-actor model, to identify the interests (that is, the goals and policies) which the state is pursuing in undertaking property development, and the constraints which it encounters in attempting to achieve them. However, unlike capitalists and workers, whose interests can be reasonably approximated by reference to their perceived material interests (that is, maximisation of profits and wages), the interests of the state in a capitalist society can vary considerably, depending upon its organisational structure, the values and goals of its incumbents and their electoral support, as well as the relations of power and influence connecting it with the different classes and interest groups in that society (see Saunders, 1980a, pp. 201–8ff; Dunleavy, 1980, Chapters 4–5; Clark and Dear, 1981; Cox, 1983). It follows from this that the precise interests and goals which the state pursues in a capitalist society cannot be affirmed *a priori*; they can only be known through empirical investigation. Nevertheless, following the lead of such writers as Offe and Ronge (1975), it is possible, by making some simplifying assumptions, to identify some of the constraints which typically limit the state's freedom of action in a capitalist society, and thereby limit its freedom of action in relation to property development.

The logic of the analysis of Offe and Ronge is that the state, in a society of capitalist commodity production, will tend to be constrained to protect the interests of capitalists (or certain sectors of them) above all other classes, since it is their investment decisions which result in profits (and hence satisfy capitalists' interests), employment (and hence satisfy, to some extent, workers' interests) and state revenue (and hence satisfy, to some extent, state interests). Thus the protecting of capitalists' interests tends to be the logical outcome of the state's position *vis-à-vis* the different interests in a capitalist society. In practical terms, this protection frequently takes the form of legislation, grants, trade protection, tax reliefs, and so on, as well as the provision of physical infrastructure (roads, telecommunications, energy, water, and so on) which are favourable to the interests of capitalists. It is in this sense that the state in a capitalist society is a capitalist state (see Offe and Ronge, 1975, pp. 139ff). However, in most advanced capitalist countries, the state has also found it necessary, in pursuance of its interest, to increasingly protect the interests of workers (employed and unemployed as well as the old, sick and the young) through social welfare payments and other facilities (schools, hospitals, houses, parks, and so on).

It follows from this that certain state activities involve the expenditure of relatively large amounts of state revenue. Since the latter normally depends upon taxation (or, more rarely, on the profitability of state enterprises), state expenditure may be constrained fiscally because of resistance to increased taxes or because the state – congruent with, and probably influenced by, certain class interests – acts to maintain low tax rates. In such situations, fiscal constraints may result in certain types of state expenditure being constrained more than others, depending upon the configuration of class forces involved. Thus, for example, Saunders found that in Croydon, when the local state was faced with limited revenue in 1973, it reduced expenditure on health, education and social services while increasing expenditure on roads and carparks (see Saunders, 1980a, p. 303). In this example, those aspects of state property development which directly benefited business interests were privileged *vis-à-vis* those which would have benefited working-class interests (see also O'Connor, 1973, and Habermas, 1976, for a more general discussion of the fiscal constraints on state expenditure).

These considerations suggest that state property development should be understood, not only by reference to the values and relations which are internal to the state but also in terms of its external relations to the various classes and interests in the society. While this methodological principle is no substitute for concrete, empirical analysis, it does provide a framework for understanding the 'interests' of the state in relation to property development and the constraints which it encounters in attempting to achieve them.

8.6 PRIVATE PROPERTY DEVELOPMENT

8.6.1 Introduction

The three principal actors involved in the private property development process (see Figure 8.1) are the developer, the landowner and the state planning authority and, for simplicity, the analysis in this section will focus primarily upon these three actors. The interest of the private property developer is in making a profit by producing either buildings or infrastructures, while the interest of the landowner is in selling or leasing land for the highest obtainable price. The interests of the state planning authority, by contrast, can vary considerably, due to the forces and factors identified in the preceding section (8.5). Thus the state planning authority in a capitalist society can have a variety of interests or goals, such as: attracting jobs to their area, maintaining low property tax rates, promoting civic pride and tourism, conserving its architectural heritage, preserving green spaces, and so on. This variety of goals was exemplified in Croydon where Saunders found that the interest of the planning authority, and of the local government generally, involved maintaining a low property tax rate, preserving the green belt and ensuring low housing densities (all of which were congruent with the interests of middle-class owner occupier), as well as in promoting civic pride and free enterprise (which were congruent with city centre business interests) see Saunders 1980a, pp. 244, 307). Despite this variety of goals and interests, local authorities usually face constraints from other actors in the process of private property development and, using examples from Britain, these will be discussed in subsection 8.6.4.

Other actors, too, notably state agencies, environmental groups and final consumers, can also be sources of constraint and conflict in the development process. These various constraints are summarised in matrix form in Table 8.1. The constraints operating upon private developers, landowners and the state planning authority will now be analysed respectively.

8.6.2 Constraints upon the Interests of Private Property Developers

Table 8.1 reveals that the interests of private property developers in a capitalist society can be constrained in six different ways. First of all, they can be constrained by competition from other property developers, which ensures that their rate of profit is maintained at a competitive level. This constraint may, however, be reduced in the case of larger developers where the number of actual and potential competitors is smaller and, correspondingly, the possibility of monopolistic or oligopolistic profits is greater.

Secondly, private property developers can be constrained by landowners, both private and state. This can occur in a number of ways. It can occur if private landowners refuse to sell their land except at an extortionate price, that is, above the price set in a competitive market. This possibility could arise if the developer is in the process of assembling a number of different sites, each of which is essential to a development project, but is hindered by one landowner who demands a price which reflects the redeveloped rather than the existing value of the site. This is known as 'price gouging' (Davis and Whinston, 1961, p. 111; see also Elkin, 1974, pp. 71–2).

Private property developers can also be constrained by state landowners who may refuse to sell suitable development land. This occurred in the City of Nottingham between 1979 and 1980 where 'more than two-thirds of the potential residential sites in the inner city were found to be in the ownership of the Nottingham City Council' (Nicholls, *et al.*, 1982, p. 332) but the 'Labour Council adopted a policy of no disposal of land for private housebuilding' (ibid., p. 339). Alternatively, private property developers may be constrained by the collective actions of landowners who are opposed to a particular type of development within their area (for example, owner-occupier residents opposed to an office or factory development in their area). Such collective action could cause a delay or even a cancellation of the proposed development and hence a thwarting of the developer's interests.

Thirdly, the developer is constrained by the state planning authority. This occurs because the planning authority, through its powers of zoning and development control, effectively controls the supply of development land; in Britain this has occasionally led to scarcities in the supply of 'suitable' development land (see Drewett, 1973, p. 177; Goodchild, 1978, pp. 13–14).[3] In addition, the developer is also constrained by the costs of making a planning application (for example, ascertaining the requirements likely to prove acceptable), the delay in obtaining a decision (see Drewett, 1973, pp. 177–8; Neilson, 1976, p. 161; Goodchild, 1978, pp. 17–18) and, in the event of permission being granted, the conditions which may be attached to it. Alternatively, the developer may be refused planning permission as occurred in 14 per cent of all planning applications in England and Wales in 1978/79

Table 8.1 The constraints and conflicts generated in the process of private property development. Sources of constraint on actors in the development process

	Private property developer	*Landowner*	*State planning authority*	*Other state agencies*	*Environmental and other groups*	*Consumers*
Private property developer	(1) Competition keeps profits in check	(1) Refusal to sell land (2) Collective action by adjacent landowners and users	(1) Restriction on supply of land (2) Cost of application (3) Delays (4) Costly conditions (5) Possible refusal of permission	(1) Price controls (2) Taxes on profits	(1) Cause delay or refusal of planning permission (2) Cause amenities to be preserved or improved	The level of effective demand

Actors in the development process	Landowners	(1) Develop-ment may reduce the value of adjacent land	(1) Land values may be reduced by adjacent uses of land and property	(1) Refusal of planning permission to use land in the most profitable way (2) 'Planning blight'	(1) Taxation of land	(1) Prevail upon planning authority to refuse permission for the most profitable use	The level of effective demand
	The state planning authority	(1) If private land is zoned for unprofit-able uses, developers are unlikely to develop it	(1) Compen-sation to landowners (2) Collective action by landowners	(1) Exclusionary zoning and fiscal policies can adversely affect other jurisdictions (2) Competition in attracting jobs	(1) A lack of co-ordin-ation between the planning authority and other state agencies	(1) Resistance to planning decisions which could cause harm to the environ-ment	(1) Actual and anticipated political behaviour of the electorate (e.g. voting, protests, etc.)

(Department of the Environment, 1980, Table 1). In addition, the developer of offices which are above a certain size, and in certain areas, must obtain an Office Development Permit (ODP) from the Department of the Environment, which may be refused (although as Pickvance, 1981, pp. 274ff, has shown, the rate of refusal of ODP's has been quite at variance with its stated policy goals). The net effect of these constraints is to increase the costs incurred by the developer, whose development, in turn, imposes costs and benefits on others (see Ambrose and Colenutt, 1975, pp. 60–67, 159–62; Balchin and Kieve, 1982, pp. 118–19).

The fourth constraint is that posed by other state agencies such as the central government. This can arise through the taxation of developers' profits. It may also arise if there are price controls upon the sale of new buildings such as houses or offices or rent restrictions on leasing.

Fifthly, the developer may be constrained by environmental groups whose actions to protect amenities may cause the developer's planning application to be delayed or even refused. In addition, they may cause the developer, via the planning authority, to incur extra costs in preserving or improving the amenities affected by their development.

Finally, the developer is constrained by the level of effective demand. In the case of housing demand, this constraint is affected by the level of wages and employment, the availability of loans and the rate of interest as well as subventions from the state to house purchasers. In the case of factories, offices, shops, and so on, effective demand is affected by the possibility of using these properties profitably, and this depends upon such factors as wage levels, interest rates, competition, government regulations, and so on. In this sense, the level of effective demand is the ultimate constraint upon the interests of the private property developer.

8.6.3 Constraints upon the Interests of Landowners

Table 8.1 also reveals how the interests of landowners may be constrained in the development process. This can also occur, as in the case of the private property developer, in six different ways. First, the interest of landowners may be constrained by a property developer if the latter's development has the effect of reducing the value of land and property in its immediate vicinity. A possible example of this would be the development of a factory, an airport, a motorway or a dump close to a residential area. Conversely, a development may increase land values in its vicinity in which case the interest of the landowner would be advanced simultaneously with that of the developer.

The second constraint comes from other owners and users of land and derives from the fact that the value of urban land and property depends, not only upon the quality and maintenance of adjacent properties, but also upon the use to which those adjacent properties are put, as well as the status of their users. Thus, if there is prejudice against a particular status group (for example, an ethnic minority), the presence of the latter in a particular area can, *ceteris paribus*, have the effect of reducing the value of adjacent land and property.

The third constraint comes from the state planning authority which has the right and the power to determine the use to which a landowner may put his land in an urban area. This effectively means that the state may inhibit a landowner from using his land in the most profitable way so that the latter suffers a loss as a result. Additionally the planning authority may have long-term plans for an area (for example, road proposals) which may cause land and property values in an area to fall as soon as the plans become public knowledge. Moreover, they may continue to fall even if the plans are subsequently withdrawn, as long as any suspicion remains that the plans may be implemented. This phenomenon is known as 'planning blight'.

Fourthly, the interest of landowners may also be constrained by other agencies of the state. This may take the form of a central government tax on land whose value appreciates as a result of planning or development. In Britain the development land tax operated in this way until its abolition in 1985 (although in a much weaker form than was originally envisaged) (see Balchin and Kieve, 1982, pp. 135–8; Cullingworth, 1982, pp. 88–90, 97–101).

Fifthly, environmental groups may constrain the interests of landowners by prevailing upon the planning authority to refuse permission to landowners to develop their land in a profitable but environmentally damaging way (for example, housing developments on scenic mountainsides).

Finally, the interests of landowners are affected by the level of effective demand from consumers (that is, consumers of offices, factories, houses, and so on) and hence by the same factors which affect the private property developer.

8.6.4 Constraints upon the Interests of the State Planning Authority

Table 8.1 also reveals the different constraints which affect the interests of the state planning authority. The first of these comes from the private property developer and derives from the fact that developers are unlikely to undertake a property development in an area if it is zoned for uses which they regard as unprofitable. This constraint is likely to vary considerably between countries and to be greatest in those capitalist countries where virtually all development is undertaken by the private sector. In these circumstances, planners must zone land in a way which broadly accords with the expectations of developers or face the prospect of having no development at all. Planning, in such situations, according to Pickvance (1977c), becomes 'trend planning' (ibid., p. 42) as distinct from 'interventive planning' (ibid.), because 'the development plan merely reflects market trends in the allocation of land' (ibid.). This, he claims, is the predominant form of planning in Britain since 1951 largely due to the fact that 'private sector developers carried out the majority of developments' (ibid., p. 43).

The second constraint is that posed by landowners and varies from one country to another according to the laws of compensation. The planning authority is likely to be highly constrained in the type of zoning which it can enforce if, for example, the laws of compensation ensure that landowners are compensated for any zoning which reduces the value of their land to below the maximum market value. In this situation the planning authority will tend, depending upon its financial resources, to zone land according to the laws of the market, in order to avoid such compensation claims. Conversely, if the laws of compensation do not favour landowners, then the planning authority will be less constrained by the threat of compensation. In Britain, compensation is governed by the provisions incorporated in the Land Compensation Act (1973), and allows compensation to be paid in such cases as planning blight, compulsory purchase, depreciation caused by public works and revocation of an existing planning permission (see Cullingworth, 1982, pp. 88–90, 97–101).

Landowners (for example, owner-occupier residents in an area) may also constrain the planning authority by engaging in collective action to have a planning decision reversed. As a result, the planning authority is likely to take into account the potential and actual opposition which its decisions are likely to meet in a particular area and to treat that opposition as a limit to its actions.

The third constraint is that posed by other planning authorities. This constraint derives from the fact that the consequences, both intended and unintentional, of the actions of planning authorities, cannot always be confined within their jurisdictional boundaries. Thus, for example, a local authority where housing and land is scarce, is likely to be constrained in solving its housing problems if the major policies of adjacent planning authorities are to preserve green belts, maintain open spaces and permit only low density residential development (see Williams and Norman, 1971; Saunders, 1980a, pp. 247–8). Similarly, the fiscal problems of a local authority facing high expenditure demands from its residents (for example, low income residents with large families) can be exacerbated if neighbouring authorities strictly adhere to a policy of low property taxes. Since one of the ways this policy is maintained is by restricting entry of those who are most likely to be a fiscal burden (for example, by restricting the amount of housing available to low income families), its effect is to ensure that the fiscal burden is, *ceteris paribus*, unequally distributed between local governments (see Baumol, 1967; Albin, 1971; Aronson, 1974). In the same way, the efforts of a local authority to attract jobs to an area may be constrained by other local authorities who are able to offer more attractive packages to lure firms and state enterprises (see Molotch, 1976; Logan, 1978). In all of these ways, planning authorities can be constrained by the actions of other planning authorities.

The fourth constraint is that posed by other state agencies or policies where there is a lack of co-ordination and co-operation between the two (see for example, Marriott, 1969, p. 200).

The final constraint is that posed by the consumers of urban property (that is, offices, factories, houses, schools, parks, hospitals, and so on). In this case it is likely that the local authority will be subject to pressures from the various class interests within its jurisdiction while at the same time being constrained by the anticipated and actual reactions of the electorate.

8.6.5 Summary

This analysis of the three main actors in the development process reveals the mutually constraining effects which each has upon the other, as well as the constraints imposed by other actors. Although it is not strictly a Marxist analysis in the sense that the main actors are not classes, nor are the actors related to each other as deterministically as in the Marxian model, the analysis does emphasise the crucial role of conflict in the property development process and the power of the various actors involved in that process. In short, the analysis here provides a set of concepts which can be readily operationalised, thereby overcoming the disadvantages of some of the more abstract Marxian concepts.

It is now necessary to examine the second process which takes place in urban areas, namely the process by which the urban area is used in the production of commodities.

8.7 PRODUCTION IN AN URBAN AREA

8.7.1 Introduction

A large proportion of the wealth in capitalist societies (that is, 'commodities' which are both use values and exchange values, as well as 'products' which are only use values: see Marx, 1974a, Chapter 1) is produced by capitalists and the state within urban areas. However, an urban area can only be used to produce wealth if capitalists and/or the state decide to locate their production operations there and if workers live (or migrate to live) within commuting distance of those production operations. Thus the decisions to locate, migrate and commute within urban areas are an important part of the process by which the urban area is used for production. Indeed, it is these decisions which determine whether an urban area grows, declines or remains stable. In turn, they determine the quantity and type of production of goods and services in a particular urban area and, by implication, the quantity and type of employment and unemployment in that area.

The methodological procedure which shall be used in this analysis is the same as that outlined in section 8.2, and applied in the sections (8.4 to 8.6). This procedure which, for simplicity, will be applied to production by capitalist firms (that is, ignoring the public sector), involves investigating the interests which capitalists and workers pursue in making their respective decisions to locate (in the case of the former) and migrate and commute (in the case of the latter), as well as the constraints which they encounter in pursuing that interest.

The decisions and actions of capitalists and workers in relation to location, migration and commuting can be conveniently summarised in terms of the concept of a labour market: capitalists' location decisions constitute the demand side of the market while workers' migration and commuting decisions constitute the supply side. The area covered by this labour market is a labour market area and the precise relationship between an urban area and a labour market area will be clarified in the course of the analysis below. The analysis begins with an investigation of the factors affecting the supply of labour in an urban area (subsection 8.7.2) followed by an investigation of the factors affecting demand (subsection 8.7.3).

8.7.2 The Supply of Labour in an Urban Area

The supply of labour in an urban area (or in a sub-area of an urban area) consists of those living within commuting distance of work in that area.

This area constitutes a labour market area and, over time, the number of workers in that area can be increased or decreased by migration.[4]

It is well established that the size of the labour market area tends to vary between workers according to their skill, largely because of differences in their migration behaviour, but also because of differences in their commuting behaviour. In Britain, for example, the size of the labour market area tends to be much smaller for unskilled manual workers than for higher professional, administrative and managerial workers. This is because the former have lower migration rates than the latter (see Johnson, Salt and Wood, 1974, pp. 106–7; Evans and Russell, 1980, pp. 212–13; Salt, 1980, p. 258). In addition, they also commute over shorter distances (see Berthoud, 1980, pp. 244–8). In short, the labour market area for unskilled manual workers tends to be less than, or equal to, the size of the urban area within which they live. By contrast, the labour market area for professional, managerial and administrative workers tends to be coterminous with the entire national (and, in some cases, international) urban system.

It is necessary to explore in more detail the reasons for this difference in the size of labour market areas by exploring how the interests of different types of workers vary in relation to migration.[5] For brevity and simplicity the analysis will be confined to two groups of workers at opposite ends of the skill spectrum: the unskilled manual worker and the professional administrative and managerial worker.

The low migration rates of unskilled (and some skilled) manual workers arises essentially because their material interests are not likely to be significantly improved by migration. This is so for a number of reasons. First, because their job is unlikely to have a career structure so that migration from one area to another would not materially improve their position. Secondly, competition for jobs is probably greatest in the unskilled category in all areas, so that migration from one area to another would not confer any decisive advantage. Alternatively, in the case of some skilled workers (for example, coal and steel workers) their skills may be specific to a particular area. Thirdly, the worker may be living in a local authority house and is likely to encounter great difficulty in getting a replacement in another area (see Johnson, Salt and Wood, 1974, pp. 1–2; Berthoud, 1980, pp. 248–51; Hughes and McCormick, 1981) – although as Gleave and Palmer (1978) have shown, local authority tenants display a higher rate of movement within local authority areas than owner-occupiers, but a lower migration rate between regions. These are some of the reasons why it may not be in the material interests of unskilled manual workers in advanced capitalist societies to migrate. In historical terms, this represents a reversal of the high migration rates of this group in the early stages of the industrial revolution (Fielding, 1982, p. 28). The net effect of these factors is that the labour market area of unskilled manual workers tends to be less than or equal to the size of the urban area within which they live.

Professional, administrative and managerial workers generally have relatively high migration rates in Britain and Western Europe. However, as Fielding (1982, p. 28) points out, this was not always the case nor is it currently the case in the United States (see Johnson, Salt and Wood, 1974, p. 106). The reason for this essentially is that their material interests can be significantly improved by migration. This is because migration may be associated with career advancement and salary increases and the transaction costs of moving house from one area to another are likely to be small relative to total earnings, particularly when they are borne by the employer rather than the employee (see Salt, 1980, pp. 258–60; Fielding, 1982, pp. 26–7). The net effect of these factors is that professional, administrative and managerial workers have relatively high migration rates with the consequence that their labour market area tends to be coterminous with the national (and possibly also, the international) urban system.[6]

It is now possible, on the basis of this review of the literature, to clarify the nature of the relationship between an urban area and a labour market area. This relationship can be conceptualised as a continuum. At one end of the continuum, the labour market area is coterminous with a part of the urban area or, in the case of smaller urban areas, with the entire urban area so that all commuting occurs within that particular area. This end of the continuum corresponds to the labour market area of unskilled manual workers. At the other end of the continuum, the labour market may be spread over a number of urban areas so that commuting and migration occurs in various directions between each of the urban areas. This end of the continuum corresponds to the labour market area of professional, administrative and managerial workers. It follows that the labour market areas of intermediate skilled workers will fall between these two extremes, with the size of the labour market area increasing directly with skill.

This conceptualisation of the relationship between urban areas and labour market areas can also be reinforced, indirectly, by evidence on the spatial distribution of unemployment in different skill groups in Britain in the 1970s (see notably Cheshire, 1979, p. 32; Evans and Russell, 1980, pp. 212–13; Corkingdale, 1980, p. 185; Richardson, 1980, pp. 214–17; Evans and Richardson, 1981, p. 114; Elias and Keogh, 1982, p. 11). The evidence shows that the rate of unemployment in different urban areas tends to be uniform for professional, administrative and managerial workers but to vary for unskilled workers. The most plausible explanation of this, according to Evans and Russell (1980, p. 213), is that 'at the lowest skill levels, the spatial extent of the labour market is likely to be coincident with a travel-to-work area, but that the labour market tends to become a national market as the skill level increases'. Within urban areas, however, rates of unemployment tend to vary much more widely for all skill groups. In the Greater London area, for example, Evans and Russell (1980, p. 210) found that '. . . when the influence of skill level has as far as possible been eliminated, . . . there is still a persistent difference between the unemployment rates prevailing in inner London and those prevailing in outer London'.

The main reason for this seems to be that the unemployed (like the employed) live in segregated neighbourhoods depending upon such factors as their age, stage in the life cycle, skill and income. In other words, the labour market interacts with the housing market to produce a variegated pattern of intra-urban unemployment. The other factor affecting unemployment is local variations in the demand for labour, which will be considered in the next subsection.

The analysis in this subsection has revealed that urban areas and labour market areas are conceptually distinct. They should not, therefore, as frequently occurs (see, for example, Broadbent, 1977, pp. 94ff; Castells, 1977a, p. 236 and subsection 6.2.2), be treated as identical.[7]

8.7.3 The Demand for Labour in an Urban Area

The demand for labour by capitalists and the state in an urban area is the outcome of their past and present decisions to locate there and to employ the labour living there. In this subsection, the analysis will be confined to the decisions of firms in order to show how they affect the demand for labour in different areas.

In broad terms, the decisions of firms as they affect the demand for labour in an area can be classified in the following way:

1. The decisions of existing firms in an area:
   (a) to maintain existing levels of employment;
   (b) to expand existing levels of employment through:
      (b′) the creation of new jobs,
      (b″) the relocation of jobs from another area;

(c) reduce existing levels of employment through:
  (c′) layoffs,
  (c″) relocation of jobs to another area;
(d) cease employment in an area through:
  (d′) demise of the plant or firm,
  (d″) relocation of plant/firm to another area;

2. The decisions of new firms to the economy:
   (a) to locate in an area;
   (b) not to locate in an area.

The significance of this taxonomy of decision-making is that it allows the change in employment in any urban area to be broken down into two components:

1. the absolute job loss or gain (to the area and the economy) which would be the outcome of decisions 1b′, 1c′ and 1d′; and
2. the locational job loss or gain (to the area but not to the economy) which would be the outcome of decisions 1b′, 1c′, 1d′, 2a and 2b.

The value of this approach has been clearly illustrated by the work of Massey and Meegan (1978). In their study of the decline in manufacturing employment (in the electrical, electronics and aerospace equipment sectors) between 1966 and 1972 in the cities of London, Manchester, Merseyside and Birmingham, they found that the majority of job losses were absolute rather than locational and were due either to closures (decision 1d′) or layoffs (decision 1c′). This fact, coupled with the failure of new manufacturing firms to locate in the inner areas of Britain's larger conurbations (decision 2b), is one of the main reasons for the relatively higher levels of unemployment among manual workers in the 1970s and 1980s in these areas. This result has been replicated by many other studies of job losses in the manufacturing sector in Britain's major cities in the period from the mid-1960s to 1980 (see Elias and Keogh, 1982, pp. 2–7 for a review of the evidence).

The significance of this result is that the private sector demand for labour in an area is the outcome of a number of different types of decisions made by firms, each pursuing their interest. However, the demand for labour in an area can be further understood by investigating the characteristics of the firms making those decisions. Increasingly the demand for all types of labour in the private sector (both manufacturing and services) is constituted by multiplant, multiproduct and, frequently multinational firms. According to Healey (1982): 'in 1972 approximately three quarters of employees in the private sector of manufacturing industry in the United Kingdom worked for multiplant enterprises' (ibid., p. 38).

The implication of this is that the type and quantity of labour demanded in an area is increasingly being determined by the location decisions of these multiplant firms. Numerous studies of their location patterns in Britain, the United States and Sweden show that their headquarters (and hence the associated functions of financial control, research and development and top management) 'tend to be concentrated into a small number of large metropolitan complexes' (Dicken, 1976, p. 402). This applies to both national and international multiplant firms whose headquarters tend to be located at the top, or in the top tier, of the national and international urban hierarchy respectively (see Westaway, 1974; Goddard, 1978; Goddard and Smith, 1978; Massey, 1979). Conversely, there is also some evidence that multiplant firms are locating their branch plants (and their associated low-skilled assembly function) in smaller urban centres (see Goddard, 1977, 1978; Massey and Meegan, 1978, p. 287; Massey, 1979, p. 237) or even rural sites (Keeble, Owens and Thompson, 1983). The outcome of these locational decisions is that the demand for highly-skilled professional labour will tend to be concentrated in the largest urban centres (or in their outskirts), while the demand for lower-skilled manual labour is shifting down and away from the urban hierarchy. In short, the spatial distribution of the demand for different types of labour in advanced capitalist societies is changing as a result of, *inter alia*, the location decisions of multiplant firms. In other words, the way in which urban areas are being used in the production of commodities is increasingly dependent upon their size and hence upon their position in the national and international urban hierarchy.

8.7.4 Summary

This section has attempted to analyse the way in which urban areas are used in the production of commodities. This was done through the analysis of the location decisions of firms and the migration and commuting decisions of workers. These two sets of decisions were analysed in terms of the concepts of a labour market and a labour market area.

These decisions (together with those of the state, which were not examined here) determine not only the amount and type of production that takes place within a particular urban area; they are also the major determinants of the process of urbanisation itself, and hence of the forces causing the size of an urban area to increase, decrease or remain stable. In short, the entire shape of the urban system in any capitalist country is the outcome of a myriad of different decisions by firms, the state and workers, each pursuing their interest in the context of the constraints and opportunities posed by each other.

It is now necessary, finally, to analyse the process by which urban areas are used in final consumption.

8.8 CONSUMPTION IN AN URBAN AREA

8.8.1 Introduction

The act of final consumption refers to the process by which labour is reproduced through the consumption of wage goods. The conventional Marxian treatment of final consumption is the following:

> Workers are paid money wages by capitalists in exchange for their labour and this enables them to buy wage goods from capitalists. These wage goods, usually along with unpaid domestic labour, are then consumed by workers who, again, exchange their labour with capitalists for another round of money wages; and so on, the cycle of production and reproduction proceeds. (see subsections 1.1.2 and 2.3.2).

One of the important developments in capitalism since Marx's time is the growing involvement of the state in the production of wage (or final consumption) goods. These include housing, schools, hospitals, public transport, sport and recreational facilities, landscaped open spaces as well as water, sewerage and transportation networks. The state produces these goods by spending the revenue which it receives from taxes (on wages, profits and rents) and from its trading operations (when they make a surplus) and distributes them according to a variety of market and non-market mechanisms. The precise distributional effect of such state expenditure will depend, in the case of each individual citizen, on the difference between the taxes paid and the consumption goods received.

The real wages of the worker in advanced capitalist societies can thus be divided into two parts: the direct wage (that is, the money wage paid directly by the employer – that is, the firm or the state – in exchange for labour) and the indirect wage (that is, the 'wage' received indirectly from the state). In the terminology of Castells and Lojkine (subsections 6.2.1 and 7.2.2 respectively) the wage can be divided into individual consumption and collective consumption.

These considerations are part of the conventional Marxian treatment of consumption. However, there is an important spatial dimension to consumption which has not been analysed by Marx or by subsequent Marxists. This dimension derives from the fact that many consumption goods are fixed to particular locations (for example, houses, schools, hospitals, roads, parks, open spaces, and so on) and can only be consumed at those locations. The analysis below will attempt to conceptualise this spatial dimension within the framework of the constrained-actor model.

The analysis begins with a typology of consumption goods (subsection 8.8.2) followed by a description of the spatial dimension of consumption goods (subsection 8.8.3). The dwelling unit is then selected as the central element in the matrix of consumption goods on the ground that the location of one's dwelling is a major factor determining the quantity and quality of other goods which an individual consumes (subsection 8.8.4). The analysis then shows how changes in the environment of the dwelling unit affects different tenure groups differently, with significant distributional effects (subsection 8.8.5). Finally, the typical reactions of residents to changes which affect consumption goods within the area of their dwellings will also be examined (subsections 8.8.6 to 8.8.9). In this way it is hoped to provide the basis for a spatial analysis of consumption.

8.8.2 A Typology of Consumption Goods

Consumption goods – in fact all goods – can be classified as either private, state or communal according to their ownership (Macpherson, 1973, 1978). A private consumption good (for example, a house, a car, an overcoat, and so on) is defined by the fact that its owner has three related property rights over that good. These rights are:

1. The right: (a) to exclude others from it; and
   (b) to determine the use to which it is put.
2. The right to receive an income from it, if possible.
3. The right to transfer it (through sale, lease or inheritance).

These rights confer complete or pure private ownership over a good (see Alchian, 1965, p. 819; Cheung, 1978, p. 51; see also Demsetz, 1967;

Table 8.2 A typology of consumption goods

		Ownership of consumption good		
		Private	*State*	*Communal*
Effect of consumption good	Positive	*Example:* Food Clothing Furniture Household appliances, etc.	*Example:* Schools Hospitals Public transport	*Example:* Fresh Air Visually pleasant environment A residential area free from crime
	Negative	*Example:* Domestic refuse	*Example:* Noxious gases, liquids, or solids, which are owned by the state	*Example:* Polluted air Congested roads Noise

Furubotn and Pejovich, 1972; Alchian and Demsetz, 1973; Pejovich, 1982).[8] Typically, a private consumption good (like a private capital good),[9] is distributed through the market where access is based upon ability to pay, although access through non-market mechanisms such as inheritance or marriage also occurs.

A state consumption good (for example, roads, streets, footpaths, as well as public schools, hospitals, parks, houses, and so on) involves the same bundle of property rights as a private consumption good except that the way in which the state exercises its right may be very different from that of the typical capitalist or worker (since, as has been seen in sections 8.5 and 8.6, their interests are very different). Access to state consumption goods typically occurs in three different ways: through the market mechanism, that is, based upon ability to pay; through the bureaucratic mechanism, that is based upon the state's definition of need; and through the free-for-all mechanism, that is, based upon the first-come-first-served principle. It is the latter form of access which effectively – that is, *de facto* if not *de jure* – transforms a state consumption good into a communal consumption good.

A communal consumption good (for example, air, common land, weather, outer space, the visual environment, the social status of an area, and so on) is defined by the fact that everyone has the right to use it and hence to benefit from or be harmed by it. In short, no one can be excluded from its consumption (see Dales, 1975, p. 491; see also Sax, 1971).[10] The most distinctive feature of communal consumption goods is that they are distributed free of charge to those living within accessible distance from them. It is for this reason that certain types of state consumption goods (roads, footpaths, streets, parks, and so on) are, in fact, if not in law, communal consumption goods.

Consumption goods can be either positive or negative according to whether their consumption has a positive or negative effect upon the consumer's well-being. Leaving aside those borderline cases where consumption goods have both positive and negative effects (for example, alcohol, tobacco, cars, and so on), it is possible to construct a typology of consumption goods. This is done in Table 8.2.

It is now necessary to examine the spatial dimension of these various consumption goods.

8.8.3 The Spatial Dimension of Consumption

Many consumption goods are fixed to particular locations (for example, houses, schools, hospitals, theatres, pubs, scenic areas, and so on) and create a positive or negative effect – an externality [11] – around the point where they are located according to whether they are positive or negative consumption goods. It is this externality effect which gives consumption goods their spatial dimension (see Pahl, 1975, Chapters 7 and 9).

The effect created by the location of a consumption good in an area can be understood in terms of the concepts of externality field (see Harvey, 1973, p. 60; Smith, 1977, p. 91; Bale, 1978, p. 334) and externality gradient (see Bale, ibid.). An externality field refers to the area over which the consumption good has an effect, either positive or negative. Within the externality field the intensity with which the effects of a consumption good are felt are likely to vary, that is, increase or decrease, with distance from its location, and this can be depicted by the externality gradient.

The concepts of externality gradient and externality field are illustrated diagramatically in Figures 8.2 and 8.3, using the example of a negative communal consumption good (for example, smoke emissions from a factory chimney which are consumed by those breathing the affected air).

Figure 8.2 shows that the negative effect of the consumption good (measured on the oy axis) decreases with distance (measured on the *ox* axis) from its location (*o*). The externality field in Figure 8.3 is derived from the externality gradient and is based upon the assumption that the

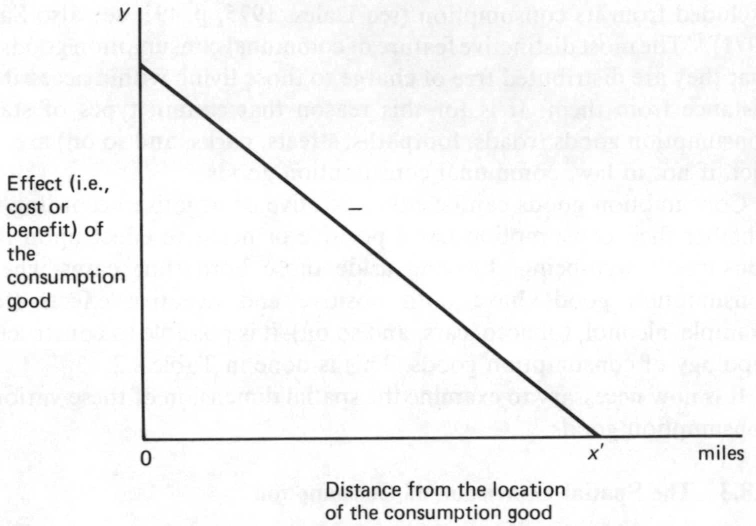

Figure 8.2 The externality gradient of a negative communal consumption good

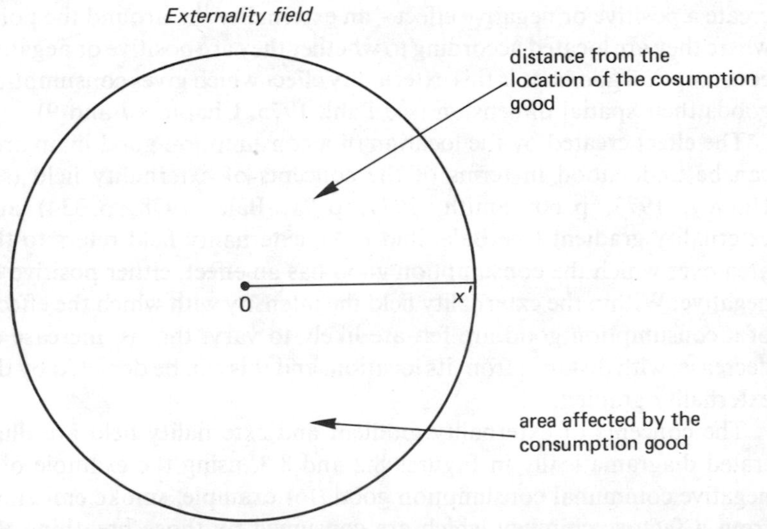

Figure 8.3 The externality field of a negative communal consumption good

effect of the consumption good is uniformly diffused in all directions from its location. Thus, since *ox′* is the distance over which the consumption good has an effect, the rotation of *ox′* through 360° from the source (*o*) defines the externality field, that is, the area affected by the

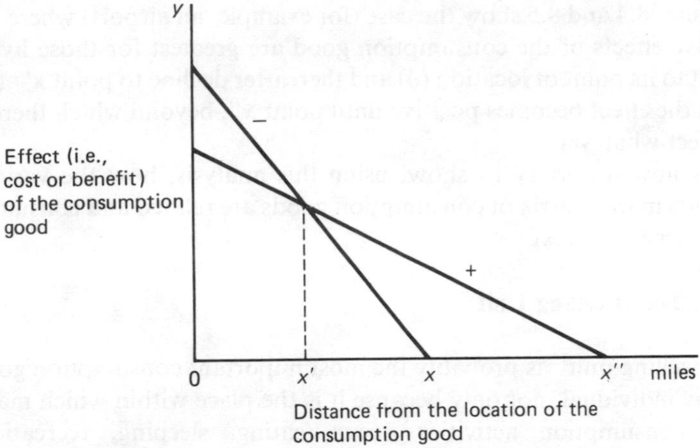

Figure 8.4 The externality gradient of a consumption good with both positive and negative effects

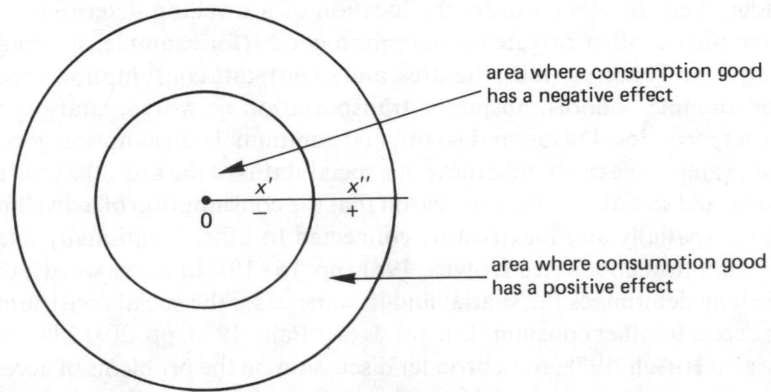

Figure 8.5 The externality field of a consumption good with both positive and negative effects

consumption good ($\pi \times (ox')^2$). It follows from this that if the population is evenly distributed in the area, then every unit increase in the distance over which the consumption good has an effect will result in a trebling of the area affected and hence a trebling of the number of people affected by the externality.

Not all consumption goods are unequivocally positive or negative, however; many have both positive and negative aspects (for example, an airport, a motorway, a pub, and so on). This is illustrated in Figures 8.4 and 8.5.

Figures 8.4 and 8.5 show the case (for example, an airport) where the negative effects of the consumption good are greatest for those living closest to its point of location (o) and thereafter decline to point x' after which the effect becomes positive until point x'', beyond which there is no effect whatever.

It is now necessary to show, using this analysis, how the various elements in the matrix of consumption goods are related and consumed in the urban context.

8.8.4 The Dwelling Unit

The dwelling unit[12] is probably the most important consumption good for any individual, not only because it is the place within which many other consumption activities occur (eating, sleeping, recreation, procreation, and so on) but also because it is the point of origin from which journeys to work as well as to other sources of consumption (schools, shops, clinics, sports centres, parks, theatres, and so on) are undertaken. In other words, the location of a dwelling determines its proximity to other private consumption goods (for example, shopping centres, golf courses, pubs, theatres, and so on) state consumption goods (for example, schools, hospitals, transportation networks, landscaped open spaces, local taxes, and so on) and communal consumption goods (for example, clean air, quietness, the social status of the area, the level of crime, and so on). It is for this reason that the consumption of a dwelling unit is spatially and inextricably connected to other locationally fixed consumption goods (see Downs, 1981, pp. 16–19). In other words, the dwelling determines the spatial and in some cases the social constraints on access to other consumption goods (see Pahl, 1975, pp. 201, 248–64; see also Hirsch, 1978, for a broader discussion on the problems of access to consumption goods). Thus, as Bourne (1981, p. 3) points out 'obtaining the key to a house, flat or apartment also brings with it the right to a given level of public services (police, schools, parks, etc); it determines one's local tax rate and in turn it delivers a set of benefits (security, etc.) or disbenefits (crime, vandalism, etc.) to both the individual household and the larger community'.[13]

The location of consumption goods, in turn, normally has a simultaneous effect upon a number of contiguous sites within a given area. Using the concepts of externality gradient and externality field, these locationally fixed consumption goods (for example, shopping centres, public parks, noise, pollution, and so on) can be seen as creating a field of effects, which normally decline with distance. In this way, the unequal distribution of locationally-fixed consumption goods within an urban area gives rise to different but internally homogenous sub-areas.

Numerous studies have attempted to quantify the effect which the location of various types of consumption goods can have upon the price of dwellings within a particular area. These studies have focused upon such consumption goods as pollution (Ridker and Henning, 1967), expenditure on education (Oates, 1969) and status (Bailey, 1966), and have shown how the proximity of dwellings to these goods can affect the price of those dwellings. This confirms that an intimate connection exists, and is perceived to exist (see Agnew, 1978), between the dwelling and other locationally-fixed consumption goods (see also Saunders, 1978, p. 247; Nicholls, *et al.*, 1982, p. 338). In a capitalist market economy, the price of a dwelling, which is determined not only by its location *vis-à-vis* other consumption goods but also by such factors as the scarcity of sites, the cost of building materials, the availability of mortgage finance, and so on, acts as the mechanism governing access to that dwelling, and hence access to different parts of the urban area. One of the outcomes of this process is that the inequalities in income within and between classes, as a result of their position in the sphere of production, are spatially reflected by their location in the different parts of the urban area. Urban sociologists and urban geographers have devoted considerable attention to documenting, through the use of social area analysis and factorial ecology, the existence of these various sub-areas, though less attention had been given, at least up until the late 1960s, to the processes by which they are created (Ambrose, 1977, p. 39).

The significance of these considerations from the point of view of the constrained-actor model is that it is possible to identify at least three different actors (or tenure groups) whose interests in relation to housing are different and who are therefore affected in different ways by changes in the value of their dwellings. These three tenure groups, that is, owner-occupiers, local authority tenants and private sector tenants are defined by their property rights over dwellings and may be referred to as 'housing classes' because they constitute different sets of interests.[14]

Although there are significant differences within each of these tenure groups in terms of income and the quality of their dwellings and its environment, each nevertheless shares a common material interest in relating to housing, not only because they tend to be similarly affected by changing property values, but also because state subventions to housing are distributed primarily on the basis of tenure (although the size of the subvention is affected by income and other factors). Other tenure groups – such as housing association tenants – may also be identified if it can be shown that their material interest in relation to housing is different from that of other tenure groups.

8.8.5 Tenure Groups and Changes in the Site Value of Dwelling Units

In Britain there are three main types of housing tenure: owner-occupation; rental from a private landlord; and rental from the local state. (Housing associations and co-operatives are yet another form of tenure but, unlike some European countries, this sector is very small in Britain.) The precise mechanism by which access is gained to these different tenurial positions is determined ultimately by income and stage in the life cycle and proximately by the 'gatekeepers' or 'managers' of the housing supply (see Pahl, 1975, Chapter 13; see also Williams, 1978).

In the private sector, where dwelling units are purchased or leased from private landlords, these managers are estate agents, mortgage managers, and landlords, who ensure that dwellings are distributed according to market criteria (that is, ability to pay) so that those with the highest (earned or unearned) income will obtain the best dwelling units and vice versa. In the state sector, where dwelling units are rented from the state, the manager is the local state authority who ensures that the dwellings are distributed according to the state's definition of need.

Each tenure group is affected differently by changes in the price of their dwelling unit. These changes are caused by spatial factors (that is changes in the location and quality of private, state and communal consumption goods) and by non-spatial factors (for example, inflation, interest rates, state subventions, and so on). The analysis here will focus only upon those changes caused by spatial (or environmental) factors for two reasons: first, in order to highlight the spatial interdependencies involved in the consumption of urban dwellings, and secondly, in order to demonstrate that the differences in material interests between different tenure groups or housing classes are not solely 'contingent' upon such non-spatial factors as high inflation, low interest rates and state subventions as Dunleavy (1979, p. 420), Saunders (1980a, pp. 97–8) and Pratt (1982, pp. 485–8, 495) have claimed. These different interests are a direct result of the operation of different sets of property rights within a built-up area.

The price of a dwelling, as has been seen, can be affected spatially by changes in the location of private consumption goods (for example, the change may relate to a shop, a golf club, or any other privately-owned amenity), state consumption goods (for example, the change may relate to the siting of a motorway, an airport, a dump, a park, and so on), or communal consumption goods (for example, the change may relate to the pollution of the air by smoke, noise, or smells, or to the increase in crime in the area, and so on). Some of these changes may increase the site-value of a dwelling unit while others may reduce it. If they increase it then owner-occupiers receive, *inter alia*, an increase in their imputed income from home ownership while tenants in the private sector will have an increase in the actual rent which they pay to the landlord, as long as competitive market conditions prevail (see Downs, 1981, Chapter 6). The effect in the case of local authority tenants cannot be determined *a priori* since it depends upon the rent policy of the local authority and the constraints imposed upon it, in turn, by central government. Conversely, if the price of the dwelling is reduced then owner-occupiers suffer a reduction in their imputed rent while private sector tenants get a reduction in their actual rent, assuming normal market conditions. The effect, in the case of local authority tenants depends again upon the rent policy of the local housing authority (see Neutze, 1976, pp. 85–6 for a useful discussion of the way in which increases in land and house prices affect different tenure groups.)

The property rights of an individual over a dwelling are thus an important consideration in assessing the distributional consequences of changes in the positive and negative consumption goods affecting that individual's area. The implication of this is that a group of individuals (for example, manual and non-manual workers) may have the same material interests in relation to production but quite different material interests in relation to housing if their tenure positions are different. These different class positions may lead, depending upon the way in which they are seen by each individual, to different types of individual and collective action at both the national and neighbourhood level. The evidence in Britain suggests that, at both these levels, there is a significant difference between owner-occupiers and tenants in their political allegiances (see Dunleavy, 1979) and also in terms of the goals of local community action (see Saunders, 1978, 1980a and b; Silburn, 1975).

It is now necessary to analyse more fully the individual and collective reactions of different tenure groups to changes which affect the site value of their dwellings, and hence affect their material interests.

8.8.6 Individual and Collective Reaction to Changes in Consumption

Residents of an area, irrespective of their tenurial position, have an obvious interest in increasing the positive consumption goods in their area and reducing the negative ones. As a result, the location of consumption goods in an area is frequently an issue around which individual and collective action arises. The way in which this occurs can be seen in the case of an area facing the threat of an increase in some negative consumption good (for example, an increase in local taxes[15] an increase in the level of crime, an increase in air and noise pollution, a deterioration in the visual environment or in the social status of an area, and so on). Although the analysis below will be illustrated by examples of negative consumption goods the same processes of individual and collective action could be applied to the location of positive consumption goods (for example, parks, crèches, schools and other desirable amenities).

The state (both central and local) is usually one of the main targets towards which individual and collective action is directed in an urban area, since it plays a crucial role in producing, distributing and regulating many of the consumption goods (both positive and negative) which are located there and which are the source of what Cox terms 'localized welfare impacts' (Cox, 1978, p. 99). It is for this reason that action over consumption in an urban area is frequently political action, as the growing body of literature on urban conflict and urban politics clearly shows (see Cox, 1973, 1978; Agnew, 1978; Dear and Long, 1978; Reynolds and Honey, 1978; Ley and Mercer, 1980; Cox, 1981; Cox and Johnston, 1982; Cox and McCarthy, 1982; Robson, 1982).

Residents in an area affected by a negative consumption good (for example, air pollution) can react in a number of different ways. They may leave or stay, protest or remain silent. The full range of options, based upon a modification of Hirschman's model is outlined in Table 8.3 (see Hirschman, 1970; see also Orbell and Uno, 1972; Dear and Long, 1978).

Table 8.3 A typology of the reactions of residents to a negative consumption good in their area

	Silence	*Protest*
Stay	(1) Resignation	(3) Collective action
Leave	(2) Migration	(4) Protest in exile

In the present context only reactions (1), (2) and (3) will be considered since option (4) is more appropriate to cases such as political refugees. The first reaction is resignation and acceptance of the negative consumption good. The second is for some (or all) of the residents to migrate to another area in order to avoid the negative consumption good. The third is for residents in the affected area to engage in collective action to have the negative consumption good reduced or relocated. Each of these three reactions will now be discussed respectively (subsections 8.8.7 to 8.8.9).

8.8.7 Resignation

Resignation is possibly the most frequent response of residents to the location of a negative consumption good in their area. There are at least three reasons why residents may adopt this strategy. First, the effects of the negative consumption good may be insignificant and thus insufficient to generate either migration or collective action. Secondly, residents may feel powerless to effect a relocation or even a reduction in the negative consumption good, thus reflecting their alienation from the political process (see Mullins, 1977, p. 33). Thirdly, the residents may not have the money, time or energy to either migrate from the area, or to engage in collective political or legal action. In consequence, they may be resigned to what they see as the inevitable.

8.8.8 Migration

The choice to migrate or 'exit' (Hirschman, 1970) is determined, in this context, by the resident's perception of the size of the effect created by the negative consumption good, the possible success of collective action and the constraints of migration facing each resident. If the effect of the negative consumption good is large (for example, a rising level of crime or taxation, the location of an airport or motorway, the movement of a low status group into a high status area,[16] and so on) and if the possibility of successful collective action is low then, *ceteris paribus*, migration is likely to be considered as a rational course of action. However, as has been seen (subsection 8.7.2) those on lower incomes face major constraints to migration by comparison with higher income owner occupiers because of the costs involved in migration. Moreover, migration is likely to be a satisfactory solution for only those owner-occupiers who move before the full consequences of the negative consumption good are reflected in the price of their dwellings. The possibility of migration for local authority tenants depends ultimately upon the policy of the local authority while, in the case of private sector tenants, it depends upon such factors as the location and price of private rented accommodation in other areas (see Cox, 1978, p. 99; Cox and Johnston, 1982, pp. 200–1).

Migration, however, does not have the effect of reducing or relocating a negative externality so that the remaining residents as well as the new immigrant residents will be obliged to bear its full costs. This may still happen even if they engage in collective action (see Dear and Long, 1978, pp. 117–18).

8.8.9 Collective Action

Collective action, as the term implies, is action by a group to obtain a goal or interest shared by the group. In the present context, the exclusion of a negative consumption good from a given residential area would, by definition, be a shared material interest. Collective action requires an organisation through which the group interest can be expressed and advanced and, in the present context, this organisation is typically a residents' committee or association although it may also be the local branch of a political party or an environmental organisation.

The emergence of an organisation to advance the collective interest of a group is neither straightforward nor inevitable. Indeed, as Olson (1971, Chapter 1) has shown, if individuals are economically self-interested, they will be unable, because of the 'free-rider problem', to form an organisation to protect or advance their collective interest – unless they resort to special incentives or coercion to ensure organisational membership. If, by contrast, individuals act from moral motives (for example, from a sense of justice or compassion) then an organisation to further the collective interest is likely to form more easily through the altruism of its members.

In the case of residents' associations, the furtherance of collective interests may also encounter the obstacle that the interests of all the residents may not be entirely identical. This could happen for a number of reasons. First, there may be variations in the age, stage in the life cycle or tenure status of the residents. As has been seen (subsection 8.4.5) negative (and positive) consumption goods affect each tenure group differently; owner-occupiers are more likely than other tenure groups to bear the full costs (and benefits) of these goods and, other things being equal, they may be more likely to engage in collective action than other tenure groups.[17] Secondly, certain consumption goods (for example, a motorway, a railway line, an airport) may be of the type whose effects are predominantly negative for those living closest to them, and predominantly positive for those living at greater distances (subsection

8.4.4). This creates a divergence (and possible a conflict) of interest between two different groups of residents. Thirdly, some negative consumption goods (for example, those relating to the social status of an area) are crucially dependent upon the belief or attitude that certain racial, religious, ethnic or income groups are of inferior status and this attitude may not be universally shared by all the residents of an area. Fourthly, the negative consumption good may affect a large area and hence a large number of residents and, as a general rule, large groups are much more difficult to organise than small groups. These four considerations reveal the types of impediment which are likely to confront the emergence of a common interest in a given urban area.

The fact that an organisation emerges in a residential area, in spite of these impediments, does not guarantee, however, that it will be effective in furthering the interests of residents. The effectiveness of an organisation in mobilising opposition depends upon a number of factors of which the following are the principal ones: the amount of money at its disposal; the quality of leadership; the internal structure of the organisation; its linkages (both vertical and horizontal) with other organisations, for example, political parties, trade unions, the media, other residential associations, and so on (see Pickvance, 1975, pp. 40–41); its contacts with influential individuals (for example, senior personnel in central or local government); its choice and number of tactics and the type and cost of the demands being made. Any one of these factors could mean the difference between the success or failure of an organisation in attaining its goals.

An investigation of the way in which residents collectively attempt to exclude negative consumption goods from their area reveals that a wide range of exclusionary strategies have been used. These strategies vary according to the source and type of the consumption good and from one country to another. The following are some of the main exclusionary strategies (apart from the market, which is also an exclusionary strategy, but does not require collective action).

1. Controlling the sale of dwelling units to new residents. This strategy, according to Cox (1973, p. 25), is used in the US by white residents in 'neighbourhoods threatened by racial transition' (ibid.). In such cases, 'residents planning to sell property are frequently asked to place it in the hands of an agency expressly established by a neighbourhood association for the purpose of limiting the business carried on by block busters' (ibid.; see also Wolf and Lebeaux, 1969, Chapter 3). This technique facilitates the racial residential segrega-

tion of neighbourhoods as well as ensuring that the supply of housing is more restricted for non-whites than for whites so that, *ceteris paribus*, the former pay more for the purchase or lease of housing than the latter (see Ridker and Henning, 1967, pp. 250–51, 255–6; Kain and Quigley, 1975, p. 540; see however, Bailey, 1966, pp. 218–20).

2. Exclusionary land-use zoning. This strategy, which is widely used in the US, involves zoning land according to certain criteria which effectively exclude low income groups. These criteria include the requirement that the size of the site and the building must be large, the prohibition of mobile homes and multiple family dwellings, restriction on the number of bedrooms, and so on (see Williams and Norman, 1971). Alternatively the area may be zoned for open space (see White, 1981).
3. The creation of physical barriers. Physical barriers in the form of roads, rivers, walls, railway lines, and so on, act as boundaries between different residential areas. These barriers may be important in 'protecting' a higher status neighbourhood from what it regards as too close proximity to a lower status neighbourhood. Where such barriers are not present, they may be erected. The most famous example of this occurred in Oxford, England, in the 1930s, when a middle-class housing estate constructed a wall – the Cutteslowe Wall – to reduce their proximity to an adjacent local authority housing estate (see Collison, 1963).
4. The use of vigilante groups. The residents in an area may adopt this type of strategy to combat crime and vandalism. However because it is illegal it is likely to be covert and of short duration.
5. The use of political pressure. This strategy is most likely to be used when it is within the power of the (central or local) state to reduce or relocate a negative consumption good (for example, the flight path of aircraft over a particular residential area). A large number of tactics may be used in the furtherance of this stragegy. Pickvance (1975, p. 37) has classified these into 'institutional', that is, those within the framework of the law (for example, voting, petitions, deputations, demonstrations, creation of media interest, and so on) and 'non-institutional', that is, those outside the framework of the law (for example, violent or illegal demonstrations, sit-downs and sit-ins, rent strikes, and so on). The effectiveness of any particular tactic is likely to be highly dependent upon the circumstances of the

case, though Saunders' study of the actions of residents' associations in the London Borough of Croydon reveals the overriding effectiveness of institutional tactics (see Saunders, 1980a, p. 121).

8.8.10 Summary

The analysis in this section has attempted to develop a spatial dimension to the concept of final consumption by attempting an account of the fact that certain elements of the real wage (for example, houses, hospitals, schools, and so on) are fixed to particular locations and can only be consumed at those locations. The analysis focused upon the dwelling unit as the central element in the matrix of consumption goods. It was shown how changes in the value of the dwelling unit, particularly those arising from changes in its location *vis-à-vis* other consumption goods can affect different tenure groups differently, and can lead to various forms of individual and collective action. Thus the analysis of the spatial dimension of final consumption in this section has opened up new issues and problems about the nature of final consumption within urban areas.

8.9 CONCLUSION: NEW DIRECTIONS FOR MARXIST URBAN SOCIOLOGY

This chapter has outlined some new directions for Marxist urban sociology. These directions were based upon the constrained-actor model which, although not strictly Marxist, nevertheless retains the Marxian emphasis upon the role of interest and conflict in human interaction. The result is a more micro-level analysis than that contained in the works of Castells and Lojkine, and one which overcomes some of the difficulties found in their work.

The novelty of the contribution presented in this chapter lies in the application of the constrained-actor model to the analysis of the three processes constitutive of an urban area. The first of these is the process by which urban areas are produced in a capitalist society and the analysis of this involved a conceptual investigation of the logic of state and private property development (sections 8.4 to 8.6). This investigation provided a broader framework of analysis than that found in Castells and Lojkine where there is no explicit treatment of the process of private property development and where the treatment of state property development, via the concept of collective consumption, is far from satisfactory (sections 6.2 and 7.2). Thus the analysis in those sections provided a framework within which more detailed empirical studies of private and state property development in different capitalist countries can be undertaken.

The second process is the process by which urban areas are used in the production of commodities in a capitalist society. Since an urban area can only be used to produce commodities if capitalists and/or the state decide to locate their production operations there, and if workers live (or migrate to live) within commuting distance of those production operations, the analysis of this process focused upon the location decisions of firms and the migration and commuting decisions of workers. This analysis was carried out (in Section 8.7) using the concept of labour market areas and it provided the basis for a clarification of the precise relationship between urban areas and labour market areas. The significance of this analysis is that it explicitly treats the issues of industrial location, labour migration and commuting patterns which have an important bearing upon the use of urban areas and which have not hitherto been adequately incorporated within urban sociology generally or Marxist urban sociology in particular.

The third and final process constitutive of urban areas is the process of final consumption. The novelty of this part of the analysis (section 8.8) lies in its typology of consumption goods and in demonstrating that consumption goods have a spatial dimension. Many consumption goods, whether they are private, state or communal and whether they are positive or negative, are normally located and fixed at specific places and can only be consumed at those places. These considerations were conceptualised by treating the dwelling unit as the central element in the matrix of consumption goods whose value is determined, *inter alia*, by the externality effects generated by its location *vis-à-vis* other consumption goods. This analysis contrasts with the traditional Marxian view where consumption goods are treated non-spatially as bundles of wage goods. The above analysis also examined the significance of housing tenure as well as the various types of actions which residents typically undertake in order to maintain or improve the amount of consumption goods in their area.

The main conclusion to emerge from this chapter and from the book generally is that the field of Marxist urban sociology, as found in the writings of Manuel Castells and Jean Lojkine, could be considerably advanced by developing a more micro-level analysis of urban processes and conflicts. This analysis would complement rather than replace the traditional Marxist approach since both macro- and micro-level explanations are essential to all sociological analysis, including Marxist urban sociology.

Notes

General Introduction

1. One of the simplest measures of the volume of interest generated by their work is the number of citations of it which are listed in the Annual Social Science Citation Index (see Institute for Scientific Information, 1969–1984). Table N1 lists the annual number of citations of their work since their names first appeared in the index.

Table N1 Number of citations per year of the works of Manuel Castells and Jean Lojkine and the average number of citations of each cited author in the Social Science Citation Index (1969–84)

Year	*Castells*	*Lojkine*	*Average*
1969	4	1	3.34
1970	3	1	3.27
1971	7	1	3.42
1972	5	0	3.39
1973	5	0	3.41
1974	23	0	3.40
1975	42	1	3.61
1976	22	3	3.68
1977	31	8	3.66
1978	61	4	3.72
1979	80	11	3.90
1980	103	12	4.00
1981	97	12	4.28
1982	92	15	4.42
1983	110	28	3.94
1984	104	14	4.03

Source: Compiled from the Annual Social Science Citation Index for each year between 1969 and 1984 (see Institute for Scientific Information, 1969–1984).

Although Table N1 reveals the volume of interest generated by these two authors it does not indicate whether that interest is favourable or unfavourable. However, three facts can be clearly discerned from the table. The first is that Castells's work has generated much greater interest than that of Lojkine. This is due not only to the slightly larger volume of Castells's work (although Castells frequently publishes the same material in slightly modified form in a number of different places) but also because Castells's work has been widely translated into English, Spanish, Portugese, Italian and Danish (see UNESCO 1974–1977). Lojkine's work has not been as widely translated. The second fact is that there has been a fairly steady increase in interest in both authors, particulary since the mid-1970s. The third fact is that the number of citations of Castells's work, with the exception of 1970, has been consistently above the average of other authors cited in the Social Science Citation Index, while the number of citations of Lojkine's work has also been above average since 1977. The writings of both authors are listed in the Bibliography below.

1 Marx's Labour Theory of Value

1. Walker comments, appositely: 'By socially necessary Marx means, of course, commercially necessary. In other words, an industrialist cannot, because of competition, use a productive method less mechanized than that prevalent in his industry generally, without eventually losing money' (Walker, 1978, p. 162).
2. The reason for Marx's preference must be seen in the context of his distinction between the use value and the exchange value of labour (which is discussed later in this section). To anticipate: when Marx speaks of the use value of labour power he refers to the value of the output which that labour power creates and describes it by the term 'the value of labour' (see Marx, 1974a, Chapter 7, pp. 173–92; 1975, section 7, pp. 43–6). By contrast, when he speaks of the exchange value of labour power he refers to the value of the wages which are necessary to reproduce that labour power and describes it by the term 'the value of labour power' (ibid.).
3. There is in turn an important distinction, within the concept of constant capital, between the stock of constant capital (that is, fixed constant capital) and the flow of constant capital (that is, circulating constant capital). Fixed constant capital (k) refers to the value of fixed equipment, stocks of raw materials and half-finished goods net of depreciation which last for more than one period of production. Circulating constant capital (c) refers to the value of the depreciation of fixed capital equipment plus the value of raw materials, fuel, etc. which is used up in one production period. It is usually assumed by Marxists (though perhaps not always justifiably: see Purdy, 1973, p. 18; and Hodgson, 1974a, pp. 57–8) that all fixed constant capital is used up during one production period (that is, $k = 0$), so that constant capital is equal to circulating constant capital (that is, $C = c$) (see Howard and King, 1975, p. 199). In the present analysis, total capital is assumed to be equal to circulating constant capital. This is an assumption of convenience, which is appropriate for the present elementary analysis.
4. Morishima (1973, Chapter 1) distinguishes between two different definitions of the value of a commodity which are present in Marx. The first definition, which is the one just outlined, defines the value of a commodity as equal to the value of those constituent elements which become embodied in it, while the second defines the value of a commodity as equal to the socially necessary

labour which is required to produce one unit of the net output of that commodity. Morishima remarks that: 'At first sight these may look like identical definitions, and Marx actually regarded them as synonymous. They are, however, found to be different views of value, their equivalence being established only if rigorous proof is provided' (ibid., p. 11). The distinction between these two definitions will not be pursued here: it will be assumed, following the convention in these matters, that the first definition is the correct (if not the only) definition.

5. Marx's assumption about money is, evidently, no longer correct. Money is no longer a produced commodity (like gold) whose value/price is determined by its value/price of production. Money now takes the form of pieces of paper and plastic whose worth is fixed by convention. Marx's assumption that all money is gold adds an additional complexity to his analysis in the sense that the money value or money price of a commodity can change, not only as a result of changes in the production of that commodity but also as a result of changes in the production of gold.

6. It is sometimes argued that the dualism between values and surplus value on the one hand, and prices and profit on the other, corresponds not only to two levels of reality but also to two different historical eras (see, for example, Meek, 1956, 1976b; Sherman, 1970, p. 278; Marx, 1974c, p. 177; Engels, 1974, pp. 895ff). The argument here is that in the preceding historical era of simple commodity production commodities were exchanged at their values, whereas in the contemporary era of capitalist commodity production, commodities exchange, not in terms of their values, but in terms of prices. Thus, the argument goes, values are not only theoretically and ontologically prior to prices, but also historically prior.

   Morishima and Catephores (1975; 1976) provide a simple refutation of this argument by showing that the historical era of simple commodity production could never have existed. They point out that simple commodity production involves a society of independent producers who are independent in three senses: first, there is no ex-ante co-ordination; second, each has individual ownership over his/her own means of production and third, there is mobility of producers among jobs. By applying this definition to the historical evidence they conclude that: 'Simple commodity production has never been realised in history in its full or pure form, or even in a tolerably approximate form, because of the lack of mobility of producers among jobs in the pre-capitalist age' (ibid., p. 315).

7. There is some disagreement over the question of Marx's mathematical ability. Engels's (1959) view was that Marx was 'well versed in mathematics' (ibid., p. 19) while Bortkiewicz (1952) refers to the 'scantiness' (ibid., p. 55) of Marx's knowledge of mathematics. Morishima's (1974a) judgement is perhaps the most balanced in pointing out that while *Capital* is not explicitly mathematical, many passages can be translated into rigorous mathematical language and that, 'mathematical problems, even new mathematical problems are concealed in his economics' (ibid., p. 612).

8. Those who attempt to defend Marx's labour theory of value by separating the issue of prices from the issue of profit have acquired the label 'fundamental-

ist' in contrast to the label 'neoRicardian' which has been reserved for those who reject the labour theory of value and adopt the Sraffa approach (see Fine and Harris, 1976, p. 144). However, the neoRicardian label is misleading since Sraffa's work demolishes the labour theory of value, held by both Marx and Ricardo, which claims that prices and profit are regulated exclusively by the quantities of labour embodied in commodities (see Hodgson, 1976, p. 20; 1977b, pp. 90–92; Roncaglia, 1978, pp. xvi–xix, 131–47; Bhaduri and Robinson, 1980, p. 104)

9. It should be noted that not all of the arguments relevant to this debate have been considered here. Possibly the most important argument relates to the effect of joint production (that is, pure joint production and fixed capital) upon the transformation of values into prices and surplus value. Steedman has shown that, when there is joint production, it is possible to have a capitalist economy where there is, simultaneously, positive profits and negative surplus value and vice versa (see Hodgson and Steedman, 1975; Steedman, 1975b and 1977, Chapter 10; however, see also Morishima, 1976 and Steedman, 1976). This is a highly anomalous result and proves that the labour theory of value breaks down in the case of joint production. Similarly the existence of a choice of techniques seriously undermines the primacy of the labour theory of value. This is because the value of a commodity can only be calculated once the technique of production is known. However, when there is a choice of techniques, the technique that is actually used will be determined by capitalists based upon current prices and profit rates. In other words, prices and the rate of profit must be known before values can be calculated. In this case, therefore, prices and profit are prior to values rather than the reverse (see Steedman, 1977, pp. 64–5; Elster, 1985, p. 136).

2 Marxian Crisis Theory

1. Glyn and Sutcliffe (1972) measured profits (including interest but less stock appreciation and depreciation) arising from production in the company sector in the UK. They found that the before-tax share of profits in net output fell from 25.2 per cent in 1950 to 12.1 per cent in 1970 (ibid., Table 3.2, p. 58), while the before-tax rate of profit fell from 16.5 per cent in 1950 to 9.7 per cent in 1970 (ibid., Table 3.3, p. 66). The after-tax rate of profit fell from 6.7 per cent in 1950 to 4.1 per cent in 1970 (ibid.), Glyn and Sutcliffe offer the following explanation: 'the decline in the share of profits and the rate of profit in the U.K. has resulted from the combination of international competition and wage pressure' (ibid., p. 70).
2. Boddy and Crotty (1975) based their research on a study of the St Louis Federal Reserve Bank which showed that, in the various expansionary periods between 1947 and 1972, wages managed to squeeze profits in the non-financial corporate sector resulting in 'a pronounced decline in the ratio of profits to wages' (ibid., p. 5). During this period, the percentage ratio of before-tax net profits (that is, profits less depreciation and net interest) to gross product fell from 19.4 per cent to 10.6 per cent (ibid.).

3. Weisskopf's (1979) research was based upon data collected by the US National Income and Product Accounts and related to the non-financial corporate business sector of the economy (which accounts for 60 per cent of the gross national product). Weisskopf's research shows that the rate of profit in this sector (defined as the ratio of 'before-tax net capital income including corporate profits plus net interest' to 'the net stock of capital including both fixed capital and inventories' (ibid., p. 349)) fell from an average of 11.5 per cent in 1949 to 6.5 per cent in 1975 (ibid., p. 350) amounting to an average annual decline of 1.2 per cent over the period. 'This decline' he argues 'was attributable almost entirely to a decline in profit share' (ibid., p. 352). Weisskopf's conclusion is that: 'The long-term decline in the rate of profit from 1949 to 1975 was almost entirely attributable to a rise in the true share of wages, which indicates a rise in the strength of labour' (ibid., p. 370).
4. Heap (1980) shows, on the basis of OECD data (Hill, 1979), that pre-tax profits in the manufacturing sector and in the transport and industry sector fell precipitately in all of the major industrialised countries in the period 1955–76 as a result of 'a squeeze on the share of output going to profits and a rise in the capital-output share' (Heap, 1980, p. 66).
5. The meaning of the terms 'long-run' and 'short-run' in the present context is slightly different from the conventional meaning. In the conventional usage (see Lipsey, 1971, p. 212; Bannock, Baxter and Rees, 1972, pp. 260, 273), the term long-run refers, at the microeconomic level, to the period of time which a firm requires to adjust output (and, by implication, the inputs necessary to produce that output) to a change in demand. The length of the long-run will be determined by that input which takes the longest time to adjust and will be equal to the latter. At the macroeconomic level, the term long-run is used more generally to refer to the period of time required for underlying 'structural' changes (for example, in employment, output, investment, and so on) to occur in the economy. By contrast, the term short-run refers, at the microeconomic level, to the period of time during which it would be impossible for a firm to adjust its output (and, by implication, the inputs necessary to produce that output) to a change in demand. The length of the short-run will be determined by that input which takes the longest time to adjust and will be less than the latter. At the macroeconomic level, the term short-run is used more generally to refer to the period during which underlying 'structural' change could not possibly occur.

   In the present context, the problem arises with the term long-run since it cannot be assumed to end endogenously. As a result, its length remains indefinite. Thus it is necessary to specify that the long-run can only be ended exogenously (for example, by state intervention) and it is this which determines its length. (Weisskopf, 1978, p. 242, uses a similar definition.) It is only because of this additional specification that it is possible to describe Marx's law of the falling rate of profit as a long-run phenomenon.
6. It should be emphasised that the issue here is not whether there exists a tendency for the rate of profit to fall and a counter-tendency for it to rise (since Marx clearly acknowledged that both tendencies exist) but whether

one tendency is actually dominant. If neither is dominant then it makes no sense to speak of a 'law' (see Steedman, 1975a, pp. 79–80; Hodgson, 1974a, pp. 97–8).

7. It may be of some interest to recall one of the few studies which have attempted to test Marx's theory against the empirical evidence of a particular capitalist economy. Gillman (1957) made one such attempt by measuring the organic composition of capital and the rate of profit (in terms of prices rather than values) for the manufacturing sector in the US for the period 1849–1952. He found, in brief, that neither the organic composition of capital nor the rate of profit consistently changed in the direction which Marx's law would have predicted. However, even if Gillman's evidence had shown a pattern identical to that predicted by Marx, there would still be the question of the appropriateness of using price data as a measure of Marx's 'law', particularly since Marx always defined the rate of profit and its tendency to fall in value terms (see Hodgson, 1974a, pp. 70–75; Desai, 1979, pp. 193–8).
8. Another cause of realisation crisis, not discussed here for reasons of space, arises from the fact that different parts of constant fixed capital 'have different durabilities' (Marx, 1974b, p. 457; see also pp. 453–73). This case is discussed extensively by Kenway (1980). The reason for this type of realisation crisis is that capital goods depreciate at different rates so that the demand for the output of the sector producing those goods is likely to be discontinuous and fluctuating, thereby giving rise to periods of overproduction (when demand is low) and underproduction (when demand is high). This possibility arises even in the case of simple reproduction, contrary to the interpretation of Bleaney (1976, p. 106) and Desai (1979, p. 41).
9. Marx's models of reproduction, like most models in economics, abstracts from what Robinson calls 'historical time' (Robinson, 1980, p. 223; see also Bhaduri and Robinson, 1980, p. 105) in the sense that it does not consider the historical process by which the economy has reached its current state of equilibrium. It is assumed, for analytical purposes, that the present (as distinct from the future) equilibrium has always existed and is identical in each preceding period, stretching back indefinitely through what Robinson calls 'logical time' (Robinson, 1980, p. 220; see also Bhaduri and Robinson, 1980, p. 105).
10. The same effect, it should be noted, would arise if the commodity – assuming it is indispensable and non-substitutable – entered final consumption as a wage good.
11. Malthus's *Essay on Population* was published in 1798 and put forward the theory that population size would always be limited by the scarcity of resources. His argument was that population would tend to increase at a compound rate (like a geometric progression) whereas resources would tend to increase at a simple rate (like an arithmetic progression) (see Blaug, 1962, Chapter 3). As a consequence, if population were not voluntarily controlled it would ultimately be controlled by starvation. This point can be illustrated graphically by plotting the curve of an arithmetic progression (correspond-

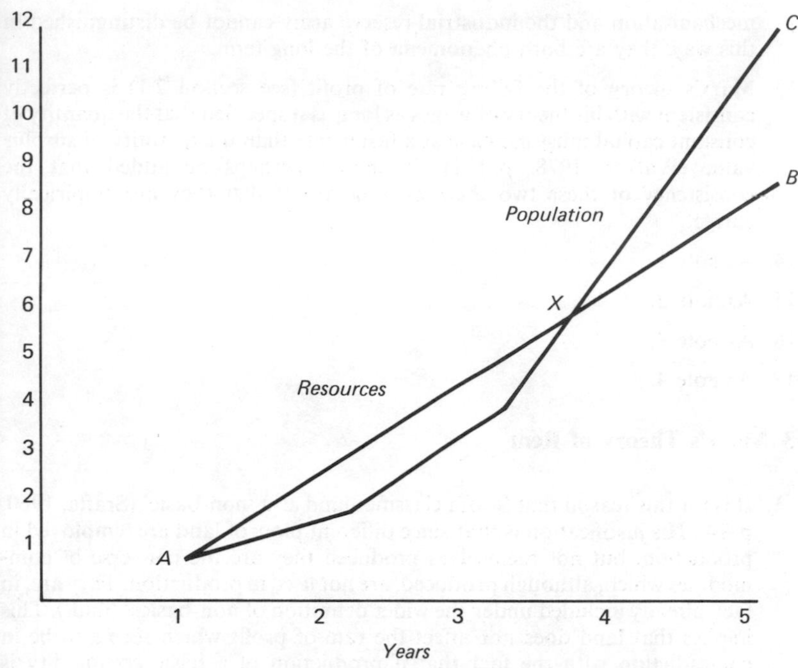

Figure N1 The growth of population and resources according to Malthus

ing to the growth of resources) and the curve of a geometric progression (corresponding to the growth of population). From Figure N1 it can be seen that the line *AB* describes the growth path of resources over time while the line *AC* describes the growth path of population over the same time. It follows from that that *X* is the point where the growth in population and resources are in equilibrium. The area to the left of *X* represents periods of plenty, while the area to the right of *X* represents periods of scarcity (that is, surplus population). The level of wages is the mechanism which determines the balance (or imbalance) between population and resources. Marx's main criticism of Malthus was that a surplus population (in relation to the available resources) was not necessarily due to natural increase alone; it could also be due to capital-using/technical innovation within capitalist society itself.

12. Morishima and Catephores (1978) distinguish between a short-term and a long-term theory of the supply of labour in Marx's work (ibid., p. 121). They claim that the industrial reserve army is the key element in Marx's short-term theory while mechanisation is the key element in his long-term theory. However this view is highly dubious since it is mechanisation which gives rise, *ceteris paribus*, to the industrial reserve army. In other words

mechanisation and the industrial reserve army cannot be distinguished in this way: they are both phenomena of the long-term.

13. Marx's theory of the falling rate of profit (see section 2.1) is perfectly consistent with his theory of wages as long as it specified that the quantity of constant capital must increase at a faster rate than the quantity of surplus value (Walker, 1978, p. 171). It should perhaps be added that the consistency of these two theories is no proof that they are empirically correct.
14. As note 1.
15. As note 2.
16. As note 3.
17. As note 4.

3 Marx's Theory of Rent

1. It is for this reason that Sraffa classifies land as a 'non-basic' (Sraffa, 1960, p. 74). His justification is that since different plots of land are 'employed in production, but not themselves produced they are the converse of commodities which, although produced, are not used in production. They are, in fact, already included under the wider definition of non-basics' (ibid.). This implies that land does not affect the rate of profit which seems to be in contradiction with the fact that if production of a basic commodity is extended to land of inferior quality then, *ceteris paribus*, it will cause a decline in the rate of profit (see section 3.1). There is, however, no contradiction since Sraffa's distinction between basic and non-basic commodities applies to commodities being produced at a given point in time and under given technical and social conditions of production (land being one such given condition). Once these given conditions change (as occurs, for example, when production is extended to inferior land), then the relationships between wages, prices and profits, postulated by Sraffa, also change (see Roncaglia, 1978, Chapter 3, especially p. 61).
2. It is possible to construct a typology of land according to its quantity and quality from which it is possible to deduce the type of situations where rent will arise if that land is owned by landowners and leased to capitalists for the production of commodities (see Table N2).

Table N2 A typology of land

		Quantity of land	
		Scarce	*Plentiful*
Quality of land	Variable	(1) Rent	(2) Rent
	Invariable	(3) Rent	(4) No rent

It can be seen from this typology that rent will arise in all cases irrespective of the variability in quality ((1) and (3)) and will also arise, even when land is plentiful (2), as long as there are not unlimited quantities of one particular type of land. The only case where no rent will arise is where land is invariable in quality and plentiful in quantity (4). The typical situation in capitalist societies is where land is scarce and variable in quality (1), or plentiful but variable in quality with the supply of each type of land being limited (2). The correctness of this typology and its implications will become apparent as the analysis of rent unfolds in the subsequent sections (3.1 to 3.4).

3. The terms input, output, net input and net output refer throughout to a quantity of goods 'calculated at the ruling levels of the rate of profits, wages and prices' (Sraffa, 1960, p. 75).
4. It should be noted that the fertility of any plot of land in a capitalist society can only be known after it has been used in the production of commodities and, consequently, its profitability has been established. Thus fertility, far from being an invariable and inherent property of the land, as Ricardo and Marx believed, is crucially dependent upon the prevailing profit (and wage) rates in each capitalist economy (see Sraffa, 1960, p. 75; Montani, 1975, pp. 71–9; Kurz, 1978, pp. 20–23).
5. In a capitalist system, the scarcity of land, and hence of corn, could arise in a situation of simple reproduction (that is, a zero rate of economic growth) if workers gained an increase in real wages (assuming corn to be the only wage good) or in a situation of extended reproduction (that is, a positive rate of economic growth) if further expansion was curtailed because of the scarcity of corn. Thus, a basic precondition of differential rent I (and, indeed of all rent) is that land is scarce (see Sraffa, 1960, p. 76) or, more precisely, that land is perfectly inelastic in supply (see Keiper *et al.*, 1961, pp. 108–10).
6. If the first option is adopted the consequences which follow will depend upon whether the efficiency of the new technology (as measured by the output per unit of input) is greater than, less than, or the same as the old technology. If the new technology is more efficient than the old and if wages are constant, then the consequence will be a high rate of profit. The effect of this, in turn, will be that competition between capitalists will reduce the rate of profit to its level before the technological innovation and the owner of the land will receive a rent. If the new technology is of the same efficiency, then there will be no change. In other words, the rate of profit will remain the same and no rent will be paid. If the new technology is less efficient then it will not be adopted.
7. There are two alternatives to this assumption. The first is that the commodity being produced is a basic but the wage is variable (both upwards and downwards) depending on workers' power. If, for example, it is assumed that workers' are powerless, then the effect of extending production from type (i) to type (ii) land will be an increase in the unit price of production of the commodity leading to a corresponding reduction in real wages (since the commodity is a basic). This will lead, in turn, to a higher rate of profit for the capitalist(s) producing on type (i) rather than on type

(ii) land. This will lead, in turn, through competition, to the emergence of differential rent I on type (i) land since the capitalist(s) producing on type (ii) land would be willing to pay a rent for the least of type (i) land up to the point where the rate of profit was the same on both plots. In this case differential rent I would arise without any reduction in the overall rate of profit.

The second possible assumption is that the commodity is a non-basic and, in this case, the effect will be to increase the price of production of the commodity (because of the higher unit costs of producing on type (ii) land), thereby giving rise to a higher rate of profit for those capitalists producing on type (i) land. However, this higher rate of profit will be reduced to that attainable on type (ii) land since the capitalists producing on type (ii) land would be willing to pay a rent for the lease of type (i) land up to the point where the rate of profit on both types of land was the same. In this way differential rent I emerges on type (i) land, although the rate of profit throughout the economy will not be affected.

8. The fact that differential rent I arises independently of the existence of the actual ownership of land (whether the owners be the state, landowners or capitalists) means that it will exist in any system of production where land is scarce and where there is more than one technique of production (due either to the variable quality of the land or to the different combinations of inputs invested in it). The fundamental difference between differential rent I in a capitalist economy, and in a centrally planned economy, stems from the way in which the prices of commodities are determined in these two economies: a centrally planned economy would not include profit in the capitalist sense and this would evidently affect prices as well as the size and calculation of differential rent I. A centrally planned economy could not abolish differential rent I without also abolishing a price system where each commodity has a single and uniform price throughout the economy.

   One implication of this is that differential rent I is perfectly consistent with the capitalist economy in the sense that it does not hinder the process of capital accumulation. Ball argues otherwise, claiming that if capitalists (notably farmers) owned land rather than leasing it from landowners, that this would lead to more investment in land and hence to more capital accumulation. He uses two arguments to support this contention. The first is that if farmers owned their own land then 'the drive for accumulation by capitalist farmers would result in additional capital being invested in each soil type until prices of production had been equalized across all lands under cultivation' (Ball, 1977, p. 390). This argument implies that those capitalist farmers who appropriate differential rent I (that is, surplus profits) will continue to invest until this surplus disappears. No rational calculating capitalist would undertake such a course of action and there are no competitive forces obliging him/lher to do so.

   Bail's second argument is that when a tenant farmer (as distinct from the capitalist farmer) pays a differential rent I to a landowner he/she is hindered from making any additional investment since 'there is no reason why the landlord should acquiesce to a loss of rent which must ensue if the farmer were to increase output by additional investment of capital at the expense of rent' (ibid., p. 391). This assertion is dubious for three reasons. First, because any investment which increases output will actually result in an increase in rent, leaving the rate of profit unchanged (assuming that the commodity being produced is a basic and that real wages are constant). Second, although tenant farmers cannot possibly increase the rate of profit (because of the combination of constant wages and competition) they may still be obliged to invest and innovate if only to maintain the existing rate of profit. Third, the period of the lease is a crucial factor here and this, as will be seen in section 3.2, could allow the tenant farmer appropriate differential rent II for the duration of the lease which may be a sufficient incentive to invest.

9. This is probably the reason why Ricardo expected the stationary state to emerge. Ricardo's prognosis of the stationary state was based on the premise that a growing economy would give rise to a growing population which, in turn, would give rise to a growing demand for food (typically, corn). As a result of this, the production of corn would have to be extended to land of inferior quality, thereby giving rise to diminishing returns. This in turn would cause corn prices to rise which, given a constant real wage, would cause profits to fall and rents to rise. This declining profit could only be arrested, Ricardo argued by a fall in the price of corn made possible by either (a) a fall in real wages or (b) improvements in agriculture or (c) the discovery of new markets. Ricardo was particularly concerned with (c), which formed the basis of his argument against the Corn Laws. He regarded wages as 'more or less permanent' (Ricardo, 1966, p. 22) and improvements as unable to 'overcome the natural impediments' (ibid., p. 32) of poor lands. The result was that, given the persistence of the Corn Laws, and given that the rate of profit in manufacture moves in the same direction as that in agriculture (ibid., p. 12) the rate of profit in the economy as a whole will fall continually, leading inevitably to the 'stationary state'. The fact that the increase in the price of agricultural commodities may not be inevitable, as Marx pointed out, thus severely undermines Ricardo's case that the stationary state is inevitable.

10. There is one difficulty with Marx's formulation of this point. This difficulty arises because Marx tends to regard two different technologies as involving two different amounts of capital: the more efficient the technology the larger the amount of capital and vice versa. This is Marx's characteristic view of technology which led him, as has been seen (section 2.1), to the erroneous view that technical change within capitalism would inevitably lead to a rising organic composition of capital (and, *ceteris paribus*, to a falling rate of profit). The relevant point here is that a technical change does not necessarily imply a larger amount of capital; it could equally well involve a smaller amount or even the same amount. It is thus important to avoid describing different techniques in terms of their amounts of capital; the economically relevant description is in terms of their efficiency.

11. The term 'monopoly rent I' is used here, in preference to Marx's term 'absolute rent', because it brings out clearly the fact that this type of rent arises from monopolistic practices, that is, collusion, rather than competition, between landowners. As with differential rent, there are two types of monopoly rent.

12. Marx also believed that this inhibited investment in agriculture although as Gibson and Esfahani (1983) point out, this depends upon the savings and investment behaviour of landlords. They write: 'if landlords have the same savings behaviour as capitalists, it is not at all clear how total investment is supposed to diminish. If, on the other hand, landlords consume more of their total income, which historically does seem to have been the case, investment will fall' (ibid., p. 95).

4 Marx's Theory of Productive and Unproductive Labour

1. The use of the terms 'Definition I' and 'Definition II' to distinguish between the two different ways in which Marx used this distinction, does not imply any chronological sequence in his usage nor does it imply that he was even aware of these different usages.
2. Ibid.
3. Marx uses the terms productive and unproductive in the 'capitalist sense' (Marx, 1969, p. 153). In other words, they are categorisations of labour from the point of view of capitalist production. He distinguishes this from the 'absolute sense' (ibid.; ibid., p. 393) of the terms which treats labour as productive (or unproductive) if it produces (or fails to produce) a use-value.
4. The distinctive feature of the capitalist sector (in contrast to the non-capitalist sector) is that surplus labour is accumulated as capital (rather than in some other form). This is clearly revealed by Marx's example of the self-employed tailor working for a client. He writes

   > It may be that the quantity of labour performed by the jobbing tailor is greater than that contained in the price he gets from me . . . This, however, is all the same as far as I am concerned . . . it is in no way a means to any enrichment, any more than any other way for spending money for personal consumption is a means of enrichment to me (Marx, 1969, p. 402).

   In other words, for labour to be productive, it must not only produce surplus value, but in addition this surplus value must be accumulated by the capitalist. Marx's argument, it will be apparent, assumes that the self-employed tailor does not accumulate his own surplus labour as capital. In this case his labour is unproductive according to 'Definition I'.
5. By definition, wages can never function as capital since they are wholly consumed to meet the subsistence requirements of the workers.
6. Marx points out that there are two 'contradictory definitions' of productive labour in Adam Smith (Marx, 1969, p. 156; see also Dobb, 1973, p. 61). On the other hand there is the 'correct' definition where Smith defines as productive all labour which 'produces surplus value for the capitalist' (Marx, 1969, p. 152). Marx regarded this definition of productive labour as one of Smith's 'greatest scientific merits' (ibid., p. 157). On the other hand, there is Smith's 'wrong conception of productive labour' (ibid., p. 155)

where the latter is defined as that which produces a 'vendible commodity' in contrast to 'services which generally perish in the very instant of their performance' (ibid., p. 163).

Marx's first definition of productive labour corresponds to Smith's 'correct' definition. However, there is some evidence, as Bullock (1973, p. 88) and Hunt (1979, p. 314) have pointed out, that Marx adopted Smith's second criterion of the material nature of the product in his later work as a 'second, different and subsidiary definition' (Marx, 1969, p. 155). Hunt concludes from this that 'the issue of whether productive workers create a physical commodity is treated in a very confusing, if not contradictory, manner by Marx (ibid., p. 314). Bullock, by contrast, defends Marx on this usage with the highly questionable assertion that 'immaterial products cannot be accumulated' even though 'individual capitalists may accumulate money capital through their control of the production and sale of such commodities' (Bullock, 1973, p. 89). Subsequently, however, Bullock (1974) abandons this position in favour of that advanced here.

7. Marx's failure to consider the effect of the non-capitalist sector upon the rate of accumulation in the capitalist sector can also be seen in his discussion of petty commodity producers (that is, handicraftsmen and peasants). These, according to Marx, 'belong neither to the category of productive nor unproductive labourers' (Marx, 1969, p. 407). However, this is true only if it is assumed that there is no trade between petty commodity producers and the capitalist sector. The existence of trade between the two would clearly have an effect on capital accumulation and hence, in this case, would make petty commodity producers, either productive or unproductive (according to 'Definition I'). Harrison makes a similar mistake to that of Marx by labelling as 'non-productive . . . all wage labour not performed under the capitalist mode of production but financed out of revenue generated in the capitalist sector' (Harrison, 1973, p. 74).

8. Marx did not classify all storage costs as circulation costs and hence as unproductive according to 'Definition II'. He classified as unproductive those storage costs which are 'due merely to the time required for the conversion of existing values from the commodity form into the money form' (Marx, 1974b, p. 142). By contrast, those costs of storage which, strictly speaking, form part of the production process (such as distilling) he classified as productive. By the same argument he also classified transport costs as productive since they too are the 'continuation of a process of production within the process of circulation' (ibid., p. 155).

9. Gough (1972, p. 66) acknowledges that these two different definitions of productive and unproductive labour coexist in Marx but he fails to note or tease out their inconsistencies while O'Connor (1975, p. 305) is apparently unaware of any inconsistency.

10. Lebowitz, in an attempt to explore the contemporary relevance of Marx's tretament or circulation costs refers to 'the tension between the desire to reduce circulation costs to a minimum and the requirements of realization' (Lebowitz, 1972, p. 337) which results in 'the secular growth in wasteful,

unproductive activity' (ibid.). Lebowitz accepts unquestionably the Marxian assumption that circulation costs are unproductive and, as a result, fails to address the crucial problem with Marx's second definition, that is, the problem of distinguishing between those costs which are technically indispensable to the production of a commodity in any mode of production and those which are necessary only in a capitalist mode of production. As a result, Lebowitz's characterisation of circulation costs as 'wasteful' is open to question.

5 The Different Marxist Traditions of Castells and Lojkine

1. Two qualifications to this characterisation of Marx's historical materialism are necessary. The first is that Marx himself never fully or rigorously developed the theory of historical materialism. Indeed the term 'historical materialism' was never used by Marx, and only first appears in the writings of Engels (see Giddens, 1971, p. 4). The second qualification is that Marx's empirical use of historical materialism, particularly in *The Eighteenth Brumaire* (Marx, 1979) is a great deal more nuanced and sophisticated than his theoretical sketch of it in 'Preface to a Contribution to the Critique of Political Economy' (Marx, 1976).

   Both of these qualifications suggest that Marx's nascent theory of historical materialism does not necessarily imply a simple (or simplistic) determinism of the superstructure of the base. Althusser's work is devoted precisely to clarifying the nature of the determinism between the base and the superstructure.

2. Although this homology exists in capitalism, it is not present in earlier modes of production and it is this, according to Balibar, which 'explains' (Althusser and Balibar, 1970, p. 215) why Marx constantly confounds them in a single concept' (ibid.). In feudal society, according to Balibar, the peasants generally retained control of the means of production (that is, the relation of real appropriation) while the feudal ruling class maintained economic ownership (that is, the relation of property). In capitalism, by contrast, the capitalist performs the 'double function' (Althusser and Balibar, 1970, p. 214) of being the owner of the means of production and hence the ultimate exploiter of labour (that is, the relation of property) and the direct organiser and controller of production (that is, the relation of real appropriation).

3. Both Balibar (Althusser and Balibar, 1970, p. 215) and Poulantzas (1973, pp. 24–5) once argued that the various instances of any mode of production could be analysed in terms of a set of 'invariant' elements which were combined by a 'variable' set of relations. Following criticisms of formalism (see, *inter alia*, Laclau, 1975, pp. 103ff; Glucksman, 1974, p. 298) this claim has been weakened to the assertion that every instance is composed of various elements and relations which may vary from one mode of production to another (Poulantzas, 1976, pp. 78–80).

4. In view of this it is perhaps curious that the Althusserian school should consistently and vehemently reject that their position is structuralist (Althusser and Balibar, 1970, pp. 7, 226; Poulantzas, 1973, p. 26; Castells and de Ipola, 1976, pp. 128–31). The reason for their rejection of the structuralist label is that they associate it exclusively with the work of Lévi-Strauss (1972). The term is evidently not confined to the latter and it does appear to be an appropriate label to describe the Althusserian position.

5. Thus, for example, in Althusserian terminology, the state consists of a political structure and a set of political practices which, in French, are translated as *le politique* and *la politique* respectively.

6. It should be noted here that there is a basic inconsistency between the Althusserian distinction between structures and practices on the one hand, and their rejection of historicism and humanism on the other. This inconsistency arises in the following way: since structures, according to the Althusserians, impose limits on the variability of practices, the question arises as to the cause (and hence explanation) of this variability. The only plausible answer to this question is that this variability is due to historical and subjective factors. However, such factors are labelled by the Althusserian school as historicism and humanism respectively, and are rejected as having no explanatory role in relation to practices.

7. One of the major problems with this definition is that it fails to grasp what Poulantzas himself terms 'the very specificity of the political' (Poulantzas, 1973, p. 38). This is because practically everything can be construed as a factor of cohesion (and hence part of the state); and in fact practically everything is included as part of the state, according to Poulantzas's definition. The result is that the political is not treated as a structure (in the strict Althusserian sense but rather as, to quote Laclau, 'a quality which pervades all the levels of a social formation' (Laclau, 1975, p. 100; see also Miliband, 1972, p. 262; Jessop, 1977, p. 355).

8. Kirk (1982, p. 142) is clearly misinformed in writing that 'Lojkine . . . like Castells . . . based his work on a structuralist reading of Marx following that of Althusser'. Lojkine's work is based upon the theory of state monopoly capitalism.

9. Lojkine use the terms monopoly firm, multinational firm and large firm as if they were interchangeable, which they are not, since a monopoly firm is not necessarily a multinational firm, and a multinational firm is not necessarily a monopoly firm, and a large firm is not necessarily either a multinational or a monopoly firm.

10. However, much of the disagreement is more apparent than real. This was also the conclusion reached by Pickvance (1977a, pp. 219–27) in his review of the debate between Lojkine and Poulantzas. He writes: 'What emerges from our examination of the Poulantzas-Lojkine debate is that there remain important differences of emphasis between the two writers, but that to a striking extent the debate goes round in circles, with each accusing the other of positions they deny' (ibid., p. 226).

6 The Marxist Urban Sociology of Manuel Castells

1. It is controversial on two grounds. The first is that the precise nature and extent of the continuities and discontinuities between Marx, Hegel and the classicals, upon which Althusser bases his proof that Marxism is scientific, is a matter of some controversy between Marxists. In other words, Althusser's 'proof' that Marxism is scientific rests upon a particular interpretation of Marx which is not shared by all Marxists. The second controversy is that a theory which serves certain ideological functions may not necessarily be unscientific, contrary to the Althusserian view. The distinction between scientific and non-scientific theories depends ultimately upon the decisions of scientists, rather than upon the ideological effects of those theories.
2. Others, however, have been less impressed. Elliot (1980, p. 153) has described it as 'a pretentious and . . . a profoundly irritating book', while Glass (1977, p. 669) has described it as 'a load of humbug'.
3. It should perhaps be emphasised that Castells does not explicitly state that collective consumption is unprofitable because it requires a high (that is, higher than average) organic composition of capital. However, this would seem to be implicit in his argument.
4. All of this assumes that facts matter, yet this is an assumption which may not be applicable to Castells's discussion of the law of the falling rate of profit. He writes: 'That we are not able to find a long-term secular trend for the organic composition to increase and the rate of profit to decrease does not contradict the theory; an intrinsic part of the theory is that reality is the result of conflicting forces' (Castells, 1980a, p. 40).
5. In his original characterisation of the urban system (Castells, 1976b, p. 79; 1976c, p. 154), Castells refers to four elements (*P*, *C*, *E*, *A*) only. The element (*S*) is only included in a later publication (Castells, 1977a, p. 238).
6. In a footnote to his elaboration of the concept of 'urban actors' Castells claims to reject 'the formalism of universal taxonomies' (Castells, 1969a, p. 442, fn43) and emphasises the need for 'theoretical relevant variables' (ibid.) Such evident inconsistency between Castells's claims and his actual achievements suggests the contemporary relevance of Locke's observation which seems to apply aptly to all of Castells's work: 'Vague and insignificant forms of speech, and abuse of language, have so long passed for mysteries of science; and hard and misapplied words, with little or no meaning, have, by prescription, such a right to be mistaken for deep learning and height of speculation, that it will not be easy to persuade either those who speak or those who hear them that they are but the covers of ignorance, and hinderance to true knowledge' (Locke, J., 1964, p. 58).
7. The title of this article is: 'Theoretical Propositions for an Experimental Study of Urban Social Movements' (Castells, 1976c). Castells's justification for using the term 'experimental' is that he assumes 'as constant all elements not included in a particular analysis' (ibid., p. 172). However, an analysis can only be experimental if certain variables are controlled and they can only be

controlled by manipulation not by assumption. As Schnore has pointed out: 'To ignore a factor is not to control it' (Schnore, 1965, p. 388). Thus Castells's use of the term 'experimental' in this context is unjustified.

7 The Marxist Urban Sociology of Jean Lojkine

1. Lojkine is here implicitly (Lojkine, 1977a, p. 124) and later explicitly (ibid., pp. 145–6) critical of the way in which Castells defines an urban area in terms of collective consumption, thus limiting it to only one of the general conditions of production (see section 3.2.2). Lojkine rejects this definition as 'one of the dominant themes of bourgeois ideology' (Lojkine, 1977a, p. 124).
2. Lojkine actually contradicts this claim in one place when he describes the growth in investment in property (particularly urban property) by monopolistic companies as 'an important instrument for warding off, the fall in the rate of profit in the industrial sectors' (Lojkine, 1977a, p. 287; see also p. 282). This statement clearly contradicts claim (b) above.
3. The acronym PADOG is an abbreviation of *Plan d'aménagement et d'organisation generale*. It was, in 1960, the plan for the organisation and development of the Paris region whose notable feature was a policy (ultimately unsuccessful) to contain the growth of Paris.
4. The acronym SDAU is an abbreviation of *Schema directeur d'aménagement et d'urbanisme*. It became, in 1965, the successor to PADOG (1960) and was itself, in turn, revised in 1969 in the light of the 1968 census, as well as in the light of the notable political events of that year. The most characteristic feature of SDAU (1965) was the creation of eight new towns in the Paris region.
5. The acronym ZEAT is an abbreviation of *Zone d'études et d'aménagement du territoire*. There are eight such zones in France which were devised under the 5th National Plan (1971–5) by the Commissariat au Plan for planning purposes in the context of both France and the EEC.
6. The *Commissariat au Plan* is a technical body whose function it is to prepare long and medium-term plans for the central government. It has, to date, prepared seven national plans.
7. The acronym DATAR is an abbreviation of *Delegation a l'aménagement du territoire et a l'action regionale*. It was set up in 1963 for the purpose of co-ordinating area and regional plans. Although it is attached to the Ministry of the Interior, it has no direct powers.
8. This is not the only weakness which has been identified in Lojkine's study of Paris. Pickvance (1977a, pp. 238–45) has shown, in a painstaking and thorough critique, that Lojkine's study is also rather weak in its analysis of the precise relationship between social classes and state policies. The critique presented here, by contrast, is primarily interested in identifying the extent to which the theoretical themes developed in Lojkine's urban sociology are also pursued in his empirical research.

8 From Marxist to Post-Marxist Urban Sociology

1. The term actor is applied to groups and organisations in the Weberian sense that the latter are 'the resultants of the particular acts of individual persons' (Weber, 1968, p. 13). Weber adds: 'When reference is made in a sociological context to a state, a nation, a corporation, a family, or an army corps, or to similar collectivities what is meant is . . . a certain kind of development of actual or possible social actions of individual persons' (ibid., p. 14).
2. Buildings and infrastructures are also found in rural areas so that the essential difference between rural and urban areas seems to lie in the degree of concentration of property (and hence in the level of spatial interdependence) rather than in the kind of property *per se*.
3. The other effect of restricting the supply of suitable land is that it increases the price of land and property and hence harms the interests of those wishing to buy property while benefiting those who already own it. In Marxian terms, this means that owners of land can appropriate monopoly rent I (in addition to differential rent I) as a result of zoning restrictions (see sections 3.3 and 3.5).
4. This apparently straightforward definition of a labour market area is extremely difficult to apply empirically because, as will be illustrated in more detail below, there are a number of different labour market areas for each of the different skill types of labour and the boundaries of each of these labour market areas tend to be imprecise and overlapping. British research (see notably Hall *et al.*, 1973; Johnson, Salt and Wood, 1974) has tried to overcome these difficulties by simply defining labour market areas in terms of the major commuting patterns within an urban area and have avoided the problem of imprecise and overlapping boundaries by adopting arbitrary (if reasonable) statistical conventions.
5. It is perhaps worth emphasising that household movement does not necessarily involve a change of job (that is, labour migration). In other words, labour migration is only a subset – and in Britain, possibly only a relatively small subset (see Johnson, Salt and Wood, 1974, pp. 5–6, 69, 113–14) – of total movement. Clark and Onaka (1983, p. 50) in a review of 18 different studies of migration in the US, UK, Canada, and New Zealand, put forward the following classification of reasons for migration:
6. The correctness of this analysis can also be confirmed, somewhat more casually, by a perusal of the job advertisements in different newspapers. Job advertisements for highly skilled, non-manual workers such as professionals and managers tend to be advertised in national newspapers, while advertisements for unskilled manual workers are normally only to be found (if at all) in local newspapers (see Johnson, Salt and Wood, 1974, p. 34; Evans and Russell, 1980, p. 213; Evans and Richardson, 1981, p. 113). This confirms, from the demand side, that the size of the area in which employers look for labour varies considerably with the level of skill of the labour being demanded.

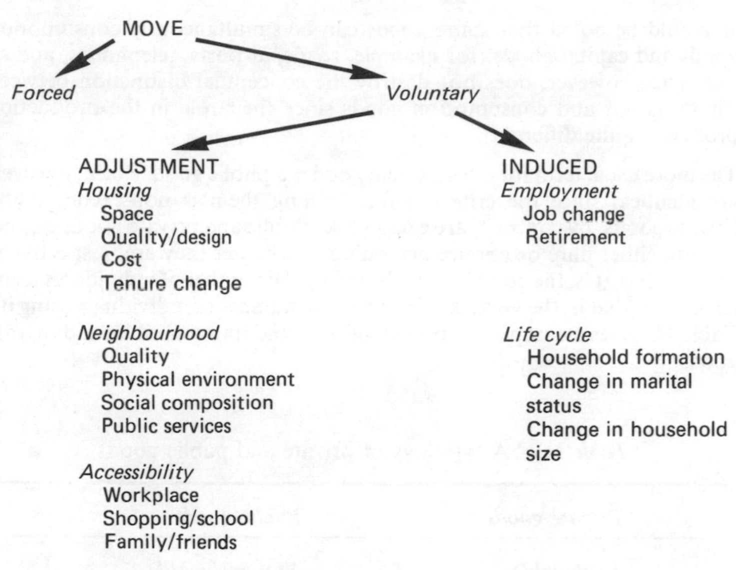

Figure N2 Reasons for household relocation

A useful survey of recent research on migration (that is, research since 1975) is contained in Clark (1982).

7. One of the implications of distinguishing between an urban area and a labour market area is that the source of unemployment should be sought within the labour market for each particular type of labour, rather than in the area where the unemployed live. The significance of this in the British context, according to Cheshire (1979), is that the high rates of unemployment among unskilled workers in the inner areas of Britain's major conurbations is due more to the lack of demand for that type of labour *vis-à-vis* the supply, rather than to the fact that this group live or are 'trapped' (ibid., pp. 36ff) in the inner city (see also Metcalf, 1975; Corkingdale, 1980, pp. 184, 190; Richardson, 1980, pp. 214–17).

8. Private ownership does not always exist in this pure form, however. For example, a proprietor may lease a house or a plot of land to a tenant, thereby temporarily ceding rights (1) and (2) to the latter (in exchange for rent). Similarly, the zoning of land by the state effectively abolishes the right (1b) of landowners over 'their' land while price and rent controls are, in effect, a reduction of right (2). Thus private ownership of property refers to a number of different empirical situations and is not an undifferentiated entity.

9. It should be noted that some goods can be simultaneously consumption goods and capital goods (for example, roads, airports, telephones, and so on). This, however, does not destroy the conceptual distinction between capital goods and consumption goods since their role in the production process is quite different.
10. The more usual term for a communal good is a public good. Both, however, are identical since the criterion for defining them is non-excludability. Private goods, by contrast, are excludable. Public and private goods can be, in turn, either pure or impure according to whether they are, respectively, non-rival (that is, the good is not affected by the number of individuals using it) or rival (that is, the good is affected by the number of individuals using it). Table N3 gives a complete typology of pure and impure public and private goods.

Table N3 A typology of private and public goods

	Private goods	*Public goods*
	Excludable	*Non-excludable*
Rival	Pure private good *Examples*: food and drink household furniture	Impure public good *Examples*: roads, streets, etc. libraries, museums, etc. schools, buses, amenity areas
Non-rival	Impure private good *Examples*: television transmissions regulated by licences	Pure public good *Examples*: national defence lighthouses airport noise air pollution

11. There is a large number of synonyms used for the term 'externality', such as: spillover effect, external effect, uncontracted effect, neighbourhood effect and third party effect. It is usually defined in the following way: 'The essence of externalities, whether in production or consumption, is that their costs or benefits are not reflected in market prices, and so the decision of the consumer or firm creating the externalities . . . generally does not take its effect into account' (Bannock, Baxter and Rees, 1972, p. 159). The concept of externality does not appear in Marx's work. It first appeared in 1890 (seven years after Marx's death) in Alfred Marshall's *Principles of*

Economics (1961) and it was Marshall's pupil at Cambridge, Arthur Pigou, who brought the concept to prominence in 1920 in his *Economics of Welfare* (1960).

12. On the term 'dwelling unit', the remark of Donnison and Ungerson (1982, p. 42) is apposite: 'At a conference called in 1966 by the United Nations Economic Commission for Europe, the definition of "dwelling" was more or less settled for the whole of Europe . . . "Dwellings" are structurally separate units built for people to live in, with an entrance opening on to the street or a space within the building to which the public has access'. The term dwelling unit will be used in conformity with this definition.

13. Thus, apart from one's dwelling, the neighbourhood is the most basic spatial or territorial entity in which one lives. However, neighbourhoods, in turn, exist within cities, cities within regions, regions within countries, and so on. These different spatial levels or places coexist in a nested fashion and, at each level, they can have an effect, independently of one's class or status position, upon the quality of one's life and life chances. It is for this reason that place, like class, can be a basis for shared interests and hence for collective action (see Molotch, 1976; Logan, 1978; see also Smith, 1977 for an insightful analysis of the independent effects of place on human welfare). The analysis in this section will be focused upon the neighbourhood level where, through housing, there can be an overlap between class-based and place-based interests.

14. There has been considerable debate in the literature over the concept of housing classes since it was first used by Rex and Moore in 1967 (see Rex and Moore, 1967). The concept has been criticised by Marxists who, using the term 'class' to refer to positions in relation to production, regard 'housing classes' as interest groups in relation to the distribution (not the production) of housing; Weberians, too, have questioned whether the differences of interest between housing classes are contingent rather than enduring (see Saunders, 1980a, Chapter 2, for a clear synopsis of this debate; see also Thorns, 1981; Pratt, 1982). As will be seen in the next subsection (8.8.5), there are real differences of interest between tenure groups in relation to housing, so that it is quite justified to refer to such groups as housing classes (in the Weberian sense of having different amounts of market power). Saunders has more recently argued that the term 'class' should be confined to production-based divisions while the term 'sector' should be used for consumption-based divisions such as divisions over housing, health, education, and so on (Saunders, 1984, pp. 206–7; see Harloe, 1984, for a critique).

15. A tax can be regarded as a negative consumption good if it reduces the real income of the consumer (that is, the taxpayer). In such cases its effect is the same as that of any other negative (state or communal) consumption good, and residents will tend to react to it in the same way. Thus there is some evidence in the US that residents (particularly affluent residents) will tend to migrate from high to low tax areas (see Cox, 1973, pp. 27ff). Aronson (1974) found similar evidence of fiscal migration in a study of the Leeds area of

England between 1965 and 1972. The Tiebout model (Tiebout, 1956) was the first attempt at explaining this type of migration within a neoclassical economic framework.

16. The usual example of this is the movement of non-whites into a white neighbourhood where the latter are prejudiced against the former. This frequently leads to a temporary fall in house prices, during the period of racial transition, followed by a rapid increase in price due to the concentration of non-white demand in those particular areas. It is this, *inter alia*, which probably explains why 'most researchers have concluded that blacks do pay more than whites for housing of comparable size and quality . . .' (Kain and Quigley, 1975, pp. 63–5ff; see also Wilkinson and Gulliver, 1971, p. 33).
17. A recent survey in Norman, Oklahoma, on attitudes to the location of mental health facilities found that owner-occupiers were more opposed than tenants to the location of such facilities in their area because of 'the potential impact of the facility on real estate values and resale possibilities' (Smith and Hanham, 1981, p. 153). This difference in attitude would, *ceteris paribus*, make owner-occupiers more likely than tenants to engage in collective action.

Bibliography

ABRAHAM-FROIS, G. and BERREBI, E. (1979) *Theory of Value, Prices and Accumulation: A Mathematical Integration of Marx, von Neumann and Sraffa* (London: Cambridge University Press) (first published in French in 1976).

AGNEW, J. A. (1978) 'Market Relations and Locational Conflict in Cross-National Perspective', in Cox, K.R. (ed.) *Urbanization and Conflict in Market Societies* (London: Methuen) Chapter 6: 128–43.

ALBIN, P. S. (1971) 'Unbalanced Growth and Intensification of the Urban Crisis', *Urban Studies*, June: 139–46.

ALCALY, R. E. (1975) 'The Relevance of Marxian Crisis Theory', in Mermelstein, D. (ed.) *The Economic Crisis Reader* (New York: Vintage Books): 132–8.

ALCALY, R. E. (1978) 'An Introduction to Marxian Crisis Theory', in The Union for Radical Political Economics (eds) *U.S. Capitalism in Crisis* (New York: Union for Radical Political Economics): 15–21.

ALCHIAN, A. A. (1965) 'Some Economics of Property Rights', *Il Politico*, 30: 816–29.

ALCHIAN, A. A. and DEMSETZ, H. (1973) 'The Property Right Paradigm', *The Journal of Economic History*, 33 (1): 16–27.

ALTHUSSER, L. (1969) *For Marx* (London: Allen Lane, The Penguin Press) (first published in French in 1965).

ALTHUSSER, L. (1971) *Lenin and Philosophy and Other Essays* (London: New Left Books, translated by Ben Brewster).

ALTHUSSER, L. and BALIBAR, E. (1970) *Reading Capital* (London: New Left Books) (first published in French in 1968).

AMBROSE, P. (1977) 'The Determinants of Urban Land Use Change', in Massey, D. and Ambrose, P. *Values, Relevance and Policy*, Section III, Units 25–6 (Milton Keynes: The Open University Press): 35–79.

AMBROSE, P. and COLENUTT, B. (1975) *The Property Machine* (Harmondsworth: Penguin Books).

ARMSTRONG, P., GLYN, A. and HARRISON, J. (1978) 'In Defence of Value: A Reply to Ian Steedman: An Extended Review of *Marx after Sraffa*, by Ian Steedman, London: New Left Books, 1977; *Capital and Class*, 5: 1–31.

ARONSON, J. R. (1974) 'Voting with Your Feet' *New Society*, 29 (621): 545–7.

BAILEY, M. J. (1966) 'Effects of Race and of Other Demographic Factors on the Values of Single-Family Homes', *Land Economics*, 42: 215–20.

BALCHIN, P. N. and KIEVE, J. L. (1982) *Urban Land Economics* (London: The Macmillan Press).

BALE, J. (1978) 'Externality Gradients', *Area*, 10 (5): 334–6.

BALL, M. (1977) 'Differential Rent and the Role of Landed Property', *International Journal of Urban and Regional Research*, 1 (3): 380–403.

BALL, M. (1980) 'On Marx's Theory of Agricultural Rent: A Reply To Ben Fine', *Economy and Society*, 9 (3): 304–39.

BANDYOPADHYAY, P. (1982) 'Marxist Urban Analysis and the Economic Theory of Rent', *Science and Society*, 46: 162–96.

BANNOCK, G., BAXTER, R. E. and REES, R. (1972) *The Penguin Dictionary of Economics* (Harmondsworth: Penguin Books).

BARAN, P. (1957) *The Political Economy of Growth* (New York: Monthly Review Press).

BAUMOL, W. J. (1967) 'Macroeconomics of Unbalanced Growth: The Anatomy of Urban Crisis', *The American Economic Review*, 57 (3): 415–26.

BAUMOL, W. (1974) 'The Transformation of Values: What Marx "Really" Meant (An Interpretation)', *Journal of Economic Literature*, 12: 51–62.

BENETTI, C. (1976) *Valeur et Repartition* (Paris: Presses Universitaires de Grenoble et Maspero).

BENTHAM, G. and MOSELEY, M. (1980) 'Socio-economic Change and Disparities within the Paris Agglomeration: Does Paris have an "Inner-City Problem"?, *Regional Studies*, 14: 55–70.

BERTHOUD, R. (1980) 'Employment in a Changing Labour Market', in Evans, A. and Eversley, D. (eds) *The Inner City: Employment and Industry* (London: Heinemann): 232–52.

BHADURI, A. (1969) 'On the Significance of Recent Controversies on Capital Theory: A Marxian View', *The Economic Journal*, 79: 532–9.

BHADURI, A. and ROBINSON, J. (1980) 'Accumulation and Exploitation: an Analysis in the Tradition of Marx, Sraffa and Kalecki', *Cambridge Journal of Economics*, 4: 103–15.

BLAUG, M. (1962) *Economic Theory in Retrospect* (London: Heinemann Educational Books).

BLEANEY, M. (1976) *Underconsumption Theories: A History and Critical Analysis* (London: Lawrence Wishart).

BODDY, R. and CROTTY, J. (1975) 'Class Conflict and Macro-Policy: The Political Business Cycle', *The Review of Radical Political Economics*, 7 (1): 1–19.

BÖHM-BAWERK, E. VON (1949) 'Karl Marx and the Close of his System', in Sweezy, P. (ed.) *Karl Marx and the Close of his System by Eugen von Böhm-Sawerk and Böhm-Sawerk's Criticism of Marx by Rudolf Hilherding* (Clifton, New Jersey: Augustus M. Kelly): 9–118 (first published in German in 1896, and in English in 1898).

BORTKIEWITC, L. VON (1949) 'On the Correction of Marx's Fundamental Theoretical Construction in the Third Volume of Capital', in Sweezy, P. M. (ed.) *Karl Marx and the Close of his System by Eugene von Bohm-Bawerk and Bohm-Bawerk's Criticism of Marx by Rudolf Hilferding*: Appendix (Clifton, New Jersey: Augustus M. Kelly): 197–21 (first published in German in July 1907 and in English in 1954).

BORTKIEWICZ, L. VON (1952) 'Value and Price in the Marxian System', *International Economic Papers*, no. 2: 5–60 (first published in German in July 1907 and in English in 1949).

BOSE, A. (1980) *Marx on Exploitation and Inequality: An Essay in Marxian Analytical Economics* (London: Oxford University Press).

BOURNE, L. S. (1981) *The Geography of Housing* (New York: John Wiley).

BREUGEL, I. (1975) 'The Marxist Theory of Rent and the Contemporary City: A Critique of Harvey', in Political Economy of Housing Workshop (ed.) *Political Economy and the Housing Question* (A first volume of papers presented to the Housing Workshop of the Conference of Socialist Economists) London, pp. 34–46.

BROADBENT, T. A. (1975) 'An Attempt to Apply Marx's Theory of Ground Rent to the Modern Urban Economy', *Centre for Environmental Studies: Research Paper No. 17*, London.

BROADBENT, T. A. (1977) *Planning and Profit in the Urban Economy* (London: Methuen).

BULLOCK, P. (1973) 'Categories of Labour Power for Capital', *Bulletin of the Conference of Socialist Economists*, 2 (6): 82–99.

BULLOCK, P. (1974) 'Defining Productive Labour for Capital', *Bulletin of the Conference of Socialist Economists*: 1–15.

BYRNE, D. and BEIRNE, P. (1975) 'Towards a Political Economy of Housing Rent', in Political Economy of Housing Workshop (eds) *Political Economy and the Housing Question* (A first volume of papers presented to the Housing Workshop of the Conference of Socialist Economists) London: 47–67.

CAIN, G. C. (1976) 'The Challenge of Segmented Labour Market Theories to Orthodox Theory: A Survey', *Journal of Economic Literature*, 14 (3–4): 1215–57.

CASTELLS, M. (1967) *Les Politiques d'Implantation des Entreprises Industrielles dans la Région de Paris: Étude Sociologique* (Thésè pour le Doctorat de 3ème Cycle en Sociologie, Faculté des Lettres et Sciences Humaines, Université de Paris, Nanterre; École Pratique des Hautes Études, VIéme Section: Sciences Économiques et Sociales).

CASTELLS, M. (1968) 'Y à-t-il une sociologie urbaine?', *Sociologie du Travail*: 72–90.

CASTELLS, M. (1969a) 'Vers une Theorie sociologique de la planification urbaine', *Sociologie du Travail*: 413–43.

CASTELLS, M. (1969b) 'Enterprise industrielle et developpement urbaine', *Synopsis*, Sept.–Oct.: 67–76.

CASTELLS, M. (1969c) 'Théorie et ideologie en sociologie urbaine', *Sociologie et Sociétés*, 1 (2): 171–91.

CASTELLS, M. (1969d) 'Le Centre Urbain: Projet de Recherche Sociologique', *Cahiers Internationaux de Sociologie*, May: 83–106.

CASTELLS, M. (1970a) 'Social Structures and Processes of Urbanization: Intersocietal Comparative Analysis', *Annales*, August: 1155–99.

CASTELLS, M. (1970b) 'La rénovation urbaine aux états-unis: synthèse et interpretation des données actuelles', *Éspaces et Sociétés*, 1: 107–35.

CASTELLS, M. (1970c) 'Les nouvelles frontières de la methodologie sociologique', *Social Sciences Information*, 9 (6): 79–108.

CASTELLS, M. (1971a) 'L'urbanisation dépendante en amérique latine', *Éspaces et Sociétés*, 3: 5–23.

CASTELLS, M. (1971b) 'La Sociologie et la question Urbaine', *L'Architecture d'Aujourd'hui*, Sept.: 92–7 (first published, in modified form, in 1969c).

CASTELLS, M. (1972a) 'Urban Renewal and Social Conflict in Paris', *Social Sciences Information*, II (2): 93–1124.

CASTELLS, M. (1972b) 'Lutte de classes et contradictions urbaines: l'èmergence des mouvements sociaux urbains dans le capitalisme avancé', *Éspaces et Sociétés*, 6–7: 3–8 (also published in 1972d, pp. 6–17).

CASTELLS, M. (1972c) *La Question Urbaine* (Paris: Maspero).
CASTELLS, M. (1972d) *Luttes Urbaines et Pouvoir Politique* (Paris: Maspero).
CASTELLS, M. (1974) 'Controverse sur le pouvoir local: remarques sur l'article de Pierre Birnbaum', *Révue Française de Sociologie*, 15 (3): 237–42.
CASTELLS, M. (1975a) 'Advanced Capitalism, Collective Consumption and Urban Contradictions: New Sources of Inequality and New Models for Change', in Lindberg, Leon N. (ed.) *Stress and Contradiction in Modern Capitalism* (Lexington, Mass.: Heath): 175–97.
CASTELLS, M. (1975b) 'Immigrant Workers and Class Struggles in Advanced Capitalism: the Western European Experience', *Politics and Society*, 5 (1): 33–66.
CASTELLS, M. (1975c) 'Urban Sociology and Urban Politics: From a Critique to New Trends of Research', *Comparative Urban Research*, 3 (1): 7–13.
CASTELLS, M. (1975d) *Sociologie de l'espace industriel*, Editions Anthropos, Paris.
CASTELLS, M. (1975e) 'La Condition Sociale de la Planification Urbaine: Le Cas de la Région de Dunkerque', *Recherches Sociologiques*, November: 401–26.
CASTELLS, M. (1976a) 'Is there an Urban Sociology?' in Pickvance, C. G. (ed.) *Urban Sociology: Critical Essays* (London: Tavistock Publications): 33–59 (first published in French in 1968a).
CASTELLS, M. (1976b) 'Theory and Ideology in Urban Sociology', in Pickvance, C. G. (ed.) *Urban Sociology: Critical Essays* (London: Tavistock Publications: 60–84 (first published in 1969c).
CASTELLS, M. (1976c) 'Theoretical Propositions for an Experimental Study of Urban Social Movements', in Pickvance, C. G. (ed.) *Urban Sociology: Critical Essays*' (London: Tavistock Publications): 147–73.
CASTELLS, M. (1976d) 'Urban Sociology and Urban Politics: From a Critique to New Trends of Research', in Walton, J. and Masotti, L. (eds) *The City in Comparative Perspective* (London: John Wiley): 291–300 (first published in 1975c).
CASTELLS, M. (1976e) 'La Crise Urbaine aux États-Unis: vers la Barbarie', *Les Temps Modernes*, February: 1177–240.
CASTELLS, M. (1976f) 'The Wild City', *Kapitalistate*, 4–5, 1–30.
CASTELLS, M. (1976g) 'The Service Economy and Postindustrial Society: A Sociological Critique', *International Journal of Health Services*, 6 (4): 596–607.
CASTELLS, M. (1976h) 'Crise de l'État, Consommation Collective et Contradictions Urbaines', in Poulantzas, N. (ed.) *La Crise de l'État* (Paris: Presses Universitaires de France): 179–208.
CASTELLS, M. (1977a) *The Urban Question: A Marxist Approach* (London: Edward Arnold) (first published in French in 1972c).
CASTELLS, M. (1977b) 'Les conditions sociale d'émergence des movements sociaux urbains (à partir d'une énquete exploratoire sur les luttes urbaine dans la région parisienne, 1968–73)', in *International Journal of Urban and Regional Research*, 1 (1): 45–75 (translated and published in English in 1978a).
CASTELLS, M. (1977c) 'Towards a Political Urban Sociology', in Harloe, M.

(ed.) *Captive Cities: Studies in the Political Economy of Cities and Regions* (London: John Wiley): pp. 61–78.

CASTELLS, M. (1977d) 'Marginalité urbaine et mouvements sociaux au Mexique: le mouvement des "posesionarios" dans la ville de Monterry', *International Journal of Urban and Regional Research*, 1 (1): 145–50.

CASTELLS, M. (1978a) *City, Class and Power* (London: Macmillan Press).

CASTELLS, M. (1978b) 'Urban Social Movements and the Struggle for Democracy: The Citizens' Movement in Madrid', *International Journal of Urban and Regional Research*, 2 (1): 133–46.

CASTELLS, M. (1980a) *The Economic Crisis and American Society* (New Jersey, USA: Princeton University Press).

CASTELLS, M. (1980b) 'Cities and Regions beyond the Crisis: Invitation to a Debate', *International Journal of Urban and Regional Research*, 4 (1): 127–9.

CASTELLS, M. (1981a) 'Toward a Sociological Theory of City Planning', in Lemert, C. (ed.) *French Sociology: Rupture and Renewal since 1968* (New York: Columbia University Press): 374–95 (first published in French in 1969a).

CASTELLS, M. (1981b) 'Local Government, Urban Crisis and Political Change' in Zeitlin, M. (ed.) *Political Power and Social Theory: A Research Annual*, 2 (Greenwich, Conn.: Jai Press) pp. 1–19.

CASTELLS, M. (1983a) *The City and the Grassroots: A Cross-Cultural Theory of Urban Social Movements* (London: Edward Arnold).

CASTELLS, M. (1983b) 'Crisis, Planning and the Quality of Life: Managing the New Historical Relationships between Space and Society', *Environment and Planning D: Society and Space*, 1: 3–21.

CASTELLS, M., CHERKI, E., GODARD, F. and MEHL, D. (1974) *Sociologie des Mouvements Sociaux Urbains: Énquête sur la Région Parisienne: Volume I: Problematique Théorique-Methodologie Analyse des Tendences Generales: Volume 2: Crise du Logement et Mouvements Sociaux* (Paris: École Des Hautes Études En Sciences Sociales, Centre d'Étude des Mouvements Sociaux).

CASTELLS, M., CHERKI, E., GODARD, F. and MEHL, D. (1978) *Crise du logement et mouvements sociaux urbains: Énquête sur la région parisienne* (Paris: Mouton) (first published in 1974).

CASTELLS, M. AND de IPOLA, E. (1976) 'Epistemological Practice and the Social Sciences', *Economy and Society*, 5: 111–44 (republished in 1979).

CASTELLS, M. AND de HIPOLA, E. (1979) 'Epistemological Practice and the Social Sciences', in Freiberg, J. W. (ed.) *Critical Sociology European Perspectives* (New York: Irvington Publishers) 217–53 (first published in 1976).

CASTELLS, M., DELAYRE, H., DESSANE, C., GODARD, F., O'CALLAGHAN, C., PUIG, G. and SKODA, C. (1970) 'Paris 1970: Reconquete Urbaine et Renovation-Deportation', *Sociologie du Travail*: 485–513.

CASTELLS, M. and GODARD, F. (1974) (in collaboration with Balanowski, V.) *Monopolville: L'éntreprise, L'État, L'urbain: Analyse des rapports entre l'éntreprise, l'État et l'urbain à partir d'une enquête sur la croissance industrielle et urbaine de la région de Dunkerque* (Paris: Mouton).

CASTELLS, M. and GUILLEMARD, A. (1871) 'La Determination des Pratiques Sociales en Situation de Rétraite; *Sociologie du Travail*: 282–307.

CHESHIRE, P. C. (1979) 'Inner Areas as Spatial Labour Markets: A Critique of the Inner Area Studies', *Urban Studies*, 16: 29–43.

CHEUNG, S. (1978) 'The Myth of Social Cost', *Hobart Paper No. 82* (London: The Institute of Economic Affairs).

CLARK, G. and DEAR, M. (1981) 'The State in Capitalism and the Capitalist State', in Dear, M. and Scott, H. J. (eds) *Urbanization and Urban Planning in Capitalist Society* (London and New York: Methuen): 45–61.

CLARK, W. A. V. (1982) 'Recent Research on Migration and Mobility: A Review and Interpretation', *Progress in Planning*, 18 (1): 1–56.

CLARK, W. A. V. and ONAKA, J. L. (1983) 'Life Cycle and Housing Adjustment as Explanations of Residential Mobility', *Urban Studies*, 20 (1): 45–57.

CLARKE, S. and GINSBURG, N. (1975) 'The Political Economy of Housing', in Political Economy of Housing Workshop (eds) *Political Economy and the Housing Question* (A first volume of papers presented to the Housing Workshop of the Conference of Socialist Economists) London: 3–33.

COCKBURN, C. (1977) *The Local State: Management of Cities and People* (London: Pluto Press).

COING, H. (1977) 'Monopolville: l'énterprise et la ville', *International Journal of Urban and Regional Research*, 1 (1): 180–85.

COLLISON, P. (1963) *The Cutteslowe Walls: A Study in Social Class* (London: Faber & Faber).

CORKINGDALE, J. T. (1980) 'Employment Trends in the Conurbations', in Evans, A. and Eversley, D. (eds) *The Inner City: Employment and Industry* (London: Heinemann): 157–92.

COX, A. (1983) 'On the Role of the State in Urban Policy-Making: The Case of Inner-City and Dispersal Policies in Britain', in Pons, V. and Francis, R. (eds) *Urban Social Research: Problems and Prospects, Sociological Review Monograph 30* (London: Routledge & Kegan Paul): 31–45.

COX, K. R. (1973) *Conflict, Power and Politics in the City: A Geographic View* (New York: McGraw-Hill).

COX, K. R. (1978) 'Local Interests and Urban Political Processes in Market Societies', in Cox, K. R. (ed.) *Urbanization and Conflict in Market Societies* (London: Methuen) Ch. 4: 94–108.

COX, K. R. (1981) 'Capitalism and Conflict around the Communal Living Space', in Dear, M. and Scott, A. J. (eds) *Urbanization and Planning in Capitalist Societies* (London: Methuen) Ch. 16: 431–55.

COX, K. R. and JOHNSTON, R. J. (1982) 'Conflict Politics and the Urban Scene: A Conceptual Framework', in Cox, K. R. and Johnston, R. J. (eds) *Conflict, Politics and the Urban Scene* (London: Longman) Ch. 1: 1–27.

COX K. R. AND MCCARTHY, J. J. (1982) 'Neighbourhood Activism as a Politics of Turf: A Critical Analysis', in Cox, K. R. and Johnston, R. J. (eds) *Conflict, Politics and the Urban Scene* (London: Longman) Ch. 10: 196–219.

CULLINGWORTH, J. R. (1982) *Town and Country Planning in Britain*, 8th edn (London: Allen & Unwin).

DALES, J. H., (1975) 'Beyond the Marketplace', *Canadian Journal of Economics*, 8: 484–503.

DAVIS, O. A. and WHINSTON, A. B. (1961) 'The Economics of Urban Renewal', *Law and Contemporary Problems*, 26: 105–17.

DEAR, M. J. and LONG, J. (1978) 'Community Strategies in Locational Conflict' in Cox, K. R. (ed.) *Urbanization and Conflict in Market Societies* (London: Methuen) Ch. 5: 113–27.

DEMSETZ, H. (1967) 'Toward a Theory of Property Rights', *American Economic Review*, 57: 347–59.

DEPARTMENT OF THE ENVIRONMENT (1980) *Development Control Statistics 1978–79* (London: Department of the Environment).

DESAI, M. (1979) *Marxian Economics* (Oxford: Blackwell).

DICKEN, P. (1976) 'The Multiplant Business Enterprise and Geographical Space: Some Issues in the Study of External Control and Regional Development', *Regional Studies*, 10: 401–12.

DICKINSON, H. D. (1957) 'The Falling Rate of Profit in Marxian Economics', *Review of Economic Studies*, 24: 120–30.

DMITRIEV, V. K. (1974) *Economic Essays on Value, Competition and Utility*, translated by D. Fry and edited with an introduction by D. M. Nuti. (London: Cambridge University Press) (Consists of three essays, first published separately, in Russian, in 1892 and 1902, and first published in book form, in Russian, in 1904 and in English in 1974).

DOBB, M. (1972) 'The Sraffa System and Critique of Neo-Classical theory of Distribution', in Hunt, E. K. and Schwartz, J. G. (eds) *A Critique of Economic Theory: Selected Readings* (Harmondsworth: Penguin Books): 205–21.

DOBB, M. (1973) *Theories of Value and Distribution since Adam Smith: Ideology and Economic Theory* (Cambridge: Cambridge University Press).

DONNISON, D. and UNGERSON, C. (1982) *Housing Policy* (Harmondsworth: Penguin Books).

DOWNS, A. (1981) *Neighbourhoods and Urban Development* (Washington D.C.: The Brookings Institution).

DREWETT, R. (1973) 'The Developers: Decision Processes', in Hall, P., Gracey, H., Drewett, R. and Thomas, R., *The Containment of Urban England: Volume 2: The Planning System: Objectives, Operations, Impacts* (London: Allen & Unwin) 163–93.

DUNLEAVY, P. (1979) 'The Urban Basis of Political Alignment: Social Class, Domestic Property Ownership, and State Intervention in Consumption', *British Journal of Political Science*, 9: 409–43.

DUNLEAVY, P. (1980) *Urban Political Analysis: The Politics of Collective Consumption* (London: The Macmillan Press).

EDEL, M. (1976) 'Marx's Theory of Rent: Urban Applications', in Political Economy of Housing Workshop (ed.) *Housing and Class in Britain* (A second volume of papers presented to the Political Economy of Housing Workshop of the Conference of Socialist Economists) London 7–23 (also published in *Kapitalistate*, 4 (1976): 100–124).

ELIAS, P. and KEOGH, G. (1982) 'Industrial Decline and Unemployment in the Inner City Areas of Great Britain: A Review of the Evidence', *Urban Studies*, 19: 1–15.

ELKIN, S. L. (1974) *Politics and Land Use Planning: The London Experience* (London: Cambridge University Press)

ELLIOTT, B. (1980) 'Manuel Castells and the New Urban Sociology', *British Journal of Sociology*, 31 (2): 151–8.

ELSTER, J. 1985 *Making Sense of Marx* (London: Cambridge University Press; Paris: Editions de la Maison des Sciences de l'Homme).

ENGELS, F. (1958) *The Condition of the Working Class in England*, translated from the German and edited by Henderson, W. O. and Chaloner, W. H. (Oxford: Blackwell) (first written and published in German in 1845; first published in English in 1892).

ENGELS, F. (1959) *Anti-Duhring* (Moscow: Foreign Languages Publishing House) (first published in German as a series of articles in *Vorwart* in 1877–8 and in book form in 1878; first published in English in 1959).

ENGELS, F. (1974) 'Supplement to *Capital*, Volume Three', in Marx, K. *Capital: A Critique of Political Economy. Volume III: The Process of Capitalist Production as a Whole* (London: Lawrence & Wishart) (first published in German in 1894; first published in English in 1909).

EVANS, A. W. and RICHARDSON, R. (1981) 'Urban Unemployment: Interpretation and Additional Evidence', *Scottish Journal of Political Economy*, 28 (2): 107–24.

EVANS, A. and RUSSELL, L. (1980) 'A Portrait of the London Labour Market', in Evans, A. and Eversley, D. (eds) *The Inner City: Employment and Industry* (London: Heinemann): 204–31.

FIELDING, A. J. (1982) 'Counterurbanization in Western Europe', *Progress in Planning*, 17 (1): 1–52.

FINE, B. (1979) 'On Marx's Theory of Agricultural Rent', *Economy and Society*, 8 (3): 241–78.

FINE, B. (1980) 'On Marx's Theory of Agricultural Rent: A Rejoiner', *Economy and Society*, 9 (3): 327–39.

FINE, B. and HARRIS, L. (1976) 'Controversial Issues in Marxist Economic Theory', in Miliband, R, and Saville, J. (eds) *Socialist Register* (London: Merlin Press): 141–78.

FLYNN, B. (1981) 'Managing Consensus: Strategies and Rationales in Policy-Making' in Harloe, M., (ed.), *New Perspectives in Urban Change and Conflict*, (London: Heinemann Educational Books): 50–62.

FREYSSENET, M., REGAZZOLA, T. and RETEL, J. (1971) *Ségregation spatiale et déplacements sociaux dans l'agglomeration parisiénne* (Paris: Centre de Sociologie Urbaine).

FURUBOTN, E. G. and PEJOVICH, S. (1972) 'Property Rights and Economic Theory: A Survey of Recent Literature', *The Journal of Economic Literature*, 10: 1137–62.

GAREGNANI, P. (1972) 'Heterogeneous Capital, the Production Function and the Theory of Distribution', in Hunt, E. K. and Schwartz, J.G. (eds) *A Critique of Economic Theory: Selected Readings* (Harmondsworth: Penguin Books): 245–91.

GARNIER, J. P. (1974) 'À propos de "la question urbaine", *Éspaces et Sociétés*, 8–9: 123–9.

GIBSON, B. and ESFAHANI, H. (1983) 'Nonproduced Means of Production: Neo-Ricardians vs. Fundamentalists', *Review of Radical Political Economics*, 15 (2): 83–105.

GIBSON, B. and MCLEOD, D. (1983) 'Non-Produced Means of Production in Sraffa's System: Basics, Non-Basics and Quasi-Basics', *Cambridge Journal of Economics*, 7: 141–50.

GIDDENS, A. (1971) *Capitalism and Modern Social Theory: An Analysis of the writings of Marx, Durkheim and Max Weber* (London: Cambridge University Press).

GILLMAN, J. (1957) *The Falling Rate of Profit: Marx's Law and its Significance to Twentieth Century Capitalism* (London: Dobson)

GLASS, R. (1977) 'Verbal Pollution: Review of *The Urban Question* by M. Castells', *New Society*, 41 (782): 667–9.

GLEAVE, D. and PALMER, D. (1978) 'Mobility of Labour: Are Council Tenants Really Handicapped?', *Centre for Environmental Studies Review*, 3: 74–77.

GLUCKSMAN, M. (1974) *Structuralist Analysis in Contemporary Social Thought: A Comparison of the Theories of Claude Lévi-Strauss and Louis Althusser* (London: Routledge & Kegan Paul).

GLYN, A. and SUTCLIFFE, B. (1972) *British Capitalism, Workers and the Profits Squeeze* (Harmondsworth: Penguin Books).

GODARD, F. CASTELLS, M., DELAYRE, H., DESSANE, C. and O'CALLAGHAN, C. (1973) *La Rénovation Urbaine a Paris: Structure urbaine et logique de classe* (Paris: Mouton).

GODDARD, J. B. (1977) 'Urban Geography: City and Regional System', *Progress in Human Geography*, 1: 296–303.

GODDARD, J. B. (1978) 'Urban and Regional Systems', *Progress in Geography*, 2: 309–17.

GOODCHILD, R. (1978) 'The Operation of the Private Land Market', in Pearce, B. J., Curry, N. R. and Goodchild, R. N., *Land, Planning and the Market*, Department of Land Economy, University of Cambridge, Occasional Paper no. 9: 11–47.

GOUGH, I. (1972) 'Marx's Theory of Productive and Unproductive Labour', *New Left Review*, 76: 47–72.

HABERMAS, J. (1976) 'Problems of Legitimation in Late Capitalism', in Connerton, P. (ed.) *Critical Sociology: Selected Readings* (Harmondsworth: Penguin Books): 363–87.

HALL, P., THOMAS, R., GRACEY, H. DREWETT, R. (1973) *The Containment of Urban England*, vol. I and II (London: Allen & Unwin).

HALLETT, G. (1979) *Urban Land Economics: Principles and Policy* (London: Macmillan Press).

HARLOE, M. (1977) 'New Trends in Urban Sociology: Weberian and Marxist Approaches', in Harloe, M. (ed.) *Captive Cities: Studies in the Political Economy of Cities and Regions* (London: John Wiley): 1–47.

HARLOE, M. (1979) 'New Perspectives in Urban and Regional Research: Progress and Problems', in Harloe, M. (ed.) *New Perspectives in Urban Change and Conflict* (London: Heinemann Educational Books): 1–26.

HARLOE, M. (1984) 'Sector and Class: A Critical Comment', *International Journal of Urban and Regional Research*, 8 (2): 228–37.

HARRIS, D. J. (1983) 'Accumulation of Capital and the Rate of Profit in Marxian Theory', *Cambridge Journal of Economics*, 7: 311–30.

HARRISON, J. (1973) 'Productive and Unproductive Labour in Marx's Political Economy', *Bulletin of the Conference of Socialist Economists*, 2 (6): 70–82.

HARVEY, D. (1973) *Social Justice and the City* (London: Edward Arnold).

HARVEY, D. (1976) 'Labour, Capital and Class Struggle around the Built Environment in Advanced Capitalist Societies', *Politics and Society*, 6 (3): 265–96.

HARVEY, D. (1978a) 'Labour, Capital, and Class Struggle Around the Built Environment in Advanced Capitalist Societies', in Cox, K. (ed) *Urbanization and Conflict in Market Societies* (London: Methuen) 1: pp. 9–37.

HARVEY, D. (1978b) 'The Urban Process under Capitalism: A Framework for Analysis', *International Journal of Urban and Regional Research*, 2 (1): 101–31.

HARVEY, D. (1981) 'The Urban Process under Capitalism: A Framework for Analysis', in Dear, M. and Scott, A. J. (eds) *Urbanization and Urban Planning in a Capitalist Society* (London: Methuen) chapter 5: 91–121.

HARVEY, D. (1982) *The Limits to Capital* (Chicago: The University of Chicago Press).

HARVEY, D. and CHATTERJEE, L. (1974) 'Absolute Rent and the Structuring of Space by Governmental and Financial Institutions', *Antipode: A Radical Journal of Geography*, 6 (1): 22–36.

HEALEY, M. J. (1982) 'Plant Closures in Multi-plant Enterprises: The Case of a Declining Industrial Sector', *Regional Studies*, 16 (1): 37–51.

HEAP, S.H. (1980) 'World Profitability Crisis in the 1970s: Some Empirical Evidence', *Capital and Class*, 12: 66–84.

HILL, T. P. (1979) *Profits and Rates of Return* (Paris: OECD).

HIRSCH, F. (1978) *Social Limits to Growth* (London: Routledge & Kegan Paul).

HIRSCHMAN, A. O. (1970) *Exit, Voice and Loyalty: Responses to Decline in Firms, Organizations, and States* (Cambridge, Mass.: Harvard University Press).

HODGSON, G. (1973) 'Marxist Epistemology and the Transformation Problem', *Bulletin of the Conference of Socialist Economists*, 2 (6): 47–64.

HODGSON, G. (1974a) 'The Theory of the Falling Rate of Profit', *New Left Review*, 84: 55–82.

HODGSON, G. (1974b) 'Marxian Epistemology and the Transformation Problem', *Economy and Society*, 4: 357–93.

HODGSON, G. (1975) *Trotsky and Fatalistic Marxism* (Nottingham: Spokesman Books).

HODGSON, G. (1976) 'Exploitation and Embodied Labour-time', *Bulletin of the Conference of Socialist Economists*, 4: 1–25.

HODGSON, G. (1977a) 'Sraffa, Value and Distribution: An Expository Essay on the Capital Controversy', *British Review of Economic Issues*, 1: 44–55.

HODGSON, G. (1977b) 'Papering over the Cracks' in Miliband, R. and Saville, J. (eds) *Socialist Register* (London: Merlin Press): 88–105.

HODGSON, G. (1982) *Capitalism, Value and Exploitation: A Radical Theory* (Oxford: Martin Robertson).

HODGSON, G. and STEEDMAN, I. (1975) 'Fixed Capital and Value Analysis', *Bulletin of the Conference of Socialist Economists*, 4 (3) 1–7.

HOUSE, J. W. (1978) *France: An Applied Geography* (London: Methuen).
HOWARD, M. C. and KING, J. E. (1976) *The Political Economy of Marx* (London: Longmans).
HOWARD, M. C. and KING, J. E. (eds) (1976) *The Economics of Marx: Selected Readings of Exposition and Criticism* (Harmondsworth: Penguin Books).
HUET, A., *et al.* (1973) *Role et portée economique, politique et ideologique de la Participation a l'amenagement urbain*, L'Office social et culturel de Rennes, France.
HUGHES, G. and MC CORMICK, B. (1981) 'Do Council Housing Policies Reduce Migration Between Regions'? *The Economic Journal*, 91: 919–37.
HUNT, E. K. (1979) 'The Categories of Productive and Unproductive Labour in Marxist Economic Theory', *Science and Society*, 43: 303–25.
INSTITUTE FOR SCIENTIFIC INFORMATION (1969–1984) *Annual Social Science Citation Index 1969–1984* (Philadelphia, Penn.: Institute for Scientific Information).
JESSOP, B. (1977) 'Recent Theories of the Capitalist State', *Cambridge Journal of Economics*, 1: 353–73.
JOHNSON, J. H., SALT, J. and WOOD, P. (1974) *Housing and the Migration of Labour in England and Wales* (Lexington, Mass. Saxon House; Lexington Books).
KAIN, J. F. and QUIGLEY, J. M. (1975) *Housing Markets and Racial Discrimination: A Microeconomic Analysis* (New York: National Bureau of Economic Research).
KEEBLE, D., OWENS, P. L. and THOMPSON, C. (1983) 'The Urban–Rural Manufacturing Shift in the European Community', *Urban Studies*, 20 (4): 405–18.
KEIPER, J. S., KURNOW, E., CLARK, C. D. and SEGAL, H. H. (1961) *Theory and Measurement of Rent* (Philadelphia, Penn.: Chilton Company).
KENWAY, P. (1980) 'Marx, Keynes and the Possibility of Crisis', *Cambridge Journal of Economics*, 4: 23–35.
KIRK, G. (1982) 'Theoretical Approaches to Urban Planning', in Blowers, A., Brook, C., Dunleavy, P. and McDowell, L. (eds) *Urban Change and Conflict: An Interdisciplinary Reader* (London: Harper & Row) pp. 135–47 (first published in 1980).
KURZ, H. D. (1978) 'Rent Theory in a Multisectoral Model', *Oxford Economic Papers*, 30 (1): 16–37.
LACLAU, E. (1975) 'The Specificity of the Political: The Poulantzas–Miliband debate', *Economy and Society*, 5 (1): 87–110.
LAMARCHE, F. (1976) 'Property Development and the Economic Foundations of the Urban Question', in Pickvance, C. G. (ed.) *Urban Sociology: Critical Essays* (London: Methuen) ch. 4, pp. 85–118 (first published in French in 1972).
LAMBERT, J., PARIS, C. and BLACKABY, B. (1978) *Housing Policy and the State: Allocation, Access and Control* (London: The Macmillan Press).
LANGE, O. (1968) 'Marxian Economics and Modern Economic Theory', in Horowitz, D. (ed.) (1968) *Marx and Modern Economics* (New York: Monthly Review Press): 68–87 (first published in *The Review of Economic Studies*, June 1935.)

LAURIA, M. (1984) 'The Implications of Marxian Rent for Community – Controlled Redevelopment Strategies', *Journal of Planning Education and Research*, 4 (1): 16–24.

LAUTMAN, J. (1974) 'Review of Lojkine, J., 1972, *La Politique Urbaine dans la Region Parisienne 1945–1971*, *Revue Francaise de Sociologie*, 15 (2): 27–7.

LEBAS, E. (1981) 'The New School of Urban and Regional Research: Into the Second Decade', in Harloe, M. and Lebas, E. (eds) *City, Class and Capital: New Developments in the Political Economy of Cities and Regions* (London: Edward Arnold): ix–xxxiii.

LEBAS, E. (1982) 'Urban and Regional Sociology in Advanced Industrial Societies: A Decade of Marxist and Critical Perspectives', *Current Sociology*, 30 (1): 1–271.

LEBAS, E. (1983) 'The State in British and French Urban Research, or the Crisis of the Urban Question', in Pons, V. and Francis, R. (eds) *Urban Social Research: Problems and Prospects, Sociological Review Monograph 30* (London: Routledge & Kegan Paul): 9–30.

LEBOWITZ, M. A. (1972) 'The Increasing Cost of Circulation and the Marxian Competitive Model', *Science and Society*, 36: 331–8.

LEFEBVRE, H. (1968) *Le Droit à la Ville* (Paris: Anthropos).

LEFEBVRE, H. (1972) *La Pensée Marxiste et la Ville* (Paris: Caterman).

LEFEBVRE, H. (1973) *Éspace et Politique: Le Droit à la Ville II* (Paris: Anthropos).

LÉVI-STRAUSS, C. (1972) *Structural Anthropology* (London: Harmondsworth). (First published in French in 1958.)

LEY, D. and MERCER, J. (1980) 'Locational Conflict and the Politics of Consumption', *Economic Geography*, 56: 89–109.

LIPSEY, R. G. (1971) *An Introduction to Positive Economics*, 3rd edn (London: Weidenfeld & Nicolson) (first published 1963).

LOCKE, J. (1964) *An Essay Concerning Human Understanding* edited by A. D. Woozley (London: Collins) (first published in 1690).

LOGAN, J. R. (1978) 'Growth, Politics and the Stratification of Places', *American Journal of Sociology*, 84 (2): 404–16.

LOJKINE, J. (1969a) 'Pour une analyse marxiste du changement social', *Sociologie du Travail*, July–Sept.: 259–73.

LOJKINE, J. (1969b) *Contribution à une théorie marxiste des ideologies* (Paris: Cahiers du Centre d'etude et de recherche marxiste).

LOJKINE, J. (1971) 'Y à-t-il une rente foncière urbaine?', *Éspaces et Sociétés*, 2: 89–94.

LOJKINE, J. (1972a) *La politique urbaine dans la région parisienne 1935–1972* (Paris: Mouton).

LOJKINE, J. (1972b) 'Pouvoir Politique et lutte des classes à l'époque du capitalisme monopoliste d'état', *La Pensée*, 166: 142–68.

LOJKINE, J. (1972c) 'Contribution à une théorie marxiste de l'urbanisation capitaliste', *Cahiers Internationaux de Sociologie*, 52: 123–46.

LOJKINE, J. (1974a) *La politique urbaine dans la région lyonnaise 1945–1972* (Paris: Mouton).

LOJKINE, J. (1974b) 'La Politique des Transports', in Les Cahiers du Centre d'Études et de Recherches Marxistes (CERM), *Urbanisme Monopoliste, Urbanisme Democratique*, CERM: 191–7.

LOJKINE, J. (1974c) 'Le projet de cite financière a Paris', *Éspaces et Sociétés*, 13–14: 111–34.

LOJKINE, J. (1975) 'Stratégies des grandes entreprises, politiques urbaines et mouvements sociaux urbains', *Sociologie du Travail:* 18–40.

LOJKINE, J. (1976a) 'Contribution to a Marxist theory of Capitalist Urbanization', in Pickvance, C. G. (ed.) *Urban Sociology: Critical Essays* (London: Tavistock Publications): 119–46 (first published in French in 1972c).

LOJKINE, J. (1976b) *Stratégies des grandes entreprises et politique urbaine: le cas des banques et des assurances* (Paris: Centre Nationale de la Recherche Scientifique: Centre d'étude des Mouvements Sociaux).

LOJKINE, J. (1977a) *Le Marxisme, L'état et la Question Urbaine* (Paris: Presses Universitaires de France).

LOJKINE, J. (1977b) 'Big Firms' Strategies, Urban Policy and Urban Social Movements', in Harloe, M. (ed.) *Captive Cities: Studies in the Political Economy of Cities and Regions* (London: Wiley): 141–56.

LOJKINE, J. (1977c) 'L'analyse marxiste de l'état', *International Journal of Urban and Regional Research*, 1: 19–23.

LOJKINE, J. (1977d) 'L'état et L'Urbain: Contribution à une analyse materialiste des politiques urbaines dans les pays capitalistes developpés', *International Journal of Urban and Regional Research*, 1 (2): 256–71.

LOJKINE, J. (1977e) 'Crise de l'État et Crise du Capitalisme Monopoliste d'État', *La Pensée*, 193: 113–26.

LOJKINE, J. (1978) 'Sur l'usage du concept de contradiction dans une analyse materialiste d'état', *La Pensée*, 197.

LOJKINE, J. (1980) 'Politique urbaine et Pouvoir local', *Revue de Sociologie Française*, 21 (4): 633–51.

LOJKINE, J. (1981a) 'For a Marxist Analysis of Social Change', in Lemert, C. C. (ed.) *French Sociology: Rupture and Renewal Since 1968* (New York: Columbia University Press) pp. 355–69 (first published in French in 1969a).

LOJKINE, J. (1981b) 'Urban Policy and Local Power: Some Aspects of Recent Research in Lille', in Harloe, M. and Lebas, E. (eds) *City, Class and Capital: New Developments in the Political Economy of Cities and Regions* (London: Edward Arnold): 89–104.

LOJKINE, J. and PRETECEILLE, E. (1970) 'Politique urbaine et stratégie de classe', *Éspaces et Sociétés*, 1: 79–84.

LORIMER, J. (1972) *A Citizen's Guide to City Politics* (Toronto: James, Lewis & Samuel).

MACPHERSON, C. B. (1973) 'A Political Theory of Property', in Macpherson, C. B. *Democratic Theory: Essays in Retrieval* (Oxford: Clarendon Press): 120–40.

MACPHERSON, C. B. (1978) 'The Meaning of Property', in Macpherson, C. B. (ed.) *Property: Mainstream and Critical Positions* (Oxford: Blackwell): 1–13.

MANDEL, E. (1968) *Marxist Economic Theory* (London: Merlin Press).

MARKUSEN, A. R. (1978) 'Class, Rent and Sectoral Conflict: Uneven Development in Western U.S. Boomtowns' *Review of Radical Political Economics*, 10: 117–29.

MARRIOTT, O. (1969) *The Property Boom* (London: Pan Books).

MARSHALL, A. (1961) *Principles of Economics* (London: The Macmillan Press) (first published in 1890).

MARX, K. (1969) *Theories of Surplus-value* (Vol. 3 of *Capital)* Part II, Moscow: Progress Publishers (first written in German between 1861–1863; first published in German in 1905; first published in English in 1963).

MARX, K. (1973) *Grundrisse: Foundations of the Critique of Political Economy* (London: Penguin Books, in association with New Left Books) (first written in German between October 1857 and March 1858; first published in German, in two volumes, in 1939 and 1941, and again in 1952; first translated and published in English in 1973).

MARX, K. (1974a) *Capital: A Critical Analysis of Capitalist Production, vol. I* (London: Lawrence & Wishart) (first written in German between 1865 and 1867; first published in German in 1869; first published in English in 1887).

MARX, K. (1974b) *Capital: A Critique of Political Economy, vol. II: The process of circulation* (London: Lawrence & Wishart) (first written in German between 1865 and 1867; first published in German in 1885; first published in English in 1919).

MARX, K. (1974c) *Capital: A Critique of Political Economy, vol. III: The Process of Capitalist Production as a whole* (London: Lawrence & Wishart) (first written in German between 1863 and 1865; first published in German 1894; first published in English 1909).

MARX, K. (1975) *Wages, Price and Profit* (Alternative title: *Value Price and Profit*) (Peking: Foreign Language Press) (first written in English and delivered as a speech, in June 1865, to the General Council of the First International; first published in 1898).

MARX, K. (1976) *Preface and Introduction to A Contribution to the critique of Political Economy* (Peking: Foreign Language Press) (first published in German in 1859 and in English in 1951).

MARX, K. (1977) 'Economic and Philosophical Manuscripts', in Marx, K. *Early Writings* (London: Penguin Books and *New Left Review*): 279–400 (first written in German between April and August 1844; first published in German in 1932; first complete translation, by T. B. Bottomore, and publication in English in 1963).

MARX, K. (1979) 'The Eighteenth Brumaire of Louis Bonaparte', in Marx, K. and Engels, F. *Collected Works, Vol. II, 1851–1853* (London: Lawrence & Wishart): 99–197 (first written in German in December 1851 to March 1852; first published in German in 1852; first published in English in 1979).

MARX, K. and ENGELS, F. (1955) 'Letter from Marx to Engels in Manchester, August 2, 1862, London', in *Selected Correspondence of Marx and Engels* (Moscow: Progress Publishers) pp. 128–33.

MASSEY, D. (1979) 'In What Sense a Regional Problem?' *Regional Studies*, 13: 233–43.

MASSEY, D. and CATALANO, A. (1978) *Capital and Land: Landownership by Capital in Great Britain* (London: Edward Arnold).

MASSEY, D. B. and MEEGAN, R. A. (1978) 'Industrial Restructuring versus the Cities', *Urban Studies*, 15: 273–88.

MEDIO, A. (1972) 'Profits and Surplus-Value: Appearance and Reality in Capitalist Production', in Hunt, E. K. and Schwartz, J. G. (eds) *A Critique of Economic Theory: Selected Readings* (Harmondsworth: Penguin Books).

MEDIO, A. (1977) 'Neoclassicals, Neo-Ricardians and Marx', in Schwartz, J. (ed.) *The Subtle Anatomy of Capitalism* (Santa Monica, Cal.: Goodyear Publishing Company): 381–411.
MEEK, R. (1956) 'Some Notes on the "Transformation Problem"', *The Economic Journal*, 66: 96–107.
MEEK, R. (1976a) 'The Falling Rate of Profit', in Howard, M. C. and King, J. E. (eds) (1976) *The Economics of Marx: Selected Readings of Exposition and Criticism* (Harmondsworth: Penguin Books): 203–18.
MEEK, R. (1976b) 'Is there an "Historical Transformation Problem"?: A Comment', *The Economic Journal*, 86: 342–7.
METCALF, D. (1975) 'Urban Unemployment in England', *The Economic Journal*, 85: 578–89.
MILIBAND, R. (1972) 'Reply to Nicos Poulantzas', in Blackburn, R. (ed.) *Ideology in Social Science: Readings in Critical Social Theory* (London: Fontana/Collins): 253–60.
MOLOTCH, H. (1976) 'The City as a Growth Machine: Toward a Political Economy of Place', *American Journal of Sociology*, 82 (2): 309–32.
MONTANI, G. (1975) 'Scarce Natural Resources and Income Distribution', *Metroeconomica*, 27: 68–101.
MORISHIMA, M. (1973) *Marx's Economics: A Dual Theory of Value and Growth* (Cambridge: Cambridge University Press).
MORISHIMA, M. (1974) 'Marx in the Light of Modern Economic Theory', *Econometrica*, 42 (4): 611–32.
MORISHIMA, M. (1976) 'Positive Profits with Negative Surplus Value – A Comment', *The Economic Journal*, 86; 599–603.
MORISHIMA, M. and CATEPHORES, G. (1975) 'Is There an "Historical Transformation Problem"?', *The Economic Journal*, 85: 309–28.
MORISHIMA, M. and CATEPHORES, G. (1976) 'The "Historical Transformation Problem": A Reply', *The Economic Journal*, 86: 348–52.
MORISHIMA, M. and CATEPHORES, G. (1978) *Value Exploitation and Growth: Marx in the Light of Modern Economic Theory* (London: McGraw-Hill).
MULLINS, P. (1977) 'The Social Base, Stake, and Urban Effects of a Brisbane Urban Social Movement', *Australian and New Zealand Journal of Sociology*, 13 (1): 29–35.
MURRAY, R. (1977) 'Value and Theory of Rent: Part One', *Capital and Class*, 3: 100–22.
MURRAY, R. (1978) 'Value and Theory of Rent: Part Two', *Capital and Class*, 4: 11–33.
NAQVI, K.A. (1960) 'Schematic Presentation of Accumulation in Marx', *Indian Economic Review*, 5 (1): 13–22.
NEILSON, L. (1976) 'Developers as Conservative Decision-Makers', in McMaster, J. C. and Webb, G. R. (eds) *Australian Urban Economics: A Reader* (Sydney: Australia and New Zealand Book Company): 151–73.
NELL, E. (1972) 'The Revival of Political Economy', *Australian Economic Papers*, 11 (8): 19–31.
NEUTZE, G. M. (1976) 'Policy Instruments in the Urban Land Market', in McMaster, J. C. and Webb, G. R. (eds) *Australian Urban Economics: A Reader* (Sydney: Australia and New Zealand Book Company): 78–128.

NICHOLLS, D. C., TURNER, D. M., KIRBY-SMITH, R. and CULLEN, J. D. (1982) 'The Risk Business: Developers' Perceptions and Prospects for Housebuilding in the Inner City', *Urban Studies*, 19: 331–41.

NUTI, D. M. (1972) '"Vulgar Economy" in the Theory of Income Distribution', in Hunt, E. K. and Schwartz, J. G. (eds) *A Critique of Economic Theory: Selected Readings* (Harmondsworth: Penguin Books): 222–32.

OATES, W. E. (1969) 'The Effects of Property Taxes and Local Public Spending on Property Values: An Empirical Study of Tax Capitalization and the Tiebout Hypothesis', *Journal of Political Economy*, 77: 957–71.

O'CONNOR, J. (1973) *The Fiscal Crisis of the State* (New York: St. Martin's Press).

O'CONNOR, J. (1975) 'Productive and Unproductive Labour', *Politics and Society*, 5 (3): 297–336.

OFFE, C. and RONGE, V. (1975) 'Theses on the Theory of the State', *New German Critique*, 6: 137–47.

OKISHIO, N. (1961) 'Technical Change and the Rate of Profit', *Kobe University Economic Review*, 7: 85–99.

OLSON, M. (1971) *The Logic of Collective Action: Public Goods and the Theory of Groups* (Cambridge, Mass.: Harvard University Press) (first published in 1965).

ORBELL, J. M. and UNO, T. (1972) 'A Theory of Neighbourhood Problem Solving: Political Action versus Residential Mobility', *American Political Science Review*, 61: 471–89.

PAHL, R. E. (1975) *Whose City? And Further Essays on Urban Society* (Harmondsworth: Penguin Books).

PAHL, R. E. (1977) '"Collective Consumption" and the State in Capitalist and State Socialist Societies', in Scase, R. (ed.), *Industrial Society: Class, Cleavage and Control* (London: Allen & Unwin): 153–71.

PAHL, R. E. (1978) 'Castells and Collective Consumption', *Sociology*, 12: 309–15.

PEJOVICH, S. (1982) 'Karl Marx, Property Rights School and the Process of Social Change', *Kyklos*, 35: 383–97.

PERRONS, D. C. (1981) 'The Role of Ireland in the New International Division of Labour: A Proposed Framework for Regional Analysis', *Regional Studies*, 15 (2): 81–100.

PICKVANCE, C. G. (1974a) 'Review Essay: Toward a Reconstruction of Urban Sociology', (Review of Castells, 1972c), *American Journal of Sociology*, 80 (4): 1003–8.

PICKVANCE, C. G. (1974b) 'On a Materialist Critique of Urban Sociology', *The Sociological Review*, 22 (2): 203–20.

PICKVANCE, C. G. (1975) 'On the Study of Urban Social Movements', *The Sociological Review*, 23 (1): 29–44.

PICKVANCE, C. G. (1976) 'On the Study of Urban Social Movements' in Pickvance, C. G. (ed.) *Urban Sociology: Critical Essays* (London: Tavistock Publications): 198–218.

PICKVANCE, C. G. (1977a) 'Marxist Approaches to the Study of Urban Politics: Divergencies Among some Recent French Studies', *International Journal of Urban and Regional Research*, 1 (2): 219–55.

PICKVANCE, C. G. (1977b) 'Physical Planning and Market Forces in Urban

Development', *National Westminster Bank Quarterly Review*, August: 41–50.

PICKVANCE, C. G. (1978) 'Review of: *The Urban Question: A Marxist Approach* by Manuel Castells, Edward Arnold, London, 1977', *The Sociological Review*, 26 (1): 173–6.

PICKVANCE, C. G. (1981) 'Policies as Chameleons: An Interpretation of Regional Policy and Office Policy in Britain', in Dear, M. and Scott, A. J. (eds) *Urbanization and Urban Planning in Capitalist Society* (London and New York: Methuen): 231–65.

PICKVANCE, C. G. (1984), 'The Structuralist Critique of Urban Studies', in Smith, M. P. (ed.) *Cities in Transformation: Class, Capital and the State*, Urban Affairs Annual Reviews, vol. 26 (Beverly Hills and London: Sage Publications): 31–50.

PIGOU, A. (1960) *The Economics of Welfare* (London: Macmillan Press) (first published in 1920).

POULANTZAS, N. (1972) 'The Problem of the Capitalist State', in Blackburn, R. (ed.) *Ideology in Social Science: Readings in Critical Social Theory* (London: Fontana/Collins): 238–53 (first published in 1969).

POULANTZAS, N. (1973) *Political Power and Social Classes* (London: New Left Books) (first published in French in 1968).

POULANTZAS, N. (1975) *Classes in Contemporary Capitalism* (London: New Left Books) (first published in French in 1974).

POULANTZAS, N. (1976) 'Problems actuels de la recherche marxiste sur l'état', Dialectiques, 13: 30–43.

PRATT, G. (1982). 'Class Analysis and Urban Domestic Property: A Critical Examination', *International Journal of Urban and Regional Research*, 6 (4): 481–502.

PURDY, D. (1973). 'The Theory of the Permanent Arms Economy', *Bulletin of the Conference of Socialist Economists*, 6: 12–32.

QUADRIO-CURZIO, A. (1980) 'Rent, Income Distribution and Orders of Efficiency and Rentability', in Pasinetti, L. L. (ed.) *Essays on the Theory of Joint Production* (London: The Macmillan Press): 218–40 (first published in Italian in 1977).

REX, J. and MOORE, R. (1967) *Race, Community and Conflict: A Study of Sparkbrook* (Oxford: Oxford University Press).

REYNAUD, E. (1974) 'Review of *La Question Urbaine* by M. Castells', in *Revue Française de Sociologie*, 15 (4): 617–26.

REYNOLDS, D. R. and HONEY, R. (1978) 'Conflict in the Location of Salutary Public Facilities', in Cox, K. R. (ed.) *Urbanization and Conflict in Market Societies* (London: Methuen) Ch. 7: 144–60.

RICARDO, D. (1966) 'An Essay on The Influence of the low Price of Corn on the Profits of Stock showing the Inexpediency of Restrictions on importation, with Remarks on Mr. Malthus' Two last publications: "An Inquiry into the Nature and Progress of Rent" and "The Grounds of an Opinion, on the Policy of restricting the Importation of Foreign Corn" ' (Abbreviated Title: 'Essay on Profits') in Sraffa, P. (ed.) *The Works and Correspondence of David Ricardo, Volume IV*; Pamphlets and Papers 1815–1823 (London: Cambridge University Press): 10–41 (first published in Feburary, 1915).

RICARDO, D. (1970) *On the Principles of Political Economy and Taxation*, P. Sraffa (ed.) (London: Cambridge University Press) (first published in 1817).

RICHARDSON, R. (1980) 'Unemployment and the Labour Market', in Cameron, G. C. (ed.) *The Future of the British Conurbations: Policies and Prescriptions for Change* (London: Longman): 208–23.
RIDKER, R. G. and HENNING, J. A (1967) 'The Determinants of Residential Property Values with Special Reference to Air Pollution', *Review of Economics and Statistics*, 49: 246–57.
ROBINSON, J. (1965) 'Piero Sraffa and the Rate of Exploitation', *New Left Review*, 31: 28–34.
ROBINSON, J. (1967) *An Essay on Marxian Economics* (London: The Macmillan Press).
ROBINSON, J. (1973) 'The Theory of Value Reconsidered', in *Collected Economic Papers*, vol. 4 (Oxford: Blackwell) pp. 59–66 (first published in *Australian Economic Papers*, 1979, 8 (12): 12–19).
ROBINSON, J. (1980) 'Time in Economic Theory', *Kyklos*, 33: 219–29.
ROBSON, B. T. (1982) 'The Bodley Barricade: Social Space and Social Conflict', in Cox, K. R. and Johnston, R. J. (eds) *Conflict, Politics and the Urban Scene* (London: Longman) Ch. 3: 45–61.
ROEMER, J. E. (1977) 'Technical Change and the "Tendency of the Rate of Profit to Fall" ', *Journal of Economic Theory*, 16: 403–24.
ROEMER, J. E. (1978a) 'Marxian Models of Reproduction and Accumulation', *Cambridge Journal of Economics*, 2: 37–53.
ROEMER, J. E. (1978b) 'The Effect of Technological Change on the Real Wage and Marx's Falling Rate of Profit', *Australian Economic Papers*: 152–66.
ROEMER, J. E. (1979) 'Continuing Controversy on the Falling Rate of Profit: Fixed Capital and Other Issues', *Cambridge Journal of Economics*, 3: 379–98.
ROEMER, J. E. (1981) *Analytical Foundations of Marxian Economic Theory* (London: Cambridge University Press).
ROEMER, J. E. (1982) *A General Theory of Exploitation and Class* (Cambridge, Mass.: Harvard University Press).
RONCAGLIA, A. (1978) *Sraffa and the Theory of Prices* (London: John Wiley) (first published in Italian in 1975).
SALT, J. (1980) 'Labour Migration, Housing and the Labour Market', in Evans, A. and Eversley, D. (eds) *The Inner City: Employment and Industry* (London: Heinemann): 253–68.
SAMUELSON, P.A. (1971) 'Understanding the Marxian notion of Exploitation: A Summary of the So-called Transformation Problem between Marxian Values and Competitive Prices', *Journal of Economic Literature*, 9: 399–431.
SAUNDERS, P. (1978) 'Domestic Property and Social Class', *International Journal of Urban and Regional Research*, 2: 233–51.
SAUNDERS, P. (1980a) *Urban Politics: A Sociological Interpretation* (Harmondsworth: Penguin Books).
SAUNDERS, P. (1980b) 'Local Government and the State', *New Society*, 51 (910): 550–51.
SAUNDERS, p. (1984) 'Beyond Housing Classes: The Sociological Significance of Private Property Rights in Means of Consumption', *International Journal of Urban and Regional Research*, 8 (2): 202–27.
SAX, J. L. (1971) 'Takings, Private Property and Public Rights', *The Yale Law Journal*, 81 (2): 149–86.

SCHNORE, L. F. (1965) 'The Spatial Structure of Cities in the Two Americas', in Hauser, P. M. and Schnore, L. M. (eds) *The Study of Urbanization* (London and New York: John Wiley: 347–98.

SCOTT, A. J. (1976a) 'Land and Rent: An Interpretative Review of the French Literature', *Progress in Geography: International Reviews of Current Research*, 9: 102–45.

SCOTT, A. J. (1976b) 'Land Use and Commodity Production', *Regional Science and Urban Economics*, 6: 147–60.

SCOTT, A. J. (1979) 'Commodity Production and the Dynamics of Land-use Differentiation', *Urban Studies*, 16: 95–104.

SCOTT, A.J. (1980) *The Urban Land Nexus and the State* (London: Pion).

SETON, F. (1976) 'The Transformation Problem', in Howard, M. C. and King, J. E. (eds) *The Economics of Marx: Selected Readings of Exposition and Criticism* (London: Penguin Books): 162–76.

SHAIKH, A. (1978) 'An Introduction to the History of Crisis Theories', in The Union for Radical Political Economics (eds) *U.S. Capitalism in Crisis* (New York: Union for Radical Political Economics): 219–40.

SHERMAN, H. J. (1970) 'The Marxist Theory of Value Revisited', *Science and Society*, 34: 257–92.

SILBURN, R. (1975) 'The Potential and Limitations of Community Action', in Lambert, C. and Weir, D. (eds) *Cities in Modern Britain: An Introductory Reader* (Glasgow: Fontana/Collins): 391–7.

SMITH, A. (1976) *The Wealth of Nations* (Harmondsworth: Penguin Books) (first published in March, 1776).

SMITH, C. J. and HANHAM, R. W. (1981) 'Proximity and the Formation of Public Attitudes towards Mental Illness', *Environment and Planning A*, 13: 147–65.

SMITH, D. M. (1977) *Human Geography: A Welfare Approach* (London: Edward Arnold).

SOVANI, N. V. (1964) 'The Analysis of "Over-Urbanization"', *Economic Development and Cultural Change*, 12 (2): 113–22.

SOWELL, T. (1960) 'Marx's "Increasing Misery" Doctrine', *The American Economic Review*, 50: 111–20.

SOWELL, T. (1976) 'Marx's Capital after One Hundred Years', in Howard, M. C. and King, J. E. (eds) *The Economics of Marx: Selected Readings of Exposition and Criticism* (Harmondsworth: Penguin Books) pp. 49–76 (first published in *Canadian Journal of Economics*, 33 (1967): 50–74).

SRAFFA, P. (1960) *Production of Commodities by Means by Commodities. Prelude to a Critique of Economic Theory* (London: Cambridge University Press).

STEEDMAN, I. (1972) 'Marx on the Rate of Profit', *Bulletin of the Conference of Socialist Economics*, 4: 104–9.

STEEDMAN, I. (1973) 'The Transformation Problem Again', *Bulletin of the Conference of Socialist Economists*, 2 (6): 37–42.

STEEDMAN, I. (1975a) 'Value, Price and Profit', *New Left Review*, 90: 71–80.

STEEDMAN, I. (1975b) 'Positive Profits with Negative Surplus Value', *The Economic Journal*, 85: 14–23.

STEEDMAN, I. (1976) 'Positive Profits with Negative Surplus Value: A Reply',

The Economic Journal, 86: 604–8.
STEEDMAN, I. (1977) *Marx after Sraffa* (London: New Left Books).
STEEDMAN, I. *et al.* (1981) *The Value Controversy* (London: Verso Editions and New Left Books).
SWEEZY, P. (1942) *The Theory of Capitalist Development: Principles of Marxian Political Economy* (New York and London: Monthly Review Press.
SWEEZY, P. M. (1973) 'Some Problems in the Theory of Capital Accumulation', *Bulletin of the Conference of Socialist Economists*, 2 (6): 25–36.
THERET, B. (1982) 'Collective Means of Consumption, Capital Accumulation and the Urban Question: Conceptual Problems Raised by Lojkine's Work', *International Journal of Urban and Regional Research*, 6 (3), 345–71.
THORNS, D. C. (1981) 'The Implications of Differential Rates of Capital Gain from Owner Occupation for the Formation and Development of Housing Classes', *International Journal of Urban and Regional Research*, 5: 205–17.
TIEBOUT, C. B. (1956). 'A Pure Theory of Local Expenditures', *Journal of Political Economy*, 64: 416–24.
TOURAINE, A., AHTIK, V., OSTROWETSKY-ZYGEL, S. and CASTELLS, M. (1967) 'Mobilité des Entreprises et Structures Urbain', *Sociologie du Travail*: 369–405.
TOURAINE, A., AHTIK, V., OSTROWETSKY-ZYGEL, S. and CASTELLS, M. (1968) *Mobilité des Entreprises Industrielles en Région Parisenne* (Paris: Cahiers de l'Institut d'Aménagement et d'Urbanisme de la Région Parisienne) Volume II.
UNESCO (1974–1977) *Index Translations, 1974–1977, Vols 27–30*, UNESCO, 7 Place de Fontenoy, 75700, Paris.
VAN PARIJS, P. (1980) 'The Falling-Rate-of-Profit Theory of Crisis: A Rational Reconstruction by way of Obituary', *The Review of Radical Political Economics*, 12 (1): 1–16.
WALKER, A. (1978) *Marx: His Theory and its Context* (London: Longman).
WALKER, R. (1974) 'Urban Ground Rent: Building a New Conceptual Framework', *Antipode: A Radical Journal of Geography*, 6 (1): 51–9.
WALKER, R. A. (1975) 'Contentious Issues in Marxian Value and Rent Theory: A Second and Longer Look', *Antipode: A Radical Journal of Geography*, 7 (1): 31–53.
WEBER, M. (1968) *Economy and Society: An Outline of Interpretive Society*, vols 1 and 2 (translated by Roth, G. and Wittich, C.) (Berkeley: University of California Press) (first written in German in 1910–14; first published in German in 1922; first published completely in English, 1968).
WEBER, M. (1974) *The Protestant Ethic and the Spirit of Capitalism* (London: Unwin University Books) (first published in German in 1904–5; first published in English in 1930).
WEISSKOPF, T. E. (1978) 'Marxist Perspectives on Cyclical Crisis', in The Union for Radical Political Economics (eds) *U.S. Capitalism in Crisis* (New York: Union for Radical Political Economics): 241–60.
WEISSKOPF, T. E. (1979) 'Marxian Crisis Theory and the Rate of Profit in the Post-war U.S. Economy', *Cambridge Journal of Economics*, 3: 341–78.
WESTAWAY, J. (1974) 'The Spatial Hierarchy of Business Organizations and its Implications for the British Urban System', *Regional Studies*, 8: 145–155.

WHITE, M. J. (1981) 'Self-Interest in the Suburbs: The Trend Toward No-Growth Zoning', in Tropman, J. E., Dluhy, M. J. and Lind, R. M. (eds) *New Strategic Perspectives on Social Policy* (New York: Pergamon Press): 434–49.

WILKINSON, R. K. and GULLIVER, S. (1971) 'The Impact of Non-Whites on House Prices', *Race*, 13 (1): 21–36.

WILLIAMS, N. and NORMAN, T. (1971) 'Exclusionary Land Use Controls: The Case of North-Eastern New Jersey', *Syracuse Law Review*, 22: 475–507.

WILLIAMS, P. (1978) 'Urban Managerialism: A Concept of Relevance?' *Area*, 10 (3): 236–40.

WINTERNITZ, J. (1948) Values and Prices: A Solution to the So-called Transformation Problem', *The Economic Journal*, 58: 276–80.

WIRTH, L. (1951) 'Urbanism as a Way of Life', in Hatt, P. K. and Reiss, A. J. (eds) *Cities and Society: The Revised Reader in Urban Sociology* (New York: The Free Press of Glencoe) pp. 46–63 (first published in *The American Journal of Sociology*, 1938, July, Vol. 44).

WOLF, E. P. and LEBEAUX, C. N. (1969) *Change and Renewal in an Urban Community: Five Case Studies of Detroit* (New York: Praeger Publishers).

WRIGHT, E. O. (1978) *Class, Crisis and the State* (London: New Left Books).

ZETTER, R. (1975) 'Les Halles: A Case Study of Large Scale Redevelopment in Central Paris', *Town Planning Review*, 46 (3) 267–94.

Author Index

Abraham-Frois, G. 18, 56
Agnew, J. A. 221, 224
Albin, P. S. 207
Alcaly, R. E. 24, 35, 36
Alchian, A. A. 216
Althusser, L. 81–4, 91–2, 95, 97, 244–5n, 246n
Ambrose, P. 197, 204, 221
Armstrong, P. 21
Aronson, J. R. 207, 251n

Bailey, M. J. 221
Balanowski, V. 125
Balchin, P. N. 204
Bale, J. 217, 228
Balibar, E. 81–3, 244–5n
Ball, M. 56, 240–1n
Bandyopadhyay, P. 56
Bannock, G. 149, 235n, 250n
Baran, P. 74
Baumol, W. J. 10, 207
Baxter, R. E. 149, 235n, 250n
Beirne, P. 56
Benetti, C. 60
Bentham, G. 121
Berrebi, E. 18, 56
Berthoud, R. 209
Bhaduri, A. 20, 234n, 236n
Blaug, M. 8, 47, 236n
Bleaney, M. 236n
Boddy, R. 24, 53, 234n
Böhm-Bawerk, E. Von 8, 13–18, 22, 33, 35, 49, 233n
Bose, A. 18, 56
Bourne, L. S. 209
Breugel, L. 56
Broadbent, T. A. 56, 211
Bullock, P. 243n
Burgess, 94
Byrne, D. 56

Cain, G. C. 136
Cataphores, G. 13, 17, 18, 36, 46, 13, 17, 18, 36, 46, 233n, 237n
Catelano, L. 56
Chatterjee, L. 56
Cheshire, P. C. 210, 249n
Cheung, S. 215
Clark, G. 198
Clark, W. A. V. 248n
Clarke, S. 56
Coing, H. 132
Colenutt, B. 204
Collison, P. 228
Corkingdale, J. T. 210, 249n
Cox, A. 198
Cox, K. R. 224, 226, 227, 251n
Crotty, R. 24, 53, 234n

Dales, J. H. 217
Davis, O. A. 201
Dear, M. J. 198, 224, 226
Demsetz, H. 215, 216
Desai, M. 12, 236n
Dicken, P. 213
Dickinson, H. D. 30
Dmitriev, V. K. 14
Dobb, M. 20, 242n
Donnison, D. 251n
Downs, A. 220, 223
Drewett, R. 201
Dunleavy, P. 198, 22, 223

Edel, M. 56
Elias, P. 210, 212
Elkin, S. L. 201
Elliot, B. 246n
Elster, J. 18, 24, 36, 249n
Engels, F. 95, 233n
Esfahani, H. 56, 242n
Evans, A. 209, 210, 248n
Evans, A. W. 209, 210, 248n

Fielding, A. J. 215
Fine, B. 56
Flynn, B. 133
Freyssenet, M. 161
Furubotn, E. G. 216

Garegnani, P. 20
Garnier, J. P. 90
Gibson, B. 56, 242n
Giddens, A. 244n
Gillman, J. 74, 236n
Ginsberg, N. 56
Glass, R. 246n
Gleave, D. 209
Glucksman, A. 83, 244n
Glyn, A. 21, 24, 53, 234n
Godard, F. 81, 96, 97, 101, 105, 109, 114, 119–21, 125–34, 161, 186
Goddard, J. B. 154, 213
Goodchild, R. 201
Gough, I. 74, 243n
Guillemard, A. 114
Gulliver, S. 252n

Habermas, J. 55, 199
Hall, P. 248n
Hanham, R. W. 252n
Harloe, M. xvii, 90, 97, 186, 251n
Harris, D. J. 35
Harrison, J. 21, 74, 243n
Harvey, D. 56, 195, 217
Healey, M. J. 212
Heap, S. H. 24, 53, 235n
Hegel, G. 91, 246n
Henning, J. A. 221, 223
Hill, T. P. 53, 235n
Hirsch, F. 220
Hirschmann, A. O. 204, 225
Hodgson, G. 15, 16, 18, 22, 35, 232n, 234n, 235n, 236n
Honey, R. 224
House, J. W. 174
Howard, M. C. 15, 24, 28, 31, 33, 35, 36, 47, 52, 232n
Huet, A. 161
Hughes, G. 209
Hunt, E. K. 72, 74, 243n

Ipola, E. de 245n

Jessop, B. 86, 245n
Johnson, J. H. 204, 210, 248n
Johnston, R. J. 224, 226

Kain, J. F. 228, 252n
Keeble, D. 154, 213
Keiper, J. S. 68, 239n
Kenway, P. 236n
Keogh, G. 210, 212
Kieve, J. L. 204
King, J. E. 15, 24, 28, 31, 33, 35, 36, 47, 52, 232n
Kirk, G. 245n
Kurz, H. D. 56

Laclau, E. 244–5n
Lamarche, F. 197
Lambert, J. 133
Lange, O. 50
Lauria, M. 56
Lautman, J. 172
Lebas, E. xvii, 85
Lebeaux, C. N. 227
Lebowitz, M. A. 243–4n
Lefebvre, H. 93–4
Ley, D. 114
Lévi-Strauss, C. 245n
Lipsey, R. G. 235n
Locke, J. 246n
Logan, J. R. 207, 251n
Long, J. 224, 226
Lorimer, J. 197

McCarthy, J. J. 24
McCleod, D. 56
McCormick, B. 209
Malthus, T. 50, 60, 236–7n
Markusen, A. R. 56
Marriot, O. 207
Marshall, A. 13, 250–1n
Massey, D. 56, 154, 21, 213
Medio, A. 21
Meegan, R. A. 154, 212, 213
Meek, R. 30, 233n
Mercer, J. 224
Metcalf, D. 249n
Miliband, R. 245n
Molotch, H. 207, 251n
Montani, G. 239n
Moore, R. 251n
Moseley, M. 121
Moroshima, M. 13, 17, 18, 36, 46, 23–23n, 234n, 237n
Mullins, P. 225
Murray, R. 56

Navqi, K. A. 38
Neilson, L. 201
Nell, E. 20
Neutze, G. M. 223
Nicholls, D. C. 201, 221
Norman, T. 69, 228
Nuti, D. M. 20

Oates, W. E. 221
O'Connor, J. 55, 199, 243n
Offe, C. 198, 199
Okishio, N. 33
Onaka, J. L. 248n
Olson, M. 226
Orbell, J. M. 224
Owens, P. L. 154

Pahl, R. 97, 144, 186, 217, 220, 222, 223
Palmer, D. 209
Pejovich, S. 216
Perrons, D. C. 154
Pickvance, C. 85, 87, 90, 92–3, 95, 97, 112, 186, 194, 204, 206, 227, 228, 245n, 247n
Pigou, A. 251n
Poulantzas, N. 81–4, 244–5n
Pratt, G. 222, 251n
Preteceille, E. 87, 161
Purdy, D. 32

Quadrio-Curzio, A. 56
Quigley, J. M. 228, 252n

Rees, R. 149, 235n, 250n
Retel, T. 161
Reynaud, E. 90
Reynolds, D. R. 224
Rex, J. 251n
Ricardo, D. 13, 56, 57, 60, 234n, 241n
Richardson, R. 210, 248n, 249n
Ridker, R. G. 221, 228
Robinson, J. 8, 20, 52, 234n, 236n
Robson, B. T. 224
Roemer, J. E. 18, 35, 54
Roncaglia, A. 234n, 238n
Ronge, V. 198, 199
Russell, L. 209, 210, 211, 248n

Salt, J. 209, 210, 248n
Samuelson, P. 22, 33
Saunders, P. 144, 191, 193, 198, 199, 200, 297, 221, 222, 223, 229, 251n
Sax, J. L. 217
Schnore, L. F. 247n
Seton, F. 16
Shaikh, A. 24, 35, 47
Sherman H. J. 233n
Silburn, R. 223
Smith, A. 67, 71, 242–3n
Smith, C. J. 252n
Smith, D. M. 217, 251n
Sovani, N. V. 94
Sowell, T. 24, 36, 52
Sraffa, P. 17–23, 56, 72, 234n, 238–9n
Steedman, I. 12, 18, 22, 30, 35, 234n, 236n
Sutcliffe, B. 24, 53, 234n
Sweezy, P. 8, 15, 16, 24, 31, 35, 36, 42, 50

Theret, B. 144
Thompson, C. 154, 213
Thorns, D. C. 251n
Tiebout, C. B. 252n
Tugan-Baranowsky, M. 42
Touraine, A. 107, 114, 116–18

Ungerson, C. 251n
Uno, T. 224

Van Parijs, P. 35

Walker, A. 47, 52, 232n, 238n
Walker, R. 56
Weber, M. 194, 248n
Weisskopf, T. E. 24, 35, 53, 235n
Whinston, A. B. 201
White, M. J. 228
Wilkinson, R. K. 252n
Williams, N. 69, 207, 228
Williams, P. 222
Winternitz, J. 16
Wirth, L. 92
Wolf, E. P. 227
Wood, P. 209, 210, 248n
Wright, E. O. 31

Zetter, R. 121

Subject Index

Althusser 224n: scientific knowledge 91–2, 246

Althusserianism xviii, 81–5, 88, 189: Castells and 90–2, 95, 97, 101–3, 104, 126, 140, 180, 245n

Balibar: characterisation of economic systems 82

Basic commodities, 17–18, 57, 59, 61, 66, 65, 73, 158, 238–41n; non-basic commodities 17–18, 64–6, 73, 158, 238–41n

Bortkiewicz: critique of Marx's solution to Transformation problem 13; solution to Transformation problem 14–18; and Bortkiewicz Corollary 17–18

Capital: constant capital 5–6, 13, 14, 27, 28, 30–1, 38–9, 86–7, 145, 151, 152, 153, 236n (Marx's theory of 5–6, 13, 14, 27, 28–31, 232n, 238; price coefficient of 14; value of 9, 14, 21, 27; over-accumulation of 27, 86–87, 153); variable capital 5–6, 27, 28, 30, 38–9, 70, 87, 145, 151, 152, 153 (Marx's theory of 5–6, 28, 30, 70; price coefficients of 14; value of 13, 14, 21, 27)

Capitalist production: Marx's characterisation of 4; Sraff's characterisation of 18

Castells: Althusserianism 90–92, 95, 97, 101–3, 104, 126, 140, 180, 245; Chicago school 91; class fractions 128–9, 132–3, 134; collective consumption 25, 95–101, 139–40, 165, 186, 187–8, 215, 229, 246n (definition of 96; effects of 98–101); housing 121, 132, 138; functionalism 140, 186; ideology 90–2; immigrant workers 134–6; index of differentiation 119–21; industrialisation 92; interest in work of 231–2n; law of falling rate of profit 35, 98–9, 127, 135, 186; location of industry 107–8, 115–18; Marxian crisis theory 25, 55, 98–101, 139, 187; Marxist political economy 89–90, 101–2, 103, 104, 106, 108–9, 113, 188–9, 192; methodology 116, 118–20, 123, 125–6, 129, 131, 132, 134, 135, 136, 137, 138–9, 186, 188, 189, 192; property relations 108, 110; real appropriation 110; realisation crises 47, 99–100; research on Dunkirk 109, 125–34; science 90–2; state monopoly capitalism 126, 129; trade union power 100–1, 188; transport 132, 134; urban actors 106, 11, 121, 140, 246n; urban areas 89, 92–3, 94, 101, 104, 105, 137, 139, 247n (definition of 95–7, 139, 185–6); urban culture 92; urban planning 81, 104, 105–9, 122, 126, 132–3, 139–40, 189–90 (definition of 105); urban politics 81, 104–5, 133; urban protests 121–5, 126, 132, 136–8, 140; urban renewal 118–21; urban social movements 81, 104, 109–13, 139, 190–1 (social base of 112–13, 123, 138, 191; social force of 112–13, 138, 191); urban sociology 89–140; critique of 89, 90–5, 139, 141, 185, 191 (formulation of Marxist urban sociology 95–113, 139,

Castells: Althusserianism – *contd.* 195); urban systems 81, 101–5, 106, 111, 132, 140, 246n) urbanism 90–1, 92–94; urbanisation 90, 91, 94–5, 96
Chicago School 91
Circulation, costs of 73–5, 243–4n
Class fractions 85, 161, 163, 167, 173, 174, 176–7: Castells's theory of 128–9, 132–3, 134; Lojkine's theory of 161, 163, 167, 174, 176–7, 178, 180, 247n
Collective action 226–30, 251n
Collective consumption 25, 187–9, 196, 229: Castells's theory of 25, 95–101, 139–40, 165, 186, 187–8, 215, 229, 246n (definition of 96; effects of 98–101); dwelling unit 215, 220–9, 230; falling rate of profit 98–9; Lojkine's theory of 25, 88, 142–50, 151–2, 186, 187–8, 215, 229, 247n; Marxian crisis theory 25, 139, 187; realisation crisis 99–100; trade union power 100–1
Commodities 67: Marx's definition of 3; value of and price of 8, 12–13, 16, 18, 49
Commuting 97, 128, 167, 186, 195, 208–11, 230
Competition 10, 16, 17, 38, 49, 59, 61–62, 64, 68, 135, 136, 201, 241n, 248n: Marx's theory of 10, 16, 17, 49, 59, 61–2, 64, 68, 136
Composition of capital: organic 6–7, 8, 10, 27, 28–33, 35, 50, 66, 87, 99, 135, 150–3, 155, 157, 236n, 246n; Marx's theory of 8, 10, 27, 28–32, 50, 66; technical 27, 31–2; value 27, 31
Constrained-actor model xvii, 192–5, 196, 198–207, 215–29
Consumption goods: Communal 186, 216–17, 220, 222, 230, 250n; negative 216–20, 224–5, 226–7, 228, 230, 251n; positive 216, 220, 224, 226, 230; private 216–17, 220, 222, 230, 250n; reactions to changes in consumption of 223–29; state, 216, 220
Crisis: Marx's theory of xviii, 24–6; Castells's and Marxist crisis theory 25, 55, 98–101, 139, 187; Lojkine and Marxist crisis theory 25, 55, 187

Dwelling unit 215, 220–9, 230, 251n, 239n

Exploitation of labour 71: Marx's theory of 4, 6; rate of 8, 28–9, 30, 32–3, 46, 152–3
Extended reproduction 44–6, 239n, 251n: Marx's model of 40–2
Externalities 217, 230, 250–251n: fields 191, 217–19, 220; gradients 217–19, 220; negative 192, 194, 217–20

Fiscal crisis 55

Housing 133–4, 165, 170, 175–6, 171–8, 190: and Castells 121, 132, 138; and Lojkine 173, 175–6, 177–8
Housing classes (*see* Tenure groups)

Ideological state apparatuses 84–5
Industrial reserve army 48, 50, 53, 54: Marx's theory of 48, 50
Interests 106, 107, 108, 121, 125, 129, 132, 134, 140, 166, 171, 192–4, 196, 198–207, 208–11, 212, 221, 223, 226–7, 229, 251n

Labour markets 97, 136, 168, 186, 208–11, 230, 248n
Labour power 27, 82, 97, 108: as a commodity 48–50, 54; Marx's definition of 4–6; reproduction of 97, 101, 107, 132, 143, 145, 146, 147, 165, 186, 214; shortage of 36, 46–7, 128
Labour theory of value: Marx's theory of 3–7, 18, 21–22, 56, 66, 234n

Land 56–69: ownership of 57, 64, 240n; price of 57, 248n; rent of 57–69

Landowners: constraints on 204–5

Land-use 173: planning of 105, 110, 132, 190; zoning 69, 108, 190, 201, 206, 228, 248n, 249n

Law of falling rate of profit 24–35, 85, 127, 150–1, 153, 158, 181, 186: Castells's interpretation of 35, 98–9, 127, 135, 186; Lojkine's interpretation 35, 85, 150, 151–3, 173, 180; Marx's theory of 24–35

Lefebvre, theory of suburbanism 93–4

Legitimation crisis 55

Location of industry 107–8, 117, 150, 154, 180–1, 189, 195, 196, 211–13, 230: Castells's research on 107–8, 115–18; Lojkine's research on 150, 154, 180, 181, 186

Lojkine: class fractions 161, 163, 167, 174, 176–7, 178, 180, 247n; collective consumption 25, 77, 88, 165, 170, 180–1, 187–8, 215, 229, 247n; collective means of consumption 142–50, 151–2, 153, 176, 180–81; housing 173, 175–6, 177–8; functionalism 186; interest in work of 231–2n; law of falling rate of profit 35, 85, 150, 151–3, 173, 180; location of industry 150, 154, 180, 186; Marxian crisis theory 25, 55, 187; Marxist political economy 141, 147, 151, 159, 182, 188–9, 192; Marx's theory of productive labour 70, 144–7, 187–8; means of material circulation 142, 151, 152, 153; means of social circulation 142, 145, 146, 151, 153; methodology 152–3, 157, 159, 168, 171, 172–3, 174, 175, 176, 178–9, 180, 186, 188, 189, 192; rent 56, 69, 150, 154–9, 173, 178, 179–80, 181; state monopoly capitalism 81, 85–8, 129, 141, 160–1, 177, 179, 181, 189, 245n; transport 149, 167, 170, 171, 175–176, 178; urban areas 141, 180, 247n (definition of 142–3, 186–7, 191); urban development 150, 167–80, 189; urban planning 160–3, 167–8, 169–72, 174, 180, 181, 182, 185, 189–90; urban politics 180; urban protests 190, 191; urban segregation 159, 167, 169, 170, 171, 173; urban social movements 163–6, 173, 180, 181–2, 185, 190–1 (social base of 164–5, 166, 191; social force of 164–5, 166, 191); urban sociology 141–82, 182, 185, 191, 195; urbanisation 142;

Macroeconomic planning: absence of 25, 36, 40–2

Marx: barter 37; constant capital 5–6, 13, 14, 27, 28–31, 232n, 238 (value of 9, 14, 21, 27; over-accumulation of 27); capitalist production, characterisation of 4; commodities (definition of 3; value of and price of 8, 12–13, 16, 18, 49, 232–233n); competition 10, 16, 17, 49, 59, 61–2, 64, 68, 136; composition of capital (organic 8, 10, 27, 28–32, 50, 66; technical 27, 31–2; value 27, 31) crisis, theory of xviii, 24–6; exploitation of labour 71 (theory of 4, 6; rate of 8, 28–30, 46); extended reproduction 44–5 (model of 40–2); industrial reserve army 48, 50, 53, 54, 237–238; labour power 4–6, 27 (as a commodity 48–50, 54; shortage of 46–7); labour theory of value 3–7, 18, 21–2, 56, 66, 233–4n; law of falling rate of profit 24–35, 86–7,

Marx: barter – *contd.*
98–9, 181, 235–6n, 238n, 241n; productive labour, theory of xviii, 69, 70–77, 146, 188, 242–4n; profit 4–5, 7, 9, 16, 17, 18, 27, 28–29, 51, 66, 68, 71, 193, 233n; 241n (rate of 8, 9, 10, 11, 12, 16, 15, 17, 22, 27, 28–9, 31, 41, 43, 45, 47, 49, 54; actual rate of 27, 30; average rate 9, 10, 49); maximum rate of 27, 29, 30, 52; price rate of 12–13, 14; value rate of 12–13, 14); realisation crisis 24–5, 35–47, 236n; rent 56–69, 154–5, 157, 181, 193 (differential rent I 57, 58–61, 157; differential II 57, 61–4, 157; monopoly rent I 57, 64–6, 157, 241n; monopoly rent II 57, 66–67, 157; theory of xviii, 55, 56–69, 238–42n); rising real wages 24–5, 26, 47–54; simple reproduction 44–6 (model of 38–9); surplus value 9, 10, 11, 13, 14, 16, 18, 21, 22, 28, 39, 66, 233n, 238n, 242n (absolute surplus value 6, 30; relative surplus value 7, 30; rate of 6, 28, 30; theory of 4–7); technical innovation 27, 29–31, 50; transformation problem (formulation of 7–9; solution to 9–12; critique of solution 12–14); use value 3–5, 232n, 242n; value, theory of xviii, 151; variable capital 5–6, 28, 30, 70 (value of 13, 14, 21, 27); wages 4, 20–2, 26, 46, 70–1, 193, 232n (Marx's theory of 50–1, 238n)

Okishio's theorem 33
Over-urbanisation 94

Planning authorities 106, 132, 162, 167, 170–2, 194, 196, 200, 201, 205: constraints on 205–7; interests of 200
Population growth: lack of 46; Malthus's theory of 236–7
Poulantzas, theory of capitalist state 84–5
Price gouging 201
Prices 3, 7, 9, 12, 21, 65, 68, 234n
Productive labour: Marx's theory of xviii, 69, 70–7, 146, 188, 242–4n; Lojkine's theory of 70 144–7, 187–8
Price coefficients 14
Profit 4–5, 7, 9, 16, 17, 18, 27, 28–9,31, 51, 65, 66, 68, 71, 100, 152, 155, 162, 234–5n, 239n: rate of 8, 9, 10, 11, 12, 16, 15, 17, 22 24, 26, 27, 28–9, 32–5, 41, 43, 45, 46–7, 54, 59, 60, 62, 63, 68, 73, 127, 146, 152, 155, 156, 201, 234n, 236n, 238–241n (actual rate 27, 30; average rate 9, 10 49, 157; maximum rate 27, 29–30; price rate of 12–13, 14, 236n; Sraffa's theory of 20–1; value rate of 12–13, 14, 236n)
Property development 132, 142, 181, 186, 187, 190, 192, 194, 196–207, 229: private 106, 168 181, 195, 197, 200–7, 229–30; state 105, 106, 108–9, 195, 197–200, 229–30
Property developers 196: constraints on 200–4

Realisation crisis 35–47, 99–100: and Castells's theory of 47, 99–100; and Marx's theory of 24–25, 35–47, 236n
Relations of property 82, 108, 244n, 249n: Castells's interpretation of 108, 110
Relations of real appropriation 82, 110, 244n: and Castells 110
Relative autonomy 82, 87
Rent 56–69, 150, 162, 238–42n: differential rent I 57, 58–61, 68–9, 157–8, 178, 179, 239–40n 248n; differential rent II 57, 61–4, 68–9, 157–8, 178, 179; Lojkine's theory of 6, 69, 150, 154–9, 173, 178, 179–80, 181; Malthus's theory 60; Marx's

Rent – *contd.*
theory of xviii, 55, 56–69, 154–5, 157, 181, 193; monopoly rent I 57, 64–6, 68–9, 157–8, 178, 179, 248n; monopoly rent II 57, 66–7, 68–9, 157–8, 178, 179; Ricardo's theory of 58, 60–1, 239n, 241n
Repressive state apparatuses 84–5
Rising real wages 24–5, 26, 47–54

Sector I, II, III 14–15, 17, 38–41
Simple reproduction 44–5, 236n, 239n: Marx's model of 38–9
Simultaneous equations 13, 15
Socially necessary abstract labour 3, 48, 232–3n
Sraffa: basic and non-basic commodities 17–18, 19–20, 238n; capitalist production, characterisation of 18; Marx's labour theory of value 20–1, 233–4n; profits and prices 18–22, 238n, 239n; and zero wages 29–30
State expenditure 72, 76–7, 99–100, 127, 150, 161–2, 174–6, 198, 199, 214
State monopoly capitalism xviii, 81, 85–8, 126, 189, 245n; and Castells 126, 129; and Lojkine 81, 85–8, 129, 141, 160–1, 177, 179, 181, 189, 245n
Surplus value 9, 10, 11, 13, 14, 16, 18, 21, 22, 28, 66, 151, 152, 153, 155, 188: absolute surplus value 6, 30, 135; Marx's theory of 4–7; price coefficients of 14; rate of 6, 28, 30, 35, 135; relative surplus value 7, 30, 135

Technical conditions of production 21
Technical innovation 24–5, 26, 27, 29–35, 36, 42–4, 49, 50, 58, 61
Tenure groups 215, 221–3, 225, 226–7, 229, 230, 239n, 251n
Trade union power 25, 26, 48, 53–4, 100–1: and Castells 100–1, 188
Transformation problem 3, 7–9, 233–234n; Bortkiewicz's critique of Marx's solution 13; Bortkiewicz's solution 14–18; invariance postulates 16; Marx's formulation of 7–9; Marx's solution 9–12; Meek's solution 16; Steedman's critque of Marx's solution 12; Winternitz's solution 16
Transport 132, 134, 149, 165, 167, 169, 173, 175–6, 178, 190: and Castells 132, 134; and Lojkine 149, 167, 170, 171, 175–6, 178

Urban actors 106, 111, 121, 140, 194: definition of 196, 248n; Castells's theory of 106, 121, 140, 246n
Urban areas 89, 92–3, 94, 101, 104, 113, 137, 166, 185–7, 190, 195–6, 214, 230: Castells's theory of 89, 92–3, 94, 101, 104, 105, 137, 139, 247n (definition of 95–97, 139, 185–6); final consumption in 214–29; Lojkine's theory of 141, 180, 247n (definition of 142–3, 186–7, 191); production of 208–214, 229; property development in 196–207, 229
Urban development 150, 167–180, 189: control of 162, 201; Lojkine's research on 150, 167–80, 189
Urban planning 81, 104, 155, 185, 189–90, 196: Castells's theory of 81, 104, 105–9, 122, 126, 132–3, 139–40, 189–90 (definition of 105); Lojkine's theory of 160–3, 167–8, 169–72, 174, 180, 181, 182, 185, 189–90
Urban politics 81, 104: Castells's theory of 81, 104–5, 133; Lojkine's theory of 180
Urban protests 111, 133–4, 190–1: Castells's theory of 121–5, 126,

Urban protests – *contd.* 132, 132, 136–8, 140; Lojkine's theory of 190–1
Urban renewal, Castells's research on 118–21
Urban social movements 81, 104, 185, 196: Castells's theory of 81, 104, 109–13, 139, 190–1 (social base of 112–13, 123, 138, 191; social force of 112–13, 138, 191); Lojkine's theory of 163–6, 173, 180, 181–2, 185, 190–1 (social base of 164–5, 166, 191; social force of 164–5, 166, 191)
Urban sociology: definition of xvii–xviii; 142, 181, 186, 195; Castells 89–140 (Castells's critique of 89, 90–5, 139, 141, 185, 191; formulation of Marxist urban sociology 95–113, 139, 195); growth of Marxist urban sociology xviii, 185, 192; Lojkine 141–82, 182, 185, 191, 195
Urban systems 81: Castells's theory of 81, 101–5, 106, 111, 132, 140, 246n
Urbanisation 94–5, 214: and Castells's theory of 90, 91, 94–5, 96
Urbanism 90–1, 92–94: Wirth's theory of 92–3; Castells's theory of 90–1, 92–4; Lojkine's theory of 142

Value 32: exchange 3–5, 75, 208; use 3–5, 75, 144, 145, 148, 149, 208; Marx's theory of xviii, 151

Wages 21, 32–4, 46, 48–54, 58–9, 60, 63, 65, 68, 70–1, 72, 100–1, 135, 136, 162, 214–15, 234–5n: Marx's theory of 50–1; zero wages 29–30, 32
Weather conditions 26, 36, 44–6
Wirth, theory of urbanism 92–3